Contemporary
Mexican Politics

Contemporary Mexican Politics

Second Edition

Emily Edmonds-Poli and David A. Shirk

ROWMAN & LITTLEFIELD PUBLISHERS, INC.
Lanham • Boulder • New York • Toronto • Plymouth, UK

Published by Rowman & Littlefield Publishers, Inc.
A wholly owned subsidary of The Rowman & Littlefield Publishing Group, Inc.
4501 Forbes Boulevard, Suite 200, Lanham, Maryland 20706
www.rowmanlittlefield.com

Estover Road, Plymouth PL6 7PY, United Kingdom

British Library Cataloguing in Publication Information Available

Library of Congress Cataloging-in-Publication Data

Edmonds-Poli, Emily, 1970–
    Contemporary Mexican politics / Emily Edmonds-Poli and David A. Shirk. —
2nd ed.
        p. cm.
    Includes bibliographical references and index.
    ISBN 978-1-4422-0756-1 (cloth : alk. paper) — ISBN 978-1-4422-0757-8
    (pbk. : alk. paper) — ISBN 978-1-4422-0758-5 (electronic : alk. paper)
    1. Mexico—Politics and government—2000– I. Shirk, David A., 1971–
II. Title.
F1236.7.E36 2012
320.972—dc23   2011037035

♾ ™ The paper used in this publication meets the minimum requirements of
American National Standard for Information Sciences—Permanence of Paper for
Printed Library Materials, ANSI/NISO Z39.48-1992.

Printed in the United States of America

Contents

Part III: Key Domestic Policy Issues

Part IV: Mexican Foreign Relations

Illustrations

FIGURES

TABLES

TEXTBOXES

Preface

In the three years since the publication of the first edition of this book, Mexico has experienced some serious challenges to democratic governance. Foremost on people's minds when they think about Mexico is the extreme and almost continuous wave of violence that has affected the country since President Felipe Calderón took office in 2006. The Calderón administration's strategy of using the military and federal police to combat drug-trafficking organizations (DTOs) has generated important successes, including the arrest of major organized crime bosses and record drug seizures. The United States has continued to support Mexico's efforts by extending aid and tactical support in the fight against drug trafficking, both at home and in Mexico. However, the failure to reduce levels of violence in Mexico or to produce any meaningful reduction in the flow of drugs to U.S. consumers has produced sharp criticism of the war on drugs in both countries.

The issue of combating DTOs has led more than a few observers to argue that Mexico is a failed state. Given that Mexico exhibits lower levels of violence than found elsewhere in the hemisphere (including Brazil and Colombia), we think that these claims are much exaggerated. Indeed, Mexico's situation is a far cry from the political, social, and economic chaos that characterizes a truly failed state, such as Somalia. Still, there is little doubt that the Mexican government's fight against organized crime groups has met with only mixed success, at best, and has inadvertently created a climate of extreme public insecurity in some parts of the country.

Meanwhile, contemporary Mexico faces other critical challenges. After the world slipped into recession in 2008, Mexico's GDP declined a precipitous 6.5 percent in 2009. Adding to its financial difficulties were a decline in tourism (subsequent to the outbreak of the H1N1 flu virus) and a drop in the price of oil, the country's top two sources of foreign capital. At the same time, the economic slowdown in the United States means that employment north of the border cannot be an effective pressure-release valve to address these needs for the foreseeable future, as exhibited by a significant slowdown in undocumented immigration and migrant remittances sent back to Mexico. Combined, these trends have contributed to a very difficult economic climate for most ordinary Mexicans, and they may result in significant political pressure on the government to provide jobs and services. Considering that a well-educated population and decent employment opportunities can help provide a foundation for the rule of law, Mexico's economic challenges are closely intertwined with its security situation.

How Mexico responds to these challenges in coming years will determine its alternative political futures and will be of great importance to the United States. Given its strategic advantages and close relationship to the United States, Mexico has the potential to become one of the great success stories of the global economy. With more than $300 billion in cross-border commerce, Mexico is the third largest U.S. trading partner and the second most important destination for U.S. exports. Mexico is also the country of origin for one in ten U.S. residents, and the country of residence for one in five U.S. citizens living abroad. What happens to Mexico also happens to the United States, and vice versa. We hope that the 2012 edition of *Contemporary Mexican Politics* helps underscore this connection, and helps readers deepen their understanding of Mexico's fascinating political history and contemporary landscape. Throughout the book, we have expanded our discussion and analysis of recent events such as these and their implications for Mexican politics. As Mexico heads into an exciting presidential election year, we remain cautiously optimistic about the country's future and the continued consolidation of Mexico's democracy.

Like other authors of a work of this nature, our book benefited enormously from those of other scholars across a wide range of disciplines who have made enormous contributions to the study of Mexican politics. Hence we must recognize those who have shaped and contributed to its development. We wish to begin by thanking those to whom we have dedicated this text, Wayne Cornelius and Ann Craig, who wrote the textbooks we read while learning about Mexico, and cochaired each of our doctoral dissertation committees. Their contributions—not only as great scholars of Mexican politics, but as extraordinary mentors and friends—have greatly shaped our personal and professional development and inspired us to follow in their footsteps. Their consistent guidance and constructive feedback on our research and scholarship, including this book, is deeply appreciated.

We also wish to acknowledge the many colleagues and friends who illuminated, cajoled, and inspired us in various ways too numerous to detail here. In particular, we are indebted to Manuel Aguilar, Elena Azaola, John Bailey, Caroline Beer, Roderic Ai Camp, Senator Pedro Joaquín Coldwell, Ambassador Jeffrey Davidow, Robert Donnelly, Federico Estévez, Jim Gerber, Senator Rosario Green, Ken Greene, Joy Langston, Armando Mejia, Kevin J. Middlebrook, Marcos Pablo Moloeznik, Dag Mossige, David Nájera, Eric Olson, José Antonio Polo Oteyza, Charles Pope, Luis Miguel Rionda, Alejandra Ríos Cázares, Viridiana Ríos, Victoria Rodríguez, Marc Rosenblum, Daniel Sabet, Miguel Sarre, Andrew Selee, María Fernanda Somuano Ventura, Rose Spalding, María Eugenia Suárez, Peter Ward, Jeffrey Weldon, and Steve Wuhs, as well as our University of San Diego colleagues and students. We are also grateful to U.S. Ambassador Carlos Pascual and the representatives of the U.S. State Department and Mexican Foreign Ministry who shared their insights on binational relations. Susan McEachern, Jehanne Schweitzer, Grace Baumgartner and Catherine Bielitz at Rowman & Littlefield provided great support and enthusiasm for what we hope is an ongoing project. Finally, without the unwavering support of our families, none of this would be possible. Thank you all. Hopefully, we have corrected some of the errors identified in the first edition and improved upon it the second time around. In any case, despite all this tremendous support, any errors or omissions remain our responsibility.

Abbreviations

AC	Alianza Cívica (Civic Alliance)
AFO	Arellano Félix Organization
AFORES	Administradoras de Fondos para el Retiro (Retirement Funds Administrators)
AMLO	Andrés Manuel López Obrador
APEC	Asia Pacific Economic Cooperation
APPO	Asamblea Popular de los Pueblos de Oaxaca (Popular Assembly of Oaxacan Peoples)
ATF	Bureau of Alcohol, Tobacco, Firearms, and Explosives
BECC	Border Environment Cooperative Commission
BIP	Border Industrialization Program
BRIC	Brazil, Russia, India, and China
CCE	Consejo Coordinador Empresarial (Business Coordinating Council)
CCRI	Comité Clandestino Revolucionario Indígena (Committee of the Clandestine Indigenous Revolution)
CD	Corriente Democrática (Democratic Current)
CFE	Comisión Federal Electoral (Federal Electoral Commission)
CMHN	Consejo Mexicano de Hombres de Nogocios (Mexican Council of Business Executives)
CNC	Confederación Nacional Campesina (National Agrarian Confederation)
CND	Convención Nacional Democrática (National Democratic Convention)
CNDH	Comisión Nacional de Derechos Humanos (National Human Rights Commission)

CNDP	Comité Nacional de Defensa Proletaria (National Committee for Proletarian Defense)
CNOP	Confederación Nacional de Organizaciones Populares (National Confederation of Popular Organizations)
COCOPA	Comisión de Concordia y Pacificación (Commission for Concordance and Peace)
COECE	Coordinadora de Organismos Empresariales de Comercio Exterior (Coordinating Body of Foreign Trade Business Associations)
COFIPE	Código Federal de Instituciones y Procedimientos Electorales (Federal Code of Electoral Institutions and Procedures)
CONASUPO	Compañía Nacional de Subsistencias Populares (National Company for Popular Subsistence)
CONEVAL	Consejo Nacional de Evaluación de la Política de Desarrollo Social (National Council for the Evaluation of Development Policy)
CPI	Corruption Perceptions Index
CRMDT	Confederación Revolucionaria Michoacana del Trabajo (Revolutionary Workers Confederation of Michoacán)
CROM	Confederación Regional Obrera Mexicana (Regional Confederation of Mexican Workers)
CTM	Confederación de Trabajadores de México (Confederation of Mexican Workers)
DF	Distrito Federal (Federal District)
DIF	Desarrollo Integral de la Familia (Comprehensive Family Development Program)
DTO	drug-trafficking organization
EFTA	European Free Trade Association
EPA	Environmental Protection Agency
EPR	Ejército Popular Revolutionario (Popular Revolutionary Army)
EU	European Union
EZLN	Ejército Zapatista de Liberación Nacional (Zapatista Army of National Liberation)
FDI	foreign direct investment
FDN	Frente Democrático Nacional (National Democratic Front)
FMLN	Frente Farabundo Martí para la Liberación Nacional (Farabundo Martí National Liberation Front)
FOBAPROA	Fondo Bancario de Protección al Ahorro (Savings Protection Banking Fund)
FTAA	Free Trade Area of the Americas
FUPDM	Frente Unico Pro Derechos de la Mujer (Sole Front for Women's Rights)

G3	Group of 3
GATT	General Agreement on Tariffs and Trade
GDP	gross domestic product
HDI	Human Development Index
ICESI	Instituto Ciudadano de Estudios Sobre la Inseguridad (Citizens' Institute for the Study of Public Insecurity)
IFAI	Instituto Federal de Acceso a la Información Pública (Federal Institute for Access to Public Information)
IFE	Instituto Federal Electoral (Federal Electoral Institute)
IMF	International Monetary Fund
IMSS	Instituto Méxicano del Seguro Social (Mexican Social Security Institute)
INCD	Instituto Nacional para el Combate a las Drogas (National Institute for Combating Drugs)
INEGI	Instituto Nacional de Estadística y Geografía (National Institute of Statistics and Geography)
INFONAVIT	Instituto del Fondo Nacional de la Vivienda para los Trabajadores (National Workers' Housing Fund Institute)
INMujeres	Instituto Nacional de las Mujeres (National Women's Institute)
IPN	Instituto Politécnico Nacional (National Polytechnic Institute)
IRA	individual retirement account
IRCA	Immigration Reform and Control Act
ISI	import substitution industrialization
ISSSTE	Instituto de Seguridad y Servicios Sociales de los Trabajadores del Estado (Institute of Security and Social Services for Government Employees)
ITESM	Instituto Tecnológico y de Estudios Superiores de Monterrey (Monterrey Technological Institute)
ITESO	Instituto Tecnológico de Estudios Superiores del Oriente (Eastern Technological Institute for Higher Studies)
IVA	impuesto al valor agregado (value-added tax)
LFC	Luz y Fuerza del Centro (Central Light and Power)
LFOPPE	Ley Federal de Organizaciones Políticas y Procesos Electorales (Federal Law of Political Organizations and Electoral Processes)
LNDLR	Liga Nacional de la Defensa de la Libertad Religiosa (National League for the Defense of Religious Liberty)
MLAT	Mutual Legal Assistance Treaty
MUCD	Mexico Unido contra la Delincuencia (Mexico United against Crime)
NADBank	North American Development Bank
NAFTA	North American Free Trade Agreement

NGO	nongovernmental organization
NIEO	New International Economic Order
OECD	Organisation for Economic Co-operation and Development
PAN	Partido Acción Nacional (National Action Party)
PANAL	Partido Nueva Alianza (New Alliance Party)
PARM	Partido Auténtico de la Revolución Mexicana (Authentic Party of the Mexican Revolution)
PASC	Partido Alternativa Socialdemócrata y Campesino (Social Democratic and Agrarian Alternative Party)
PCM	Partido Comunista Mexicano (Mexican Communist Party)
PEMEX	Petróleos Mexicanos (Mexican Petroleum)
PIPSA	Productora e Importada de Papel, Sociedad Anónima (Paper Products and Imports)
PISA	Programme for International Student Assessment
PNR	Partido Nacional Revolucionario (National Revolutionary Party)
PPP	purchasing power parity
PR	proportional representation
PRD	Partido de la Revolución Democrática (Party of the Democratic Revolution)
PRI	Partido Revolucionario Institucional (Institutional Revolutionary Party)
PRM	Partido de la Revolución Mexicana (Party of the Mexican Revolution)
PROCAMPO	Programa de Apoyo Directo al Campo (Program for Direct Assistance in Agriculture)
PRONAFIM	Programa Nacional de Financiamiento al Microempresario (National Small Business Financing Program)
PRONASOL	Programa Nacional de Solidaridad (National Solidarity Program)
PSD	Partido Socialdemócrata (Social Democratic Revolutionary Party)
PSE	Pacto de Solidaridad Económica (Economic Solidarity Pact)
PT	Partido del Trabajo (Labor Party)
PVEM	Partido Verde Ecologista de México (Mexican Green Ecological Party)
SAGARPA	Secretaría de Agricultura, Ganadería, Desarrollo Rural, Pesca y Alimentación (Ministry of Agriculture, Livestock, Rural Development, Fishing, and Food)
Salud	Secretaría de Salud (Ministry of Health)
SAR	Sistema de Ahorro para el Retiro (Retirement Savings System)
SAS	Secretaría de Asistencia Social (Ministry of Social Assistance)
SEDESOL	Secretaría de Desarrollo Social (Ministry of Social Development)

SEM	Servicio Exterior Mexicano (Mexican Foreign Service)
SEMARNAT	Secretaría de Medio Ambiente y Recursos Naturales (Ministry of Environmental and Natural Resources)
SMD	single-member district
SME	Sindicato Mexicano de Electricistas (Mexican Syndicate of Electricians)
SNPSS	Sistema Nacional de Protección Social en Salud (National System for Social Protection in Health)
SNTE	Sindicato Nacional de Trabajadores de la Educación (National Union of Education Workers)
SP	Seguro Popular (Popular Insurance Program)
SPP	Security and Prosperity Partnership
SRE	Secretaría de Relaciones Exteriores (Ministry of Exterior Relations)
SSA	Secretaría de Salubridad y Asistencia (Ministry of Health and Assistance)
TRIFE	Tribunal Federal Electoral (Federal Electoral Tribunal)
UNAM	Universidad Nacional Autónoma de México (National Autonomous University of Mexico)
VAT	value-added tax
WTO	World Trade Organization

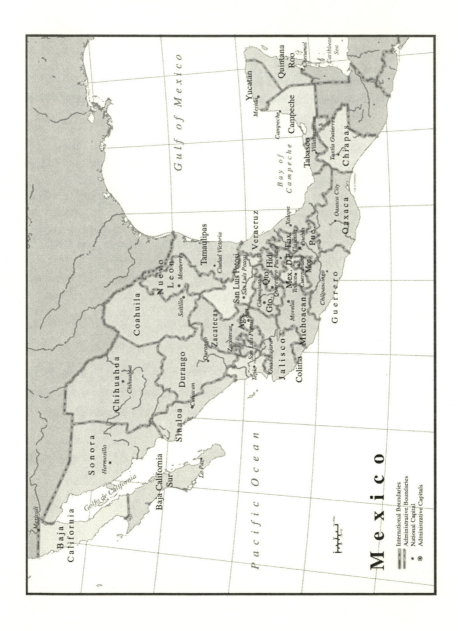

Mexico

International Boundaries
Administrative Boundaries
★ National Capital
⊙ Administrative Capitals

Baja California

Sonora
Hermosillo

Baja California Sur
La Paz

Chihuahua
Chihuahua

Sinaloa
Culiacán

Durango
Victoria

Coahuila
Saltillo

Nuevo León
Monterrey

Tamaulipas
Ciudad Victoria

Zacatecas
Zacatecas

San Luis Potosí
San Luis Potosí

Aguascalientes

Guanajuato
Guanajuato

Querétaro

Jalisco
Guadalajara

Tepic

Colima

Michoacán
Morelia

Mex. D.F.
Toluca

Hidalgo
Pachuca

Oto.

Mor.
Guerrero
Chilpancingo

Veracruz
Xalapa

Puebla
Puebla

Tlax.

Oaxaca
Oaxaca City

Guerrero

Tabasco
Villahermosa

Chiapas
Tuxtla Gutiérrez

Campeche
Campeche

Yucatán
Mérida

Quintana Roo
Chetumal

Gulf of Mexico

Bay of Campeche

Caribbean Sea

Pacific Ocean

Golfo de California

Mexicali

Introduction

C omo México no hay dos. Like Mexico there is no other. Mexico was the birthplace of the several major indigenous civilizations of Mesoamerica and the foundation of Spain's empire in the New World. After launching the first major social revolution of the twentieth century, it produced the world's longest-lasting single-party-dominant political system. Today, Mexico is an emerging democracy, with the twelfth largest economy in the world. No other country has as powerful and direct an impact on the United States as Mexico, whose economic, social, and political influences stretch far across the border. For this reason, not only are Mexico's rich past, present circumstances, and future possibilities of interest to historians and political scientists, they are of great relevance to all students of world politics. Only by studying Mexico in depth is it possible to appreciate its full appeal, complexity, and significance.

Let's start, for example, with Mexico's people and geography. Although the majority of Mexicans are mestizos (of mixed white European and indigenous ancestry), other ethnicities, including Jewish, Middle Eastern, African, and Asian, make up a small but significant portion of the nation's population. As a result, from architecture to food to language, Mexico is a unique amalgamation of various traditions and cultural influences. Mexico's geography and climate are similarly diverse. Roughly 760,000 square miles, or one-fifth the size of the United States, Mexico is the fifteenth largest country in the world and has a varied landscape of peaks, valleys, and plateaus. While Mexico's north is characterized by arid deserts and the lowlands and the rain forests of the southeast experience tropical conditions

1

without a cold season, the central plateau's latitude and altitude bring it rainy summers and mild winters.

Mexico is also one of the world's most fascinating case studies for comparative political analysis, with features that are relevant to other countries: religious and military conquest and colonialism, class and ethnic divisions, revolutionary struggles and civil wars, corporatist state-society relations, dueling forces of economic nationalism and promarket liberalism, and powerful transnational crime syndicates. Perhaps the most significant consideration for comparative analysis is Mexico's recent democratization and ongoing processes of democratic consolidation. For many years, Mexico was considered to have the "perfect dictatorship," thus described because one political party, the Institutional Revolutionary Party (Partido Revolucionario Institucional, or PRI), ruled single-handedly—often by restricting political competition and participation—while maintaining considerable popular support and an outward appearance of democratic competition.

Beginning in the late 1960s, Mexico began a slow and sometimes painful transition from single-party dominance toward a more open and competitive political system. For many, the proof that democracy had arrived came on July 2, 2000, when opposition candidate Vicente Fox defeated the PRI in a free and fair presidential election. Six years later, Fox's party, the National Action Party (Partido Acción Nacional, or PAN), triumphed a second time when Felipe Calderón Hinojosa defeated his closest challenger by a razor-thin margin. But the PAN has not replaced the PRI as Mexico's "official party." Indeed, no political party has won a majority in Congress since 1997, and the 2012 presidential elections are likely to be competitive. Since its impressive showing in the 2009 midterm elections, the PRI has appeared poised to recapture the presidency in 2012. But in order to win, the party must remain unified and overcome fears that its return to power will set back the clock on Mexican democratic governance.

For now, Mexico's ability to move, in one generation, from a single-party-dominant system to one with vibrant electoral competition is remarkable. Many countries, especially those also struggling with the challenge of economic development, are unable to achieve democratic governance or make it last. One need only look at recent history to understand how elusive and fleeting democracy can be. During the twentieth century, almost every country in Latin America moved from authoritarian rule to a more open political system, only to see dictatorships return (often led by the military) before democracy could really take hold. Although the latter part of the twentieth century brought a slow return to democratic pluralism, many countries continue working to consolidate these gains, and others—like Venezuela and Honduras—have suffered significant setbacks.

Like all things Mexican, the country's path toward more democratic governance has been unique. After a prolonged and uncertain transition, single-party dominance has given way to highly institutionalized electoral competition, newfound political transparency, and substantial checks and balances in government. The key question many observers are asking today is whether Mexico's democracy has matured enough to withstand the onslaught of organized crime, the hardship of global recession, and a possible PRI victory in 2012. Our aim in this book is to provide a thorough discussion of Mexican political development, evaluate the prospects for Mexico's continued democratic consolidation, and underscore its special relationship with the United States. Overall we are optimistic about the future of democracy in Mexico, given important institutional, societal, and economic changes that have occurred in recent years. However, some important challenges and obstacles remain, which we will discuss in detail throughout this book.

The first part of this book provides a historical overview of Mexican political development. After a brief discussion of pre-Columbian society, chapter 1 chronicles the difficult process of modern Mexican state formation, from Spanish colonialism to independence. Chapter 2 examines the course and consequences of the 1910 revolution, from the overthrow of the authoritarian ruler Porfirio Díaz to the emergence of the PRI as Mexico's dominant political party. Chapter 3 explores the "classic" PRI system that facilitated the party's electoral hegemony for more than seventy years. Chapter 4 analyzes the reasons for the PRI's decline and the confluence of factors that contributed to the emergence of democratic competition in Mexico.

The second part of the book examines Mexico's political institutions, culture, and society. On paper, Mexico's presidential system, with a bicameral legislature, multilayered federalism, and elections, appears strikingly similar to that of the United States. Still, while Mexico's postindependence constitutions were significantly influenced by the example of the United States, the two systems function very differently. To help understand why, chapter 5 examines Mexico's government institutions and processes, while chapter 6 explains party and electoral systems. Society is the focus of chapters 7 and 8. Chapter 7 describes Mexican values and beliefs, attitudes and feelings, and norms and behaviors in relation to politics, while chapter 8 examines the nature and role of Mexican civil society. Together, these four chapters demonstrate how far the Mexican state and society have come since the days of single-party rule.

That said, the future of Mexico's democracy will depend on its ability to address some major domestic and foreign policy challenges, which are the subject of the third and fourth part of this book, respectively. In the third part, chapters 9 and 10 focus on Mexico's difficulties in achieving macroeconomic stability, sustaining economic growth, reducing poverty, and promoting equity. Unless Mexico successfully overcomes these challenges, it is unlikely that democracy will deepen. Likewise, without the rule of law, the subject of chapter 11, Mexico will find it difficult to consolidate its recent democratic gains. In the final part of the book, chapter 12 examines Mexican foreign policy outlook and its mechanisms for engaging the rest of the world, while chapter 13 explores its close ties with the United States, with particular attention to migration, trade, security, and the countries' shared border.

Part I

MEXICAN POLITICAL DEVELOPMENT

1

Mexico's Historical Foundations

M exico has a long and fascinating history. To this day, contemporary Mexico is rich with the archeological remnants, languages, and descendants of several advanced indigenous civilizations. The conquest and decimation of those civilizations by Spanish invaders in the early fifteenth century constituted one of the most dramatic and lamentable examples of cultural conflict in world history. For three hundred years after the conquest, Mexico became a colony of the Spanish Crown and fed the development of one of Europe's greatest empires. Eventually, as elsewhere in the Americas, the efforts of the Spanish Crown to gain a stronger hold on its colonial territories—including laws and bureaucratic measures that squeezed the colonists and sharpened class distinctions—inspired insurrection and calls for independence. The bloody struggle to separate from Spain left Mexico to wrestle with the dilemmas of self-governance and the territorial encroachments of the United States. It was not until the late nineteenth century that Mexico achieved some reasonable semblance of order, and only at the cost of the ideals of freedom and equality that had inspired some of its greatest patriots.

This chapter explores Mexico's historical foundations by surveying events leading from its earliest civilizations up to the prerevolutionary period at the start of the twentieth century. No brief account of this sort can do justice to Mexico's rich and captivating history. The purpose here is therefore to provide readers with sufficient background to understand some of the factors that contributed to the formation of Mexico's political development. We first discuss Mexico's ancient indigenous civilizations and some of their political and cultural contributions to modern society. We then turn to the legacy created by three hundred years of Spanish colonialism. In particular,

7

legacy of Spanish Colonialism

we emphasize the roles of the mercantilist economic model, the hierarchical imperial bureaucracy, extreme social stratification, and tensions between the Catholic Church and secularists. All of these significantly shaped the foundations of contemporary Mexican politics.

PRE-COLUMBIAN CIVILIZATIONS

Prior to the arrival of Europeans, several major civilizations made up the region known as Mesoamerica or "Middle America," the area that is today occupied by Mexico and the six countries that make up Central America. These civilizations developed over the course of several thousand years in four distinct regions of contemporary Mexico: the Gulf Coast (Olmec), the Oaxaca Valley (Zapotec, Mixtec), the Yucatán Peninsula (Maya), and the Central Plateau (Teotihuacán, Toltec, and Aztec) (see figure 1.1). Becoming familiar with Mexico's ancient indigenous civilizations helps us understand Mexico's long-standing regional and cultural diversity, and provides background on personalities and events that are important cultural referents in contemporary Mexico. Doing so also acquaints us with the history and heritage of indigenous people, who represent a significant portion of Mexico's population today and continue to struggle for justice and equality.

importance to poli sci

The histories of these ancient civilizations remain somewhat incomplete. Physical evidence and archeological remains are still the subject of scientific rediscovery and investigation, as researchers try to uncover and explain the mysteries of the past. Indigenous written histories—of which there were many—were initially indecipherable or were lost to the ravages of time and conquest. Among the best accounts available are those written by the Spanish, whose cultural interpretations and deliberate revisions were often self-serving and denigrating to their subjects. Hence the material presented here represents our effort to combine multiple and sometimes conflicting sources on the subject.

According to the best available estimates, the story of Mexico's indigenous peoples began approximately 20,000 to 25,000 years ago, when humans first settled in Mesoamerica. Like their nomadic ancestors who crossed the ice-covered Bering Strait from Asia as long as 30,000 years before them, the first people of Mesoamerica engaged in primitive hunting and gathering. Over the next several thousand years, these early Mesoamericans relied on basic tools and technologies—fire, coarsely crafted stone instruments, rope, and woven baskets—and lived lives similar to those of primitive humans around the world.[1] Mesoamerican settlements increasingly relied on domesticated crops that were unique to the region and eventually became staples. Corn, in particular, developed and maintains a deep cultural significance in Mexico. Early Mesoamericans also domesticated other plants

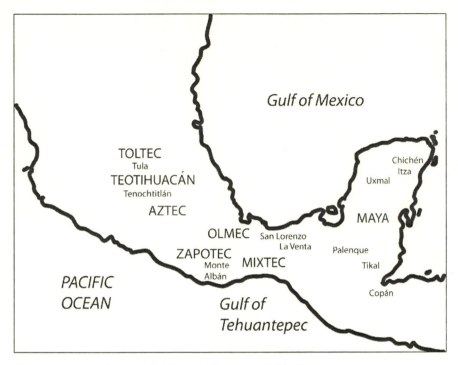

Figure 1.1. Map of Mexico's Major Indigenous Civilizations

that are commonly identified with Mexico today: chili peppers, beans, avocados, cocoa (chocolate), and henequen (sisal). With the advance of agricultural production came larger and more established settlements, and the foundations for Mesoamerica's great civilizations. The people learned to make tools and crafts—knives, millstones, and pottery—and basic structures, and eventually developed advanced technologies, architecture, and systems of governance that rivaled the early civilizations of Europe, Asia, and Africa.

Mesoamerican civilizations developed unique identities and legacies that found representation in great monuments, majestic pyramids, and impressive religious structures. To accomplish these feats, most Mesoamerican civilizations relied on hierarchical political systems, which featured specialized economic production that was marked by stratified social divisions between elites (nobles, priests, and military leaders) and commoners (merchants, artisans, farmers, and slaves).[2] While elites typically had a monopoly on scientific, intellectual, and ritualistic achievements in these ancient societies, they depended on the labor, ingenuity, and tribute of their subjects to develop highly sophisticated civilizations, as we discuss below.

The Gulf Coast: The Olmecs

The first major civilization to emerge in Mesoamerica was that known as the Olmecs (1500 to 400 B.C.E.), during what archeologists call the Pre-Classic Era.[3] Some estimates suggest that there were as many as 350,000 inhabitants of the Olmec civilization. At its peak, the size of some of the largest Olmec settlements—such as San Lorenzo, La Venta, and Zapotes on the Gulf Coast of what is now the state of Veracruz—may have exceeded 1,000 inhabitants, making them the largest conurbations in Mesoamerica up to that point, and most likely the first major civilization in all of the Americas.[4] Indeed, many scholars have described Olmec society as one of only six "pristine" or sui generis civilizations in human history, though they surely also had interactions with and influences from other people in Meso-america. Still, the Olmec are believed to be the first people in Mesoamerica to have constructed crude pyramids, used advanced mathematical concepts (such as the use of zero), and developed sizable settlements with organized methods of planning and design for urban communities.[5]

One of the most distinctive aspects of Olmec civilization was their con-struction of colossal carved-stone heads with thick, broad facial features, thirteen of which have been discovered in different settlements. Among the most significant subsequent influences of the Olmecs were their spiritual beliefs. Sacred images of jaguars and mixed human-jaguar figures occupied a central place in Olmec sculpture and artwork. Later Mesoamerican cul-tures combined the Olmecs' reverence for the jaguar and the eagle as sacred symbols, and they adopted similar religious practices. Olmec shamans also produced balls from local rubber trees to conduct ritualistic games involv-ing competition between two opposing teams in specially constructed ball courts. Ball courts and other aspects of Olmec culture were widely adopted in Mesoamerica by later civilizations.

The Oaxaca Valley: The Zapotecs and Mixtecs

The Zapotec people, centered in modern-day Oaxaca, began to develop their initial settlements around the same time as the Olmecs. By ap-proximately 500 B.C.E., centuries before the rise of the Maya, the Zapotecs eclipsed the scale of any Mesoamerican civilization to that point. By its peak between 450 and 700 C.E., the Zapotec city of Monte Albán grew to as many as 25,000 inhabitants, traded actively with neighboring resi-dents of Teotihuacán, and held dominance over surrounding settlements in the Oaxaca Valley. The Zapotecs likely originated some of the most important and widely diffused aspects of Mesoamerican culture, including hieroglyphic writing, masonry, and advanced astronomy. Indeed, Zapotec astronomers are credited with inventing a complex but highly accurate 365-day solar calendar (eighteen months with 20 days, plus a period of 5 additional "unlucky" days), as well as a sacred cyclical calendar (with 260 days drawn from thirteen cycles of 20 named days), later used by the Olmecs and throughout Mesoamerica.

The causes of Zapotec decline are unknown, but it is clear that the fall of Monte Albán coincided with and was likely linked to the decline of its major trading partner, Teotihuacán. Over time, Monte Albán's influence waned and the Zapotecs were gradually eclipsed by the cultural influence and military superiority of the Mixtec civilization. The Mixtecs were a distinct linguistic and ethnic grouping that first grew out of mountainous central areas of the Oaxaca Valley as early as 7000 B.C.E. and later spread to the northern highlands and coastal areas. By the fall of the Zapotec civilization, the Mixtecs had developed a series of small kingdoms that achieved important accomplishments in writing, artisan work, and construction between 1000 and 1400 C.E. Yet during this period, the Mixtecs also faced the encroachment of militaristic expansion from their neighbors.[6]

The Yucatán Peninsula: The Maya

During the Classic Era (from around 250 to 900 C.E.) Mayan civilization grew to become one of the most expansive and enduring in Mesoamerica. At its apex, around 600 C.E., Mayan civilization likely consisted of as many as 2 million people, speaking more than two dozen languages. Tik'al, the largest Mayan city of the time, may have had as many as 60,000 inhabitants, with an additional 30,000 people in surrounding rural areas. Eventually, through a loose agglomeration of city-states or kingdoms, the Maya came to occupy most of the Yucatán Peninsula, southern Mexico, and present-day Guatemala, Belize, El Salvador, and western Honduras.

Early Mayan civilization was likely influenced in important ways by trade, migration, and related interactions with other Mesoamerican peoples, though the nature and extent of these influences are debated by experts.[7] Mayan civilization stood out for its size, sophistication, and longevity. Adaptation of various agricultural methods—including fertilization, terracing, hydrology, draining, and crop rotation—allowed the Maya to develop a large, densely populated civilization in a difficult tropical environment.[8] Major Mayan cities also featured uniquely designed and lavishly ornamented pyramids, temples, and other architectural structures, built at steep angles from the white limestone prevalent throughout the Yucatán Peninsula. The Mayans, like the Zapotecs, also developed a written language of elaborate hieroglyphs, leaving important Mayan texts, or codices, that still survive and help document their history.

Mayan civilization fell into decline and disarray beginning in the Late Classic Period, probably as the result of the combined influences of drought, overexploitation of the region's natural resources, increased warfare, famine, social dissolution, and (later) invasion and conquest by the Toltecs of central Mexico.[9] However, the people and remnants of Mayan civilization survived until the arrival of the Europeans in the early sixteenth century and even today constitute an important component of Mexican society.

The Central Mexican Plateau: Teotihuacán, Toltec, and Aztec Civilizations

The Central Plateau of Mexico gave rise to a series of prominent and influential civilizations that arguably dominated much of Mesoamerican history and modern-day fascination with pre-Columbian times. The first major civilization was based in the city of Teotihuacán and located northeast of present-day Mexico City. It rose to prominence between 300 and 100 B.C.E. and began to decline after 700 C.E. At its peak, Teotihuacán was inhabited by as many as 200,000 people, making it one of the largest cities in the world at that time. By then, the city boasted more than six hundred pyramids, thousands of dwellings, and hundreds of workshops. The most significant structure, the Pyramid of the Sun—completed around the time of Christ in the Western calendar—was of great religious significance; it was believed to establish a connection to the underworld through the caves beneath it.[10] Teotihuacanos succeeded in dominating nearby peoples, like their neighbors to the east, the Tlaxcalans, and established trading relationships that extended throughout central and southeast Mexico. Moreover, long after Teotihuacán fell into decline, the city retained a prominent place in Toltec and Aztec civilizations, who called it the City of the Gods.

Following the decline of Teotihuacán, a second major civilization, the Toltecs, arose in central Mexico between 900 and 1100 C.E., and was centered in the city of Tula in the present-day state of Hidalgo (just north of Mexico City). By its zenith, the Toltec capital of Tula may have reached as many as 60,000 inhabitants. While less populous than Teotihuacán, Tula nonetheless achieved remarkable influence throughout Mesoamerica. The Toltecs expanded militarily, and traded with and otherwise influenced people of the Gulf Coast, the Yucatán, southwestern Mexico, Central America, and even native peoples in North America. Toltec influences can be seen in the dissemination of religious practices and mythology, including their worship of the feathered serpent god Quetzalcoatl, the continued use of Olmec-style ball court games, and their use of some religious symbols. Above all, the Toltecs are remembered for their militaristic orientation.[11]

Toltec accomplishments were documented, extolled, and possibly embellished by the Aztecs, who emulated Toltec militarism and ferocity. In actual fact, the Aztecs descended from the Mexica people (the source of Mexico's modern name), who arrived in central Mexico in the aftermath of Toltec decline. These early Aztecs initially served as mercenaries for the people of Colhuacan. However, in 1325 C.E. when the Mexica purportedly killed a Colhuacan princess in a religious ritual they were banished, whereupon they relocated to the marshlands of Lake Texcoco. Aztec legend suggests that this site was foreseen by prophecy and revealed by the sighting of an eagle perched on a cactus and consuming a serpent (from which Mexico's national seal was derived). The Aztecs began to reclaim the marshes of Lake Texcoco by erecting artificial agricultural fields (*chinampas*), constructing canals, and building dikes to separate salt and freshwater systems. The lake's islands, Tenochtitlán and Tlatelolco, were connected to the mainland by three extended causeways and an aqueduct.[12]

Within a century, the Aztecs established themselves as the predominant power in central Mexico, thanks to the establishment of the so-called Triple Alliance between three great kingdoms centered in Tenochtitlán, Texcoco, and Tlacopan. While the three entities ostensibly shared power equally, the great city of Tenochtitlán became the center of this loosely administrated political system. Led by a series of fierce and audacious leaders, notably Itzcoatl (1427–1440) and Ahuitzotl (1486–1502), the Aztecs established an expansive sphere of influence—some might say an empire—that stretched from the Gulf Coast to the Pacific. Aztec expansion was achieved through alliances with the willing and the military conquest of the defiant, both of which were required to pay tribute and sometimes became the victims of ritual sacrifices. By its peak in the early sixteenth century, under the reign of Moctezuma II, who led the kingdom from 1502 until the arrival of the Spanish, the Aztec capital of Tenochtitlán numbered as many as 300,000 people.[13]

SPANISH EXPLORATION AND CONQUEST IN MEXICO

In Europe and Africa, half a world away from Mesoamerica, impressive civilizations also rose, fell, and competed for dominance. In the struggle for dominance among civilizations, the year 1492 was an auspicious one for the Spanish: Christian nobles reconquered the last Moorish stronghold and reestablished Spanish sovereignty after three hundred years of domination by Muslims from Northern Africa. Spain's attempt to reclaim its identity, particularly with respect to religion, contributed to the strength of the Catholic Church—and the zealousness of the Spanish Inquisition to root out the unfaithful—under the reestablished monarchy. When King Ferdinand and Isabella "La Católica" came to the throne, however, Spain was a latecomer to the game of exploration and imperialism in which other European powers—especially the Italians and the Portuguese—were already much advanced. The exploration of the New World, in actuality a search for alternative access to lucrative trade with Asia, therefore represented the efforts of the Spanish Crown to catch up with other parts of Europe. The discovery of a new continent gave Spain an opportunity to plunder new sources of wealth and enabled its ascent as Europe's strongest power by the end of the seventeenth century.

The Great Clash of Civilizations

The Spanish conquest (1492–1533) in Mexico began as explorers moved from the Caribbean coast and inward to the mainland empires of the Mayans and the Aztecs. The man we know as Christopher Columbus—an Italian named Cristóbal Colón—led the way in the era of Spanish exploration and expansion. He was later followed by Hernán Cortés, the principal actor in the conquest of what became known as New Spain (contemporary Mexico and Guatemala). Cortés sailed from Cuba to Mexico in 1519 with just a few hundred men and sixteen horses, authorized by the governor of Cuba, Diego Velázquez, to explore the coast of the "island" of Yucatán. Going well beyond this, within two and a half years Cortés had conquered millions of native people. What made Cortés so successful so quickly and against such overwhelming odds? The answer lies in the technological, biological, and strategic advantages favoring the Spanish, and the particular circumstances of the Aztecs, the dominant indigenous civilization of the time.

Most obviously, the Europeans benefited from technologies—guns, steel armor, and horses—that were unknown in the New World. The blunt stone and wooden weapons of indigenous peoples, often primarily intended to stun or subdue an opponent, were outmatched by steel swords and armor. Still, despite the real and psychological advantages these weapons gave the Spanish, the sheer number of their opponents would have easily overwhelmed the Spanish if not for other factors.[14] In particular, the Europeans brought unfamiliar diseases, such as smallpox and syphilis, inflicting devastating plagues that rapidly decimated the native population. While demographers continue to debate the number of people in the Americas in the 1490s, it was certainly no less than 13 million and possibly well above 100 million. Whatever the total, many scholars estimate that depopulation occurred at a horrifying rate, and within 130 years of the arrival of the Europeans, as few as 3 million indigenous people remained.[15]

Cortés and other conquerors also benefited from the political fragmentation of the Aztec empire and the resentments harbored by the groups it dominated. Cortés skillfully capitalized on anti-Aztec sentiments to forge alliances, most notably with the Tlaxcalans, to overthrow the Aztecs.[16] Furthermore, Cortés benefited from the invaluable skills and assistance of an indigenous woman whose given name is unknown but who was called "Marina" by the Spanish, and is known today as "La Malinche" or "Malintzin." Likely born near modern-day Coatzacoalcos, Malinche was enslaved as a young girl and taken to the Gulf Coast by her captors. Later she became one of twenty female slaves awarded to Cortés's expedition as tribute from a local chieftain. Initially, Cortés had enlisted the services of a Spaniard named Jerónimo, who had lived shipwrecked for several years among the Maya and learned their language. Because Malinche spoke Mayan and Náhuatl, the language *translator* of the Aztecs, she was able to work with Jerónimo to provide Cortés with translation. However, Malinche quickly learned Spanish and thus became an indispensable asset as both a confidante and consort to Cortés. Her place in history is one that many Mexicans equate with betrayal of all indigenous people. Yet, confronted with limited options, Malinche likely made the same strategic choices other indigenous people made during this troubled time. Had it not been this particular indigenous woman who aided Cortés, some other indigenous speaker might have become a similar instrument of Spanish power.[17]

With these advantages, Cortés and his men battled against hostile indigenous tribes for months as they made their way inland from the Yucatán coast. Upon landing at Veracruz, Cortés hastily established a local government in the name of the Crown—La Villa Rica de la Vera Cruz, known today as Veracruz—giving himself some measure of legal autonomy from Governor Velázquez. Cortés famously tested his men by offering safe passage to Cuba for those disinclined to continue. His ruse was actually intended to expose the fainthearted and the disloyal, whereupon Cortés burned the ships, left a small battalion to defend his base, and marched on to the interior.

As was likely his intent, the news of Cortés's advance toward the Aztec capital preceded him. The message was not lost upon Moctezuma, the ninth Aztec ruler of the city of Tenochtitlán and the leader of the Triple Alliance. Moctezuma was the great-grandson of the Aztec ruler Moctezuma Ilhuicamina (1440–1468), who had introduced the universal military training that facilitated Aztec hegemony.[18] According to Spanish accounts, Moctezuma believed that Cortés was the Toltec god Quetzalcoatl, and that a series of mysterious events—a comet, silent lightning flashes striking a fire in a temple, and ghostly apparitions—served as supernatural omens of his second coming.[19] This portrayal of Moctezuma as a naive, superstitious leader may merely reflect the biases of the Spanish themselves or convenient retrospective interpretations of the conquest. Indeed, it would be a mistake to presume that Moctezuma was a fool. Like his predecessors, Moctezuma was a warrior king; he had dramatically expanded Aztec influence and consolidated their reach into Mixtec territory. Moctezuma's realm likely held three times the population of Spain and more than any other European nation—roughly 30 million people. With a thousand concubines and three thousand servants, Moctezuma enjoyed every possible luxury for his time. He was an accomplished scholar, a careful student of history, and widely regarded as a great leader until his ultimate downfall.[20]

Yet, despite multiple opportunities to crush Cortés and avert his own defeat, Moctezuma hesitated to do so. Possibly the Aztec leader miscalculated or misinterpreted the unprecedented situation before him. Wary, and perhaps uncertain as to whether Cortés was indeed a returning god, Moctezuma initially attempted to dissuade the Spanish. Moctezuma sent Cortés warnings of the hardships of the journey to the highlands, and he offered gifts of gold to encourage the Spaniards to turn back. It is also possible that Moctezuma's overtures were a strategic delay tactic. Since most able-bodied men were in their fields tending to the harvest, the readiness of the Aztec army may have been limited.[21] For his part, Cortés sought to intimidate Moctezuma by enlisting the support of thousands of Tlaxcalan warriors and displaying his willingness to use extreme force. In Cholula, Cortés butchered an estimated three hundred of the town's leaders in a public square, on rumors that they were plotting to kill the Spaniards. By his arrival in Tenochtitlán, Cortés had amassed considerable military strength and a forceful reputation. Hence, Moctezuma decided that the best approach was to offer Cortés an audience and evaluate the situation for himself.[22]

As Cortés and his men crossed the great causeway over the lake and into the Aztec city, Moctezuma greeted him personally with a dramatic procession in the plaza of Tlatelolco. Yet, once within the walls of Moctezuma's palace, Cortés took the emperor hostage and forced him to issue decrees that effectively abdicated power to the Spaniards. For a time, the Aztecs were reluctant to attack while their leader was held hostage. However, the tide turned after Spaniards evidently misinterpreted an Aztec religious rite as an impending attack and responded violently. After the ensuing melee, Moctezuma was killed and the Spaniards, together with their Tlaxcalan allies, fought to make their way out of the seething Aztec capital. Over half of Cortés's men and hundreds of Tlaxcalans died. The rest made a miraculous escape on June 30, 1520, on a turbulent and rainy evening that the Spanish called the Sad Night (*La Noche Triste*). According to legend, that night Cortés wept beneath an *ahuehuete* tree—a conifer that is today Mexico's national tree—lamenting the loss of blood and treasure.[23]

In the months that followed, while the Aztecs suffered a major outbreak of smallpox that killed Moctezuma's immediate successor, Cuitlahuac, and dramatically weakened Aztec forces, Cortés and his Tlaxcalan allies plotted to retake the city. Together, they constructed a miniature armada of boats—large enough to transport horses and soldiers—that could be disassembled over land and deployed into Lake Texcoco. With these technological innovations and some new allies, the Spaniards and Tlaxcalans laid siege to Tenochtitlán. After the Spaniards captured Cuauhtémoc, Moctezuma's nephew and the newly designated leader of the Aztecs, they were able to force the final surrender.

SPANISH COLONIALISM

After the surrender of the Aztecs, Cortés rapidly asserted Spanish authority by extracting the allegiance of neighboring native peoples—sometimes by replacing existing chieftains with leaders who vowed their support—and by extending the conquest to the rest of the mainland and present-day Guatemala. Those Spanish fortune seekers who prevailed during the conquest and continued the exploration of the New World were rewarded with *fueros* land grants (*encomiendas*) and privileges that enabled them to exploit the people and resources of the New World. Spain's colonial holdings in the Americas—of which Mexico was its greatest asset—made it the dominant power in Europe for most of the next three hundred years. Meanwhile, the indigenous people of the New World had a very different perspective on Spanish colonialism. The Spanish gradually undermined and usurped the power of even their elite indigenous allies, eventually reducing all indigenous people—including those with whom the Spanish cohabited—to a category of inferior social status.[24]

While numerous important developments unfolded over the course of Spanish colonial history, we focus our analysis on four key features of the time period: the mercantilist economic model, the colonial bureaucracy, the stratification of social classes, and the significant role of the Catholic Church. Each of these phenomena had a direct impact on Mexican political development that lasted after independence in 1821 and into the twentieth century.

Mercantilist Economic Model

The decision by European monarchs to fund expeditions such as those led by Columbus and Cortés was driven above all by the desire to achieve economic and political dominance on the home continent. Thus, once the task of defeating indigenous armies was complete, the conquerors immediately set about establishing a colonial economy that served the Spanish Crown. This economic model, known as mercantilism, held that all economic activity should enhance the wealth and power of the state. In practice it meant that the colonial economy was based on the production of primary goods (e.g., precious metals, textiles, foodstuffs) to be exported to Europe, while providing a foreign market for the sale of Spain's manufactured goods (e.g., clothing, processed foods, luxury items). However, while the mercantilist model greatly benefited Spain and other European empires, it had several detrimental effects on the colonies themselves.[25]

low economic diversity

First, because mercantilism was based on the extraction of resources for the benefit of Spain, there was almost no attention given to promoting the development of a robust, diversified economy in the colonies. Second, all economic infrastructure was concentrated in areas that served Spanish economic and political demands. Together, the lack of economic diversification and infrastructure (including roads, administrative institutions, and local financial institutions) put Mexico at a severe disadvantage once it secured its independence from Spain. Faced with the task of restarting the economy after independence, the new ruling elite, perhaps quite naturally, later chose to replicate many aspects of the mercantilist model, including a dependent trade relationship with Europe. Though the Mexican version of mercantilism had the advantage of bringing wealth and power to Mexico rather than to a foreign Crown, it perpetuated repressive labor conditions, extreme income inequality, and dependence on foreign capital investment. As we will see in the coming chapters, throughout the course of Mexican history, these three characteristics have served as a source of social and political instability.

future social and political instability

Colonial Bureaucracy

Successful administration of the mercantilist system required an organizational apparatus to monitor and regulate activities in the colonies and protect the interests of the Crown. The development of the administrative bureaucracy was especially necessary to counter the power of *encomendados*—conquistadors who were granted ownership of vast land holdings (*encomiendas*) and their populations (sometimes including entire towns and villages)—who had a great deal of autonomy from the Crown. The Spanish Crown appointed viceroys (*virreyes*), who were supervised by the king's representatives in an appointed body known as the Council of the Indies. There were viceroyalties for New Spain (Mexico), Peru, New Granada (Venezuela, Ecuador), and La Plata (Argentina).

The viceroys helped oversee the vast administrative bureaucracy created to regulate the customs and duties of the Crown with regard to economic transactions in the colonial economy. In addition, the viceroys commanded the military, the coercive apparatus that served as both an exploratory force for expanding Spain's territorial holdings and the protector of the Crown's interests in the New World. Gradually, the Crown did away with the *encomiendas*, and local mechanisms of colonial administration became institutionalized under the authority of the viceroys. Governors headed the more populated territories, which became the basis for the subsequent development of state governments in the nineteenth century. Similarly, hundreds of local government districts (*ayuntamientos*) emerged, with power centered in the figures of the mayor (*alcalde*) and city counselors (*corregidores*).[26]

Thus, the colonial bureaucracy laid the foundation for subnational administrative and political divisions in Mexico that persisted well after the colony of New Spain won her independence.

Social Stratification

Another important aspect of Spanish colonialism was the extreme social stratification that developed in Mexico over three hundred years. The fact that Spanish colonization of the New World initially took the form of a series of military campaigns meant that, for the most part, the conquistadors did not bring their wives and families to the Americas. Consequently, many Spaniards cohabitated and bore children with native women. Even after the conquest, mixing between the New World's three races—the socially constructed categories of white, black, and Indian—produced a diverse array of class and ethnic identities. Indeed, during this period there developed a hierarchical "pigmentocracy," in which an individual's social status (and perceived value) was determined entirely by place of birth and racial background.[27]

At the top of the pigmentocracy were "whites": both *peninsulares* (pure-blooded Europeans born on the Iberian Peninsula) and *criollos* (Europeans born in the Americas). By virtue of their European birth, education, and socialization, the *peninsulares* were the smallest group, but they dominated virtually all positions of economic and political power. Even their offspring, the *criollos*, were considered inferior in their readiness to govern and were relegated to midlevel positions in the bureaucracy (as lawyers, accountants, etc.) and in business (as merchants, import-exporters, bankers, etc.). At the bottom of the social pyramid were the full-blooded indigenous people and the African slaves, imported to offset labor shortages after the decimation of local populations. Mixing among these "lower" races produced a colorful social caste system with mestizos (white-Indian), mulattos (black-white), and zambos (black-Indian), who tended to work as manual laborers, artisans, and domestic servants in colonial society. While mestizos eventually became the vast majority in Mexican society, in the long run this pigmentocracy created patterns of social and economic interaction that sustained asymmetrical power relations and, even today, mitigates against the development of equal political rights in Mexico.

The Catholic Church

The Catholic Church was an important facilitator of the colonization of Mexico and the rest of Latin America. Indeed, Spanish military explorers and the agents of the Church worked together with sword and cross to settle untamed lands through an integrated network of fortresses (*presidios*) and missions (*misiones*). The dissemination of religion was vital to the overall effort of the conquest, and the success of the Church was enormous: in a few years millions of indigenous people converted to the Catholic faith.[28]

Religion had long been an agent of cultural diffusion among various indigenous civilizations. Religious icons and practices were commonly disseminated and blended through various cultural interactions—and directly imposed by civilizations that conquered neighboring peoples. When conquering other civilizations, they tore down enemy shrines and constructed new temples on top of the remains, often using the same stones to rebuild. Hence, while not necessarily immediately embraced by native peoples, the phenomena of cultural conquest and religious blending were hardly unfamiliar when later perpetuated by the Spanish, who similarly constructed new Catholic sanctuaries from the indigenous temples that they destroyed. The native people adapted to the new religion with relative ease, and agents of the Church appeared eager to blend Catholic and native religious symbols, a phenomenon known as "syncretism," to win converts to the Church. For example, the existence of a wide array of Catholic saints made it relatively easy to map the religious symbols of Christianity onto the pantheon of indigenous gods.[29] Perhaps the best-known example of syncretism in Mexico is the deeply revered Virgin of Guadalupe—a brown-skinned, Náhuatl-speaking image of the Madonna. (See textbox 1.1.)

While the Church can be rightly seen as closely tied to the Spanish Crown, some members of the clergy made important efforts to promote the rights of indigenous people. Two prominent examples are Juan de Zumárraga, the first bishop of New Spain and the Protector of the Indigenous, and Father Bartolomé de las Casas, whose revelatory book *History of the Indies* and activism in Spain were instrumental in creating special protections for native people through the New Laws in 1542. Such ministry and activism won many converts and helped make Catholicism the primary religion for the vast majority of Mexicans and the rest of Latin America. On the other hand, representatives of the Church also committed significant abuses, amassed enormous wealth, and acquired huge tracts of land for agricultural production. Over time, the power of the Church contributed to a series of contentious church-state conflicts that lasted into the twentieth century, as anticlerical elements worked to divest the Church of its holdings and influence in secular matters.

INDEPENDENCE AND POSTCOLONIAL INSTABILITY

At the beginning of the eighteenth century, the Spanish Crown fell under the control of the Bourbon dynasty of France. The Bourbons allied Spain with France in its conflicts with other European powers, notably England,

Textbox 1.1. THE VIRGIN OF GUADALUPE

According to Catholic teachings, the Virgin of Guadalupe appeared to Juan Diego, an early convert to Christianity, three times, beginning on December 9, 1531, on the hill of Tepeyac, close to the destroyed Aztec temple honoring the goddess Tonantzin. Speaking to Juan Diego in his native tongue, the apparition asked him to appeal to the bishop, Juan de Zumárraga, to build a church for her over the ruins of Tonantzin's temple. Despite multiple entreaties, the bishop initially denied Juan Diego's request and demanded proof of his vision. Hence, upon her final apparition, the Virgin provided proof by directing Juan Diego to gather a crop of Spanish roses—miraculously blooming in the dead of winter. When Juan Diego opened his cloak to reveal to the bishop the roses he was carrying, emblazoned on the cloak was the image of the Virgin that appears here. Bishop Zumárraga immediately began building the Basilica of Guadalupe in her honor. In 1745 the Vatican officially recognized the appearance of the Virgin of Guadalupe as a miracle. Juan Diego was venerated in 1987, beatified in 1990, and canonized as a saint in 2002.

The Virgin of Guadalupe has acquired such a significant following in Mexico that her image is nearly as popular as the country's flag. She was the symbol behind which Father Miguel Hidalgo rallied his cry for Mexican independence in 1810, and behind which the revolutionary forces of Zapata fought in the 1910 Mexican revolution. Today, the feast day of the Virgin of Guadalupe on December 12 continues to be celebrated by an estimated 11 million visitors to the Basilica of Guadalupe in Mexico City.

and imposed a series of new regulations to impose order and extract greater resources from the colonies. These regulatory changes, which further heightened the political and economic status of *peninsulares* at the expense of *criollos*, exacerbated existing tensions between the two groups and ultimately contributed to the latter's quest for expanded opportunities via independence from Spain.[30] *peninsulares vs Criollos*

[margin note: Criollo rebellion]

Miguel Hidalgo, a priest who had lost his lands and was relegated to a remote parish because of his *criollo* status, developed a loyal following of *criollos*, mestizos, and indigenous people. Resentful of the repression of these groups in the colonial hierarchy, Hidalgo joined other liberally minded *criollos* in plotting for Mexican independence. In September 1810, Hidalgo was warned by Ignacio José Allende Unzaga, a fellow *criollo* and coconspirator, that Spanish officials planned to arrest him. In the first hours of September 16, 1810, Hidalgo rallied his supporters and parishioners by tolling the church bells of the small town of Dolores, Guanajuato, and issuing the rallying cry "Death to the Spaniards, long live the Virgin of Guadalupe" (*¡Mueran los gachupines, Viva la Virgen de Guadalupe!*).[31] So began an independence movement that quickly mobilized more than eighty thousand people to Hidalgo's cause. Although Hidalgo's forces captured important cities such as Morelia and Puebla, Spanish reinforcements easily defeated the poorly armed and untrained peasants and then executed Hidalgo (whose head was placed on display). Soon after, José María Morelos—a mulatto priest who supported Hidalgo—took up the mantle of independence (along with the zambo military commander, Vicente Guerrero).[32]

[margin note: el grito de Dolores]

As it turned out, Mexican independence was stalled by events in Europe. With the defeat of Napoleon's armies in 1812, Ferdinand VII was restored to the Spanish throne; he moved swiftly to deploy Spanish forces to put down the rebellion in the New World. With these reinforcements, the Spanish succeeded in capturing Morelos; they executed him in 1815 and significantly reduced insurgent forces over the next few years. Yet by this point life had deteriorated significantly in the colonies as economic production was severely disrupted, and wealthy Mexican elites found themselves increasingly supporting the royal treasury out of their own pockets.

Ironically, it was these same conservative elites who revived the independence movement in 1820. Concerned by the efforts of liberals in Spain to restrict the Crown under the 1812 Constitution of Cadiz, Mexican conservatives believed that a weaker monarch would threaten their privileges and began to favor independence. A conservative general named Agustín de Iturbide led the break from Spain, issuing the Plan de Iguala, a proclamation favoring Mexican independence, the establishment of a constitutional monarchy, and a guarantee that merit, not race or place of birth, would be the sole criterion used to fill economic and political positions. Under these principles, Iturbide secured both liberal and conservative support and with minimal force succeeded in liberating Mexico in 1821, becoming its first independent head of state.

The Dilemmas of Self-Governance

Along with political autonomy, independence brought considerable chaos and strife, and ground Mexico's economy to a virtual halt by severing the newborn country's trade with the Old World. War had destroyed much of the country's agricultural output and severely disrupted mining activity. Indeed, the production of gold and silver—which had reached its peak in Mexico by the 1790s and into the early eighteenth century—fell to less than half capacity by the end of the war. Broader Mexican society was plagued by high levels of unemployment, lack of access to land, and miserable living conditions; as a result, peasant and worker revolts were common during this period, often numbering in the thousands. Under these unenviable circumstances, Mexico's new leaders negotiated a series of unfavorable foreign loans and issued bonds that Mexico was later unable to repay.

Meanwhile, independence created a political free-for-all, with no clear leader or group having sufficient power to govern effectively. In place of the old colonial bureaucracy, there emerged a series of *caudillos*, or strongmen, who took power and maintained their position by use of force. The highly personalistic rather than institutional nature of power after independence became an enduring characteristic of politics in Mexico and elsewhere in Latin America. Immediately after independence, General Iturbide declared himself emperor of Mexico and pillaged the national treasury—a move that led to his swift removal thanks to the forces of Vicente Guerrero, who advocated the creation of a constitutional republic with a popularly elected president and legislature. Yet even after the promulgation of the 1824 constitution, political stability remained elusive, and power remained concentrated in the figure of the Mexican president and an array of powerful individuals at the regional and local level. Between 1824 and 1857 there were nearly fifty different governments (and more than twenty-five different heads of state), at least half of which came to power as the result of violent insurrection.[33]

Within this context General Antonio López de Santa Anna emerged as one of Mexico's most famous *caudillos* and was both respected and reviled. Santa Anna had proved himself an effective military leader during the wars of independence, and he ruled Mexico (either directly or indirectly) between 1824 and 1855 with a devastating combination of opportunism, corruption, and authoritarianism. In retrospect, Santa Anna's character should have been ominously clear when, after being elected for the first time in May 1833, he unabashedly spent government resources on frivolous affairs of state, posh public works (e.g., an elegant opera house), and his own luxurious lifestyle.

Beyond this, Santa Anna left the actual task of governing to his vice president, Valentín Gómez Farias, at least until Gómez Farias sought to curtail the power of the Church and the military. Santa Anna staged a coup against Gómez Farias in June 1833, and then, paradoxically, restored Gómez Farias to govern in his place. This pattern of personalistic intervention repeated itself multiple times over the next several years, as we discuss below.

The War of the North American Invasion (1845–1848)

Compounding Mexico's problems as a new nation was its geographic location next door to the United States, an ambitious young power with a fifty-year head start on independence. The origins of the War of North American Invasion (known in the United States as the Mexican-American War) are found in Texas. In the 1820s, the Spanish Crown had encouraged settlement in its northern territories in an effort to dissuade U.S. expansionism. Settlers of any nationality could obtain land for next to nothing in exchange for becoming Mexican citizens and Catholics. A group of Anglos led by Stephen F. Austin settled in Texas while actively resisting the terms of the agreement, refusing to become Mexican citizens or convert to Catholicism. Initially these Anglos posed little threat to Mexican interests, but by the 1830s, they outnumbered Mexicans five to one. Supported by the United States, leaders like Austin began calling for independence from Mexico, which was increasingly trying to exert its authority on the remote territory. In order to put down the budding insurgency, in 1835 Santa Anna led his troops to Texas and decisively defeated the rebels at the Alamo. The Mexican victory prompted a fierce response by the Texans and the U.S. government, which actively supported retribution, and in 1836 Texas captured Santa Anna and won its independence from Mexico. To secure his release, Santa Anna agreed to withdraw his troops south of the Rio Grande—a move that would encourage the United States to greatly exaggerate its actual boundaries and add to Mexico's territorial losses just ten years later.[34]

Had Texas remained independent, Mexico might have eventually relinquished its claim and recognized Texas's sovereignty. However, the U.S. decision to annex Texas and its later encroachment into still disputed territories provoked outrage in Mexico. In May 1846, U.S. forces led by General Zachary Taylor encroached on Mexican territory and clashed with Mexican forces in an encounter that left several dead. Claiming that Mexico had "invaded" U.S. territory, when in fact the opposite had occurred, U.S. president James Polk declared war on Mexico. For a year the two armies battled over the location of their countries' shared border. The United States steadily advanced into Mexican territory from the north and east through the gulf port of Veracruz. After a bloody battle, U.S. forces made their way to Mexico City. Santa Anna's poor strategic decisions and inability to command the loyalty of regional leaders or ordinary citizens allowed the United States to defeat Mexico relatively easily, despite fierce final shows of resistance in Mexico City.[35] In the end, Mexico was forced to surrender and accept the terms of the Treaty of Guadalupe Hidalgo (1848), which ceded more than one-third of Mexico's northern territory to the United States in exchange for $15 million in war indemnities. In the wake of his humiliating defeat at the hands of the North American armies, Santa Anna was forced into exile. Meanwhile, to the dismay of Mexicans and at the expense of Mexico, the United States had established itself as the larger and more powerful of the two countries.[36]

La Reforma: The Conservative-Liberal Divide

The nationalism generated by the Mexican-American War intensified the domestic tensions between Mexico's two opposing elite factions, the liberals and the conservatives. Each had a different vision of how Mexico should assert its national identity. The liberals were primarily *criollos* who claimed to stand for the defense of liberal democratic practices, advocated the separation of church and state, and called for the integration of indigenous people into modern society. The conservatives traced their roots to the traditional beliefs of *peninsulares* and favored maintaining autocratic forms of governance, preserving the privileged status of the Catholic Church, and upholding strict social divisions.

While the conservatives had the upper hand at the outset of Mexican independence, political backlash against Santa Anna's abuses of power advantaged the liberals, who took power after his exile. They quickly convened a constitutional convention and drew up a new charter that reinforced the liberal commitment to a federalist republic, free elections, clear separation between church and state, and access to public education. In order to bring the constitution of 1857 into force, the liberals also enacted a series of reforms—known as the Reform Laws (La Reforma)—to strip the military and the Catholic Church of their power. In particular, the Reform Laws eliminated exemptions given to the military and the clergy from being tried in civil courts; forced the Church to sell off all property except for churches and monasteries; and removed birth, death, marriage, and other registries from Church control and gave them to the state. By December 1857, conservatives responded by declaring General Félix Zuloaga president in an attempt to oust the liberals from power. The liberals responded in kind by declaring Benito Juárez, a well-respected Zapotec lawyer and Oaxacan governor, president. What followed was a brutal three-year civil war between liberals and conservatives, called the War of Reform, which ended with a liberal victory and the installation of Juárez as Mexico's first indigenous president. (See textbox 1.2.)

Textbox 1.2. BENITO JUÁREZ

Benito Juárez, a Zapotec Indian, was born March 21, 1806. He was one of only a few ethnically indigenous Mexicans to serve as president, a position he held for a total of five terms. Trained as a lawyer, he served as governor of Oaxaca, where he focused on public works projects. He was later expelled and went into exile in the United States for opposing the Santa Anna regime. There he helped draft the Plan of Ayutla, a strong foundation of the liberal revolutionary movement, which called for the removal of Santa Anna as dictator and the drafting of a Mexican constitution. In 1855 Juárez was appointed minister of justice and public education, a position he utilized to eliminate *fueros,* the special privileges of the military and clergy. In a very short time he also served as minister of the interior and president of the Supreme Court of Justice.

Juárez was first elected president in 1857, and he focused on limiting the power of the Roman Catholic Church and the military, promoting citizen equality, and establishing a federalist constitution. He also reduced the size of the military and introduced educational reform. Juárez was ousted by the invasion of the French in 1863 but returned to power after the defeat of Napoleon's forces and the execution of Emperor Maximilian. Today, Juárez is regarded as a great Mexican hero because of his opposition to Santa Anna's corrupt regime and his dedication to democracy, equality for indigenous populations, and defense of nationalism. His death in 1872 created a political vacuum that allowed Porfirio Díaz to reintroduce autocratic rule and ignore socioeconomic inequality, two important contributors to the Mexican revolution.

Unfortunately, the young liberal republic remained saddled with debt. In 1861, Benito Juárez declared that Mexico's economic situation would prevent it from paying its sizable foreign debt to countries like France, Britain, and Spain. Unhappy with this pronouncement, France's Napoleon III sent troops to collect the debt, at the eager invitation of bitter conservatives longing for a return to monarchy. After a major defeat at the battle of Puebla on May 5, 1862, the French returned with 24,000 reinforcements and succeeded in installing Maximilian von Hapsburg of Austria as emperor of Mexico in April 1864.

Maximilian proved to be a sore disappointment to conservatives who believed that monarchical rule was the only way to reestablish the correct order of things. Showing decidedly liberal tendencies, he upheld the Reform Laws, restored communal lands to indigenous villages, and outlawed debt peonage. Yet these acts were not enough to appease the liberals, who continuously attacked his royal forces. With virtually all Mexicans opposed to his rule, Maximilian sat uncomfortably on what one historian has referred to as a "cactus throne." As Napoleon III's power began to wane in Europe, the unfortunate Maximilian's days were numbered. By 1867, liberal forces recaptured northern Mexico and forced Maximilian's surrender. He was tried, found guilty of violating Mexico's sovereignty, and executed by firing squad.[37]

The restoration of the republic paved the way for Juárez's return. With the conservatives soundly defeated, Juárez enjoyed widespread popular support, in part because of his solid reputation but also because he shrewdly managed to secure the backing of many of society's most powerful groups, whose interests often contradicted each other. Moreover, true to liberal principles, Juárez actively promoted honest elections and greater access to free public education, and brought greater economic progress by investing in infrastructure and increasing exports. Despite the relative peace and prosperity that followed, a number of domestic tensions were brewing, and not everyone was pleased with Juárez or his decision to seek reelection in 1871. Indeed, one of his most notable detractors was General Porfirio Díaz, another Oaxacan of indigenous heritage. Díaz was a war hero who had served Juárez in the battle of Puebla and later became a member of Congress. Arguing that Juárez's reelection violated liberal principles, Díaz campaigned against him using the slogan "Effective Suffrage, No Reelection."

While Juárez handily won the 1871 election, his term came to an abrupt end when he died of natural causes in July the following year. Sebastián Lerdo de Tejada, the president of the Mexican Supreme Court, was named as the interim replacement for Juárez. Though he too had run for president in 1871, Lerdo was a close ally of Juárez and was strongly committed to the liberal project. Indeed, the Reform Laws requiring the sale of Church properties were his brainchild, and were also known as the Lerdo Laws. By December 1872, Lerdo was formally appointed by the Mexican Congress to serve as president; he was reelected in July 1876. Lerdo's aspirations to a third term and Mexico's progress toward becoming a liberal republic came to an abrupt end when Porfirio Díaz seized the presidency by force in November 1876.

THE PORFIRIATO

General Porfirio Díaz governed Mexico for thirty-four years before finally relinquishing power in 1910. For a brief, four-year period, Díaz ruled from the sidelines when his friend and military comrade Manuel González sat as president (1880–1884). However, throughout the Porfiriato—the period of Díaz's uncontested rule—there was little doubt about who dominated Mexican politics. With regard to civil liberties and religion, Díaz pragmatically positioned himself between liberals and conservatives. In the process, Díaz successfully transformed the model and motto of the Mexican republic from "Liberty and Progress" to "Order and Progress." For Díaz, political stability ("order") was essential for economic modernization and growth ("progress"), and the dictator successfully achieved both to an unprecedented degree during Mexico's independence. In this sense, one of the most important accomplishments of the Porfiriato was the development of national unity and a sense of nationalism in a long-fragmented country. Still, the inequity and repressiveness of the Díaz regime would bring about its own undoing in the 1910 Mexican revolution.

dev. of national unity — nationalism

Order: The Pax Porfiriana

The Porfiriato was characterized by a strong central government headed by Díaz and fortified by his hierarchical, highly personalized style of rule. One of Díaz's first tasks after taking power was to develop a loyal base of support by placing faithful allies and military comrades in key positions in the legislature, courts, government ministries, and state governments. He also used his military rank and personal connections to blur the civil-military relationship and channel all institutional lines of authority to the executive. The practical result was that the military answered to him and other branches of government lacked the authority or the will to check his actions. Overall, Díaz's efforts to centralize power in his own hands and use force to maintain order effectively rendered moot the constitution of 1857, and made it easy to liken the general to other Latin American *caudillos*, par excellence.[38]

As documented in John K. Turner's 1908 book *Barbarous Mexico*, Díaz did not hesitate to use the military, rural police, secret police, and even death squads to assert the state's power to impose order and crush dissidents.[39] One tool of repression was the notorious *ley fuga* or escape law, which permitted authorities to execute any prisoner who attempted to flee and led to numerous extrajudicial killings. On a grander scale, Díaz was particularly unmerciful in his repression of a Yaqui rebellion (1876–1910) in the northeastern state of Sonora; thousands of captives were sent to enslavement and a rapid demise in Yucatán and Quintana Roo.[40] To maintain the support of wealthy elites and local strongmen, Díaz selectively bestowed favors and state resources upon those who favored him. He also assumed the role of a political godfather, brokering solutions for the disputes among elites that he had, in effect, played an important role in creating. To ensure the support of the most prominent local elites, Díaz allowed them considerable autonomy in controlling their strongholds on the condition that they reserve their ultimate loyalty for him. Many elites readily embraced the terms of a bargain so favorable to them, and they relied on Díaz to defend their privileged positions in the face of the popular uprisings, indigenous revolts, and peasant land invasions that became common during this era. Díaz's rural police (*rurales*), sometimes called *federales,* acquired a dubious reputation as they helped bring disgruntled and disobedient peasants and laborers back in line with the demands of their employers and the government. In this way, Díaz created the conditions, bases of support, and pockets of resistance that ensured rapid but inequitable economic growth through the turn of the century.

Progress: Economic and Social Modernization

At the heart of Díaz's approach to modernization was the European philosophy of positivism, which posited that a country's economic and social problems could be solved using rational, scientific, and systematic methods. Díaz filled his government with *científicos,* trained professionals who espoused the positivist view that Mexico had the potential to become a modern, prosperous state. In economic terms, "progress" meant infusing the Mexican economy with foreign capital, which would introduce technologies and production methods to increase growth. Therefore, the Mexican government created attractive incentives for foreign investors, such as tax and legal exemptions and subsoil rights of ownership, to ensure high profits. And because political order was virtually guaranteed under Díaz, Mexico became one of the most attractive investment opportunities in Latin America.[41]

It is hardly a surprise, then, that international investors, mainly from the United States, Britain, and France, flocked to Mexico and foreign investment increased dramatically. Indeed, by 1910, 90 percent of investments in mining, electricity, oil, and banking were foreign owned. The United States accounted for the greatest share of all foreign investment over the course of the Porfiriato, buying the lion's share of Mexican exports (see figure 1.2). The dramatic increase in capital modernized most sectors of the Mexican economy, especially those most targeted by foreigners: infrastructure, mining, and commercialized agriculture. To support these industries, Díaz developed a vast communications and transportation network. When Díaz took power in 1876, there were 400 miles of railroad in Mexico; by 1911, there were 15,000 miles.[42] Over the same period, the number of mines tripled and output expanded greatly, due to new machinery and processes.[43] Because of these developments, Mexico's economy boomed and became significantly more integrated into the overall world economy, with exports expanding nearly tenfold (from 25,000 pesos to roughly 225,000 pesos) and imports increasing by nearly sixfold (from 40,000 pesos to 155,000 pesos) between 1876 and 1909.[44] At the same time, Mexico's dependence on foreigners and the emerging global economy made it vulnerable to

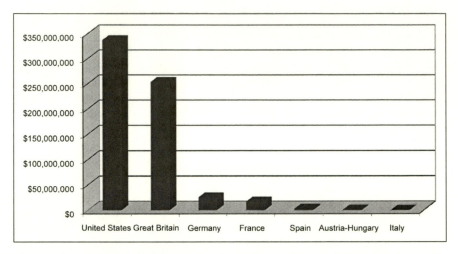

Figure 1.2. Foreign Capital Investment in Mining and Industrial Companies, 1886–1907

Source: José F. Godoy, *Porfirio Díaz, President of Mexico: The Master Builder of a Great Commonwealth* (New York, London: Knickerbocker Press, 1910), 128.

instability in the international economy, and the privileges granted to foreigners in Mexico would later become a point of serious resentment.

An integral part of the positivist philosophy of Díaz and the *científicos* was a firm belief in the tenets of social Darwinism, which posited that certain races, such as black Africans and indigenous Americans, were physically, intellectually, and morally inferior to white Europeans. Therefore, for Mexico to overcome its "Indian problem," it would have to "whiten" itself to successfully achieve modernity. To this end, the regime actively encouraged the immigration of Europeans, who, generally speaking, possessed more labor skills, higher levels of education, and cultural traits believed to be necessary to move the country forward. Furthermore, the government made an effort to incorporate what were perceived to be superior architectural styles and materials, while the elites emulated everything French, from education to cultural practices and fashions, hoping to mirror what they saw as the height of sophistication. In sum, during the Porfiriato, government and society embraced modernity as a cultural aspiration that was exclusionary and decidedly inorganic.[45]

CONCLUSION

Despite its significant shortcomings, the Porfiriato made Mexico into a more politically stable, economically successful, and socially vibrant modern polity. The political and economic instability of the independence and reform eras were distant memories, and at the turn of the twentieth century, Mexico appeared to have a very bright future. Mexico City had become a booming cosmopolitan capital with majestically constructed buildings and monuments, many of which survive even today as a testament to the grandeur of the Porfiriato. However, to focus solely on the great strides Mexico made in state formation and economic stability during the Porfiriato ignores the deep problems wrought during the same era.

Indeed, at almost every level of society, there were simmering resentments against the Díaz regime. Within the elite, many domestic owners of capital were frustrated that foreign investors enjoyed so many advantages at their expense. Similarly, some industrialists felt that the government's economic policies overwhelmingly favored agricultural exporters. Within the middle classes there was resentment because, although they had benefited from greater economic prosperity, the elite still tightly controlled access to capital and higher education. Further, many in the middle classes objected to being effectively locked out of important political positions in a country that was ostensibly a liberal republic. Artists and intellectuals began to chafe at restrictions on free speech and freedom of expression, and questioned the perceived superiority of European trends and thought. At the bottom, the working classes experienced little of the greater economic prosperity enjoyed by the upper and middle classes, and were instead exploited by labor practices that blatantly favored employers. In their traditional roles as indentured servants on elite-owned haciendas, indigenous people were viewed as inherently inferior, and they had no prospects for social mobility or access to land. These resentments, combined with the contractions in the international market on which Mexico had grown highly dependent, ultimately coalesced to produce a meaningful effort to bring about change, known as the 1910 Mexican Revolution.

2

The Mexican Revolution
and Its Legacy

1910-17

From 1910 to 1917, the Mexican Revolution mobilized hundreds of thousands of men, women, and children, resulting in at least one million deaths (more than one in ten Mexicans), a brief U.S. invasion, the elimination of entire towns, and the extended disruption of the Mexican economy.[1] Despite the upheaval it entails, revolutionaries tend to view violent political change as a means to achieve greater freedom and equality. Yet ironically, as in other major social revolutions of the twentieth century—Russia (1917), China (1949), Cuba (1959)—the Mexican Revolution produced an authoritarian order that lasted for several decades.[2] Understanding contemporary Mexican politics and the effects of violent regime change requires a solid grasp of the causes and course of the revolution, the major figures involved, and the long-term consequences of postrevolutionary regime consolidation. This chapter examines the course of the Mexican Revolution in three phases: the breakdown and overthrow of the ancien régime, the struggle for control in the postrevolutionary period, and the gradual consolidation and institutionalization of power under a new revolutionary government.

BREAKDOWN AND OVERTHROW OF THE PORFIRIATO

Few people expected that Mexico would experience a full-scale social revolution just after the turn of the century. However, the evident order and progress of the Díaz regime disguised some of the underlying problems with Mexico's turn-of-the-century political system. In particular, Mexico's heavy dependence on foreign investment—most banks, mines, railroads, and electric power were under foreign control—made its economy particularly vulnerable to the series of international economic crises and contractions of capital that occurred in 1904 and 1907. As crops were shifted to promote exports like henequen (sisal), everyday Mexicans suffered from the resulting price increases and occasional shortages in staple products like corn, which was increasingly imported to meet domestic needs. At the same time, a deep resentment toward foreigners grew from the persistent inequality and mistreatment of Mexicans in their own country. In some foreign companies operating in Mexico, for example, wages paid to foreigners were as much as double those earned by Mexican laborers doing the same work.[3] As in the case of other twentieth-century revolutions in Russia, China, and Iran, one historian observes, Mexico experienced "growing foreign influence and abuses; humiliating subordination to foreign regimes; state collaboration with international financiers while excluding domestic capitalists; and the social, political, cultural, and economic displacement of provincial and local elites, artisans, and peasants."[4]

Meanwhile, the persistence of poverty and severe inequalities in this era of "prosperity" made sustainable and widespread economic progress ultimately unfeasible under the Porfirian model. The everyday lives of Mexicans were compromised by limited economic opportunities, harsh working conditions, high infant mortality rates, rampant disease, and occasional food shortages. By mid-decade, a growing number of food riots and strikes—by tens of thousands of miners, textile workers, and other industrial workers—illustrated the many economic hardships faced by ordinary Mexicans. Meanwhile, over the course of the Porfiriato, small family farmers found themselves increasingly squeezed out by encroachment from wealthy foreigners and hacienda owners. Indeed, by the time of the revolution, more than two-thirds of the population was employed in the agricultural sector, but most found themselves working for wealthy landowners on the roughly eight hundred enormous haciendas that occupied half of Mexico's workable land. Furthermore, despite its abolition in 1814, slavery persisted for hundreds of thousands of indigenous people—sold at $50 a head—in parts of southern Mexico.[5]

In the end, however, it was not the economic inequality or repressiveness of the Díaz regime that sparked the revolution. Rather, it was the frustration and ambition of relatively wealthy elites. Some young elites, especially, felt that their upward political mobility and influence in the regime was circumscribed by the power structure: a network of generals, political bosses, and cronies that was as enduring and impervious as the great dictator himself. By the later part of the Díaz regime, only 8 percent of Mexico's population was over the age of fifty, yet the power structure overwhelmingly represented an older demographic: the average age of ministers of

Díaz's government was nearly sixty-eight, and few of them appeared likely to retire anytime soon.[6] Thus, among ambitious young elites, opportunities for advancement to the positions of power occupied by Díaz and his fossilized cronies must have seemed very far away. Nevertheless, even as late as 1910, very few people—perhaps Díaz least of all—seemed to even imagine the possibility of a complete revolutionary overthrow in Mexico.

The course of Mexico's revolution began innocently enough, with a casual but fateful remark made by Díaz in an English-language interview conducted by reporter James Creelman for *Pearson's Magazine* at Díaz's residence, Chapultepec Palace, in 1908. The interview produced a glowing portrayal of the Díaz regime, describing the great dictator as the "hero of the Americas" and "the greatest man of the continent" and emphasizing Díaz's commitment to "the democratic idea." Indeed, in the interview, Díaz expressed that he welcomed opposition candidates to run against him in the next election, and would gladly step down if defeated. To be sure, since Díaz had run virtually uncontested and still employed blatant fraud in the previous eight elections, the invitation was most likely insincere. Yet his remark drew interest from many in Mexico, most importantly, from a young man named Francisco Ignacio Madero.

As the grandson of one of the five richest men in Mexico, Madero came from a privileged background. He was foreign educated (Paris and University of California, Berkeley) and came from a wealthy northern family from Coahuila with a fortune in cattle and mining. Like many other progressive Mexican intellectuals of his generation, Madero was inspired by the liberal vision of Benito Juárez and the Reform Era, and by the democratic experiences of the United States. Yet as a man of means, Madero's initial intention was not to generate a full-scale social revolution to benefit the masses. Rather, his goal was to find a way to facilitate the transition from Díaz's oligarchic power structure into a liberal democratic system that would incorporate new elites through the application of democratic practices. His plan for this transition—which he outlined in his book *The Presidential Succession of 1910*—was for Díaz to choose someone from Mexico's young, progressive elite to serve as his running mate in the next presidential election. Ideally, that someone could learn from Díaz and pick up the reins of power once he was gone. Yet when Madero approached the president to propose himself as the vice presidential running mate, Díaz cordially but firmly declined.[7]

Frustrated but ambitious, Madero viewed Díaz's interview with Creelman as an open invitation to challenge the dictator in the upcoming election. Madero opted to run for president under the slogan: "Effective suffrage, no reelection" (*Sufragio efectivo, no reelección*)—the same slogan Díaz had used to run against Benito Juárez decades before. However, when Madero's campaign began to attract popular support, he was arrested by Díaz supporters in Monterrey. After Díaz won the election handily, Madero escaped from prison with the help of his supporters. He then issued the Plan de San Luís Potosí, a call to arms to overthrow the Díaz regime, and fled to the United States to prepare for the implementation of his plan.

VIOLENT STRUGGLE FOR POLITICAL CONTROL

The Mexican Revolution was a violent struggle to replace the existing political order, and it killed at least a million people over the course of roughly a decade. Yet the start of the violent phase of the revolution was rather unimpressive. On November 20, 1910, Francisco I. Madero returned to Mexico with just ten men and a hundred rifles, prepared to launch a revolution. He was supposed to meet with four hundred reinforcements but found only ten more men. Rather than attack, Madero returned to the United States and traveled to New Orleans to plan a second invasion. By the time Madero returned a few months later, now with 130 armed men, he was in a better position to challenge the regime, benefiting from critical allies and other armed insurgent groups now working to overthrow the Díaz regime. Along with Madero, several of the key figures who emerged in the process became icons of the revolution itself.[8]

One of Madero's most important sources of support was a man known as Francisco "Pancho" Villa, who became one of the revolutionary champions of the poor and disenfranchised. Villa was born to a poor family on a hacienda in the north-central state of Durango, and given the name of Doroteo Arango. The details of his early life are much debated. However, it seems that Arango became a fugitive at the age of sixteen after he shot at Augustín López Negrete—the owner of the hacienda—allegedly in retaliation for his advances toward Arango's sister. Arango turned to illegal activities like rustling cattle and stealing horses, evading the forces of the Díaz regime in the mountainous areas of Chihuahua. During this time, Arango changed his name to Villa and acquired a reputation as a bandit and folk hero. By the age of thirty-two, Villa made the switch from bandit to revolutionary, when he joined Madero in the struggle against the Díaz regime in 1910.[9] A fine sharpshooter and a superlative horseman—known by some as the Centaur of the North—Villa proved himself a bold military commander and an innovative strategist. He quickly became the head of Madero's forces in Chihuahua, eventually forming what became known as the Northern Division (División del Norte). Villa began collaborating with other rebel units under the command of Pascual Orozco, and their forces gradually grew from a few hundred guerrillas to thousands of seasoned troops, with large numbers of women and children in tow (see textbox 2.1).

**Textbox 2.1. MEXICO'S *SOLDADERAS*:
WOMEN IN REVOLUTION**

The violent upheaval from 1910 to 1917 mobilized not only men but thousands of women. Mixed in with both federal troops and the irregular forces of various revolutionary factions, these women took on versatile roles as wives, mothers, nurses, spies, arms smugglers, and even armed combatants. Many *soldaderas* fought bravely alongside the men, and some even rose to the rank of officer. However, most women brought onto the battlefield performed less glamorous and more grueling tasks, such as cooking, cleaning, doing laundry, and burying the dead. Nevertheless, the contributions of all *soldaderas* were essential, if less well known than they should be, to the story of the Mexican revolution.

Also important in this early phase of the revolution were the agrarian forces that arose in southern Mexico to demand land redistribution and property rights. The predominant symbol of these social forces was Emiliano Zapata. Zapata, a farmer and horse trainer orphaned at age sixteen, came from a small village in Morelos. Dark skinned and contemplative, Zapata spoke both Spanish and Náhuatl fluently. In character and appearance—with his excellent horsemanship, his enormous sombrero, his cigars, and his thick mustache—he conjured up visions of the *charro* bandits who roamed his region. Zapata's village had appealed to the Díaz government for many years to defend their land rights from large commercial farmers. When Zapata was selected as the leader of his village in 1909, he began to use force to take back the lands that his village had lost. These land seizures were quickly followed by similar efforts in other towns, and soon Zapata commanded a revolutionary army of several thousand rural fighters throughout Morelos. These guerrilla forces often quickly attacked enemy troops and immediately resumed normal agrarian activities to avoid detection. But having an agrarian base was also a serious limitation of the Zapatistas, since they were unable to stray far from their home communities. In the end, Zapata's primary goal in participating in the revolution was to win land and freedom for his people.[10]

Confronted with these uprisings as well as other separate attacks by rebels in northeast Mexico, Díaz began to realize the seriousness of the situation, which was clearly spiraling out of his control. By early 1911, his advisers warned that the strength of rebel forces in Chihuahua alone required that he amass thirty thousand troops if he hoped to control the state.[11] Over the course of his administration, Díaz had cut the size of the armed forces by more than half, and he now had only about fourteen thousand men under his command. The prospect of increasing the number of federal troops was unattractive, since arming unwilling conscripts would have simply placed more weapons in the hands of potential rebels who now enjoyed the support of some of the wealthy northern elites.

As the rebels redoubled their efforts and the conflict spread throughout the country, Díaz realized that defeating the rebels would be next to impossible. Consequently, he proposed sweeping reforms in April 1911 to regain favor. But even his purge of high-ranking officials and pledge to redistribute land merely revealed his weakness and served to embolden the rebels, who continued their assault in both the north and the south. In Chihuahua, Madero's forces began to use the regime's own infrastructure against him by seizing control of railroads as a means of deploying troops in attacks on the city of Agua Prieta. Soon after, they captured the city of Casas Grandes and moved on to lay siege to Ciudad Juárez, a critical military stronghold for Díaz. With Zapata's forces also gaining ground in Morelos, Díaz offered a truce and began negotiations with Madero. Madero initially only demanded political representation for his supporters in the government. Both Villa and Orozco, however, pressured Madero to demand Díaz's resignation, a point on which Madero halfheartedly conceded.

When they later seized control of Ciudad Juárez, Villa and Orozco were again at odds with Madero when he pardoned General Juan Navarro, the commander of Díaz's forces in Chihuahua, instead of executing him for atrocities committed against their men. The incident illustrated an important rift. Madero had mild, reformist intentions and basically accepted the Porfirian order, with modifications; other revolutionaries had a more radical vision of comprehensive change. While Villa remained fiercely loyal to Madero despite this fact, other revolutionary forces eventually turned against him. Indeed, Orozco and Zapata later disavowed Madero for his general acceptance of the existing order and his failure to press for more radical change.

In the meantime, thanks to the initial support of the insurgent forces, Madero emerged victorious. On May 17, 1911, Díaz reluctantly ceded to the terms of the Treaty of Ciudad Juárez, including the terms for an interim presidency and a transfer of power through national elections. On May 25, 1911, Díaz resigned as president and departed from Veracruz on a ship bound for Europe, where he would be lauded till the end of his days. Before he left, however, Díaz made the fateful observation "Madero has unleashed a tiger, let us see if he can control him." Indeed, getting rid of Díaz was just the beginning of a long contest to achieve political control and consolidate a new regime. Even before he was elected president in a landslide election in October 1911, Madero clashed with Zapata over the issue of land rights and refused to return properties that had been taken from agrarian workers by large landowners. Hoping to assuage the concerns of those landowners, whose support he needed to reestablish order, Madero sent a general named Victoriano Huerta to Morelos to disarm the Zapatistas. In response, in November 1911, Zapata issued his Plan de Ayala, demanding land and liberty for Mexico's rural sector and declaring Madero a traitor to the revolution.

Zapata's insurgence was soon complemented, in March 1912, by a larger, more serious challenge from Pascual Orozco. In his Plan Orozquista, Orozco called for major labor concessions (such as wage increases, a ten-hour workday, stronger child labor laws), nationalist protections (especially for railroads), local autonomy, and agrarian reform and land redistribution. Strongly in agreement with these objectives, Zapata quickly aligned himself with Orozco, whom he viewed as the rightful leader of Mexico. Together, Orozco and Zapata viewed revolution as a movement to promote greater social equality in Mexico through land, labor, and educational reform. While Villa shared this view, he nonetheless stayed loyal to Madero, whose main objectives were far less progressive. Indeed, for Madero, the real purpose of the revolution was to return to the glorious era of Mexican liberalism: reinvigorating Mexico's liberal democratic republic by strengthening the legislature and courts, fostering democratic contestation, and allowing greater freedom of the press. Madero's efforts to promote social reform—agrarian, labor, and educational reforms in particular—were extremely limited, poorly funded, and clearly not a major priority.

In a sense, Madero's failure to embrace a social reform agenda and his strong commitment to liberal democratic reform became his undoing. While Madero battled his erstwhile supporters, he was perhaps democratic to a fault toward his enemies. Indeed, political deadlock and the proliferation of opposition forces in the legislature plagued and undermined his government. Meanwhile, heckled by a newly liberated media, Madero was badly maligned and ultimately appeared to be a weak and ineffective president. In this context, Madero's apparent weakness invited two coup attempts. But rather than execute the traitors, Madero ordered their imprisonment, enabling his detractors to conspire for a third, successful coup attempt in February 1913.

In responding to these rebellions, Madero regularly called on General Victoriano Huerta, his military chief of staff, to help defend his government. However, during the 1913 coup attempt, Huerta seized the opportunity to betray Madero and take power for himself. Huerta's takeover was supported by U.S. Ambassador Henry Lane Wilson, who detested Madero and viewed him as incompetent. The lack of U.S. support for Madero was attributable in part to his alliances with forces advocating land redistribution, however limited, and the constraints he was considering for foreign businesses (especially oil). In Mexico, however, Huerta was seen as a usurper by revolutionary forces, and he only held Mexico City for eighteen months, from February 1913 to July 1914.[12]

Chief among Huerta's opponents was the governor of Coahuila, Venustiano Carranza, leader of the "Constitutionalist" forces that sought to restore order. Carranza was a large landholder in Coahuila and had been a senator during the Porfiriato. Carranza seems to have seen himself as a modern-day Benito Juárez whose main objective was to return to the legal framework originally established under the 1857 constitution. With dutiful respect to procedure, Carranza had obtained legislative approval to rebel against Madero's usurpers. His Plan de Guadalupe denounced Huerta and proposed himself as leader of the Constitutionalist army, and provided a basis for him to become president when he finally defeated Huerta in August 1914. However, after vanquishing Huerta, Carranza refused to give due recognition to Villa and Zapata, who responded by ousting his fledgling government from Mexico City in November 1914. Villa tried to hold the city while Zapata returned to Morelos for reinforcements. The forces of Carranza supporter Álvaro Obregón retook the city in January 1915, driving Villa into hiding in the north, while Carranza sent General Pablo González to pursue Zapata in the south.

The 1917 Constitution

In 1916, in the midst of the battle against Villa and Zapata, Carranza assembled delegates in the city of Querétaro for the promulgation of a new constitution, approved on February 5, 1917. In accordance with Carranza's objectives, the 1917 constitution was modeled after the liberal reform constitution of 1857. Rooted in liberal democratic principles intended to ensure a representative democracy composed of elites, the 1917 constitution also stipulated the protection of basic political liberties, such as free speech (Article 6), a free press (Article 7), freedom of peaceful assembly (Article 9), religious freedom (Article 24), rights of the criminally accused (Article 20), and provisions for the division and balance of political power in government (Article 49 and subsequent articles).

Yet the 1917 constitution also went further, to include important socially progressive goals associated with more radical revolutionaries, like Orozco and Zapata. These progressive provisions included universal public education (Article 3), national ownership and redistribution of lands and natural resources like minerals and petroleum (Article 27), local autonomy (Article 115), and recognition of worker rights (Article 123). These revolutionary provisions went against Carranza's own designs and had been forced onto the agenda by sympathizers of Villa, Zapata, and Obregón, making it one of the most progressive founding charters ever produced. In the short run, however, the constitution of 1917 was largely symbolic because the government had neither the resources nor the will to enforce many of the new laws. The weak state of the economy made worker protections difficult to sustain.

Furthermore, after 1917, landowners regularly allied with the Church to oppose land redistribution and takeovers. Foreign interests, which still owned a substantial portion of agricultural lands, also opposed reform.[13]

Thus the vision of social justice for the poor, peasants, and workers of Mexico was undermined by a new ruling coalition that included Carranza's revolutionary generals, wealthy industrialists, and turncoats from the old landed elite. Meanwhile, within a few years, Carranza was able to neutralize the two major forces fighting for revolutionary social justice. Zapata was tricked and killed by Carranza's forces in 1919. Villa was driven into hiding and later retired to civilian life by 1920; he was finally murdered three years later (possibly because of a land dispute or his philandering). Over the next eight decades, both the liberal democratic and revolutionary provisions of the 1917 constitution were eroded, as vested interests and political convenience led to its frequent abrogation and amendment.

Still, by the end of his term in 1920, Carranza was unable to fully consolidate his control of the political system. In May of that year, with the evident intention of ruling from behind the scenes in the next administration, Carranza attempted to impose his successor, an obscure fellow Sonoran named Ignacio Bonillas. Obregón, who had supported Carranza against Huerta, felt slighted and issued the Plan de Agua Prieta, a proclamation urging Mexico to rebel against the president. In addition to popular support among workers, Obregón had the overwhelming support of the military, including General Plutarco Elías Calles, who helped Obregón drive Carranza from office. Carranza fled Mexico City to Veracruz, taking with him 50 million pesos from the national treasury. Ultimately Carranza did not escape. Conflicting accounts suggest that he was assassinated by one of his own guards or caught by Obregón's supporters and shot. Whichever the case, Carranza's ouster was the last successful armed uprising in Mexican history and led to a new phase of postrevolutionary consolidation in which subsequent governments maintained a monopoly on coercive force.

POSTREVOLUTIONARY CONSOLIDATION

After Carranza's ouster, an interim president oversaw new elections in 1920 that brought Álvaro Obregón to the presidency (1920–1924). Hailing from Sonora, Obregón continued the Northern Dynasty of prominent strongmen from the north who dominated national politics after Díaz's fall. Because Obregón's political orientation lay somewhere between those of elite interests and those of the more progressive revolutionary forces, he was considered a dangerous conservative by some and a dangerous radical by others. During his term of office, President Obregón spent most of his efforts ensuring international recognition of the new regime and consolidating his power vis-à-vis potential rebels against the government. However, Obregón made relatively little progress in implementing the revolutionary ideals that toppled the Porfiriato. His major contribution to the revolution was his ability to restore political order and initiate the consolidation of the new regime. It was Calles, his close collaborator and successor, who would put the finishing touches on this process of regime consolidation and lay the institutional foundations to secure the legacy of the revolution.

Álvaro Obregón and the End of Extralegal Succession

Although Obregón received much of his support from the working classes and the Regional Confederation of Mexican Workers (Confederación Regional Obrera Mexicana, CROM) founded during his administration, his government gave few concessions to workers and even harassed communist- and anarchist-led unions.[14] Obregón was also fairly conservative on land distribution; he mostly protected the interests of large landholders and was personally skeptical of the efficiency of redistributing land in small plots. Furthermore, Obregón's administration was friendly toward foreign business interests, particularly those in the United States. Though President Wilson had refused to recognize Obregón's new government after Carranza was murdered, under the administration of President Warren G. Harding (1921–1923), Obregón launched a series of prolonged negotiations that were finalized in 1923 with the Bucareli Agreement. This pact established that the United States would recognize Obregón's government in exchange for guaranteed protections for U.S.-owned agricultural lands and concessions to foreign oil interests. Many Mexicans perceived this as a breach of revolutionary nationalism and protested loudly. However, after Obregón easily quashed a revolt by one of his generals, he preempted other possible revolts by downsizing the military and its budget by roughly 40 percent.

These efforts gradually consolidated Obregón's power and established the authority of the new revolutionary government. As a result, in 1924, Obregón became the first postrevolutionary president to successfully complete a four-year term. To ensure a peaceful transfer of power, Obregón asserted himself in the selection of his successor, backing fellow Sonoran General Plutarco Elías Calles as Mexico's next president. The imposition of Calles provoked an uprising by several military commanders, but with renewed support from the United States, Obregón's government put down the rebellion in a few months. The quelling of this rebellion clearly demonstrated Obregón's monopoly on coercive force and gave his government an upper hand in securing political support for the final ratification of the Bucareli Agreement. Significantly, it also established a tradition of presidential imposition in the succession process, which lasted for most of the twentieth century.

Plutarco Elías Calles

For some, President Calles represented a more progressive orientation than his predecessor in that he openly proclaimed his commitment to socialism, provoked foreign oil companies with new reforms, introduced significant agrarian reforms, and invoked anticlerical provisions of the Mexican constitution. Calles also gave increased influence to the CROM and named its leader, Luis N. Morones to the cabinet post of minister of industry, commerce, and labor (a position Calles had himself occupied under Carranza). Under the Agrarian Law of 1925, Calles also implemented a more ambitious program of land redistribution than his predecessor, distributing more than 3 million hectares of land, compared to less than 1 million hectares distributed by Obregón. In addition, as a former schoolteacher, Calles placed heavy emphasis on educational reform. Yet Calles's evident commitment to progressive revolutionary goals confronted significant opposition and obstacles. Indeed, Calles ultimately removed Morones from his cabinet due to pressure from Obregón's supporters, who still controlled the Congress. Calles also later abandoned his minor efforts at agrarian reform to deal with other pressing challenges.

One such challenge was to smooth relations with the United States, which viewed Calles's self-professed socialism with suspicion. Mexico had recognized the Soviet Union in 1923 and enjoyed very amiable relations with Moscow, thanks to the efforts of envoys such as Alexandra Kollontai (1926–1928), the first female ambassador in the Western Hemisphere. However, at the height of the Red Scare, U.S. politicians and oil interests grew increasingly concerned about Mexico's leftward drift, particularly as the Calles administration sought to restructure laws regulating foreign petroleum companies beginning in 1925. When Calles later actively opposed U.S. foreign policy in Nicaragua, Mexico and the United States slid dangerously close to war. These tensions were eased by an eventual shift in Soviet policy toward Mexico (due to clashes between Stalinist and Trotskyist factions), a juggling of the U.S. diplomatic corps, and Calles's shift toward more business-friendly policies. The establishment of new laws (e.g., income tax, banking, credit) and investments in infrastructure put Mexico on a more solid economic footing and helped assuage the fears of the U.S. government and international investors.

If Calles's efforts to smooth political and economic relations with the United States were considered antirevolutionary by some, his commitment to the revolutionary goal of separating church and state was unquestionable. With his approval and encouragement, various state governments enacted policies that called for government registration of priests, the prohibition of priestly garments in public, and restrictions on worship services. In response, outraged Catholics founded the National League for the Defense of Religious Liberty (Liga Nacional de la Defensa de la Libertad Religiosa, LNDLR) with the implicit sanction of the Church. When the president called for a package of anticlerical policies—dubbed the Calles Laws—that included a suspension of church services, Catholic opposition became increasingly vocal and assertive. Tensions grew when the press reported that Archbishop José Mora y Ríos opposed the 1917 constitution, which provoked the government to close religious schools and deport two hundred foreign priests and nuns. The LNDLR collaborated with Church officials to implement a nationwide boycott of businesses and government services. By late summer, however, Catholic activism boiled over into violence. Fury over government restrictions and persecution of the clergy led to a series of uprisings in central Mexico known collectively as the Cristero rebellion (see textbox 2.2).

Textbox 2.2. THE CRISTERO REBELLION

The Cristeros consisted mainly of devout Catholics and a few priests who engaged government forces in a violent guerrilla war between 1926 and 1928. Under the battle cry *"Viva Cristo Rey"* ("Long live Christ the King"), the Cristeros were primarily concentrated in Jalisco and the Bajío region, an agricultural zone in central Mexico that historically served as the center of mining and industry. At the peak of the Cristero rebellion, also known as the Cristiada, the religious combatants numbered as many as fifty thousand irregular troops. Clashes with government forces led to as many as seventy thousand deaths (including nearly a hundred priests), and more than half a million Mexicans were displaced in the conflict. A diaspora of Catholic activists fled to urban centers and the farthest reaches of Mexico—including Baja California and Yucatán—and the United States.

Perhaps the best-remembered Cristero is José de León Toral, the young seminary student who assassinated President-elect Álvaro Obregón. Evidently he feared that the persecution of Catholics would continue unabated if Obregón, a close ally of the hated Calles, returned to the presidency. However, these concerns were likely misplaced. By 1928 a mediated settlement between the Church and the state was already under way, thanks to the intervention of the U.S. embassy and U.S. Catholics designated by the Vatican to facilitate a peaceful resolution of the conflict. The murder of the president-elect set these negotiations back for more than a year and solidified in the minds of many Mexicans the notion that the Catholic Church has no place in the national political arena.

Source: Jean A. Meyer, *La Cristiada*, vol. 1 (Mexico City: Siglo Veintiuno Editores, 1976).

Meanwhile, in the midst of this great conflict, Obregón and his supporters maneuvered to position the former president as Calles's successor. In 1926, the Obregonistas, who dominated the legislature, passed constitutional amendments to permit nonconsecutive reelection and to increase the presidential term to a full *sexenio*, or six-year term (to become effective during the next term). In 1927, in reaction to these developments, two generals plotted to overthrow Calles and prevent Obregón's return to power. However, over the course of a brief rebellion, both generals were captured and executed for treason. Obregón also survived two assassination attempts before winning the election on July 1, 1928. Two weeks later, however, he was fatally shot by a twenty-six-year-old Catholic seminary student posing as a sketch artist.

Obregón's assassination presented a severe political crisis for the new regime, creating a power vacuum that needed to be filled carefully and with renewed deference to the revolutionary maxim "Effective suffrage, no reelection." Initially suspected (though quickly exonerated) of being the architect of Obregón's assassination, President Calles was under pressure to step down. In his presidential address on September 1, 1928, Calles called on the Congress to name an interim president for the next term, declaring himself out of the running. Moreover, Calles emphasized his renewed commitment to the principle of no reelection: "Never again will an incumbent president of the Mexican Republic return to occupy the presidency." Calles argued earnestly that this was a critical juncture in Mexican history; in his words, it was an "opportunity to direct the country's politics toward a true institutional life."[15]

The *Maximato* and Birth of the Revolutionary Party

Three weeks after President-elect Obregón's assassination, the legislature selected a civilian, Emilio Portes Gil, to serve as interim president. Portes Gil was favored by many because of his commitment to socialist ideology, his public criticism of CROM corruption, and his past efforts to promote land reform in his home state of Tamaulipas. Serving for little more than a year, Portes Gil was primarily charged with the task of holding new elections in 1929. He was the first of three interim or provisional presidents over the next six years, a period that many have since described as the *maximato* because of the ongoing influence of former president Calles, who was referred to as the *jefe máximo*, or "maximum chief."

Indeed, soon after Obregón's assassination, Calles had set about creating a new political party to assemble what he called the "revolutionary family" of previously unconnected military leaders, regional political bosses (caciques), and other subnational political interests under one national umbrella. It was implicit in Calles's vision, of course, that the *jefe máximo* would be holding that umbrella to ensure Mexico's continued postrevolutionary stability and progress. However, at the time, the destiny of Calles's National Revolutionary Party (Partido Nacional Revolucionario, or PNR) was by no means certain. In the preceding decade, literally hundreds of minor political parties had vied for power at the state and national level. Since 1910, each president had run on a different party's ticket, and legislative coalitions were built more around the personal power of national and regional *caudillos* than around programmatic or policy agendas.[16]

The PNR was further hindered by concerns about Calles's blatant personal ambition to retain control of the organization. For this reason, the former president avoided taking a formal leadership role in the party and actually abstained from its founding convention, held in March 1929. Still, when another Calles follower, Pascual Ortiz Rubio, received the PNR's nomination for the presidency, renewed opposition and violence followed. Over the course of the next six months, ambitious military generals, Catholic zealots, and traditional liberals mobilized in opposition to the emerging regime. Each in turn failed to prevent the continued influence of Calles and, more important, the institutionalization of the PNR as a political force.[17] Meanwhile, Calles's continued influence was facilitated by the relative weakness of Ortiz Rubio, who was shot in the jaw in an assassination attempt on the day of his inauguration. As a result of this injury, which some attributed to a plot by the *jefe máximo* himself, Ortiz Rubio continued to suffer physical and mental anguish until he finally resigned prematurely in 1932.

More than halfway into the term for which Obregón was elected, it was now constitutionally possible for Congress to appoint a new interim president without holding a special election. From a list of Callista favorites, the PNR selected General Abelardo L. Rodríguez to serve in this capacity. Rodríguez's term, short as it was, laid an important foundation for the future: the no-reelection clause was formally and permanently reintroduced to the constitution. This shift prompted the PNR to adopt (at its second national convention to select a presidential candidate) a plan to ensure the continuity of its programs into the next administration. In its first six-year plan, the PNR proclaimed its commitment to the subdivision and redistribution of agricultural lands; improved irrigation and access to water, and modernized agricultural methods; more effective conservation and regulation of forestry; vigorous application of federal labor laws; new protections for domestic industries to help substitute imports from abroad; investments in transportation and communications infrastructure; greater federal resources to promote health care and proper hygiene; greater public investments in education (as well as the promotion of nonreligious, socialist education in public schools); and federal involvement in the development of the country's minerals and energy policy.

This renewed emphasis on key revolutionary and even socialist objectives demonstrated a shift in the political orientation of the ruling coalition and hinted at the coming downfall of the *jefe máximo*. In the aftermath of the revolution, the interests of agrarian and industrial workers seemed to fall by the wayside. To be sure, under Calles and throughout the *maximato*, modest labor and land reforms were enacted, and limited attempts were made to check foreign interests in the energy sector. Over time, Calles grew resistant to radical labor demands and skeptical of the merits of land redistribution as a means of modernizing Mexican agriculture. By the end of that decade, fewer than 4 million hectares of agricultural land had been redistributed and numerous industrial and mineral holdings remained in foreign hands. Revolutionary goals took a backseat to Calles's primary objective: personal power.[18] In this sense, Calles himself had become the biggest obstacle to what he called for in his outgoing presidential address in 1928: for Mexico to move toward being a "nation of institutions and laws." Ultimately, the Great Depression gave revolutionary ideals fresh appeal, and the influence of the *jefe máximo* would be undone by one of his own followers, General Lázaro Cárdenas.

CARDENISMO AND REVOLUTIONARY MEXICAN NATIONALISM

By explicitly adopting the 1910 Mexican Revolution in its name, the PNR symbolically embraced the hopes, themes, and heroic struggles of the revolution. However, well into the 1930s, many of the revolution's socially progressive goals remained largely unrealized. The PNR's selection of Lázaro Cárdenas as its presidential candidate in 1934 reflected three important shifts in Mexico. First, it represented a geographic shift of some significance. Unlike most previous postrevolutionary presidents, Cárdenas did not hail from the Northern Dynasty. Instead, Cárdenas came from the central state of Michoacán, and his presidency marked the beginning of a new era; virtually all subsequent presidents similarly came from Central Mexico.

Second, the selection of Cárdenas reflected growing support in the PNR and in Mexico for sweeping progressive reforms. As noted above, several major reforms were introduced during the *maximato* that paved the way for unprecedented agricultural, labor, and educational reforms under Cárdenas. In 1931, under Portes Gil, a new federal labor law established a minimum wage and basic workplace protections. In 1934, under President Rodríguez, a new agrarian code was introduced to break up and redistribute large landed estates in the form of communal lands (*ejidos*). Yet by fully implementing these reforms, President Cárdenas ultimately became the avatar of progressive revolutionary reform and one of the most revered Mexican presidents of all time.

Third, Cárdenas's nomination illustrated the weakening of Calles and his influence in the PNR. Calles's chronic health ailments worked together with the corruption and ineffectiveness of the CROM, increased strikes and activism of independent unions, and a worsening economy to undermine the *jefe máximo*'s power.[19] In this context, the PNR selected Cárdenas over two other candidates with closer ties to Calles. Born to an upper-middle-class family in Michoacán but unable to go on to high school after his father died prematurely, Cárdenas joined the revolution at the age of eighteen. He quickly rose through the ranks, making his way from first lieutenant to brigadier general in just seven years. After the revolution, Cárdenas's military career and connections to both Obregón and Calles made him eligible for political office. For most of the 1920s, however, Cárdenas remained active in the military, fighting to put down the rebellion in 1923 and deployed by Calles to protect Mexico's northern oil fields when tensions flared with foreign business interests in 1925.

Later, in 1928, Cárdenas ran as the unopposed candidate for governor of his home state of Michoacán. His gubernatorial experience offered him an opportunity to develop his own programs, political vision, and style of governance. In hindsight, three aspects of Cárdenas's approach in Michoacán stand out as particularly relevant to his future presidential administration: a commitment to agrarian reform, a skillful mobilization of support from organized labor and civic groups, and a significantly greater tolerance for the Church than Calles had. Cárdenas redistributed an enormous amount of land, with many of the new landholdings organized as collective farms or *ejidos*. Michoacán was the site of assertive agrarian demonstrations in the 1920s, led by local icons such as the indigenous leader Primo Tapia, who died in the grassroots struggle for land. As governor, Cárdenas pooled the support of workers, agrarians, and teachers and intellectuals into a single union: the Revolutionary Workers Confederation of Michoacán (Confederación Revolucionaria Michoacana del Trabajo, CRMDT). Formal incorporation of interests under the CRMDT provided Cárdenas with a mass base of support and a model for the future restructuring of the official party of the revolution. As governor of Michoacán during the later years of the Cristero rebellion, Cárdenas also showed considerable tolerance toward and maintained relatively friendly relations with the local Church hierarchy.

Like other populist leaders of the 1930s, Cárdenas successfully promoted a cult of personality that brought massive support from the poor and working classes. Always inclined to travel to remote villages and hear the concerns of the people, Cárdenas eschewed the pretensions of political office and mundane affairs of state. As a result, Cárdenas's persona in Michoacán rose to the same mythic status of Vasco de Quiroga, a lawyer turned priest, who had protected local Tarascan indigenous people from the abuses of the Spanish four hundred years earlier.[20] Cárdenas's honesty, benevolent reputation, and compassion for the poor led the people of Michoacán to bestow on him the same honorific once granted to Quiroga: "Tata" (Father).[21]

As the PNR gradually developed more revolutionary and socialist objectives into the 1930s, Cárdenas's progressive record in Michoacán made him seem an ideal candidate for the presidency. In part because of a long, close personal relationship with the young general from Michoacán, but also because he was favored by the revolutionary family, Calles chose Cárdenas to be his successor. Cárdenas embraced his candidacy with unprecedented zeal. Despite the guarantee of victory provided by the PNR nomination, Cárdenas embarked on an ambitious and innovative nationwide campaign, visiting even remote rural areas and using radio to address the nation. Cárdenas's industrious campaign and his more progressive political orientation enabled the PNR to roundly defeat three minor leftist challengers.[22]

On taking office, Cárdenas initially deferred to the *jefe máximo*, incorporating key Callistas into his cabinet. However, as Cárdenas gave license for a significant increase in labor agitation over the first several months of his term, Calles grew visibly displeased and apt to intervene. By June 1935, Calles issued a vituperative public address, sharply criticizing Cárdenas. Responding with a bold move against the *jefe máximo*, Cárdenas dismissed his entire cabinet (replacing them with loyalists) and sent Calles by presidential plane for a "respite" in the then sleepy western port of Mazatlán. This provided only a temporary solution. Calles returned to Mexico City in December 1935, attempting to counter Cárdenas by rallying the support of workers in the CROM. Over the next few months, minor clashes and acts of violence by Calles supporters hinted at the possibility of a coup. However, in April 1936, backed by thousands of workers and agrarians now mobilized under the banner of the National Committee for Proletarian Defense (Comité Nacional de Defensa Proletaria, CNDP), Cárdenas had Calles escorted to exile in the United States; he moved his family to San Diego.[23]

In effect, by ousting Calles, Cárdenas succeeded in transforming and reasserting the power of the Mexican presidency. The supreme authority of every sitting Mexican president would be unchallenged for the remainder of the twentieth century. However, Cárdenas's experience showed that in order to move beyond the militant *caudillismo* of the past, effective presidential authority required a strong and coordinated power base. While Calles's PNR provided a framework for unifying regional strongmen, generals, landowners, and elites under the auspices of the revolution, the official party had failed to establish a firm basis for the support of the working class and agrarian sectors. Now unopposed, Cárdenas went to work transforming the PNR into a party that successfully harnessed these interests and more assertively promoted the goals of Mexican revolutionary nationalism.

At the December 1937 PNR convention, the party voted to dissolve and reconstitute itself as the Party of the Mexican Revolution (Partido de la Revolución Mexicana, PRM). This transformation held both emblematic and functional implications. On the one hand, the party's rechristening symbolically embraced the revolutionary and nationalistic agenda of President Cárdenas. On the other hand, the party's reconstitution established an organizational structure for the representation of key revolutionary interests. Specifically, the party was now formally divided into four sectors: military, labor, agrarian, and middle class.

The first sector comprised the roughly sixty thousand members of Mexico's armed forces in a blatant blending of the official party with the coercive apparatus of the federal government. To incorporate labor, Cárdenas lent his full support to Vicente Lombardo Toledano's Confederation of Mexican Workers (Confederación de Trabajadores de México, CTM) as the primary representative of labor interests within the ruling party.[24] The CTM was rewarded with a central role in the PRM's organizational structure. At the same time, the PRM also incorporated the National Agrarian Confederation (Confederación Nacional Campesina, CNC). While Lombardo had formerly worked to unite urban and rural workers under one union, Cárdenas supported the creation of the CNC in 1935 in part to counterbalance the growing power of the CTM. Finally, in recognition of the influence of the middle classes—particularly teachers and government bureaucrats who supported Cárdenas—the PRM incorporated a popular sector. It was loosely organized during Cárdenas's term but would later be represented by the National Confederation of Popular Organizations (Confederación Nacional de Organizaciones Populares, CNOP), formed in 1942. Ultimately the popular sector held important advantages—higher education levels, greater resources, and more effective organizational skills—relative to the CTM and CNC.

Cárdenas's model of building popular fronts to support the ruling party is an approach to coordinating interest groups in political and decision-making processes that is commonly described as corporatism. Corporatism is a top-down form of interest representation in which the government formally recognizes and incorporates organized groups in society into the policy-making process, as discussed further in chapter 3. Cárdenas's explicit objective was to provide for the inclusion and representation of the diverse forces that propelled the revolutionary government to power. Indeed, the restructuring of the ruling party provided Cárdenas with the political support to embark on an ambitious restructuring of government policy, living up to the expectations of PNR progressives by implementing the extensive reforms previously contemplated in its six-year plan. Two areas in particular—land reform and the nationalization of oil production—deserve special attention, and we consider them below.

Land Reform

One of Cárdenas's most profound national reforms was the reorganization of land tenure arrangements. Calles had redistributed nearly three times more land than Obregón or Carranza, and slightly more land was redistributed during each of the abbreviated terms of Portes Gil, Ortiz Rubio, and Rodríguez. However, the vast majority of lands redistributed during these postrevolutionary governments were poor quality, relatively small plots intended to provide individual farmers with subsistence production to subsidize their day labor. Over the course of his presidency, Cárdenas subdivided and redistributed more than 17 million hectares of land (see figure 2.1).[25]

Still, despite the far-reaching nature of land reform under Cárdenas, the initiative did not result in a long-term improvement of conditions for the rural poor because of problems with implementation and the lack of effort to maintain or improve the program beyond his administration. For example, many *ejidos* not only failed to become major producers but also declined to levels well below self-sufficiency. Hasty implementation of the land redistribution program led to miscalculations in land surveys and in the distribution of water resources for the *ejidos*. Loopholes and special provisions to protect the interests of landowners allowed many to hold on to the most valuable sections of their property, leaving the *ejiditarios*

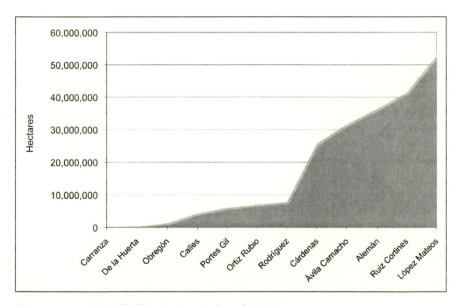

Figure 2.1. Land Redistribution in Mexico after 1916
Source: Data from 1916 through 1964 adapted from figure 2.7 in Roger D. Hansen, *The Politics of Mexican Development* (Baltimore: Johns Hopkins University Press, 1971), 33.

unproductive and fragmented parcels of land. Some large landowners subdivided their lands and sold them to members of their own family to avoid
forced redistribution. Faced with competition from large commercial farms,
collective farms were relatively inefficient: they could not benefit from
economies of scale or lay off their workers.

Collective farms also suffered from a lack of access to credit and machinery, which in many cases was still controlled by the large landowners who
had previously owned the redistributed lands. Furthermore, because *ejiditarios* were restricted by law from using their lands as collateral for private
loans, they depended heavily on government support; yet this support became sparse in the 1940s and 1950s. In contrast, government loans and investments favoring large, private commercial farms during the same period
contributed to a boom in Mexican agricultural production. Although land
redistribution in Mexico failed to have long-term positive effects, Cárdenas
is still revered by many for his efforts to uphold the spirit of the revolution
by increasing access to land.

Oil Nationalization

Cárdenas is perhaps most remembered—with admiration by many, and
with contempt by others—for his nationalization of foreign-owned oil
companies in 1938. Oil production in Mexico began in the 1890s, but it
was not until the end of the Porfiriato that the first significant oil wells were
tapped and put into operation by foreign investors. These companies had
demonstrated their influence in the 1920s—as evident from the pressure
on Obregón to negotiate the Bucareli Agreement—and drew significant
resentment from many Mexicans. In 1937, foreign oil companies became
the target of massive labor strikes protesting low wages and poor working
conditions, midway through Cárdenas's term. The dispute went before a
federal arbitration committee, the labor court, and eventually the Mexican
Supreme Court, which ruled in favor of the workers and required foreign
oil companies to abide by government terms for significantly higher wages,
hiring of Mexican managers, and improved conditions for workers. When
foreign companies refused to comply with the Supreme Court decision, the
Cárdenas administration viewed this as a violation of Mexican sovereignty.
Drawing on prior congressional authorization to use Article 27 to national-
ize private property for public use, Cárdenas expropriated the assets held by
mostly U.S. and British foreign oil companies.

Worried foreign investors reacted sharply to Cárdenas's actions, resulting
in an international boycott of Mexican goods and a significant economic
downturn. However, some feared that the boycott threatened to drive
Mexico toward a closer relationship with the Axis powers of World War II.
Hence, both the U.S. and British governments actively sought to normalize

relations with Mexico. The Mexican government went on to establish its own oil operations under the state-owned company called Mexican Petroleum (Petróleos Mexicanos, PEMEX). To this day, PEMEX remains the sole oil company in Mexico, though it has increasingly become the subject of calls for privatization.

Overall, Cárdenas had a tremendous impact on contemporary Mexican politics. He succeeded in concentrating executive power in the office of the president, rather than in the personality of its occupant or some other figure lurking in the shadows. Cárdenas also gave the official party of the revolution greater legitimacy and staying power by incorporating the revolutionary masses—especially industrial and agrarian workers—within the formal sectors of its organization. Cárdenas helped realize part of the promise of the Mexican Revolution by asserting national control of key economic assets and redistributing massive amounts of land. Finally, unlike Obregón and Calles, Cárdenas withheld any further ambition to wield political power after ceding the presidency to his handpicked successor. This particular decision established a precedent followed by every Mexican president thereafter, which effectively promoted greater loyalty and obedience from future presidential aspirants and their followers. In short, by the end of the Cárdenas administration, Mexican politics had taken on most of the characteristics that predominated throughout the remainder of the twentieth century.

CONCLUSION: THE LEGACY OF THE MEXICAN REVOLUTION

The 1910 Mexican Revolution was an explosion of popular discontent with the political constraints, economic inequality, and innate repressiveness of the Díaz regime. Yet the motivations of Mexico's revolutionaries were not uniformly aligned. The course of the revolution took many turns, had different regional manifestations, and brought together an assortment of interests that were joined only by their repudiation of the ancien régime and a desire for change. While Madero and Carranza saw the revolution as an effort to restore the nineteenth-century liberal principles enshrined in the 1857 constitution, Villa, Orozco, and Zapata were not content with merely restoring the liberal status quo ante, and sought redress for long-standing socioeconomic inequalities. Taking up arms, farmers sought "land and liberty," while urban industrial workers sought basic labor protections and redress for the long-standing injustices of Mexican capitalism. Most who fought for change desired a reduction of the disproportionate privileges that foreigners had accrued in Mexico under Díaz, and some to restore the anticlerical vision of nineteenth-century masons and secular liberal reformers.

Overall, the 1910 revolution provides an important referent for understanding contemporary Mexican politics for two reasons. On the one hand,
despite the bloodshed and mayhem that continued well beyond the initial
uprising in 1910, the revolution provided the underpinnings for a remarkably stable political system over the remainder of the twentieth century. Perhaps the most significant factor in the consolidation of that regime was the
eventual creation of a single, dominant political party that pulled together
all elements of the revolutionary family. The birth of a single "revolutionary"
party ensured that the methods of military rebellion, reactionary insurgency,
and popular uprising never again provided a path to power in Mexico. By the
same token, for seventy-one years, it would not be possible for a politician to
aspire to the nation's highest political office through any other organization
than the ruling party.

On the other hand, the revolution provides an important referent for
contemporary Mexican politics as the country engages in a different form of
regime change: a relatively peaceful transition from authoritarian to democratic politics. Even as Mexico moves away from single-party hegemony, the
heroes and ideals of the revolution are still held dear by most Mexicans.
In the next chapter, we examine the key elements of the political system
that emerged in the aftermath of the Mexican Revolution. In subsequent
chapters, we move on to consider how that system has been transformed
in contemporary Mexican politics.

[handwritten annotations:]

peaceful transition from authoritarian to democratic
politics

Juárez
Díaz
Madero
Huerta
Carranza
Obregón
Calles – PNR
Cárdenas – PNR-PRM

3

Postrevolutionary Mexican Politics, 1940–1968

PRI

From 1940 onward, Mexico held regular elections, boasted high levels of popular participation, featured a wide array of opposing political parties, and observed peaceful transfers of power from one administration to the next. Most important, unlike the Porfiriato, no one person held absolute power over time. Yet for most of the next several decades, few observers viewed Mexico as a democracy. Indeed, the irony of the Mexican Revolution was that it ultimately produced one of the most durable autocratic regimes of the twentieth century. Contributing to the antidemocratic character of postrevolutionary Mexico was the PRI's utilization of classic machine-style politics. While generating genuine support from the party's clientelistic beneficiaries, the machine also restricted competition through exclusion, fraud, and even the occasional use of coercive force. In this chapter, we explore these characteristics of Mexico's postrevolutionary system, with special attention to the institutions and practices that held it together for more than sixty years. The discussion will illustrate how the PRI's favored institutions and tactics eventually undermined its own legitimacy and set the stage for Mexico's transition to democracy during the latter part of the twentieth century.

UNDERSTANDING POSTREVOLUTIONARY MEXICAN POLITICS

Mexico's postrevolutionary political system defies easy classification. It had some of the characteristics of authoritarianism, a political system in which the government derives power primarily through force and coercion. Yet at the same time, Mexican politics also bore the trappings of a democratic political system, in which the government relies on a system of popular participation, political contestation, and representation. As a result, for much of its modern history, political scientists tended to describe Mexico alternately as either a semiauthoritarian regime or a restricted democracy.[1]

To be sure, Mexico's was not like other authoritarian regimes.[2] Mexico's revolutionary party held regular elections and relied more on a sophisticated system of cooptation than on the use of coercive force. Mexico's political system was not operated by jack-booted oppressors lording over a cowering citizenry. Indeed, in an era when many other Latin American countries fell into military dictatorships—from the 1940s to the 1970s—the Mexican military was notably absent from government, and the country's political system appeared relatively stable and even somewhat democratic. Perhaps most important, the regime genuinely enjoyed widespread popular support and achieved important accomplishments in terms of economic performance and the redistribution of wealth. Hence, despite the undemocratic features of the PRI system or "regime," many political scientists were reluctant to refer to Mexican politics as authoritarian or used various modifiers to describe Mexico's unique variant of authoritarianism.[3]

Still, in other ways, Mexico's postrevolutionary political system hardly resembled other democracies, due to severely restricted electoral competition and occasional instances of violent repression. Indeed, Mexico was an enigma for many political observers, who viewed it as a democracy with adjectives: an "electoral autocracy," a *democradura*, or (at best) an "emerging democracy."[4] By the 1940s, the ruling party had reorganized itself as the Institutional Revolutionary Party (Partido Revolucionario Institucional, PRI), which remained the sole party of government for decades to come. Since Mexican elections were anything but "free and fair," PRI candidates for public office almost always won and virtually everyone was considered to be a member of the PRI: a *priísta*. Not only did the PRI benefit from fraudulently manipulated election results, but also from the partisan support of the media and government resources to buy popular support. Moreover, the PRI's total dominance of all branches and levels of government led to widespread corruption and abuse of power. In the worst cases, when opponents could not be bested or coopted by the system, they were harassed, disappeared, or even killed. While these occurrences were rare, such a system could hardly be labeled as democratic, and—without opportunities for genuine political participation and contestation—appeared to have little prospect of changing. Even as late as 1999, a satirical film about Mexican politics was initially banned because of its critical depictions of the ruling party (see textbox 3.1).

Textbox 3.1. *HEROD'S LAW*

Written and directed by Luis Estrada, the award-winning film *La Ley de Herodes* (*Herod's Law*) is a dark political satire set in Mexico in 1949, during the administration of President Miguel Alemán. In the role of Juan Vargas, Mexican actor Damián Alcázar plays an innocent, good-natured junkyard operator who is tapped by his friend Ramírez, a midlevel bureaucrat from the ruling party, to serve as the interim replacement for a corrupt mayor (*presidente municipal*) who was driven out of office. Vargas and his wife Gloria are deeply appreciative of the opportunity and head off to the small indigenous town of San Pedro de los Saguaros. Vargas's initial efforts to play politics on the straight and narrow lead only to disappointment. On the advice of Ramírez's boss, the minister of the interior (*secretario de gobierno*), Vargas gradually comes to understand the crass reality of Mexican politics, which he calls Herod's Law: "Screw or be screwed." The film's theatrical release in 1999 was initially prohibited by the Mexican government due to its references to systemic corruption and political assassination. However, filmmakers and the press, making accusations of political censorship, successfully pressured the government to release the movie. The film provides a useful, if controversial, allegory for thinking about Mexican politics during the classic period of PRI rule.

Remarkably, this political system kept its predominant features over many years. For most of the twentieth century, the classic features of Mexico's postrevolutionary system were single-party hegemony, a virtual fusion of party and government, the centralization of power, restricted political opposition, and occasional instances of repression. Moreover, the political system presided over by the PRI appeared so steady and enduring that some observers referred to it as a "living museum."[5] Today, of course, hindsight tells us that the classic PRI political system was not so impervious to change. Indeed, Mexican politics began to undergo a significant transition toward democracy in the latter part of the twentieth century. By the year 2000, the stable, semiauthoritarian political system that grew out of the Mexican Revolution was replaced by a system that was significantly more democratic, but much less predictable.

To understand Mexico's transformation over the past few decades, it is essential to have a clear grasp of the dynamics of postrevolutionary politics and the tremendous challenge of consolidating power after a major violent upheaval. As we saw in chapter 2, reconstructing and establishing control over the state apparatus after 1910 took more than a decade. The massive mobilization of the population required Mexico's leaders to create institutions that would facilitate power sharing and decision making across the diverse sectors and interests mobilized by the revolution. Moreover, like other postrevolutionary societies in the twentieth century, Mexico found unity and long-term stability in the creation of a single, institutionalized political party. We therefore begin our exploration of Mexico's postrevolutionary system with an examination of the history and role of the Institutional Revolutionary Party.

PRI HEGEMONY IN ELECTIONS AND GOVERNMENT

As discussed earlier, the National Revolutionary Party (Partido Nacional Revolucionario, PNR) was originally founded in 1929 by Plutarco Elías Calles as a means to harness (and to promote national unity among) the forces unleashed by the revolution. The PNR was dissolved in December 1937 and later reorganized as the Party of the Mexican Revolution (Partido de la Revolución Mexicana, PRM), reflecting the desire of President Lázaro Cárdenas to empower the revolution's neglected labor and agrarian sectors. Cárdenas's successor, Manuel Ávila Camacho (1940–1946), introduced further changes to the ruling party and thereby established the enduring elements of Mexico's postrevolutionary system for the remainder of the twentieth century.

Its symbolic status as the champion of the revolution contributed to the ruling party's genuine popularity among many Mexican voters. The "party of the revolution" bore an intrinsic connection to the founding event and mythology of the Mexican political system, and to revolutionary heroes like Villa and Zapata; as such, the ruling party appealed to many voters' nationalist sentiments.[6] Indeed, the ruling party ultimately took explicit advantage of this connection by adopting the colors of the Mexican flag as its own (sometimes confusing illiterate voters who could be persuaded to simply vote for "Mexico"). Moreover, the fact that the PRI presided over a prolonged period of sustained economic growth during most of the mid-twentieth century provided a substantial degree of "performance legitimacy." Hence, although the PRI's advocacy of revolutionary goals often tended to be merely rhetorical, the widespread support of the PRI should not be underestimated.

However, the ruling party's long-term monopoly on power in Mexico was not just symbolic nor merely the result of a slavish, uneducated electorate. Rather, the dominance of the revolutionary party was the product of a sophisticated system of institutional arrangements and incentives. While several elements of this system were already in place by the beginning of the 1940s, two important changes took place in 1946 that solidified the ruling party and ensured its dominant position in Mexican politics for the remainder of the twentieth century. The first was the creation of the Federal

Electoral Law, which established the mechanisms of electoral control that ensured the party's monopoly on power. The second was the reorganization of the ruling party, which completed its evolution as Mexico's dominant political force. Below we examine these major developments, how they contributed to the institutionalization of the ruling party, and the functioning of the PRI's classic postrevolutionary system.

The Institutionalization of the Ruling Party

The long-term hegemony of the ruling party over all other rivals was in part guaranteed by the centralization of control over federal electoral procedures. Specifically, the passage of the 1946 Federal Electoral Law placed the regulation of elections for the president and all federal legislators under the control of the Interior Ministry (Secretaría de Gobernación). Prior to this reform, state governments were responsible for regulating and tabulating elections, as has been historically the case in the United States. With the 1946 electoral reform, however, Mexico's electoral system now became more centralized, since one of the president's most important cabinet ministries was now the authority responsible for registering political parties, overseeing campaigns, and reporting electoral results. This gave significant advantages to the ruling party and also greatly affected the structure of power relationships in Mexico, since the incumbent party could effectively modify electoral regulations, prohibit the registration of certain political parties, and ultimately control electoral outcomes.[7]

In effect, the Federal Electoral Law enabled the ruling party to establish itself as a nationwide political machine with an automatic or machine-like ability to consistently place its candidates in public office and exercise control over the government. Like political machines elsewhere around the world, including the U.S. political machines of the early and mid-twentieth century, the power of Mexico's ruling party was derived in large part from its control over the electoral process. Indeed, postrevolutionary governments frequently resorted to fixing electoral contests through a variety of techniques of fraud, such as having voters return to vote multiple times at the same polling place ("carousel" or "merry-go-round" voting), stuffing ballot boxes with folded wads of ballots known as "vote tacos" (*tacos de votos*), adding false names to voter rolls (e.g., Cantinflas or Mickey Mouse), bringing prestuffed or "pregnant" ballot boxes (*urnas embarazadas*) to the polls, or simply manipulating official figures. Because the party's representatives in government controlled the electoral process, there were no legal means to challenge these practices. Hence, the 1946 Federal Electoral Law provided a political instrument to ensure the ruling party's lasting monopoly on power.

The 1946 Federal Electoral Law also had an important impact on the structure of power arrangements within the ruling party. In particular, the centralization of electoral control at the national level significantly empowered federal authorities, vis-à-vis state and local officials, who might otherwise have used their control over local elections to build their own, state-level bases of power, as was the case in the United States during the era of machine politics. Instead, in Mexico's postrevolutionary context, machine politics was projected to the national level. Moreover, placing the electoral process under the supervision of the president ensured that political control was not only centralized at the national level, but within the executive branch. Would-be federal legislators and even the president's successor depended on the favor of the sitting president. Indeed, as we discuss below in more detail, the organizational structure of the PRI created a hierarchical chain of relationships and loyalties that helped ensure a high degree of party loyalty and predictability.

PRI Organizational Structures

In addition to centralizing Mexico's electoral laws, another major development occurred in 1946 when the ruling party underwent a second major reorganization. That year, President Manuel Ávila Camacho was preparing to transfer power to his handpicked successor, then interior secretary Miguel Alemán Valdés. The ruling party's rebirth as the Institutional Revolutionary Party (Partido Revolucionario Institucional, PRI) constituted an emblematic and lasting transformation. The ruling party's new moniker neatly encapsulated both its role as the champion of the revolution and the paradoxical consolidation of a permanent revolution. Moreover, so institutionalized was the ruling party that it would maintain its lock on power and its basic organizational structure for the next half century. On paper, the PRI had a national, state, and local committee structure; formally elected party leaders and appointed officers; and established internal democratic procedures for determining its candidates and platforms. In practice, the PRI was a political machine with highly centralized and autocratic features whose survival depended on its symbiotic relationship with the government.

Ávila Camacho's reorganization of the party also had the important effect of demilitarizing the ruling party, which highlighted some of the tensions that had developed in his own election in 1940. Ávila Camacho, Mexico's last president with military experience, had seen very little combat in the revolution, and therefore lacked the military cast of the presidents immediately preceding his candidacy.[8] In the 1940 election, he faced conservative General Juan Andreu Almazán, who broke from the ruling party out of objection to the policies of Lázaro Cárdenas and what he perceived to be a lack of adequate representation of military interests within the ruling party. Though the election was heavily contested and exhibited indications of fraud, Ávila Camacho was named the victor. In the aftermath, Ávila

Camacho worked deliberately to diminish the influence of the military and make way for a new breed of civilian political leadership.[9] These efforts were critical in distinguishing Mexico's political system from others in Latin America, where a prominent role in domestic politics led to military takeovers and prolonged periods of authoritarian rule by the armed forces. While the decision to reduce the power and visibility of the military sector in Mexican politics was therefore of great importance, this is not to say that the military became unimportant in Mexico, nor—as we discuss later—that it failed to support the regime when needed.

In the formal organization of interest groups within the ruling party, the armed forces were supplanted by a new "popular sector" that represented Mexico's middle class, professionals, and government bureaucrats. While Cárdenas had informally integrated these groups into the party beginning in 1938, in 1943 they were formally incorporated with the creation of the National Confederation of Popular Organizations (Confederación Nacional de Organizaciones Populares, CNOP). (See textbox 3.2.) Hence, with the reorganization of 1946, the ruling party's corporatist system now consisted of three formally recognized sectors: a labor sector most prominently represented by the CTM, an agrarian sector represented by the CNC, and a popular sector represented by the CNOP. The relative size of these three sectors could be estimated by their representation among the PRI's federal deputies, with the agrarian sector holding the largest share of seats until the 1960s. The labor and agrarian sectors were well rewarded for their organizational muscle—their capacity to mobilize large groups to support the ruling party at campaign rallies and on election day. Gradually, however, the popular sector proved an especially important source of leadership and political mobilization for the PRI, supplanting the agrarian sector and serving as the brains of the ruling party.[10]

In addition to its corporatist features, the PRI's organization relied on a complex structure of hierarchical relationships of political exchange among individuals, frequently described as clientelism. Clientelism refers to an arrangement in which individuals with access to power serve as the patrons—or providers of material benefits and services—to a certain set of constituents, or clients, in exchange for their allegiance and support (see textbox 3.3). In effect, the PRI consisted of a clientelistic power structure of personal relationships that extended through the federal, state, and local levels, from the highest levels of the political arena to everyday citizens. Within that system, a politician's prospects for advancing his own career depended on his connections to and ability to win the favor of higher-ranking politicians. That politician used his access to power to bestow political favors to his most loyal and trusted subordinates, who in turn worked to help that politician advance his goals and mobilize political support, often by drawing on their own network of clients.

Textbox 3.2. CORPORATISM

Corporatism is a system in which there is formal and structured incorporation of key interest groups into government decision-making processes. The term *corporatism* comes from the Latin word for "the body," or *corpus*, and refers to the incorporation of separate units as part of an integrated system. The concept of corporatism was first developed within the Catholic Church as a way of coordinating civic groups and unions that were not formally part of the ecclesiastical body of the Church. Corporatist practices were later applied to politics in Europe and Latin America in the mid-twentieth century, when many governments incorporated highly mobilized popular sectors in Italy (fascism), Germany (Nazism), and Argentina (Peronism). While these earlier forms of corporatism had authoritarian tendencies, contemporary corporatist arrangements, or "neocorporatism" (as in Sweden, Norway, and the Netherlands), provide for formal and structured negotiations between democratic governments and key interest groups as a means of facilitating consensus in political decision-making.

In most corporatist arrangements, the government often plays a significant role in the formation of associations and interest groups that are formally "incorporated" within the system. In effect, the government therefore determines which interest groups will have a seat at the table. Thus, in a corporatist system, interests not formally incorporated or officially recognized may be ignored and may even face harassment or discrimination because they compete with official interest groups. In contrast, pluralism is an alternative model in which autonomously formed interest groups (for example, in the United States, the National Rifle Association, the Sierra Club, chambers of commerce, etc.) vie for influence on governmental decisions, often with varying degrees of success. That is, in a pluralist system, a group's influence on government tends to be determined by its financial clout or other factors, such as the effectiveness of its lobbying efforts.

A politician's networks with his supporters therefore often reflected long-standing personal relationships accumulated over years of loyalty, trust, and close interaction. Therefore, transferring political loyalties from one faction to another was rare and likely to be viewed with suspicion. The networks of personal influence that developed around individual personalities were referred to as *camarillas,* and the more elevated a politician's position became in the PRI's "labyrinths of power," the greater the benefits and the support he could generate for his own faction within the party.[11] Meanwhile, at lower levels, individuals who failed to advance through the ranks did their best to make lateral moves, sometimes recycling and alternating their positions.[12]

Textbox 3.3. CLIENTELISM

Clientelism is a system in which certain types of goods or favors are exchanged between an individual with access to power and his supporters. The types of benefits bestowed by a "patron" to his "clients" may include tangible material benefits (such as a job, supplies, food, or small gifts) or simply preferential access to certain types of services (such as issuance of public permits, the resolution of fines, or even basic sanitation). The types of support offered by a client may include public demonstrations of support (such as attending a campaign event) or simply showing up to vote for one's patron on election day. Finally, because clientelist systems often depend heavily on long-term personal relationships and norms of deference, some of the benefits exchanged can be purely symbolic, such as a visit by the patron or the client to the wedding of a family member. Naturally, the more valuable the support rendered by the client, the greater the potential rewards a patron may offer. The concept of clientelism need not be restricted to the political arena, since patron-client relationships are often observed within social organizations, organized crime syndicates, and even in certain professions (not academia, of course). Indeed, the opening scene of *The Godfather* portrays a classic example of clientelism, as Vito Corleone offers a favor to Amerigo Bonasera, a humble mortician who asks for his intervention to solve a delicate problem. The Godfather agrees, but notes that "someday, and that day may never come, I may call on you to return the favor." Such patron-client relationships are often employed to determine "who gets what, and how" in politics. However, in the political arena, clientelism has a negative connotation because it frequently results in the unequal distribution of public resources or services that should be equally accessible to all members of society and provides some individuals with preferential access to government jobs, services, and other benefits. Individuals who do not support the patron can be deprived of these benefits. Some political observers have noted that a system of preferential access can have certain benefits, particularly for otherwise excludable minorities. For example, in the United States, the clientelistic political machines of New York and Chicago provided Irish and other minorities with access to government jobs and resources in the early part of the twentieth century. However, modern democracies strive toward a system that does not privilege one group over another but instead provides public goods for the overall benefit of society.

At the bottom of this chain of influence, of course, were individual voters (especially poor urban and rural voters in dire need of assistance) whose meager benefits of preferential access might include a sandwich (*torta*) or a T-shirt for showing up to vote, or a chance to resolve an administrative matter through their connections in the ruling party. Yet even such ordinary citizens demonstrated remarkable loyalty and support for the PRI. Given the PRI's proclivity for electoral fraud and given that voter support was often contingent on a system of tangible rewards and punishments, it is of course difficult to determine whether political support for the PRI was legitimate. What is clear is that, for the better part of the twentieth century, large numbers of Mexicans regularly backed the PRI at the ballot box, in opinion polls, and in other public demonstrations of support.

Party Discipline, Power Sharing, and Ideological Flexibility

Given Mexico's particular institutional context and the prevalence of clientelistic relationships, it is not surprising that there was a very high degree of party discipline within the PRI. The pressure to demonstrate loyalty to the party—for example, by supporting the PRI's candidates, official decisions, and legislation—was especially acute because of Mexico's constitutional prohibitions on immediate reelection. Mexico's virtually sacred commitment to the principle of no reelection ensured a high degree of turnover (and a low degree of continuity) in public administration. That is, from one administration to the next, incoming presidents, governors, and mayors would redistribute the spoils of public office—political appointments, bureaucratic positions, and government staff jobs—to their own networks of clientelistic supporters. Thus, at the end of one's term in office, the only hope for career advancement in the next administration was to have the favor of other politicians at higher levels in the party hierarchy. A powerful patron could guarantee an appointment to a new, higher-ranking post or could influence the party officials with the formal authority over nominations for elected office. Hence in many cases, a politician's merit and ability mattered less for his career advancement than his personal connections and fealty to the system.[13]

One natural result of the consistent maneuvering by PRI politicians vying for power was a significant degree of factionalism and internal competition within the ruling party. Indeed, as in other systems where a single party dominated the political system, different *camarillas* within the PRI necessarily competed for influence within a given administration, or from one administration to the next.[14] Hence, the PRI's longevity as a political party depended in part on its ability to minimize the frictions resulting from this competition and its ability to ensure a certain degree of power sharing within and across different government administrations. For most of the twentieth century, party leaders were careful to heal intraparty divisions and to woo potential defectors by providing reasonable concessions to the losing candidate or faction.

Meanwhile, although PRI factions were highly personalistic, they also frequently represented a wide array of ideological currents. A certain degree of ideological tolerance within the PRI facilitated the expression of these diverse perspectives and frequently muddled the differences between left and right in Mexico. At the same time, the PRI's broadly inclusive organization and its ability to facilitate power sharing among divergent factions gave the party important advantages vis-à-vis potential competitors by incorporating diverse sectors of society and therefore leaving little ideological space for the opposition to organize around. When outside opposition did arise, the PRI's wide range of political currents also enabled it to shift political positions in order to draw support away from potential opponents. In fact, some observers have noted that, as different factions within the PRI alternated power across different administrations, they tended to move gradually from one end of the political spectrum to the other, oscillating between left and right.

While the PRI began as fundamentally leftist under Lázaro Cárdenas, the party moved to the political center under his successor, Manuel Ávila Camacho, who adopted a more favorable position toward business interests and the United States than Cárdenas had. His successor, Miguel Alemán (1946–1952), moved even further to the right by not only favoring private capital and industry, but strongly opposing communism and severely repressing labor activists.[15] Partly in response to the reactionary nature of Alemán's government, the PRI shifted moderately to the left during the 1950s and early 1960s, under Presidents Adolfo Ruiz Cortines (1952–1958) and Adolfo López Mateos (1958–1964).[16] Hence, whatever the PRI's symbolic references to revolutionary rhetoric, the party's ideology was quite flexible. Moreover, as we shall see in the next chapter, the actions of outgoing presidents very often made it necessary for incoming presidents to adopt positions that directly contradicted those of their predecessors.

In short, by the 1940s, Mexico's ruling party acquired the basic organizational characteristics and political advantages that ensured its hegemonic position in the Mexican political system for the remainder of the twentieth century. As the official party of the revolution, the explicit connection between the party and the postrevolutionary government, which some scholars have described as a kind of PRI–government symbiosis, provided the ruling party with tremendous political advantages.[17] Through a sophisticated system of favors and influence, government officials maintained close connections with and depended on the support of the PRI's organizational apparatus, which in turn relied heavily on government resources to help sustain the party's clientelistic networks. Its success as a political machine was derived from its effective control over the electoral process, a highly centralized and disciplined political hierarchy, the formal incorporation of key sectors of society, and a degree of ideological flexibility that gave the party the ability to adapt to changing political circumstances. Access to government resources and services provided a means of obtaining political support from the public, and PRI government officials were able to offer their endorsement and resources to the party's candidates for public office. Thus, rather than serving as an agent of political interests in society (as in many democratic countries), in its relationship with society the PRI served primarily as a mechanism for generating political support for the government.

CENTRALIZATION OF POWER

Mexico's postrevolutionary political system today comprises thirty-one state governments, a federal district, and over 2,400 municipal governments. At the federal, state, and municipal level, power is divided among the executive, legislative, and judicial branches of government. Yet despite all of these structural characteristics, political authority in Mexico has traditionally been highly centralized (see textbox 3.4). Indeed, for most of its history all roads led metaphorically to Mexico City, where political decisions were made, governmental resources were concentrated, and whence the better part of Mexico's ruling elite emanated. As elsewhere in Latin America, most Mexican presidents dominated the legislature and judiciary to such an extent that there were few real checks and balances across branches of government. Moreover, Mexican presidents had the de facto ability to influence the selection of gubernatorial candidates and to replace sitting governors practically at will, giving presidents considerable influence over subnational affairs as well.[18]

While partly a continuation of Mexico's "centralist tradition" stretching back to the colonial era, the concentration of power in the postrevolutionary system exhibited particular features. Indeed, political centralization under the PRI was far more institutionalized than during the Porfiriato. As noted in chapter 1, Porfirio Díaz had relied on an extensive personal network of his own cronies to administer other branches and levels of government. While personal ties were still important under the PRI, its corporatist structures provided an institutional context for sustaining relationships and systems of clientelistic exchange that extended beyond and outlived most individual personalities. The key point of difference in the postrevolutionary system had to do with identifiable institutional factors—more than personal ties—that contributed to the power of the Mexican presidency. Specifically, the prohibition of reelection, combined with the total hegemony of the ruling party, concentrated authority in the *office* of the presidency—rather than in the personality in office—and ensured a relatively

> **Textbox 3.4. CENTRALIZATION AND DECENTRALIZATION**
>
> Organizational systems are often described as "centralized" or "decentralized." What do these terms mean? In a centralized system, decision making and policy implementation are concentrated at high levels within the system or emanated from one particular entity or division of the system. By contrast, in a decentralized system, greater decision making and authority are granted at lower levels of administration or shared more equally across different branches of an organization. Within systems of governance there is often horizontal power sharing across different branches of government, or vertical distribution of resources and authority among the national, state or regional, and local governments.

high degree of elite circulation.[19] Because no one individual or group could easily monopolize power beyond a single six-year term, control of the presidency offered that person a one-shot grab at the privileges and spoils of office for his supporters (and a lifetime of luxury for himself). At the same time, the no-reelection rule contributed to a high degree of centralization because ineligibility of governors and legislators for reelection made them heavily dependent on the sitting president and ranking party leaders for future political mobility.[20]

Indeed, in a context without reelection, executive control of the electoral process was critical in enhancing the president's powers, since it gave him complete control over the selection of his party's candidate. In effect, the president handpicked his own successor in a ritual known as the *dedazo* or "finger tap." The *dedazo* was the president's most important means of assuring party loyalty within the party, and therefore his vast power during his six-year term or *sexenio*. Until a successor was named, high-ranking PRI politicians attempted to maintain the favor of the president in the hope that they or the head of their *camarilla* or faction would benefit from the ultimate prize: the presidency itself. Once a successor was identified—through the *destape* or unveiling of the president's preferred candidate—political loyalties naturally gravitated to the man who would become the ultimate authority in the PRI system for the next six years.[21]

Thus, during most of his term, the influence of the sitting president was paramount, extended downward throughout the political system, and was reinforced by the centralization of administrative controls and fiscal revenues in Mexico. The Mexican president had extraordinary control over the federal bureaucracy, including key coercive agencies of the government, such as the military and the intelligence service. The latter agencies answered directly or indirectly to the secretary of the interior, often seen as the president's enforcer and a likely candidate for presidential succession. Indeed, of the thirteen presidents elected from the ruling party from 1928 to 2000, eight were former interior secretaries and only one, Francisco Labastida in 2000, failed in his attempt to be elected. Because they enjoyed the president's trust and because they were likely to succeed him, Mexico's interior secretaries traditionally exercised significant power and few were willing to defy them.

In effect, as we discuss further in chapter 5, Mexico's postrevolutionary political arrangements—and the dominance of a single, hierarchical dominant party—meant that the president's authority was virtually absolute and that the institutional separation of powers that theoretically permits the checks and balances of a federal system to function was practically nonexistent.[22] The president's ability to command the allegiance of other politicians and to exercise absolute control over the federal bureaucracy made the executive branch dominant over both the Mexican Congress and the federal judiciary. In effect, the PRI's virtual monopoly in the Congress made legislators a mere rubber stamp for executive legislation, budgetary approval, and even constitutional amendments. Indeed, from 1917 to the fall of the PRI in 2000, the Mexican constitution was amended more than four hundred times. Meanwhile, the federal judiciary comprised PRI appointees who had little inclination to challenge the president or the Congress. Under the PRI, the federal judiciary lacked a significant budget, and the judiciary's ability to apply judicial review to government actions or legislation was essentially limited to use of the *amparo* (an injunction or waiver from government actions or statutes that adversely affect an individual's constitutional rights). In short, neither the legislative nor the judicial branches of government provided any real check on executive power.[23] The exaggerated powers of postrevolutionary Mexican presidents have been described by Garrido (1989) as metaconstitutional and even anticonstitutional because they greatly exceeded those formally ascribed by the constitution.[24]

OPPOSITION, COOPTATION, AND REPRESSION

As noted above, the PRI was one of the world's strongest, most extensive political machines and held power longer than any other political party during the twentieth century. One secret of the PRI's success was the fact that—despite its undemocratic tendencies and significant abuses of power—the party enjoyed a remarkable degree of public support, thanks to its strategies for popular incorporation, its use of power sharing among divergent interests, and its appeal to revolutionary themes. For decades the PRI was the choice of millions of Mexicans, who appreciated the stability it provided and believed in the promise that it offered for a better future.[25] Still, as noted above, the reality of the PRI system was that its tendency to rely on fraud and repression to maintain its political monopoly diminished the overall legitimacy of the system. Moreover, there were significant sources of opposition to the PRI throughout most of its existence, both in the electorate and in society.

The PRI's approach to managing the political opposition relied on both cooptation and coercion: carrots and sticks. Indeed, many believe that the cornerstone of the PRI's dominance was its ability to achieve a careful balance between persuasive and repressive tactics. Examining the PRI's approach to managing political opposition therefore provides insights into its long-term survival. However, as we discuss below, over the years the cumulative effect of PRI coercion—including a number of particularly severe instances of violent repression—contributed to the unraveling of Mexico's perfect dictatorship. Below, we discuss the sources of political opposition in the PRI regime, as well as the strategies the ruling party employed to alternately coopt or coerce its opponents. During the classic period of PRI dominance, these organizations' relatively small followings, meager resources, and lack of experience meant that they were unlikely to wrest power away from the behemoth. Moreover, they were prevented from gaining a meaningful foothold in the political arena by the patently unfair system of rules set up by the ruling party. This discussion gives us further insights into the sources of PRI power and Mexico's gradual transition to democracy.

Political Opposition

There were effectively three main sources of opposition in the classic Mexican political system. First was the National Action Party (Partido Acción Nacional, PAN). The PAN was founded in 1939, exactly ten years after the birth of the ruling party. The founders of the PAN came from different elements of conservative opposition to the new regime. First, the PAN attracted educated, upper-middle-class professionals, who like the U.S. progressive reformers of the early nineteenth century were averse to the corruption and ineffective government service produced by machine politics. Second, the PAN attracted Catholics, who initially reacted negatively to the anticlericism of Calles and later to the socialist tendencies of Lázaro Cárdenas. Social and religious conservatives were especially incensed by Cárdenas's claims that he would socialize education in Mexico. Last but not least, the PAN initially attracted wealthy business interests that were alarmed and angered by the expropriation of properties and the loss of foreign capital during the Cárdenas administration. The PAN was by far the strongest opposition party in Mexico; however, it never came close to challenging the PRI's electoral dominance until the end of the century.[26]

A second source of opposition was the seemingly endless array of minor parties. Beginning in the 1960s, electoral rules allowed for a limited form of proportional representation and led to the creation of minor parties, also known as "third parties." This helped create an appearance of democratic competition. Yet because these parties had no real chance of winning, their existence simply fractionalized the Mexican party system. In some cases, they were described as parastatal parties because they were actually created or supported by the PRI in order to mollify or supplant real opposition groups. One classic example was the Authentic Party of the Mexican Revolution (Partido Auténtico de la Revolución Mexicana, PARM), which was created in the 1950s by disgruntled PRI members who split from the ruling party. While the PARM ran its own candidates for legislative and lower offices, it consistently supported the PRI's presidential candidates from its founding until the late 1980s. The PARM also served as an unwavering legislative ally of the ruling party, and it may have even received direct financial assistance from the PRI. In general, parastatal parties and other third parties illustrated the way the PRI was able to neutralize opposition at the height of its power, either by marginalizing or buying off its political opponents.

Finally, there were a number of unrecognized or even illegal sources of opposition. These were parties or groups that were excluded from power and considered illegal by the PRI government. The most notable illegal source of opposition was the Mexican Communist Party (Partido Comunista Mexicano, PCM), which was outlawed by the PRI's conservative governments of the 1940s and 1950s. However, there were a number of other important social movements and insurgent groups, including splinter movements from the ruling party, that formed in opposition to the political system. Long before Mexico's most famous insurgent group, the Zapatista Army of National Liberation (Ejército Zapatista de Liberación Nacional, EZLN) came into public view in 1994, small groups of irregular armies and guerrilla insurgents engaged in military campaigns against the government. In the 1960s and 1970s, homegrown, armed leftist movements like the student-run September 23 movement, the Clandestine Revolutionary Workers Party—Union of the People, and the Popular Revolutionary Army fought to provoke what they viewed as true revolutionary change in Mexico. However, while such organizations occasionally caused significant damage and loss of life through organized attacks and bombings against businesses and government facilities, Mexican insurgent groups were generally ephemeral, largely unsuccessful, and therefore of little threat to the overall political order during PRI rule.[27]

Political Cooptation

One of the major reasons why the PRI was so successful at retaining power was its ability to use cooptation to manipulate or reduce opposition to and within the PRI regime. Cooptation involves the use of persuasion or concessions to win over potential adversaries. Groups or individuals are often said to have been coopted when they receive tangible benefits in exchange for some form of tacit or explicit concession on their part. In Mexico, cooptation took a variety of forms during the PRI's hegemony. For example, party leaders often awarded important political and bureaucratic posts to political opponents within the PRI; in exchange, the internal opposition might offer its support or simply refrain from an outward challenge against the party. It was also common for the government to grant concessions to critics outside the regime. In such instances, the demands of the interest group, political party, or neighborhood might be partially met (e.g., with a subsidy or government contract, greater revenue or representation, or a public works project, respectively), with the understanding that this was as far as the government was willing to go.

On the whole, cooptation worked well for the PRI, and there is little doubt that its ability to coopt would-be critics and opponents contributed to single-party dominance, since it allowed the PRI to neutralize all but its most ardent detractors. Yet as opportunistic and undemocratic as it was to essentially buy off opponents, the PRI's widespread use of cooptation contributed in some measure to the party's inclusiveness. Indeed, it can be argued that this was another way of making the PRI more inclusive and forcing political interests to compete for access within the confines of the party rather than by challenging the system itself. Once incorporated into the party, groups and individuals were far more likely to have their concerns addressed than had they remained outside the revolutionary family.

This is not to say that cooptation yielded positive results for Mexico; rather, it is simply a point of fact that those who could be convinced to play by the PRI's rules tended to fare better than those who rejected the system outright. Of course, the line between cooptation and coercion is often very thin, and the PRI was not above using threats, intimidation, and even force when its efforts to coopt would-be opponents failed. While coercion was generally only employed as a last resort, these tactics represented real and tangible danger that effectively prevented the expression of alternative viewpoints, political protest, and freedom of choice. That the PRI used coercive force, such as arrests, torture, and martial law, with such relative infrequency was a testament to its ability to generate genuine support or, at a minimum, to persuade its opponents through cooptation. However, when these tactics failed, the PRI did occasionally resort to the use of repression, such as the intimidation of opposition candidates and the shooting of unarmed protestors. When such events occurred, they illustrated the limits of PRI power and seriously compromised its claims of legitimacy. Moreover, once subjected to its violent and repressive side, victims were not so easily won back by the PRI's charms. Below we discuss the use of coercive power by the PRI, with particular attention to a major incident of political repression that occurred during the late 1960s.

Coercion and Political Repression

In the era of PRI hegemony, the ruling party's use of coercion was relatively infrequent, thereby attesting to the effectiveness of its other tactics for retaining power. However, when applied, the PRI's use of coercion ran the gamut from threats of violence against individuals to the organized repression of groups by government forces. Government critics (e.g., journalists, artists, opposition candidates, social movements, and independent labor unions) were characteristically harassed or otherwise intimidated by threats against them and their families. More subtly, just as those who obeyed the system had opportunities to advance their careers in both the public and private sectors, those who were critical of the government found that those same doors were closed to them. Moreover, the government made significant efforts to identify and monitor its opponents, placing wiretaps on potential sources of opposition (including members of opposition parties and officials) and infiltrating social movements and popular organizations. While such tactics have been used in the United States—as in the case of intelligence efforts to monitor communist organizations, civil rights activists, and even political campaigns—in Mexico there was little legal recourse for the protection of civil liberties.

Meanwhile, outright repression—while relatively rare—could be severe. The use of police and military units to suppress labor protests was instrumental in establishing the hegemony of the PRI's official unions in the 1930s and 1940s. Over subsequent decades, as Mexico experienced stronger economic growth, there was a corresponding period of labor mobilization and organization. Mexican workers—particularly in the oil and railroad industries—organized numerous labor strikes in different parts of the country. The PRI government viewed these labor strikes as subversive and damaging to the economic interests of the country. The government responded to the unions and to other dissenting voices with severe repression. In 1958 and 1959, a railway workers' dispute caused the PRI government not only to break the strike but also to imprison numerous railroad workers and supporters from other unions. In the end, strike organizers Demetrio Vallejo and Valentín Campa were sentenced to sixteen years in prison, effectively decapitating the movement. Among those who protested the government's harsh repression was the renowned muralist David Alfaro Siqueiros, who was himself imprisoned as a result.[28]

Similarly, when Mexican opposition parties attempted to defend apparent victories by their candidates in state and local races, such postelectoral conflicts were likely to expose the PRI's authoritarian side. Such was the case when the government used violence to crack down on opposition protesters in places like León, Guanajuato, in 1945; Mérida, Yucatán, in 1967; and Tijuana, Baja California, in 1959 and 1968.[29] Yet by far the single instance of PRI repression that stands out the most was the 1968 massacre of student protesters in Tlatelolco, a middle-class neighborhood on the north side of Mexico City.

1968 Massacre at Tlatelolco

During the late 1950s and 1960s, Mexican students—like many of their counterparts in other countries—were drawn to progressive, even radical political positions by world events like the Cuban Revolution and the Vietnam War. On the university campuses of Mexico, students sought ways to get involved in addressing these issues by holding meetings and rallies to voice their discontent. This kind of activism was viewed with significant concern by Mexican authorities. Students who organized marches and became involved in left-wing organizations were closely monitored. Their events were occasionally dispersed with tear gas and the butt of a rifle, as in 1961 when students marched in Mexico City to celebrate the newly installed Castro government in Cuba. Major leaders in these kinds of activities were sometimes arrested as political prisoners, but nonetheless a growing atmosphere of student activism developed over the course of the 1960s. By 1968, the ten-year anniversary of the Cuban Revolution, student activism reached new heights and levels of sophistication that created extreme distress for the PRI government.[30]

The year 1968 was also a particularly sensitive moment for Mexico because the Olympic Games were to be hosted in Mexico City beginning in October. Mexican authorities viewed this as an opportunity to demonstrate the successes of the PRI government to the world. Indeed, the ruling party had reason to boast. After three decades of remarkable economic progress and political stability, Mexico had reestablished itself among the world's most prominent developing nations and was the shining star of Latin America. Anticipating hundreds of international dignitaries and media representatives, President Díaz Ordaz spent an estimated $240 million on preparations for the twelve-day sporting event.[31]

Despite these efforts to host a magnificent event, trouble began brewing in the months before the Olympics, as the summer brought heightened tensions between Mexican student activists and police. On June 23, 1968, a fight between two groups who appeared to be from rival high schools provoked a severe crackdown by Mexico City police. A legion of three hundred police then swarmed and violently subdued those involved in the skirmish. While it appears that the instigators of the fight were not even students, police continued their rampage by storming into an unrelated but nearby vocational school and harassing its students and faculty members. The schools in question were associated with two prominent Mexico City public universities, the National Polytechnic Institute (Instituto Politécnico Nacional, IPN) and the much larger National Autonomous University of Mexico (Universidad Nacional Autónoma de México, UNAM). In response to such an exaggerated show of force, outraged students from these two rival universities banded together in a rare demonstration of unity to protest the recent police brutality and the PRI government in general. With 250,000 students at the time, UNAM was the largest university in the hemisphere, and had been a hotbed of student activism over the course of the 1960s.

Over the next several weeks, students organized strikes and marches throughout the capital. Using their university campuses as a base of operations, they took over classrooms and hallways to produce flyers, rally support, and make public speeches. Off campus, students painted protest signs denouncing the PRI government and calling for the resignation of the Mexico City police chief. In addition to tacit (and sometimes overt) support from university administrators and faculty, what made this movement particularly successful was the fact that the students were extremely careful about the structure and organization of their movement. To prevent the government from coopting or intimidating its organizers, the students developed an elaborate system of rotating leadership and decentralized operations.

The most important innovation was the rotating National Strike Council—comprising 250 representatives from over a hundred schools—and a complex system of committees and brigades that prevented the easy identification, cooptation, or coercion of its members. No single student or group could be identified as leader of the movement, since directions were issued by different students from week to week. This enabled the student organizers to create a movement based on generally accepted ideas and strategies, rather than on individuals or personalities. Also, rather than acting through a single, easily identifiable organizational structure, the movement's separate cells and brigades could act with a high degree of autonomy. The final straw came with the violation of UNAM's hard-fought tradition of autonomy from the government, when the military sent ten thousand troops onto the UNAM campus on September 18. This set off an intense wave of protests and marches that grew increasingly strident in their criticisms against the PRI regime itself.[32]

The Mexican government responded with great concern and frustration, particularly in light of the impending Olympic Games, scheduled to begin on October 12. The government was anxious for an opportunity to show the world how much progress had been made in Mexico under the PRI. Yet the prospect of student demonstrations threatened to embarrass the PRI by projecting exactly the opposite image the Mexican government wanted. Most important, the PRI was frustrated by its inability to utilize its usual tactics to undermine political opposition. There was little the government could do to coopt the student movement according to its standard playbook for handling electoral challengers, union organizers, or armed rebels. On the one hand, the government could not readily appeal to particular leaders to buy off their support, and on the other hand it could not legitimately resort to full-scale violence against students and the ordinary citizens who supported them. In short, the PRI government found that cooptation was not an option and at the same time knew that repression would carry a high political cost.[33]

With each demonstration, the government's response was to call in more fully armed police and even the military in a massive demonstration of the state's coercive capacity. As the movement gathered momentum into September, the PRI government began interrupting marches and sending police onto high school and university campuses to try to restore order and identify dissidents. During these increasingly intense clashes, dozens of students were killed and hundreds were injured in the resulting violent conflicts with police. Tens of thousands of people rallied to the cause. Growing sympathy and support from the public soon swelled the movement as it was embraced by ordinary citizens and workers' unions, who participated in marches that now brought together tens of thousands of protesters demanding not only justice for police abuses and the release of political prisoners, but also broader calls for democratic reform in Mexico. As the movement increased in size and support, the government's frustration grew.

This continuing escalation came to a dreadful climax on October 2. Starting around 5:00 p.m., a group of six thousand protesters gathered for a march that was to begin in a residential area surrounding the Plaza of Tlatelolco—the famed site where Cortés allegedly battled the Aztecs and forged a nation of mestizos—with plans to continue over to the IPN campus. Within an hour, these students were surrounded by a massive contingent of ten thousand soldiers armed with machine guns and bayonets. Rather than risk undertaking the planned march, the protesters instead began speaking in the plaza, in the view and protection of the surrounding apartment buildings of this middle- and working-class neighborhood. As they spoke, helicopters and armored cars began to arrive, as soldiers moved into fortified positions in and above apartment complexes and buildings surrounding the plaza. Some students also noticed the arrival of plainclothesmen bearing a single white glove and haircuts that seemed to indicate some sort of military affiliation.

Soon after surrounding the plaza, the soldiers opened fire on the stage and the front of the crowd. Soldiers aimed first at the speakers and then at the panicked crowd. Soon soldiers flooded the plaza and began beating and arresting the demonstrators. Those believed to be members of the National Strike Council were lined up along walls and forced to strip to their underwear. Students, ordinary citizens, and journalists alike were assaulted, abused, and otherwise terrorized in the police rampage. One terrified witness in the plaza was a young future politician by the name of Ernesto Zedillo, who would become Mexico's president a quarter of a century later. In the end, official government figures claimed that only a few dozen protestors were killed and asserted that these individuals had provoked and fired on police. Yet independent, international media sources and activists believed the toll to be much higher, not least because dozens of protesters and student leaders simply disappeared in the wake of the incident.

Whatever the number of people who were killed or injured in the assault, the incident came to be aptly described as the 1968 student massacre. What was especially disturbing is that the massacre appeared to be part of a well-orchestrated and premeditated plan that could only have been organized and authorized at the highest levels of the Mexican government. Indeed, in addition to participation by the military, the white-gloved agents who took part in the massacre turned out to be members of a branch of the Mexican secret police known as the Olympia Battalion. Many critics now believe that the massacre was ordered directly by the Office of the President, though it remains unclear who specifically issued the order. While President Gustavo Díaz Ordaz was much criticized for his administration's actions, human rights activists have focused primary responsibility on then interior secretary Luis Echeverría Álvarez for planning and ordering this and subsequent acts of government repression. Over the past several years, Mexico's new democratic government and civil rights activists have worked together to sort out the details through the Mexican court system. Still, it will take many years until allegations against high-ranking officials are resolved.

Part of the problem of assigning responsibility is that the incident was effectively covered up by the PRI. Most domestic and international media sources were dissuaded or diverted from covering the story, as the government successfully focused greater attention on the 1968 Olympic Games. To the dismay of Mexican journalist Elena Poniatowski, one of the few who reported extensively on the story, the incident was effectively buried in the media within hours. To the extent that it was covered in the media, official explanations blamed the students and even foreign terrorists for the "incident."[34] Over the next ten days, the blood and protest signs were wiped away and Mexico City made itself up to shine before the international community. Indeed, the Olympics went on as scheduled. In the immediate aftermath of the games, the most notable memory of Mexico's Olympic games for most of the world was a tribute to black power and human rights issued jointly by African American U.S. gold and bronze medalists Tommie

Smith (who had just set a new world record for the 200-meter dash) and John Carlos, with support from Australian silver medalist Peter Norman.

In short, the PRI minimized immediate scrutiny and diverted the negative impact of the massacre. Yet in retrospect this repressive incident appears to have had long-term negative effects for the PRI regime. First, for a large number of Mexicans who were directly involved or subsequently learned about the massacre, the incident dramatically reduced the legitimacy of the PRI regime. Second, this major instance of repression created a new generation of opposition activists fiercely committed to undermining the PRI regime. And third, over the course of the 1970s, it led the Mexican government to make further crackdowns and somewhat imprudent (and largely ineffective) overtures to bolster its political support. In this sense, the repression of the 1968 student movement was for some observers of Mexican politics an incident that ultimately contributed to the downfall of the PRI regime.[35]

CONCLUSION

During most of the twentieth century, Mexico was at best a democracy with adjectives—a "limited" or "restricted" democracy; at worst Mexico was an authoritarian regime with only the trappings of democracy and none of its substance. Yet, from the revolution until the late 1960s, Mexico was characterized by institutions of political control that generated political stability and economic prosperity during a period of unprecedented growth and development. Widespread cultural acceptance and a revolutionary mythology helped build support for the PRI. Also, the regime's ability to incorporate a wide array of societal groups and coopt would-be detractors provided an essential source of support and political stability.

However, in 1968, the PRI regime showed signs of weakness and failed to respond effectively to key challenges. In the face of the 1968 student protests, the PRI's ability to use cooptation failed, and it was forced to use violence. In the eyes of many, it was the first major illustration of the limits of PRI power. In the aftermath, the PRI would spend decades trying to restore its credibility and control. Over the next three decades, the PRI's power would gradually erode and give way to a more open and democratic political system. In the next chapter we discuss this prolonged transition.

4

Mexican Democratization, 1968 to the Present

DEMOCRATIZATION IN MEXICO

In many ways the culmination of social unrest that started brewing in the 1950s, the events of 1968 were also the beginning of a slow transition. Over the next thirty years, Mexico would move away from single-party dominance and toward more open democracy, coalescing in 2000 with the election of the first opposition candidate to the presidency. Yet these changes to the Mexican political system happened so gradually that only in retrospect did they appear to constitute a linear transition away from authoritarianism and toward democracy. In fact, during the decades that the political opening took place, there were many points at which Mexicans and outsiders alike wondered whether the PRI would manage to salvage and further consolidate its hegemony, allowing democracy to elude Mexico indefinitely. We know now that this did not happen: in 1997 the "official" party lost its majority in Congress, and less than ten years later, placed last in a three-way race for the presidency.

How can we explain Mexico's transition from a single-party-dominant system to one that is now highly competitive? How did a firmly entrenched party that was accustomed to winning elections with over 60 percent of the vote for more than half a century lose so much support and power? The purpose of this chapter is to explore these questions. We suggest that the PRI's fall from grace and the subsequent emergence of greater political competition occurred as the result of three interrelated factors: the inability of the government to effectively promote economic redistribution and stability, the PRI's loss of cohesion and legitimacy, and the institutional changes that created openings for the opposition parties to gain footholds that eventually allowed them to challenge the PRI head on and boost themselves into power. Each of these factors is outlined briefly below as a prelude to a longer discussion of how they combined to erode the PRI's dominance and foster the rise of the opposition. Together these developments led to the creation of the competitive electoral environment in Mexico that persists today.

DECLINING PRI LEGITIMACY

As discussed earlier, the PRI's hegemony was rooted both in its ability to incorporate and coopt a wide range of otherwise disparate interests and in its electoral dominance. However, another critical factor in the party's success was the strong performance of the national economy between 1940 and 1970. The so-called Mexican Miracle was impressive by any standards: for thirty years, the economy grew at an annual rate of more than 6 percent. (See chapter 9.) The political benefits of sustained growth proved immeasurable. In addition to gaining genuine popular support at the polls from "pocketbook" voters, plentiful resources allowed the government to use material benefits and social services to reward the loyalty of its supporters. As the national economic model began to visibly falter in the 1970s, the PRI's performance legitimacy eroded and it became increasingly difficult for the ruling party to use material rewards to sustain its power base.[1] Many began to question the benefit of demonstrating allegiance to the PRI—especially when it had shown itself to be a corrupt organization that undergirded a corrupt system. But it was not just the exhaustion of Mexico's economic miracle that undermined the PRI's position; it was also that the national economic gains produced between 1940 and 1970 were not evenly distributed within society. While the private and industrial sectors did very well, most Mexicans suffered from the side effects of growing inflation, stagnant wages, high unemployment, and inadequate public services. Moreover, between the mid-1970s and the mid-1990s, the country experienced a cycle of economic booms and devastating busts that created great uncertainty for ordinary Mexicans and eroded public confidence in the political system. By itself, economic instability was not sufficient to produce political change because support for the PRI was rooted in more than a simple exchange of material goods for votes. But the government's inability to deliver economic stability greatly undermined its practice of using patronage to ensure popular support and contributed to the second source of the PRI's decline—its loss of legitimacy.

From the time of its creation and subsequent institutionalization in the first half of the twentieth century, the PRI claimed to embody the principles of Mexico's revolution. These principles, while sometimes vague, consistently called for inclusion, redistribution, and stability. Mexicans long supported the PRI because it made an effort to create and sustain the revolutionary family. The events of 1968 had made clear that the regime would use force against those who were too critical or sought too much independence. In the aftermath of the 1968 massacre, the government's continued use of force against its detractors in the 1970s, combined with the pervasive and unabashed use of graft, patronage, and abuse of power by government officials at every level, created a deep distrust of the PRI government among some Mexicans. Meanwhile, although the party had always been internally divided, competition among its various factions for control of the organization became more fierce as the strain of losing popular support set in. By the mid-1980s, disputes among factions led to the public airing of differences, accusations, and dirty laundry, and this further tarnished the party's image.

In this context, the PRI enacted a series of institutional reforms that appeared to open the political system. Specifically, from the 1970s through the 1990s, PRI leaders offered three major types of reforms as concessions to members of the opposition: first, increasing the size of the legislature in 1977; second, decentralizing power to state and local governments in the 1980s; and third, creating an independent electoral authority in the early 1990s. While these three reforms were intended to give the Mexican political system a semblance of democratic legitimacy, each one preserved enormous advantages for the ruling party. The introduction of proportional representation in the 1970s led to the creation of a host of "parastatal" parties that often actually received resources from and directly supported the PRI. While national politicians touted the benefits of decentralization, most real power and resources remained centered at the federal level. Moreover, even after important changes to Mexico's electoral laws, the PRI continued to influence electoral outcomes at all levels through a variety of means.

Even so, Mexico's political opening after 1968 was significant. Providing expanded opportunities for political representation—albeit initially more symbolic than real—ultimately gave opposition parties the political experience needed to effectively compete and govern in the future. Increasing the power of states and municipalities was also important in the democratization process because it meant that when opposition parties won contests in subnational elections, they had greater autonomy and sometimes more resources with which to govern. This helped them establish a track record that helped their candidates run for higher office. Finally, perhaps the most important step in leveling the electoral playing field for the opposition was the creation and subsequent strengthening of an independent electoral authority in the early 1990s. Before the creation of the Federal Electoral Institute (Instituto Federal Electoral, IFE), it was the minister of the interior, the right-hand man of the president, who oversaw all elections and decided all electoral disputes.

Without independent oversight of elections, the opposition never stood a chance of making meaningful electoral gains. But with a set of independent institutions widely acknowledged to be impartial, Mexico's inchoate democracy made significant strides. The opposition was no longer always reliant on the PRI's goodwill in order to win an election. Instead, parties could focus on the challenges of getting elected and know that victories were almost certain to stand.

Hence, our discussion thus far suggests that the PRI's demise was, in large part, its own doing; without the government's unilateral decisions to reform the system, it might have held on to power indefinitely. However, this captures only part of the story. Although the process of political change in Mexico was in many ways a top-down phenomenon orchestrated by the PRI, the degree of pressure exerted by opposition parties, independent social movements, and other critics of the status quo also greatly influenced the course and pace of democratization. Indeed, such pressure was often the only means of forcing the PRI's hand, since otherwise the ruling party would have obviously preferred to maintain the status quo. These and other issues become much clearer with a more comprehensive account of Mexico's transition to democracy between 1970 and 2000, the subject we will now explore in more detail.

EARLY POLITICAL OPENING (1970–1988)

With the election of Luis Echeverría to the presidency in 1970, almost everyone expected his administration to try to recapture public support by using the PRI's traditional methods of incorporation, cooptation, and coercion.[2] Indeed, as the minister of the interior under the Díaz Ordaz government, Echeverría had played a determining role in the decision to use force against the demonstrators. In fact, many believed that he, rather than Díaz Ordaz, had orchestrated the government's repressive response to the demonstrations. Yet, upon being selected the party's presidential candidate, Echeverría made a concerted effort to brand himself as a different kind of *priísta*: one who was willing to speak publicly about the failures of past administrations and the shortcomings of the revolution, and one who was genuinely concerned about making life better for the poor. Echeverría was also quick to state that the economic advances of the previous thirty years had come at the expense of the peasantry and working classes. Upon taking office, he announced his intention to address the regime's failings and redeem his party. To that end, he proposed numerous changes that ranged from reforming the legislature to promoting the redistribution of wealth.

The legislative reform enacted in 1973 was ostensibly designed to make it easier for opposition parties to win seats in the Chamber of Deputies by lowering the minimum threshold for obtaining a party seat. While the reform did create new spaces for the opposition in the legislature, this was something of a double-edged sword. The low threshold for obtaining representation in government had the (not-unintended) effect of encouraging the proliferation of small fringe parties that either presented little threat to the PRI or even colluded directly with the ruling party. Thus, while ostensibly promoting democratic competition, the reform of 1973 had the effect of further fractionalizing and coopting the opposition, rather than creating meaningful alternatives to the PRI.

Echeverría's other reforms included anticorruption measures; significant increases in government spending for education, housing, and other public services; and greater resources for rural development (e.g., expanded credit, subsidized fertilizers, seeds, and irrigation infrastructure). At the same time, he stated in no uncertain terms that the time had come for the wealthy elite to give back to the country. He introduced tax hikes that required the rich to pay more in income taxes than they had in the past, and he set about reducing the availability of tax breaks and government subsidies that significantly lowered the costs of production for industrialists and large agribusinesses. Further, the government tightened restrictions on foreign capital and investment and redistributed more land to agrarian workers. Despite the apparent comprehensiveness of Echeverría's reforms, they produced little real change, in part because many of the reforms did not go deep enough to alter existing power structures or address pervasive administrative shortcomings, and also because elites undermined the president's reforms by removing their capital from the national economy. Halfway through his *sexenio*, Echeverría was forced to curtail many of his programs and to court the favor of the private sector and others in the ruling class.

In part because of the limits of his reforms and also because of global economic trends, by the time Echeverría left office in 1976, Mexico was facing its most serious economic crisis ever. The once-booming Mexican economy suffered from a mushrooming public deficit, rising inflation, a currency devaluation that resulted in the peso's loss of half its value, and stagnant real wages. In the end, Echeverría had failed to recapture public support for the PRI, and Mexico was no better off in 1976 than it had been six years earlier. The vast majority of Mexicans had seen no improvement in their standard of living or any real reform of the political system, and the selection of José López Portillo as Echeverría's successor suggested no radical departure from the past. If anything, the future promised to be more difficult because the new president inherited an economic disaster. Moreover, the PRI faced a serious blow to its legitimacy when López Portillo ran unopposed in the 1976 presidential election. After he won with nearly 100 percent of the vote, Mexico could hardly claim to be a plural polity.

López Portillo immediately set out to address both the economic and political weaknesses of the system. He began by selecting a fiscally conservative cabinet and pledging to drastically reduce government spending on public services, development projects, and wage increases, while at the same time limiting the foreign debt and tightening the money supply to control inflation and avoid overvaluing the peso—in other words, he set out to dismantle much of what Echeverría had put in place. These moves met with the instant approval of many in the private sector, including international investors and lenders such as private banks and the International Monetary Fund. Many at home and abroad lauded him for his pragmatism and sound approach to bringing about economic stability, but few had forgotten the embarrassing circumstances under which López Portillo had assumed the presidency. In the 1976 presidential election, the failure of the most coherently organized opposition party, the PAN, to run a candidate had robbed the PRI of its "loyal" opposition, while all other opposition parties backed the PRI. The absence of any real opposition exposed the regime's lack of legitimacy as a truly competitive democracy and prompted further electoral reforms.

Specifically, López Portillo introduced the Federal Law of Political Organizations and Electoral Processes (Ley Federal de Organizaciones Políticas y Procesos Electorales, LFOPPE) in 1977. The LFOPPE was designed to increase the access of smaller opposition parties by increasing the size of the Chamber of Deputies and making it easier for them to participate in and win elections. Much like the 1973 legislative reform, the LFOPPE facilitated increased participation and representation of the opposition; indeed, in the next few years five new parties obtained official registration. But the reforms also encouraged the formation of many small parties, rather than a unified opposition, and therefore made it highly unlikely that the PRI would ever be seriously threatened. Thus its overall effect was to revive the legitimacy of the Mexican political system, and therefore of the PRI, by making it look like the regime was promoting true electoral competition when in fact it was undermining the opposition.

Despite the largely symbolic nature of the LFOPPE, it placated many in the opposition and redeemed the PRI because it coincided with an impressive economic boom brought about by the discovery of sizable oil deposits in the Gulf of Mexico at the outset of López Portillo's term. This event, more than any political maneuvers by the government, was responsible for Mexico's political stability in the late 1970s and early 1980s. The deposits made Mexico the world's fourth largest oil producer, with an average annual rate of economic growth of more than 8 percent, and the government once again had resources to spare. However, even an economic boom of this magnitude was not enough to put Mexico on solid economic ground or to definitively rescue the PRI. Despite López Portillo's efforts to avoid the negative effects of a dramatic and rapid economic growth—runaway inflation, an overvalued currency, and in this case, overreliance on oil as a source of revenue—Mexico quickly suffered from all of the above and, for all practical purposes, squandered its incredible good fortune. Although revenue increased significantly once the production and export of oil was ramped up, so too did government spending. The government invested heavily in the petroleum industry and other high-priced industrial development projects, and spent millions on basic food imports. Amazingly enough, oil revenue, which reached $6 billion in 1980—up from $500 million in 1976—was insufficient to cover the government's spending, and López Portillo began to expand the money supply and borrow from abroad to pay debts.

By early 1982, the internal and external pressures for devaluation were strong enough to force the government's hand, and the peso lost 30 percent of its value. This meant not only that Mexicans' purchasing power declined substantially—the rate of inflation had increased to a whopping 100 percent— but also that Mexico's foreign debt nearly doubled, to $80 billion. As if this were not enough, in April, international oil prices dropped sharply, bringing Mexico less than half the amount of government revenue originally predicted for that year. This confluence of events created an untenable situation, and by the end of the summer Mexico declared that it would be unable to meet its foreign debt obligation: it was, in essence, bankrupt. Mexican economic growth, an enviable 8 percent in 1981, fell to zero by 1982. In order to prevent mass capital flight and further destabilization, the López Portillo administration nationalized all domestically owned banks—a move that went over well with the poor and working classes but sent shockwaves through the private sector.

Thus, with the country on the verge of economic collapse, the end of the López Portillo *sexenio* looked remarkably like the end of that of his predecessor. The PRI had been further discredited by rampant and unabashed corruption and its dismal failure to manage a plentiful endowment of the most valuable resource a country could hope to possess. In this context, López Portillo selected Miguel de la Madrid, his minister of budget and planning, as his successor. De la Madrid was viewed as a "technocrat"— a U.S.-trained bureaucrat with sophisticated technical skills in economic administration—who was committed to reducing state involvement in the economy to facilitate growth. This approach harkened back to the liberal principles of Adam Smith, David Ricardo, and the so-called classical school of economic theory. International lenders were willing to renegotiate the terms of Mexico's outstanding $80 billion in debt only if it reduced its fiscal deficit and embraced a neoliberal, free-market approach. Therefore de la Madrid filled his cabinet with technocrats like him, especially young professionals trained at U.S. institutions, and together they initiated a new era of economic reform in Mexico.

De la Madrid's policies focused on stabilization and structural reorientation of the economy. Economic restructuring included the dismantling of trade protectionism for domestic production, and an opening to international trade through Mexico's entry into the General Agreement on Tariffs and Trade (GATT) in 1986. At the same time, the de la Madrid administration made drastic reductions in public expenditures in all areas, from public works to education and from government subsidies for domestic industries to price controls on essential food items. His government also sought to increase its revenue by raising existing taxes and introducing a 15 percent value-added tax (VAT) on the sale of most items, as well as price hikes on utilities and public transportation. In addition, his government began working to tighten the money supply in order to rein in inflation and increase investor confidence. De la Madrid initially stated that it would take at least three years of fiscal austerity to put Mexico back on track. The reality was far worse. The government could not get a firm handle on inflation or produce meaningful economic growth until the end of the decade, with the help of the Economic Solidarity Pact (Pacto de Solidaridad Económica, PSE). This pact bound its signatories—labor, agricultural workers, and business—to respect even tighter monetary policy, trade liberalization, and fixed wages and prices, a clear precursor to the economic approach that followed in the next administration.

De la Madrid's economic reforms were accompanied by a three-pronged strategy to bring about political change, or at least the appearance of change. The first part of this strategy was to call for a zero-tolerance policy toward corruption at all levels of government. This move served an important political purpose but did virtually nothing to clean up the system. In the words of Judith Adler Hellman,

> Responding in this way to the public mood of frustration at the economic humiliation Mexico was suffering, de la Madrid concentrated on the malfeasance of the previous administration as a means to personalize and focus the anger of Mexicans on a relatively limited target. . . . But no systematic investigations of "unexplained wealth" were actually undertaken. To no one's great surprise, even the most highly visible offenders from the López Portillo regime went free. However, the campaign served a short-term purpose of deflecting attention from the more profound questions that needed to be publicly addressed in this period of crisis.[3]

De la Madrid also tried to alleviate the political pressures brought about by the economic crisis by promoting decentralization, or greater power sharing among the federal, state, and local (municipal) levels of government. While the main thrust of this reform aimed to clarify the responsibilities of the three levels and, somewhat ironically, made life more difficult for local governments, it also introduced proportional representation to municipal elections.[4] As a result, it paved the way for the opposition to gain entry into, and hence valuable hands-on experience from, governing at the local level.

The third part of de la Madrid's effort to promote political change was a constitutional amendment in 1986 that once again increased the size of the Chamber of Deputies by 100 proportional representation seats. On the surface, the addition of the new seats was supposed to create more space for the opposition. However, in reality the reform protected the PRI from the gains made by the opposition since the last round of reforms because changes to the seat allocation formula gave the PRI access to the proportional representation seats for the first time, and another law guaranteed the party with the highest vote a majority in the Chamber, even if it won less than 51 percent of the national vote.[5] The latter law, commonly known as the "governability clause," meant that the PRI need only obtain a plurality in order to control the lower house of the legislature. Many in the opposition welcomed the addition of new seats to the national legislature, but they took issue with the governability clause since it virtually guaranteed that the PRI would have an absolute majority in the legislature even if other parties collectively held a majority of the votes. Given a growing number of recognized opposition victories at the state and local level, such a prospect did not seem entirely out of the question in the near future. Hence, although the political reforms enacted by the de la Madrid administration were more far reaching than any that had come before, they failed to significantly enhance the PRI's legitimacy.

Meanwhile, people in all sectors of society felt the impact of persistent inflation, stagnant wages, high rates of unemployment, and the general difficulties of making ends meet. Unfortunately, this scenario was nothing new. But the crisis of the 1980s was deeper and more lasting than any experienced in the past and took a higher toll on society. Although de la Madrid's neoliberal economic program may have met with the approval of the private sector and the international financial community, it imposed great costs on ordinary Mexicans. This, together with the government's incompetent response to the massive earthquakes that hit Mexico City in September 1985 (see textbox 4.1), led many Mexicans to organize groups that openly expressed their dissatisfaction with the ruling party. What was different this time around was that in the next presidential election, voters for the first time had a meaningful choice to make: should they vote for the PRI and invite more of the same, or support Cuauhtémoc Cárdenas, the son of Mexico's most-revered postrevolutionary hero, in his quest to destroy the monolith? Not surprisingly, many opted for the latter, and the 1988 presidential election posed the most serious threat to the PRI's dominance that it had faced to date.

Textbox 4.1. 1985 EARTHQUAKES

On the morning of September 19, 1985, a massive earthquake measuring 8.1 on the Richter scale shook Mexico City. The next day, just as the dust was settling, a second temblor, this one measuring 7.5, struck in virtually the same location. Together, these earthquakes destroyed or damaged thousands of buildings, killed or injured hundreds of thousands of citizens, and caused several billion dollars' worth of damage to a country that was already in the throes of economic crisis. There is little doubt that the Mexico City earthquakes exacerbated Mexico's already desperate economic circumstances. Less predictable was the political fallout that occurred as a result of the natural disaster.

Much like the criticisms leveled against the U.S. government for its lackluster response to Hurricane Katrina in 2005, Mexican and international observers alike were horrified at the inadequacy of the city's infrastructure and at the national government's mishandling of the tragedy. Many of those trained and employed by the government to respond in such disasters, such as the police and army, stood by and watched as ordinary citizens set about digging survivors out of the rubble. Rather than provide effective leadership, President de la Madrid appeared aloof, and he inexplicably rejected all offers of foreign assistance. Public outcry against this attempt at nationalism led de la Madrid to eventually admit international rescue teams, aid, and equipment. But once it arrived much of this help was undermined by the Mexican government's insistence on control over all rescue efforts and by its looking the other way when police and army personnel began to sell donated supplies on the black market rather than distributing them to people in need.

For all of the hardship that the earthquakes brought the inhabitants of Mexico City, the disaster had a silver lining. The government's ineptness forced ordinary citizens to take matters into their own hands and coordinate their own rescue efforts. The success of these efforts became the foundation for further collective action to demand health care, housing, and other basic needs for survivors. Thus the earthquakes served as a catalyst for organized popular mobilization that pressured the government to address public demands for services and accountability. These grassroots social movements were one of the many factors that gradually led to greater support of opposition political parties and the decline of the PRI.

Source: Judith Adler Hellman, *Mexico in Crisis* (New York: Holmes & Meier, 1988).

SALINAS AND THE RISE OF
THE OPPOSITION (1988–1994)

Perhaps the greatest irony of the powerful opposition movement that the PRI faced in the late 1980s was that it came from within the party itself. The ascent of technocrats to powerful positions in the PRI in the late 1970s and early 1980s fundamentally altered the ideological orientation and leadership of the ruling party. These young, U.S.-trained economists brought with them a belief that free-market policies were the key to stabilizing and restructuring the economy in order to produce sustained growth. Given the economic crises of the times and pressure by international governments and lending institutions to use this approach, the technocrats were considered perfectly suited for cabinet level and bureaucratic positions within the López Portillo and de la Madrid governments.[6] Once in positions of power, the technocrats sought to remake the party in their own image, pushing aside members who had long since proven their loyalty but held more traditional views about the ideological orientation of the PRI. The subsequent rift between the *técnicos* and *políticos* proved to be extremely bitter and damaging to the party.

When de la Madrid began the process of selecting his successor, it quickly became clear that no old-style *político* stood a chance of being chosen. Indeed, the final choice of Carlos Salinas de Gortari, a tried-and-true technocrat, made it undeniable that the party would continue to pursue a market-oriented approach. This prompted several high-ranking members of the PRI who were ideologically committed to the principles of redistributive justice and other revolutionary myths, to break with the party and launch a bid for the presidency. Their preferred candidate, Cuauhtémoc Cárdenas, evoked memories of his father, President Lázaro Cárdenas, whose policies in the 1930s were widely revered for their faithful embodiment of Mexico's revolutionary principles. Once Cárdenas announced his intention to run for president, he was eagerly supported by a number of small leftist parties who formed a coalition, the National Democratic Front (Frente Democrático Nacional, FDN), and together nominated him as their presidential candidate. Cárdenas's candidacy tapped into a wellspring of popular discontent with the PRI. Among the most important sources of electoral support were the myriad civic organizations that had sprung up in the 1980s, especially in the aftermath of the earthquakes, and people who simply wanted to punish the PRI. With such widespread popular support for this new leftist movement, the PRI's leadership evidently decided that it could not leave the outcome of the election to fate. On election night, the computerized vote tabulation system mysteriously crashed when Cárdenas appeared to have a 2 to 1 lead in voting. When the system came back on line, the PRI's Salinas de Gortari had mysteriously captured the lead. The official results of the election showed that Salinas won with 51 percent of the vote, a decisive victory but a far cry from the 60-plus percent of the vote obtained by all of his predecessors. Both opposition candidates participating in the election, Cárdenas for the FDN and Manuel Clouthier for the PAN, claimed that the PRI had used electoral fraud to win. Their claims appeared to be substantiated by the fact that more than seventeen hundred precincts reported Salinas receiving 100 percent of the vote—a highly unlikely outcome. Years later, President de la Madrid admitted in his 2004 autobiography that the election was fraudulent and that the PRI declared victory as a preemptive measure before even confirming the final count.[7]

At the time, despite a widespread belief that the election had been stolen, the pro-Cárdenas opposition had few avenues to contest the official outcome because of the PRI's influence on the Federal Electoral Commission, and because—as we discuss below—the PRI and the PAN voted together in Congress to certify the results of the election. While Carlos Salinas was able to take office, he had to both work quickly to deal with detractors inside his own party and also contend with the popular perception that he was an illegitimate president. To deal with members of rival PRI factions, Salinas offered both carrots and sticks. While he won over some dissenters with cabinet positions and bureaucratic posts, others were forced from positions of power; indeed, during his term, more state governors "resigned" from their posts prematurely than under any other president since 1940.

Salinas also introduced an ambitious set of economic and political reforms. In the late 1980s this project appeared to have few chances for success. However, Salinas's charisma and political acumen allowed him to implement reforms that had a huge impact on Mexico and earned him great national and international prestige, for a time. Specifically, Salinas continued the country's neoliberal reform project—keeping tight control on government spending; restoring investor confidence by reprivatizing the banks and government-run industries; renegotiating the foreign debt; and permanently reducing barriers to trade with its most important trading partner, the United States, through the North American Free Trade Agreement (NAFTA). Salinas promised a robust, diverse, market-driven economy that would eventually place Mexico among the most illustrious first world of countries. In the meantime, the president acknowledged that these reforms would disproportionately harm the poor, particularly people in the countryside, who were most likely to be displaced by structural changes in the economy. In order to soften the transition for the country's most marginalized communities, Salinas also introduced the National Solidarity Program (Programa Nacional de Solidaridad, PRONASOL), a government-funded program designed to help communities find ways to meet their most pressing public service and infrastructure needs.[8] The Solidarity program helped some of the poorest people in Mexican society, but it never went far enough or reached all of those in need. It nevertheless did do something to promote economic well-being, and it served the very important political purpose of demonstrating the commitment of the government, and therefore the PRI, to addressing poverty.[9]

Recognizing that the opposition and the Mexican people were unlikely to tolerate a repeat of the 1988 election in the future, Salinas also introduced some significant reforms to the political system. In 1990, the Federal Code of Electoral Institutions and Procedures (Código Federal de Instituciones y Procedimientos Electorales, COFIPE) was implemented and created a new voter registry with tamper-proof identification cards, and two new and independent electoral institutions, the Federal Electoral Institute (IFE) and the Federal Electoral Tribunal (Tribunal Federal Electoral, TRIFE). Also included in the COFIPE was a revision of the governability clause introduced in 1986, in which the party with the most votes in single-member districts (SMD) for the Chamber of Deputies (and a minimum of 35 percent of the total) was automatically awarded a majority of seats in the legislature.

While the opposition was widely in favor of the creation of the independent electoral bodies, it saw the governability clause for what it was: a clear attempt to preserve the position of the PRI, since no other party could, at the time, hope to win more single-member districts. Therefore many within the opposition refused to support the COFIPE, particularly those affiliated with the newly created Party of the Democratic Revolution (Partido de la Revolución Democrática, PRD), which grew out of the FDN in 1989. Yet the reforms were approved by the legislature, but not because the PRI unilaterally amended the constitution as it had in the past; it did not have the necessary two-thirds majority to do this. Rather, somewhat surprisingly, Salinas found a willing partner in the PAN. Despite its long-standing criticism of and antipathy toward the PRI, many observers believe that the PAN entered into *concertación* or a surreptitious pact with the PRI during the early 1990s. While PAN leaders vigorously denied that they secretly colluded with the PRI, such a pact could have helped the PAN obtain important political concessions, such as the electoral reforms and electoral victories that it achieved during Salinas's presidency. In the final analysis, the PAN was largely in favor of Salinas's neoliberal economic reforms, was leery of Mexico's new opposition on the left, and felt that even with the governability clause, the creation of the IFE was a meaningful step in the right direction. Pact or not, the PAN had many reasons to support the PRI's agenda, and it did so.

Meanwhile, amid a growing number of postelectoral disputes, Salinas introduced a second round of reforms in 1993 to increase opposition representation and lessen the PRI's institutional advantages.[10] These reforms doubled the size of the Senate to 128 seats and guaranteed the opposition a minimum of 25 percent of the seats, a significant number but one that would not threaten the PRI's two-thirds majority. Second, the contentious governability clause was amended so that no party could hold more than 60 percent of the seats in the Chamber of Deputies, thereby depriving any party of the ability to unilaterally amend the constitution. Third, the IFE was given the role of certifying legislative electoral results, a task that had previously fallen to the legislature itself. The impact of these reforms on Mexico's democratization is discussed in more depth in chapter 6.

By late 1993 it appeared that Carlos Salinas had done the impossible: he had placed Mexico on solid economic ground and on the verge of beginning a new era of free trade with the United States and Canada, while at the same time doing something to address the dire need of his country's most disadvantaged citizens. He had also mended fences with detractors within his party and reestablished the PRI's hegemony, and he had worked with the opposition to implement some significant political reforms. Indeed, Salinas's successes were so impressive that Mexicans openly speculated about the possibility of amending the constitution to allow him to serve a second term of office, and many in the international community revered Mexico as a model for other developing countries to emulate. However, as quickly as Salinas had won the hearts of Mexicans and foreign observers alike, on January 1, 1994, he began a precipitous slide that eleven months later left him one of the most reviled politicians in Mexican history.

Salinas's undoing began with an uprising instigated by the Zapatista National Liberation Army (Ejercito Zapatista de Liberación Nacional, EZLN) on New Year's Day. This uprising, which we discuss in more detail in chapter 8, was planned to coincide with the first day that NAFTA went into effect, in order to demonstrate that Salinas's reforms had done nothing to meaningfully address the plight of Mexico's downtrodden indigenous communities or to construct an inclusive democracy. While the leaders of the EZLN had worked for many years under a Marxist ideology, the decline of communism led the rebels to rebrand their movement as a struggle against PRI authoritarianism, the discriminatory nature of Mexican society, and the inequities of the global economy.

While the Salinas government struggled to find the right response to the Zapatistas, it suffered another blow with the assassination of Salinas's chosen successor, Luis Donaldo Colosio.[11] Because Colosio's assassination took place at the height of his campaign, Salinas found himself in the uncomfortable position of having to name a successor from a tiny pool of eligible candidates. Mexican electoral laws require candidates to resign from their government posts six months prior to an election, making Salinas's closest allies and cabinet members ineligible to run for president. The man Salinas chose to replace Colosio was Ernesto Zedillo, who had stepped down from his post as education minister to help run the presidential campaign. Zedillo was a Yale-educated technocrat, and he appeared to be a stiff, unimaginative bureaucrat poorly suited to excel in public office, much less the presidency.[12]

Salinas's popularity and his historical legacy were further tarnished after Zedillo took office. Having propped up the peso with high interest bonds throughout 1994, by the end of his term Salinas had exhausted Mexico's currency reserves, contributing to a severe economic crisis. This was partly a political decision, since devaluing the currency prior to the July elections would have certainly hurt the PRI at the polls. Yet, Salinas could have devalued the currency soon after Zedillo's victory, thereby allowing plenty of time to repair the damage before leaving office and giving Zedillo an opportunity to start his term with a clean slate. Zedillo's team reportedly urged Salinas to follow this course, but he did not. By the time Zedillo took office in December, the situation had become so untenable that the new administration had to devalue the currency just eighteen days after the new president took office. As a result of this massive devaluation, Mexicans who held their savings in the national currency lost nearly half of their wealth at the same time that they saw consumer prices and personal debt rise exponentially. While this turn of events was devastating, for many Mexicans it was somehow not as bad as finding out that the Salinas administration had fully anticipated the impending economic crisis and had knowingly allowed it to worsen rather than addressing the situation.

FROM HEGEMONY TO
POWER SHARING (1994–2000)

Like Salinas, Ernesto Zedillo was expected to be a weak, ineffective leader. And while it took some time to dispel rumors that he would not finish his term of office, eventually Zedillo managed to salvage his personal image by shepherding meaningful political reform and deepening the country's economic stability. Thanks largely to the creation of the IFE, the 1994 elections were widely regarded as the freest and fairest to date in Mexico. Seeking to build on this foundation—and to the dismay of many within his party—Zedillo set out to deepen Mexico's transition away from single-party dominance and toward democracy. Building on the reforms of the Salinas administration, in 1996 he introduced legislation that prevented any party from enjoying extreme overrepresentation in the Chamber of Deputies and ensured that half of the Senate seats would go to the second-place party in each election. Furthermore, under Zedillo the IFE became a truly independent body, governed by nonpartisan citizen councilors rather than by the minister of the interior, and assumed full authority over electoral matters. Political parties were guaranteed by law more equal access to public funds and media exposure, and at the same time were increasingly required to account for the amounts and sources of their campaign contributions as well as their campaign spending. The cumulative effect of the political reforms implemented between 1990 and 1996 was to gradually erode the PRI's electoral dominance.

The PRI's decline became painfully and undeniably clear in the aftermath of the 1997 midterm elections, when it lost its majority in the Chamber of Deputies for the first time in its existence. This development, while profoundly bruising to the PRI, proved to be instrumental in promoting Mexico's transition toward democracy because it introduced, for the first time, a system of checks and balances and forced the executive to negotiate with the legislature even for relatively minor concessions. Of similar importance were Zedillo's efforts to strengthen the judiciary, with reforms in 1994 that increased the power and independence of the judiciary.

Of all of the reforms that Ernesto Zedillo deepened or introduced, perhaps the most significant of these for the PRI was his apparent refusal to designate his successor. Under enormous pressure to continue the PRI tradition of handpicking the next candidate, Zedillo instead chose to downplay his influence and, in so doing, forced the party to adopt new internal rules for candidate selection. The importance of this move should not be underestimated, because it weakened the traditional power of the president and brought greater internal democratization to the PRI—an element sorely lacking before the late 1990s. The president's ability to choose his successor was one of the most important elements of presidential power in Mexico because it guaranteed that he could single-handedly award the highest prize for party and personal loyalty. Zedillo's decision to break with this practice may have stemmed from the fact that he represented no particular faction of the party—all had equally disdained and even challenged him during his *sexenio*—and he therefore did not feel compelled to remain true to the party's traditional practices. Moreover, given his weakness within his own party, it is possible that his chosen candidate would have faced open challenges from the losing factions with potentially devastating consequences for the party.

Whatever the reasons for Zedillo's decision, in the end it benefited the PRI by forcing it to adopt an internal primary process that modernized the party and probably made it more competitive.[13] Nevertheless, in the short term, the PRI's primary produced a bitter and damaging internal brawl as each of the four main aspirants sought to win the party's nomination. In their attempts to curry popular favor, the contenders slung mud and threw punches, accusing one another of everything from violating internal party rules to participating in the party's use of electoral fraud and corruption. In the end, Francisco Labastida, a technocrat said to be Zedillo's unstated choice, won a decisive victory, but at the personal expense of his challengers, and perhaps more importantly, at the cost of the PRI's credibility and legitimacy.[14] There is little doubt that the bruising primary campaign contributed to the PRI's loss of the presidency in 2000, culminating a long and gradual electoral decline for the ruling party (see figure 4.1).

Equally important in the PRI's defeat in 2000 was the growing strength of the opposition, in particular the PAN. While the PRD and its third-time presidential candidate, Cuauhtémoc Cárdenas, still had significant popular support in the capital, the organization's internal dynamics and infighting had prevented it from becoming a well-consolidated, disciplined political party. Although he was undisputedly among the party's most important leaders, Cárdenas was a controversial candidate in 2000 within the PRD. Many felt that after his poor showing in 1994, winning just 17 percent of the vote, and his mediocre performance as the mayor of Mexico City, the party needed a more dynamic candidate to appeal to voters. Moreover, the party's internal squabbles, public airing of dirty laundry, and perceived ambivalence toward democracy alienated voters who were otherwise sympathetic to its left-of-center ideology. In retrospect, a stronger candidate with more popular appeal and a more coherent party organization with a proven track record were absolutely necessary to counter the challenge put forth by,

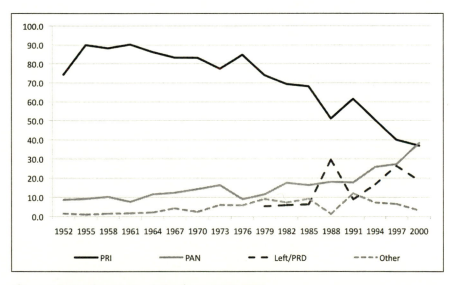

Figure 4.1. Mexican Federal Elections, 1952–2000

Source: 1961 and 1988 figures: Silvia Gómez Tagle, *La frágil democracia Mexicana: partidos políticos y elecciones* (Mexico City: García y Valadés Editors, 1993). 1964–1985 figures: Juan Molinar Horcasitas, "The 1985 Federal Elections in Mexico: The Product of a System," in *Electoral Patterns and Perspectives in Mexico*, Monograph Series, 20, ed. Arturo Alvarado (La Jolla: Center for U.S.-Mexican Studies, 1987). Figures from 1991–1997 derived from Carlos Sirvent, "Las elecciones de 1997: el voto por la alternancia," in *Estudios Políticos*, cuarta época, no. 16 (September–December 1997), 67–89. 2003 and 2006 data obtained from IFE.

on the one hand, the incumbent party with a long, if tainted, legacy and copious resources, and on the other, the PAN, with its upstart candidate, reputation for honesty and transparency, and vast campaign war chest.

To many observers of Mexico, Vicente Fox and the PAN seemed to come out of nowhere to win the presidency in 2000, when in fact Fox's victory represented the culmination of the PAN's growing electoral success throughout the 1990s. Its success in 2000 was determined by several factors, including the party's ability to capitalize on its many subnational electoral victories and solid reputation and parlay these into greater national support.[15] Yet equally important was the party's choice of candidate. In some senses, Vicente Fox was an unlikely and unexpected candidate: although he had a proven track record as a federal deputy and governor of the state of Guanajuato, he was not a member of the party leadership. Indeed, he was thought by many within the PAN to be too pragmatic and not fully committed to the party's principles or statutes. Nevertheless, thanks to his image as a businessman who was not afraid to speak bluntly, and thanks to a well-organized political action committee that amassed a small fortune in campaign contributions and began a groundswell of popular support, Fox emerged as the PAN's best chance for defeating the PRI, and even skeptics in the party became obliged to support his candidacy. Although most predictions favored the PRI, Fox's sophisticated campaign convinced voters that Labastida was no different from the party he represented—authoritarian, corrupt, and retrograde. At the same time, Fox presented himself as the best option for meaningful change by discrediting Labastida's claims of representing a new PRI and overshadowing Cárdenas's attempts to present himself as the champion of Mexican nationalism and a credible source of change. In the end, 42 percent of voters felt that Fox was their best hope for defeating the PRI and moving the country forward, and Mexico entered the twenty-first century with its first opposition president in more than seven decades.

VICENTE FOX AND THE CHALLENGES
OF POLITICAL CHANGE

During his campaign, Fox promised change for Mexico through wide-ranging reforms that included an overhaul of the tax system, modernizing and privatizing the energy sector, and labor reform. Fox also promised to create a million jobs a year, produce 7 percent annual GDP growth, resolve the lingering conflict in Chiapas, reduce crime and corruption, and deliver an immigration accord with the United States. However, he ultimately faced significant challenges resulting from his governing style, divisions within his own party, and a divided Congress. Indeed, over the course of his term, Mexico's economy muddled through with an average of about 3 percent growth, and key sectors (such as *maquiladora* production) suffered major hits from overseas competition. He was unable to gain party support for some of his major policy priorities, most notably a fiscal reform package that sought to substantially increase tax revenue by extending the national VAT to include previously exempt items such as food, medicine, school tuition, and public transportation.[16] Despite Fox's leadership on new legislation for indigenous rights, the Zapatista rebels in Chiapas refused to lay down their arms, and the arrest of several major drug traffickers, ongoing problems of crime and rising drug violence left many Mexicans feeling even less safe than at the start of his administration. Meanwhile, Fox's efforts to negotiate an immigration accord with the United States faltered in the face of newfound concerns about illegal immigration and terrorism following the terrorist attacks of September 11, 2001. Critics charged that, while he may have been an excellent candidate to win the presidency, once in office Fox lacked the political skills to achieve his goals.

The highly polarized political climate that prevailed during Fox's term was by far the greatest obstacle to his policy agenda. Fox faced a divided legislature controlled by two opposition parties—the PRI and the PRD—that were in a very strong position to recapture the presidency at the end of his term. In this context, members of the opposition were unlikely to give Fox much quarter, since voter dissatisfaction with his government could translate into support for their parties. Indeed, despite the PAN's slogan during the 2003 midterm elections—"Take the brakes off change"—voters increased their support for the opposition, especially the PRD (which nearly doubled its seats in the Chamber of Deputies from fifty in 2000 to ninety-seven in 2003). Hence the 2003 midterm elections secured Fox's status as a lame duck president and ensured that major changes would not be forthcoming over the remainder of his administration.

That said, Fox's six years in office were hardly a complete failure. On the contrary, his administration can claim credit for some important successes, chief among them economic stability. While the Mexican economy did not grow at nearly the rate promised by Fox, it did grow, and equally important, strict fiscal discipline led to a balanced budget and a significant decrease in inflation, from over 16 percent in 1999 to roughly 4 percent in 2006, remarkable accomplishments given the depth of the 1994 peso crisis and the instability of the Mexican economy in recent decades.

The Fox administration had other notable successes, including passage of the Federal Law for Transparency and Access to Public Government Information, akin to freedom of information laws in the United States and elsewhere. This law and the Federal Institute for Access to Public Information (Instituto Federal de Acceso a la Información Pública, IFAI) that it created provide access to a wide array of government documents, greatly promoting transparency and accountability in Mexico.[17] Also important was the Federal Law to Prevent and Eliminate Discrimination, a law that strengthened existing legislation and made it illegal to discriminate on the basis of "ethnic or national origin, sex, age, disability, social or economic condition, health, pregnancy, language, religion, opinions, sexual preference, or marital status." Moreover, thanks to shifting legislative coalitions among different political parties under Fox, the Mexican Congress actually passed more legislation during Fox's term than had been achieved in decades. Still, Fox's ultimate legacy will be debated for many years to come and will no doubt be shaped by the challenges faced by subsequent administrations in deepening and consolidating Mexico's democracy.

THE CALDERÓN ADMINISTRATION AND BEYOND

The 2006 presidential election proved extremely controversial, as discussed in greater detail in chapter 6, since the result was a virtual tie between PAN candidate Felipe Calderón and PRD candidate Andrés Manuel López Obrador (AMLO). Ultimately, Calderón was declared the winner by the slimmest of margins, 0.5 percent of the vote, or roughly a quarter of a million votes, and was heavily criticized by López Obrador and his supporters, who alleged electoral fraud and bias in the postelectoral legal decisions. The 2006 election revealed that Mexico was divided between those in the north and central western parts of the country, who largely supported Calderón, and those in the south and central east, who supported López Obrador. Furthermore, the country was almost evenly split between those who favored the existing economic model that called for promoting free-market reforms and those who favored a model that allowed the government to play a more active role in the distribution of resources. These divisions, together with the PAN's tiny margin of victory and López Obrador's postelectoral disputes, weakened Calderón's mandate. López Obrador claimed that the election had been stolen and that, much like Cuauhtémoc Cárdenas in 1988, he was the legitimate president. Together with the National Democratic Convention (Convención Nacional Democrática, CND), he formed a "parallel government" to monitor the actions of the "spurious government" and orchestrate meaningful reforms. López Obrador sought to stay in the public eye and eventually displace Felipe Calderón, his alleged usurper. Thereafter, López Obrador refused to meet with Calderón, and for several months his supporters held demonstrations to protest what they saw as an illegitimate takeover of the presidency.[18]

Calderón thus took office amid severe social unrest and serious questions about his legitimacy. In recognition of the millions of poor and marginalized citizens that López Obrador represented, Calderón initially asserted that his administration would help address Mexico's economic inequalities and promote better employment opportunities for all Mexicans. As he had claimed during his presidential campaign, Calderón aspired to be Mexico's "jobs" president, with a strong focus on social and economic development. Calderón also pushed forward important reforms to Mexico's pension system, taxation, electoral regulations, and the judicial sector. In the first few years of his presidency, Calderón's popularity grew significantly and the scars of the 2006 presidential election were seemingly forgotten.

Even so, Calderón will most likely be remembered for his controversial policies to combat drug trafficking and other forms of organized crime, which became the primary focus of his administration. At the outset of his term, Calderón requested an immediate 24 percent increase in the national security budget, and he promptly deployed tens of thousands of federal forces to the states most impacted by drug trafficking–related violence. Arguably, these measures reflected the fact that Calderón came to the presidency at a time of trouble and uncertainty. Even as he took office in December 2006, the southern state of Oaxaca continued to simmer with unrest after a midsummer teachers' strike erupted into violence, and the Zapatista National Liberation Army (EZLN) had returned to a state of "red alert" in reaction to a violent police crackdown on flower vendors in the city of Texcoco, outside Mexico City.

However, internecine violence among drug-trafficking organizations in states along Mexico's Pacific coast and northern border regions quickly became Calderón's primary focus. By the end of 2010, his fourth year in office, more than thirty-four thousand people had died as a result of this violence, including hundreds of police, military personnel, government officials, and ordinary citizens caught in the crossfire. As discussed in chapter 13, Calderón's efforts were welcomed and praised by presidents George Bush and Barack Obama, both of whom supported his administration through a massive security assistance package known as the Mérida Initiative. Given the toll of violence that resulted from the war on drugs, by the end of Calderón's term, many Mexicans began to question whether they were better off than at the beginning. Moreover, a majority of Mexicans also grew to believe that their government was outmatched by the narco-traffickers. Drug traffickers enjoyed at least some complicity, support, and even sympathy from certain segments of society, and in some areas of the country locals have held public demonstrations protesting the government.[19]

As the end of Calderón's term approached, many Mexicans felt that their country was headed in the wrong direction. In July 2009, Calderón suffered a major political defeat as the PRI gained ground in elections for the federal legislature, and in state and local governments around the country. Despite this major defeat, Calderón proceeded to unveil sweeping reform proposals that—if passed—would dramatically transform Mexico's system of democratic governance. Upon announcing the reforms, Calderón indicated that "our democracy is still far from being able to express and represent clearly the voice and desire of the people in legislative and public policy decisions." His proposals included the following ten major political reforms:

1. Consecutive reelection of mayors and city council members, with a proposed limit of twelve years in one post, to promote greater responsiveness to voters and to facilitate long-term planning in public administration.
2. Consecutive reelection of federal legislators with term limits set at twelve years, to increase responsiveness to their districts and the acquisition of legislative knowledge on issues important to their constituents.
3. Reduction of the number of seats in the Chamber of Representatives and the Senate, to promote greater efficiency in legislative work and better use of public funds.
4. Increased proportion of votes required for political parties to conserve their national registration and public financing, assuring that there is sufficient popular support to justify their existence.
5. Legislative initiative process, so that citizens can participate directly in proposing laws before the Congress.
6. Permission for candidates to run independently of political parties, to offer citizens a wider array of choices in elections.
7. A second round of voting for the president in highly competitive races, to promote coalition building and ensure strong electoral support for the president.
8. A constitutional provision allowing the Supreme Court to propose legislative initiatives, to strengthen the role of the judiciary and provide more direct juridical guidance to legislators.
9. Special presidential legislative initiatives and constitutional amendments (up to two per legislative session) that would take effect unless rejected by Congress before the end of the session (constitutional amendments would be submitted to a citizen referendum).
10. Possibility of segmented congressional and executive approval of the federal budget, so that disagreements over certain sections of the budget do not delay the approval of sections that are approved by all parties.

While the Calderón administration managed to obtain fifty-five reforms to the Mexican constitution during his first three years in office, the president was already widely perceived as a lame duck by the time the reform package was announced in December 2009. In the wake of the PAN's losses

in the midterm elections earlier that year, except for some minor proposals (such as independent candidates), this sweeping reform initiative was
unviable, and critics viewed it as an intentional political distraction by the
administration.[20]

Meanwhile, with the PRI resurgent in the state and midterm elections,
many pundits began to predict the return of Mexico's former ruling party in
the presidential election of 2012. Indeed, presuming that the PRI was able
to maintain internal unity for its presidential candidate—a task that proved
elusive in both 2000 and 2006—numerous public opinion polls signaled
strong support for the presidential candidacy of Enrique Peña Nieto, the
young and dashing PRI governor of the state of Mexico. Even so, electoral
uncertainty is a new and prominent feature of contemporary Mexican politics, so—unlike elections of the past—any effort to predict the final results
of Mexico's presidential election prior to July 2, 2012, would constitute
pure speculation.

CONCLUSION

Mexico's transition away from the single-party dominance of the PRI happened gradually over several decades. New students of Mexican politics are
sure to ask why, given the PRI's loss of legitimacy in almost every area, the
transition did not happen faster or earlier. With the help of hindsight, it is
possible to say that the pace and even the character of Mexico's transition
were determined largely by timing and sequence of events. That is, had the
contributing factors—economic crisis, loss of legitimacy, and institutional
openings—happened all at once, we might have expected the PRI to lose
power more quickly and definitively. But obviously this could not have
happened, because each event was a consequence of another. The PRI's
loss of legitimacy stemmed in no small part from its failure as an economic
manager and agent of redistribution, as well as its exclusionary and corrupt tendencies. The loss of legitimacy in turn made it increasingly difficult
for the PRI to use its traditional practices (e.g., cooptation and electoral
fraud) to perpetuate its power, and forced the administrations of the 1970s,
1980s, and 1990s to create the openings that gradually leveled the playing
field and made it possible for the opposition to gain entry into the political system. Meanwhile, the pace of the transition was determined by the
regime's periodic runs of good luck (the discovery of vast oil deposits in the
mid-1970s) and its understandable reluctance to dismantle the authoritarian institutions that preserved its dominance. Only when faced with serious
challenges to its power did it enact the reforms that cumulatively brought
greater democracy to Mexico. In some ways the erratic and moderate pace
of the transition may have benefited the opposition by providing it time

to gain the electoral and governing experience that was essential to its successes in the mid-1990s.

One question we are left with is whether Mexico's transition has proceeded far enough and penetrated deeply enough to establish the country as a definitive democracy. As subsequent chapters will demonstrate, the country has the foundation for a solid democracy: for example, it has some of the strongest electoral institutions in the world, the separation and balance of powers has been considerably strengthened in the past fifteen years, and Mexican voters believe they have a meaningful role to play in the electoral and political processes. However, there also remain vestiges of the past and formidable obstacles that suggest that Mexico's transition is not complete: the lines of representation and accountability between legislators and their constituents are something between fuzzy and nonexistent, the rule of law remains weak, and vast socioeconomic disparities undermine the equality purportedly offered by the Mexican constitution. Another looming question is whether a PRI victory in the 2012 presidential election would effectively reverse Mexico's many gains of the past thirty years. Finally, because Mexico's 2012 elections coincide with the U.S. presidential race—a phenomenon that happens every twelve years—the future of U.S.-Mexico relations is also very likely to be significantly shaped by the outcome in both countries. In the coming chapters, we explore these questions in greater depth, with an emphasis on the political institutions, processes, and interests that shape Mexico's political situation today.

Part II

POLITICAL INSTITUTIONS, CULTURE, AND SOCIETY

5

Government Structure and Processes

MEXICAN GOVERNMENT

Reading Mexico's 1917 constitution might lead one to believe that its political system is very similar to—if not more advanced than—the U.S. constitution, authored nearly 150 years earlier. Comprising nine title sections and 136 separate articles, Mexico's constitution provides for a presidential executive, a bicameral legislature, an independent judiciary, a federal system of states with constitutionally granted autonomy, and direct popular elections for the selection of political leaders (without a U.S.-style electoral college). Compared to the U.S. constitution, the Mexican constitution is far more progressive, since it provides special protections for indigenous minorities and grants all citizens a right to basic education, labor protections, and other social welfare provisions. *progressive in writing*

In practice, however, Mexican politics have always been quite different from those of its northern neighbor, and political practices have often deviated very significantly from Mexico's own constitutional procedures and rights. As we have seen, for most of the twentieth century, Mexico functioned more like a highly centralized authoritarian regime than a competitive democratic system, since the PRI controlled nearly all aspects of the political process. Single-party domination compromised the spirit of many formal institutions (e.g., legislative and judicial independence), and virtually eliminated the possibility of power sharing. Additionally, the PRI's hegemony made it almost impossible for the opposition to pose a serious challenge to the status quo. Yet by the mid-1980s the PRI's power began to decline, as Mexicans increasingly questioned its effectiveness and legitimacy. Over the course of the next two decades, the Mexican political system experienced significant changes that signaled the end of single-party hegemony and the beginning of Mexico's new, pluralistic democracy. This chapter discusses Mexico's main governmental structures and describes how they have changed during the country's transition to democracy.

EXECUTIVE BRANCH

During most of the period of PRI rule, Mexico's president enjoyed the authority and legitimacy of an autocrat. This power was not granted by the constitution, which outlines fewer powers for the Mexican executive than many other Latin American presidents enjoy.[1] Yet during the rule of the PRI, the power of the Mexican president typically exceeded the de jure or legal responsibilities of the office (see textbox 5.1). According to political scientist Jeffrey Weldon, the Mexican president's historically exaggerated powers—described as "hyperpresidentialism" or *presidencialismo*—stemmed from the coincidence of three conditions that predominated during PRI rule: unified government, a high level of party discipline, and presidential leadership of his political party. Together these elements allowed the president to exercise an inordinate amount of influence in the Mexican political system.[2] Today, Mexican presidential power is much more limited, and the executive must forge political consensus with other branches and levels of government.

Hyperpresidentialism in Mexico

Weldon's allusion to unified government refers to the fact that a single party, the PRI, held an absolute majority in both houses of Congress from the 1930s until 1997, giving the president legislative support for all of his proposals. However, unified government by itself was not enough to produce *presidencialismo*. Another essential condition was strong discipline within the ruling party, since the president needed PRI legislators to consistently toe the party line. Party discipline within the PRI was traditionally strong, thanks to the ban on consecutive reelection. A ban on reelection gives politicians little motivation to pay attention to constituents in their districts, but it provides a strong incentive to demonstrate loyalty to party leaders who can help advance their careers. Loyalty to the PRI was especially important because candidates for office were almost always selected by the party leadership rather than through a primary system. Party discipline and *presidencialismo* were also a consequence of the president's dual role as the head of government and the formal head of his party. As head of the party, the president had the de facto power to nominate nearly all PRI candidates,

Textbox 5.1. DE JURE POWERS OF THE MEXICAN PRESIDENT

The specific authority and responsibilities of the president are outlined in Article 89 of the Mexican constitution, which empowers him as follows:

- To introduce legislation and execute laws generated by the Congress
- To appoint and remove cabinet-level officials and other federal employees
- To appoint, with Senate approval, the Mexican attorney general, high-level diplomatic personnel (such as ambassadors and consular officials), and top military commanders in Mexico's army, navy, and air force
- To appoint other military personnel without Senate approval
- To serve as commander in chief of Mexico's military forces and national guard to preserve Mexico's national security, and to declare war if passed by law through the Mexican Congress
- To direct Mexican foreign policy—and, with Senate approval, the promulgation of international treaties—toward the goal of respecting the principles of self-determination, nonintervention, peaceful resolution of controversies, minimization of the use of force, the legal equality of nations, international cooperation, and the preservation of international peace and security
- To convoke extraordinary sessions of the legislature with approval by its Permanent Commission
- To assist the judiciary as needed to expedite its functions, and to nominate members of the Supreme Court, with approval by the Senate
- To establish and control all ports, customs, and border installations
- To grant pardons to criminals sentenced by federal tribunals or by the Federal District
- To concede temporary privileges to promote invention, discovery, and industrial innovation
- To make high-level appointments (not including the Supreme Court) with approval by the Permanent Commission when the Senate is not in session

including his successor. Therefore, members of the party were not simply expressing loyalty to their party, they were also demonstrating loyalty to the president in the hopes of being tapped for a future elected or appointed office. The *dedazo*—the term used to describe the practice of sitting executives handpicking their successor—epitomized the excesses of *presidencialismo*. Together, these conditions created and reinforced the power of the presidency in Mexico and endowed the office with what have often been called extraconstitutional powers—political powers that go beyond constitutional authority but stay within the bounds of the law.[3] In practice, the chief executive's extraconstitutional authority was used for a variety of purposes. Often, Mexican presidents used it to amend the constitution, to assume the role of chief legislator, to influence the judiciary in legal matters, to nominate party candidates for offices at all levels of government, and to overrule or even remove state governors and other elected officials. Today, as a result of Mexico's gradual democratization, there are significant constraints on executive power, which must be explored in greater detail.

Mexico's Diminished Presidency

[handwritten: PRI loses majority in COD]

When the PRI lost its majority in the Chamber of Deputies in 1997 the conditions that created *presidencialismo* were altered and the Mexican executive no longer enjoyed the same amount of power as his predecessors. The halcyon days of PRI hegemony were over. One of the first reality checks came in 1998, when Congress rejected a presidential proposal to establish the Savings Protection Banking Fund (Fondo Bancario de Protección al Ahorro, FOBAPROA) and instead voted to approve a different version of the bill introduced by the PAN. Yet this is not to say that the president suddenly became a weak political player or that the PRI ceased to be the dominant political power in Mexico. Indeed, the president continued to be the most powerful political actor in the country, and the party still enjoyed substantial support at all levels of government. Yet ironically, it was President Zedillo himself who further diminished the power of the presidency by refusing to exercise the office's remaining extraconstitutional powers or to name his successor, instead proclaiming that he would maintain a healthy distance (*sana distancia*) between himself and his party.

Given that Mexican presidents essentially ruled single-handedly for much of the twentieth century, other aspects of the executive branch were long overshadowed. But like other presidential systems, the executive branch in Mexico also comprises the president's cabinet of twenty ministries (see table 5.1) and other key advisers. The president appoints all members of the cabinet and only the Mexican attorney general (procurador general de la República) must be approved by the Senate. Like their counterparts in other countries, cabinet officials serve as the core of the administration, formulating and implementing the policies that become the hallmark of a particular *sexenio*. All cabinet-level officials—such as the ministers of foreign relations, treasury, and public security—specialize in specific areas, make recommendations, and oversee the bureaucratic entities that carry out the president's policy initiatives. Historically, the most important cabinet official has been the minister of the interior (secretaría de gobernación), who oversees Mexico's internal affairs. In addition to playing a pivotal role

[handwritten: minister of the interior]

Table 5.1. Executive Cabinet Ministries

Government	Social Development
Foreign Relations	Labor and Social Welfare
Attorney General	Communications and Transportation
Public Security	Environment and Natural Resources
National Defense	Energy
Armed Forces	Agriculture and Rural Development
Navy	Agrarian Reform
Treasury and Public Credit	Education
Economy	Health
Governmental Transparency	Tourism

in policy formation and the preservation of public order, serving as interior minister traditionally provided a stepping-stone to the presidency.[4]

Advisory posts within the presidential staff tend to vary in number and importance from one administration to the next, depending on a president's priorities. Two important positions are the president's personal secretary (*secretario particular*) and his chief adviser (*jefe de asesores*), who serve as his closest advisers and determine who has access to the president. Equally important is the president's legal adviser, without whom the president cannot effectively interact with legislative and judicial branches of government. The office of the president also typically relies on two offices—public opinion and communications—to gather feedback on the administration's performance and publicize its accomplishments. Other advisory positions generally report directly to the president and work alongside specialized agencies to raise the profile of particular policy areas (e.g., national security and foreign relations, public housing, indigenous affairs). In creating his inner circle, President Calderón made public security a major priority by appointing experts like Sigrid Arzt and Jorge Tello to his advisory group.

The Mexican executive and his cabinet also oversee a number of bureaucratic agencies and parastatal (state-owned) enterprises. For example, the minister of energy oversees the bureaucratic organization that manages Mexico's energy policy, including the parastatal organization known as Mexican Petroleum (Petróleos Mexicanos), better known by the acronym PEMEX, and the Federal Electricity Commission (Comisión Federal de Electricidad), which respectively control the production and distribution of oil and electricity. There are also a number of state-owned banks (e.g., BANOBRAS, NAFIN, BANCOMEXT) that work to promote development and trade. Many of these agencies and parastatal enterprises—particularly PEMEX—are a holdover from the days of state-led economic development (1940s to 1970s), and for many Mexicans, they are the last bastions of national economic pride.

Still, the Mexican presidency is no longer what it was. Economic restructuring to liberalize trade and domestic production has fundamentally transformed the role of the Mexican state, and therefore the role of the executive branch. Moreover, because of Mexico's political liberalization, the executive branch has been forced to adjust to a more democratic context where power is shared across all three major branches of government. Since 1997, when President Zedillo headed the country's first divided government—where the party that controls the executive branch faces an opposition majority in the legislature—Mexican president and legislature must now negotiate to approve legislation and budgets, or they may be unable to move forward on key policy initiatives. Indeed, divided government during the Fox administration resulted in significant disagreements between the executive and legislative branches, resulting in a total of seventeen presidential vetoes of congressional legislation (including one budget). President Calderón did not use the veto nearly as much—only five times in his first five years in office—which probably reflected the PAN's ability to gain a majority of seats in the Senate in the 2006 elections, but also the fact that his administration learned how to negotiate with the legislature behind the scenes. To better understand how the president has become more subject to legislative oversight and judicial authority, we turn to the other branches that now provide "checks and balances" against Mexico's once dominant executive.

THE LEGISLATURE

The duties and functions of the Mexican Congress are outlined in Article 73 of the Mexican constitution. Like the United States, Mexico has a bicameral legislature, with an upper house (the Senate) and a lower house (the Chamber of Deputies). The Mexican Congress meets in two legislative sessions per year, both a fall term (September through mid-December) and a spring term (mid-March through late April).

As discussed earlier, the Mexican legislature has been historically limited in its role as a check against the executive, primarily because a single, highly disciplined political party controlled both branches of government. However, as opposition parties gained strength in the legislature and ultimately came to dominate it, this branch has become a much more powerful counterweight to the executive. Still, Mexican legislators continue to face important challenges and limitations. Due to prohibitions on immediate reelection in Mexico, legislators cannot serve consecutive terms. While they can be reelected after one term has passed, most Mexican legislators have historically served only one term before moving on to some other area or level of government or running for a different public office. The prohibition on reelection creates a disincentive to develop strong relationships with their constituents and makes it difficult for them to develop legislative expertise. Below we describe the structure and function of both houses of the legislature and then discuss the evolving role of the legislature in contemporary Mexican politics.

The Senate

elected concurrently

The Mexican Senate comprises 128 members, who are elected concurrently with the president in one of two ways. Each of Mexico's thirty-one states and the Federal District elects two senators under the plurality rule, and one senator based on the principle of first minority. In any given ☆ senatorial election, the party that receives the highest vote, even if it is less than half, wins two seats and the second place (or first minority) party is awarded one seat. The remaining thirty-two Senate seats are allocated according to proportional representation (PR), that is, in proportion to each party's share of the total national vote.[5] *election procedure*

This complex method of selection for Mexican senators was intended to provide a degree of access to the Senate for minority parties. However, in practice parties are not necessarily represented in proportion to their actual electoral strength. For example, with only a plurality of the vote, a single party could win two-thirds of the seats in each state and any number of PR seats and be significantly overrepresented in the Senate. Indeed, in the 2006 election, the PAN won 33 percent of the national vote but was awarded a total of fifty-two senatorial seats, and therefore comprised 40 percent of the Senate. The PRD, on the other hand, won just under 30 percent of the national vote, but its members made up just 24 percent of the Senate.[6] Again, unlike the U.S. Senate, which elects senators during both presidential and midterm elections, the Mexican Senate is chosen along with the president and maintains the same political configuration throughout his presidency.

In terms of its internal organization, the Executive Committee (Mesa Directiva) heads the Mexican Senate. Its president is similar to the Senate majority leader in the United States and presides over Senate debates and plenary votes. The Executive Committee comprises three vice presidents and four secretaries, all of whom must be elected by an absolute majority of the Senate. Each serves a one-year term, with the possibility of reelection. Within the Senate, each political party has a Parliamentary Group (Grupo Parlamentario) for the purpose of facilitating the legislative process and doing their best to ensure party discipline by serving as party whips. The leaders of each Parliamentary Group, plus two more from the majority party and one more from the first minority party, comprise the Political Coordination Board (Junta de Coordinación Política), a multiparty group responsible for promoting agreement on legislative initiatives and proposing committee appointments to the Executive Committee. The president of the Political

Coordination Board is elected by an absolute majority of its membership and is responsible for securing agreement on the legislative agenda.

The Mexican Senate also has a number of committees (_comisiones_) that specialize in specific policy areas and play an integral role in formulating bills that are then introduced to the entire body. Committees comprise no more than fifteen seats allocated according to the proportion of representation each party has in the Senate. Each committee has a president and two secretaries and can take one of two main forms: a standing committee (_comisión ordinaria_) or permanent committee that analyzes initiatives in specific areas (e.g., trade and development, foreign relations, border issues); and an ad hoc committee (_comisión especial_), which seeks to investigate a specific transitory issue (e.g., state reform and promoting peace in Chiapas). Bipartisan committees can also be established for specific purposes. The most important bipartisan committee is the Permanent Commission (Comisión Permanente), which presides over matters during the legislative recess.

The Chamber of Deputies - 500 members

The Chamber of Deputies has five hundred members, three hundred of whom are directly elected by a plurality in single-member districts. The other two hundred are drawn from party or plurinominal candidates elected in regional districts using proportional representation. All deputies are elected every three years—at each presidential and midterm election— and cannot be immediately reelected, though (like senators) they can serve nonconsecutive terms. In Mexico, the lower house of Congress has the sole authority to approve the president's budget, though the Supreme Court has ruled that the president can issue a veto of the budget.[7] The Chamber of Deputies' power of the purse is one of the most important aspects of power sharing within the federal government.

The Chamber is organized in the same manner as the Senate, with an Executive Committee, Parliamentary Groups, and a Political Coordination Board. The Executive Committee serves a one-year term and is made up of a president, or speaker, three vice presidents, and three secretaries. Like their counterparts in the Senate, all members of the Chamber's Executive Committee must be elected with a two-thirds majority. Each political party with at least five members in the Chamber is entitled to have a formally recognized Parliamentary Group. The Political Coordination Board comprises the party leaders and is responsible for making committee nominations, proposing the budget, and presenting resolutions to the Executive Committee.

The Chamber of Deputies has a well-established committee system that allows legislators to specialize in a particular policy area. The Chamber's standing committees are very similar in focus to those found in the Senate (e.g., national defense, public education, environment, and indigenous issues). In recent years, the Congress has also established a number of special committees to investigate issues as diverse as campaign finance and the high rate of homicide of young women in Ciudad Juárez, in the state of Chihuahua. Each committee can have up to thirty members, and no deputy can serve on more than three standing committees. Since 1994, party representation in the committees has been roughly proportional to their numbers within the Chamber, and this has allowed minority parties to have an important influence on policy decisions.[8]

Mexico's Evolving Legislature

Despite the fact that the Mexican constitution clearly establishes three separate branches of government, the Mexican legislature served as a rubber stamp for presidential initiatives from the mid-1930s until 1997 because the executive effectively monopolized the electoral and legislative processes. Table 5.2 shows that until 1988, the PRI regularly won at least 75 percent of the seats in the Chamber of Deputies. Under such conditions, the president had no trouble garnering the simple majority needed to approve a bill. Members of the PRI were all too happy to support the president's legislative initiatives, given that he had the power to determine the trajectory of their future in the party. Moreover, with its two-thirds majority, the PRI could single-handedly amend the constitution. Table 5.2 also shows that the PRI retained its dominance within the Chamber into the early 1990s, though its representation dropped to roughly 50 to 60 percent. This was still enough to allow the PRI to single-handedly approve most legislation, and the president continued to enjoy an extremely high rate of approval of executive-sponsored bills.[9] But by the late 1990s, the PRI was no longer able to win even a simple majority in either the Chamber or the Senate, and since 2000, no party has held a majority in either house of Congress.[10]

As the PRI's dominance waned, the legislature became more active and independent. This trend began in earnest after 1997, when the PRI lost its majority in the Chamber of Deputies. Consequently, whereas the Chamber sponsored, on average, 195 public bills during each legislative session between 1988 and 1997, during the fifty-seventh legislature (1997–2000), it sponsored 566 initiatives. In the Senate, that number increased from roughly 2 to 38.[11] Moreover, Congress began to check the president's power. Between 1997 and 2000, President Zedillo sponsored only 29 percent of all approved bills in the Chamber of Deputies, down from 75 percent in the previous legislature (1994–1997), while the Chamber and Senate together sponsored 67.9 percent of all approved bills (up from 24 percent).[12] Equally important was the willingness of Congress to block presidential initiatives. For example,

Table 5.2. Percentage of Party Representation in the Chamber of Deputies, 1976–2012

Party/Year	1976–1979	1979–1982	1982–1985	1985–1988	1988–1991	1991–1994	1994–1997	1997–2000	2000–2003	2003–2006	2006–2009	2009–2012
PRI	81.9	74.0	75.0	72.3	52.0	64.1	59.8	47.2	42.2	44.8	20.8	48.2
PAN	8.4	10.5	12.5	10.3	20.0	17.8	23.8	24.2	41.2	30.2	41.2	28.2
PRD	–	–	–	–	–	–	13.0	25.2	10.0	19.4	25.0	13.6
PT	–	–	–	–	–	–	1.8	1.4	1.4	1.2	3.2	2.6
PVEM	–	–	–	–	–	–	–	1.2	3.4	3.4	3.8	4.2
PC	–	–	–	–	–	–	–	–	0.8	1.0	3.4	1.6
PANAL	–	–	–	–	–	–	–	–	–	–	1.8	1.4
ASC	–	–	–	–	–	–	–	–	–	–	0.8	–
PSN	–	–	–	–	–	–	–	–	0.6	–	–	–
PAS	–	–	–	–	–	–	–	–	0.4	–	–	–
PPS	5.0	3.0	2.5	2.8	10.0	2.2	–	–	–	–	–	–
PARM	4.6	3.0	–	2.8	6.6	2.8	–	–	–	–	–	–
PFCRN	–	–	–	–	7.2	4.8	–	–	–	–	–	–
PST	–	2.5	–	3.0	–	–	–	–	–	–	–	–
PDM	–	2.5	–	3.0	–	–	–	–	–	–	–	–
PSUM	–	–	–	3.0	–	–	–	–	–	–	–	–
PCM	–	4.5	–	–	–	–	–	–	–	–	–	–
PMS	–	–	–	–	4.0	–	–	–	–	–	–	–
PRT	–	–	–	1.5	–	–	–	–	–	–	–	–
PMT	–	–	–	1.5	–	–	–	–	–	–	–	–
Indep.	–	–	–	–	0.2	–	–	–	–	–	–	0.2
Total:	100	100	100	100	100	100	100	100	100	100	100	100

Source: http://www.camaradediputados.gob.mx. Accessed March 13, 2011.

in 1998, in what was mainly a symbolic gesture of newfound legislative power, the Chamber of Deputies refused to authorize two of President Zedillo's planned trips abroad. More meaningfully, the Chamber exercised its authority to review and approve the budget and, in the process, challenged the president's budget proposals.[13]

That the legislature is now more active and independent than it was in the past does not necessarily mean that it has the capacity to fulfill all of its constitutional functions and responsibilities. Indeed, many scholars agree that there remain at least three main obstacles to further strengthening and improving the quality of the legislature: low congressional budgets, the ban on consecutive reelection, and the use of proportional representation to allocate two hundred Chamber and thirty-two Senate seats. First, unlike legislators in the United States, members of Mexico's Congress do not have large budgets and extensive support staffs. Moreover, Mexico does not have a readily accessible store of congressional archives and other documents needed for legislative research.[14] As a result, the legislature often relies on the executive branch for information, and individual legislators, as well as congressional committees, have a difficult time developing independent, thoroughly researched analyses needed to formulate effective policy initiatives.[15]

The problem of creating good legislation is compounded by the second obstacle, the prohibition on immediate reelection. While the ban on reelection is of great historical importance in Mexico, it creates at least three important problems for the legislature.[16] First, it means that members of Congress have few opportunities or incentives to gain the experience needed to be professional legislators. This is especially true within the Chamber of Deputies, where members serve a short three-year term. Three years is just enough time to learn the ropes before they are turned out for a new bunch of freshman deputies. Second, the ban on immediate reelection strengthens political parties at the expense of the voters. Since members of Congress cannot be reelected, voters have no chance to either hold them responsible or reward them for their job performance. Instead, politicians see themselves as responsible to the party, which determines the fate of political careers based on how well they uphold party discipline. Therefore, Mexican legislators tend to represent their parties' interests rather than their electoral constituents' preferences. Given these consequences of no immediate reelection, it is not surprising that many Mexican politicians and academics have called for reforms that would eliminate the ban. Indeed, in December 2009, President Calderón listed the possibility of reelection for legislators and local governments among his ten proposals for a major political reform in Mexico. However, Mexico's general population appears to have little support for reelection, largely due to their deep distrust of politicians, and the perceived importance of forever banning reelection after the excesses of the Porfiriato.

③ The third obstacle to strengthening and improving the legislature is the use of proportional representation to elect thirty-two senators and two hundred deputies. While the introduction of the plurinominal seats has the positive effect of ensuring minority representation in Congress, it also prevents these members of Congress from developing a strong geographic base (particularly when combined with no reelection) and gives a significant amount of influence to the parties, again, at the expense of voters who otherwise would have the ability to hold them accountable for their performance.[17] While most Mexican politicians recognize the problems associated with the use of proportional representation in their system, there is little interest in doing away with it. This stance can be attributed to the fact that many are loath to reform an institution that has awarded them (and their parties) a place within the federal legislature.

Meanwhile, though Mexican voters are often critical of the executive-legislative deadlock that has resulted in recent years, they have not strengthened the president's hand. Indeed, Mexican voters appear increasingly disposed to split-ticket voting—dividing their ballots to elect executives and legislators from different parties—and less inclined to back the president's party during midterm elections. Such tendencies are not unusual in a democratic setting: voters in the United States often split their ballot between a presidential candidate and a legislative representative from another party, or switch party preferences from one election to another. Also, it is common in presidential systems for the opposition to regain political space against the party of the incumbent president in a midterm election. Indeed, with the advent of competitive elections in Mexico, the president's party lost seats in every midterm election since 1997.

As a result of the trend toward divided government and other factors, the Mexican Congress is no longer a mere rubber stamp for the executive. In the coming years, efforts by the Congress to assert its authority will surely continue to dramatically reshape its role in contemporary Mexican politics. A key institution in determining the constitutional limits of both presidential and legislative authority will be the Mexican Supreme Court, which we examine next.

THE JUDICIARY

Like the legislature, for much of the twentieth century Mexico's Supreme Court served to refine but above all to support presidential initiatives. Until 1994, the twenty-five justices were handpicked and could be removed only by the president. Moreover, the Court rarely considered cases of importance and did not have the power of judicial review. Hence, the Supreme Court never ruled against the interests of the president or the

PRI—a practice that directly violated the democratic principle of separation of powers.

According to Beatriz Magaloni, there were three reasons why the judiciary was subordinate to the president: a flexible constitution, presidential control over political nominations, and lack of power of judicial review.[18] While Mexico prided itself on having a progressive constitution and an active legal process, in practice the constitution could be easily altered to suit presidential interests because the PRI could easily make constitutional amendments. Furthermore, the president, as the head of the party, controlled the nomination (and dismissal) of political appointees in all areas of government, including the judiciary. Finally, the constitution did not grant the Supreme Court the power of judicial review on electoral matters or the ability to serve as an arbiter of intergovernmental disputes.

In 1994, the Law of Judicial Power was enacted to increase the power and independence of the judiciary. This law, introduced by President Zedillo and approved by Congress, mandated that the Supreme Court be composed of eleven justices who serve fifteen-year terms. The president nominates judicial appointments based on their legal experience, and candidates must be confirmed with two-thirds approval of the Senate. These changes, together with the multiparty composition of the Senate and the guarantee that no single party can hold more than the two-thirds majority needed to approve a presidential nominee, suggest that for the foreseeable future, the Mexican Supreme Court will operate independently and impartially in its role as the cornerstone of the Mexican legal system.

Another important change brought about by the 1994 constitutional reform was the introduction of two new powers of judicial review (see textbox 5.2). The Court now had the authority to decide the constitutionality of federal laws and international treaties with "constitutional actions" and also the right to resolve "constitutional controversies," or legal disagreements among different branches and levels of government.[19] Constitutional actions require the support of 33 percent of the members of Congress (or the state legislature at the state level), the attorney general, or the leadership of any official political party (for the constitutionality of electoral laws) to send a case before the Court. Constitutional controversies can be introduced by any branch or level of government seeking arbitration in an intergovernmental dispute. These powers give the Supreme Court the ability to veto legislation deemed unconstitutional and settle intergovernmental conflicts—two functions that were previously nonexistent in Mexico.

The Law of Judicial Power has paved the way for greater judicial activity and independence. Since 1995, the number of constitutional actions and controversies has increased steadily. For example, in 1995, the Supreme Court heard one constitutional action and nineteen controversies. By 1998,

Textbox 5.2. JUDICIAL REVIEW AND ACTIVISM IN CONTEMPORARY MEXICO

Mexico uses a "civil" or statutory legal system. This system is also known as Roman or Napoleonic law because it is derived from the traditions first established in ancient Rome and later reinstated in parts of Europe by Napoleon Bonaparte during the early nineteenth century. Civil legal systems differ significantly from so-called common law systems, like the one used in the United States. In a civil legal system, judicial decisions are strictly interpreted as codified by legislative statute; that is, a judge makes a decision in a case solely based on his or her interpretation of the law as it is written. In contrast, judges in a common law system also take into consideration the "common" practices and precedents established by decisions in other cases. In addition to an emphasis on the law as written, common law relies on the principle of stare decisis, which is Latin for "let the decision stand." This principle allows judges to decide a case based on precedents established by other judicial decisions in cases that have a similar fact pattern.

Critics of civil law systems argue that such systems lack the flexibility of interpretation provided in common law systems, since legislative changes to the law may be slow in coming or otherwise politically infeasible. At the same time, some domestic critics of the common law system used in the United States have charged that U.S. judges effectively "legislate from the bench" by reshaping and even overturning the decisions of democratically elected legislators. Both civil and common law systems are widely used around the world, with varying degrees of efficiency and effectiveness. In Mexico, the combination of civil law with a U.S.-style, constitutional separation of powers creates a unique—and some might say awkward—hybrid. The U.S. judiciary was able to assert its role as a check on other branches of government with the Supreme Court's landmark decision in *Marbury v. Madison*, which provided a precedent for judicial review to determine the constitutionality of government decisions. Yet in Mexico, the judiciary has not been as free to curb the power of other branches or to modify public policy through case law, in part because of its civil law tradition.

Mexican federal courts have long addressed legal controversies through the *amparo* procedure, an innovation introduced by Mexico's 1857 constitution. An *amparo*—literally, a "protection"—provides an injunction blocking government actions that encroach on an individual's rights. However, a given court's decision to grant *amparo* is only binding for the parties involved in that particular case. Binding precedents can be established through the *amparo* procedure, but only after the Supreme Court or collegiate circuit courts make five consecutive and identical majority rulings on the same topic, thereby establishing a legal norm known as a *jurisprudencia*. Reforms introduced in December 1994 expanded the Supreme Court's powers of judicial review by introducing "motions of unconstitutionality" (*acciones de inconstitucionalidad*). This innovation allowed key institutional actors—the attorney general, political parties, and a designated proportion of representatives from either the national or state level legislatures—to challenge the constitutionality of legislation or other government actions. Moreover, recent decisions—including a celebrated June 2007 verdict invalidating a piece of legislation known as the Televisa Law, in which legislators blatantly favored corporate interests—signal a growing sense of independence on the part of the Mexican Supreme Court, which may suggest the beginning of a new era of judicial activism in Mexico.

the number of cases increased to twelve actions and twenty-nine controversies.[20] The federal judiciary has also become much more active in its attempts to promote its own institutional independence. Since 2000, it has engaged in a concerted effort to establish budgetary autonomy with a constitutional amendment that guarantees it a fixed percentage of the federal budget. It has also sought a constitutional amendment that would allow the judiciary to initiate legislation on judicial matters, and it has encouraged reform of the Otero Formula, a provision in Mexican law that prevents the Supreme Court's decisions from having general effects or establishing legal precedent, unless they are approved by at least eight of the eleven justices.[21] These initiatives are clear indications of the Court's new role as an independent branch of the federal government.

Late in his term, President Zedillo learned firsthand what it meant to have an empowered Court. In an attempt to learn the truth behind the federal government's bailout of several banks in the mid-1990s, Congress had asked the government to release important government documents. The Zedillo administration refused, and the case went before the Supreme Court. The Court ordered that the documents be released, thus redefining the limits of executive power.[22] During Fox's *sexenio*, the Supreme Court also handed down some decisions that directly contradicted the president's authority. In one instance, the Court invalidated a presidential decree that sought to establish daylight savings time, instead ruling that it was the responsibility of the Congress to decide Mexico's timetable. In all, the Court struck down three of the six presidential policy initiatives it heard between 1997 and 2005, indicating its willingness to exercise much greater independence than in the past.[23]

The Supreme Court has also begun to fulfill its new role as an impartial interpreter of the constitution. In practice, this has meant that its decisions are based on legal principles rather than political interests or public opinion. For example, in 1998, the Court handed down a unanimous decision declaring a state electoral law in Quintana Roo unconstitutional. This marked the first time that the Supreme Court had ruled against the PRI and signaled the judiciary's willingness and ability to act as an independent arbiter.[24] More recently, the Court agreed with a lower court's decision that upheld the thirty-year statute of limitations on genocide. This ruling made it very difficult for prosecutors to bring genocide charges against former president Luis Echeverría, who has been accused of ordering paramilitary forces to fire on student demonstrators in the 1968 Tlatelolco massacre.[25]

In fact, the judiciary's activity and independence have not come without controversy. In late 2004, President Fox introduced his budget proposal for 2005. The Chamber of Deputies modified the bill to include an additional 112 billion pesos in spending. The Fox administration claimed that the spending increases were ill conceived because they were based on unrealistic income projections, and more importantly, that the Chamber had overstepped its authority to modify the budget when it voted to authorize approximately 4 billion pesos for projects that lay outside the scope of the executive's National Development Plan. In late December of that year, the Fox administration filed a constitutional controversy against the Chamber in order to block the new budget items thought to exceed congressional authority.[26] Because the Court was not in session, the case was sent to the single Supreme Court justice who was on duty during the recess.[27] He assigned the case to another justice, who then ruled in the president's favor and suspended the 4 billion pesos in question. Many within the Chamber of Deputies claimed that these procedures directly violated the law on two counts: first, only the Chief Justice has the authority to make case assignments, and second, the judiciary does not have the authority to modify the budget. These criticisms put the Supreme Court in the difficult position of evaluating the legality of its own actions.

At the same time, the judiciary must also work toward the establishment of rule of law. In this regard, Mexico has not changed much. Mexican citizens continue to live in a society where the law is applied arbitrarily and does not guarantee protection of individual rights. In other words, the rule of law is not institutionalized in Mexico.[28] It is extraordinarily difficult to prosecute criminals, and as a result, a large number of crimes are neither investigated nor prosecuted. Also, as we discuss in chapter 11, widespread corruption in law enforcement and the judiciary makes it even more difficult to bring criminals to justice.

The role of the judiciary in strengthening the rule of law is critical, and it has broader ramifications for the future of democracy in Mexico. As long as the government cannot credibly protect citizens' rights and impartially protect citizens from one another's actions, it is impossible for democratic principles to become institutionalized, and Mexicans may lose what little faith they have in the government and in democracy as a political goal. Moreover, without fair and predictable legal treatment of property rights, consumer protections, and basic contractual terms, private-sector firms and individuals cannot conduct business transactions or make the investments necessary to promote Mexico's economic development. Hence, the longer-term strengthening of the judiciary is a critical component to help guarantee the rule of law and democracy in Mexico.[29] We take up these issues in greater depth in chapter 11.

STATE AND LOCAL GOVERNMENTS

As we have seen in the previous sections, one of the consequences of Mexico's combination of single-party dominance and *presidencialismo* is that political authority in the country became highly centralized. That is, the federal government—and more specifically the executive branch—had a disproportionate amount of control over policy decisions and over the resources needed to implement them. Normally, a federal system is one that has independently elected and relatively autonomous governmental entities that have differing responsibilities and levels of jurisdiction. Indeed, on paper, Mexico has had a three-tiered federal system of government since soon after its independence in 1821, but in reality state and local governments had relatively little authority. The fact that most major business activity occurred in Mexico City—located in the approximate center of the country—added an economic and geographic element to the country's high level of centralization. Thus, in practice, Mexico looked much more like a unitary system of government—where political representatives at the local level are essentially appointed and directed by national-level authorities—rather than a federal system. Because much has changed in the last thirty years in terms of the relative importance of state and local governments, it is to these areas that we now turn.

Mexico comprises thirty-one states and the Federal District (see text-box 5.3). Each state has its own constitution and therefore a unique set of institutions, but all share the same general characteristics as the three branches of government: the executive, comprised of the governor, his or her cabinet, and supporting bureaucracy; a unicameral legislature or state congress; and a state judiciary.

At the local level, Mexico has close to 2,500 municipalities.[30] Each municipality elects a mayor (*presidente municipal*) and a council (*cabildo*) from a single slate for a three-year term of office.[31] The constitution grants both states and municipalities specific rights and responsibilities—though in practice, *presidencialismo* made many of these rights irrelevant. That is, like politicians at the national level, governors had few incentives to act

Textbox 5.3. THE FEDERAL DISTRICT

Mexico City, or the Federal District (DF), is the national capital of Mexico. With a population of over 20 million, it consistently ranks among the three largest cities in the world. The DF is divided into sixteen boroughs and forty electoral districts. Before 1997, Mexico City was essentially an extension of the federal government. The president appointed the head (*regente*) to implement and oversee his policy initiatives. In 1987, Congress amended the constitution to create a representative assembly charged with making some administrative decisions and advising the president on the city's policy priorities. Reforms in 1993 and 1996 paved the way for the assembly to become a true legislative body, with lawmaking and budget authority. The Legislative Assembly of the Federal District comprises sixty-six deputies, forty elected by plurality in single-member districts and twenty-six elected by proportional representation from party lists. All deputies serve three-year terms. Furthermore, the DF's head of government is now popularly elected and serves a six-year term. The PRD has strong support in Mexico City, and the first three elected heads of government of the Federal District—Cuauhtémoc Cárdenas (1997–1999), Andrés Manuel López Obrador (2000–2005), and Marcelo Ebrard (2006–2012)—were all members of this party. Two other members of the PRD, Rosario Robles (1999–2000) and Alejandro Encinas (2005–2006), have also served as interim heads of government. Financially and administratively, the DF has a special status that allows it to function as a city, but with many of the same rights enjoyed by states. In practice this means that it has more powers of taxation and hence more resources for governing. In translations, the district's special status as a federal entity also contributes to some confusion, since its head of government is often referred to as the Mexico City mayor. Mexico City is also unique because, despite attempts to introduce decentralization, the capital remains the country's most important political, economic, and cultural hub.

independently—their performance was evaluated not by their popularity or use of innovation, but rather by their ability to maintain stability and ensure overwhelming support for the PRI come election time. Governors who failed to comply or achieve this goal risked being asked to step down by the president and not advancing their career within the party. To the extent that state executives had autonomy, it was to determine who within the state would receive the resources doled out by the federal government.[32] Municipal presidents faced a similar situation, though at the local level the pressure was to demonstrate loyalty to the governor.[33]

The economic and political perils of extreme concentration became apparent in the wake of the economic crisis of the early 1980s. When

Mexico nearly defaulted on its external loans, the government's first move was to reduce spending drastically and embark on a period of economic austerity. As the federal government struggled to provide even basic services, the PRI's performance legitimacy was severely damaged, and the newly elected de la Madrid administration began to call for decentralization reforms. This first round of reforms sought to clarify the rights and responsibilities, particularly of local governments, and to deconcentrate economic production and national government agencies. While de la Madrid's reforms constituted an important effort to address some of the problems associated with overcentralization, they were only mildly successful, in part because they were designed more to recapture electoral support for the PRI than to begin a coherent plan of decentralization. The Salinas administration had the same goal in mind when it introduced the Solidarity program, which was aimed to alleviate problems associated with poverty by strengthening local organizations and governments.[34] Again, this program did make some headway in empowering local authorities, and more progress in addressing poverty, but it is difficult to ignore the strategic allocation of Solidarity funds to states and municipalities or the program's positive impact on the PRI's performance in the 1991 midterm elections.[35]

More meaningful decentralization reforms would have to wait until the mid-1990s, when President Zedillo introduced the most comprehensive plan for decentralization to date. The New Federalism project had a variety of aims, among them reform of the revenue-sharing system and boosting the power and autonomy of state and local governments. His motivation for this program surely stemmed from a combination of pressure by the opposition and his commitment to reforming the Mexican political system. Zedillo had to deal with an unprecedented number of demands from the opposition, which by then had a strong presence in state and local elected offices: by 1997, the PAN and the PRD governed ten states and the Federal District and at least half of the thirty-one state capitals. Because many of the PAN and PRD governors and mayors of the 1990s were staunch advocates of reviving federalism and promoting democracy in Mexico, Zedillo had little choice but to grant them some concessions.[36]

One of the areas of greatest concern among subnational politicians was the distribution of national revenue. Governors and mayors have long complained about the overcentralization of financial resources, claiming that there exists an 80-16-4 split, meaning that the national government hoards 80 percent of the nation's resources, leaving a paltry 16 and 4 percent for the states and municipalities, respectively. How, they ask, can subnational governments possibly hope to address their many public policy priorities and public demands with so few resources? It is true that the federal government in Mexico controls a disproportionate amount of public revenue. But this is true in most federal systems. What is different in Mexico is that its revenue-sharing system is set up in such a way as to weaken subnational governments. The Law of Fiscal Coordination (Ley de Coordinación Fiscal, LCF) stipulates that states and municipalities forfeit many of their tax powers (most notably, sales tax) in exchange for a share of federal revenue that is transferred to subnational governments.[37] For many states and especially for local authorities, this arrangement makes good financial sense because they do not have the bureaucratic infrastructure needed to levy their own taxes. Moreover, because federal transfers are allocated according to redistributive formulas, the system provides poorer states and municipalities with more funds than they might be able to collect on their own. Yet, while the existing tax and revenue systems may help redress regional inequalities, they create several obstacles to healthy federalism and good governance in Mexico.[38]

First, there is general unhappiness with the current revenue-sharing arrangement. In particular, wealthier states feel slighted because they invariably contribute the most tax revenue to the general fund but receive proportionately less than their fair share. This perceived injustice stems from the national government's obligation to redistribute resources to poorer states and promote equality among its geographic regions. On several occasions, governors of wealthier states have even threatened to opt out of the revenue-sharing system unless the formulas are revised to give greater weight to the origin of tax receipts. For their part, poorer states tend to be unhappy with the status quo because they feel that even with the redistributive formulas, they never have enough resources to address their many public policy challenges. Their most commonly voiced demand is that the central government increase the overall amount of resources given to the states and municipalities.

The second problem is that the LCF allows states to determine how to allocate a portion of the federal transfer funds among their municipalities. While this provision is an important aspect of state autonomy, it has the potential to create tension between state and municipal governments, particularly when the former chooses to allocate the bare minimum or to use political rather than objective criteria as the basis for distributing what constitutes, in many cases, more than half of the local budget. Third, the existing tax system promotes overdependence on the national government and inefficient taxation. There are few incentives for states and municipalities to exercise the tax authority they do have, when it is much easier and sometimes more lucrative to wait for a monthly check from the federal government.[39] Finally, the current system of revenue sharing undermines government accountability. Because state and local governments have little tax authority and rely so heavily on federal transfers, governors and mayors can always claim that their administrations' shortcomings are the result of too few funds rather than incompetence or unresponsiveness.

Together, these problems have set the stage for some serious intergovernmental conflicts over resource distribution, taxation authority, and states' rights. The focus on strengthening federalism has boosted the power of subnational politicians, and events in recent years have shown that governors have effectively raised their national profiles by challenging the federal government on these issues. In fact, all of the major presidential hopefuls in 2000, and most in 2006, were former governors. However, decentralization in Mexico has some important shortcomings. In particular, some claim that strengthening subnational governments has created local strongholds for governors, many of whom wield a disproportionate amount of power and have no interest in promoting democracy.[40] Moreover, as we have seen, severe economic disparities among states persist and create tension in the federal arrangement that will not be easily resolved because they pit rich states against poor and states against municipalities. There is little doubt that these issues will be at the forefront of Mexican politics for the foreseeable future.

CONCLUSION

Mexico's political system has changed significantly over the past twenty years. No longer dominated by a single political party and the executive, there is now more balance among political parties and among the various branches and levels of government. The late 1990s ushered in a period of power sharing never before seen in Mexico. The three largest political parties have since enjoyed significant representation in the legislature, and as the PAN demonstrated in 2000, it is possible for the opposition to win the presidency. Furthermore, executive dominance at the national level has waned, and both the legislature and the judiciary are willing and able to oppose the president on some of his highest-profile policy initiatives (e.g., tax reform and the privatization of energy). Likewise, states and municipalities now exercise significantly more independence than in the past, some going so far as to challenge the federal government and even the president on matters of revenue distribution and subnational autonomy.

Does this mean that the era of *presidencialismo* and extreme centralization has ended? Many argue that returning to the past is now impossible because the PAN and the PRD are so well established that the PRI, even if it were to recapture the presidency, would be unable to reestablish its near-monopoly on government. Proponents of this view point to the many important institutional changes that have been implemented since the

1990s (e.g., empowerment of the Supreme Court and the constitutional clause that prohibits any party from holding more than 60 percent of the seats in the legislature). As noted above, much of the reform of the Mexican political system has occurred thanks to the multipartisan composition of the legislature and the strong presence of the PAN and the PRD at the state and local levels. And while it is theoretically possible for a single party to capture the presidency and a majority in both legislative bodies, the current political environment in Mexico would appear to make that development unlikely without a preelectoral coalition. Indeed, it is much more likely that the country will continue to experience greater shared governance, with all the benefits and drawbacks that this entails.

6

Political Parties and Elections in Mexico

Before 1988, any discussion of political parties and elections in Mexico inevitably centered on the PRI. During most of that period, Mexico's official party was much like the powerful parties found in other non-communist, hegemonic party systems. Like the KMT in Taiwan, the People's Action Party in Singapore, the People's Democratic Party in Nigeria, and even the Democratic Party in New York's Tammany Hall era, the PRI maintained power through a combination of genuine popular support, electoral fraud, institutional manipulation, and careful coordination of organized political interests. This formula made it possible for the PRI to achieve a relatively high degree of political stability and control. In this context, political opposition was tolerated but it was largely futile, because the PRI was the only party with a realistic chance of winning elections: those who spoke out against the regime were effectively marginalized, and those who truly threatened PRI power were severely repressed. However, as discussed in chapter 5, support for the opposition grew dramatically in the 1980s and 1990s, resulting in the eventual defeat of the ruling party in the 2000 presidential election.

To understand contemporary Mexican politics in the period after PRI hegemony, it is necessary to be familiar with all of the country's political parties and what they seek to achieve in government. Also, because electoral rules greatly influence the number and behavior of political parties, it is essential to examine how the design—and frequent redesign—of Mexican electoral institutions has shaped the country's unique multiparty system. Accordingly, the first section of this chapter provides a detailed examination of Mexico's three major parties (the PRI, the PAN, and the PRD), as well as other minor parties that currently play a role in Mexican electoral politics and in government. Next we focus on the electoral process and the specific electoral institutions that contributed to the making and eventual unmaking of PRI hegemony. Finally, we close this chapter with a discussion of the key trends in Mexican elections today, with particular attention to the dynamics of the 2012 presidential election.

MEXICAN POLITICAL PARTIES

Like most countries in Latin America today, Mexico has a multiparty system, in which more than two significant parties compete for power. However, because of the PRI's longtime dominance, Mexico's multiparty system did not become truly competitive until the 1980s, when the National Action Party (PAN) and the Party of the Democratic Revolution (PRD) began to obtain a much greater share of the vote in elections. Likewise, even the relative importance of Mexico's minor parties has grown as elections have become more competitive; minor parties like the Mexican Green Ecological Party (Partido Verde Ecologista de México, PVEM) and the Labor Party (Partido del Trabaja, PT) have increasingly served as vital coalition partners in electoral campaigns and legislative negotiations. Table 6.1 provides a snapshot of the main political parties in the contemporary Mexican political arena.

In this section we discuss the origins, ideological orientation, organizational structure, and support base of the three major parties, though we give relatively less attention to the PRI because it has been covered substantially in previous chapters. We then turn to briefly examine the role of minor parties in the Mexican political system, focusing primarily on those that currently have representation in the federal legislature. While each of Mexico's political parties has evolved considerably from the era of single-party hegemony, some degree of uncertainty remains about the future direction of Mexico's party system.

The PRI

As we saw in previous chapters, the party that governed Mexico for most of the twentieth century originated from the National Revolutionary Party (PNR), which was founded in 1929 by President Plutarco Elías Calles in order to forge a revolutionary family from the disparate political and military elements that emerged victorious from the 1910–1917 conflict. By 1937, to more formally incorporate peasants, urban laborers, and middle-class professionals, President Lázaro Cárdenas and his followers reorganized the ruling party as the Party of the Mexican Revolution (PRM), a corporatist entity that integrated Cárdenas's agenda to defend national economic interests. In 1946 under Manuel Ávila Camacho, the party was reborn as

Table 6.1. Mexican Political Parties, 2000–Present

	Convergence	National Action Party (PAN)	New Alliance Party (PANAL)	Party of the Democratic Revolution (PRD)	Institutional Revolutionary Party (PRI)	Labor Party (PT)	Mexican Green Ecological Party (PVEM)
Spanish Name:	Partido Convergencia por la Democracia	Partido Acción Nacional	Partido Nueva Alianza	Partido de la Revolución Democrática	Partido Revolucionario Institucional	Partido del Trabajo	Partido Verde Ecologista de México
Year Formed/Official Registration:	1999	1939	2005	1989	1929 as PNR 1938 as PRM 1946 as PRI	1993	1993
Platform/Ideology:	Social democracy. Favors free market economics but argues for some state role in order to ensure equality, social justice, and respect for basic human rights.	Conservative with a strong Catholic base. Committed to free markets, low government spending, transparency, decentralization to subnational governments, and conservative on social issues.	Emphasizes education as a key element in economic development, as well as moderate state intervention in the market economy.	Leftist. Skeptical of neoliberalism, emphasizes need for attention to the plight of the poor. Calls for wider social welfare programs and poverty alleviation.	Flexible: rhetoric centers on revolutionary nationalism but since early 1980s, has used free market policies to "modernize" the country. Still occasionally appeals to economic nationalism.	Socialist roots. Advocates mass participation, economic nationalism, increased redistributive spending, and decreased economic dependence on the United States.	No clear ideology beyond environmental protection. Some emphasis on sustainable development, protection of human rights, and "just distribution of resources to guarantee the consolidation of democracy."

Note: The Social Democratic Party (Partido Socialdemócrata, PSD) a progressive social democratic party, with emphasis on agrarian issues, lost its registration after polling less than 2% of the vote in the 2009 midterm election.

the Institutional Revolutionary Party (PRI). This rechristening proved to be remarkably apt, since the PRI truly became a lasting and institutionalized legacy of the revolution. From its founding until its decline in the 1990s, the ruling party was an indomitable political force in Mexico.[1]

Guided directly by the hand of the Mexican president, the ruling party provided a forum for elite power sharing and political negotiation among hierarchically organized factions (*camarillas*) and interest groups. The PRI also served as a political machine that mobilized voters in support of the regime during electoral campaigns, and with the help of fraud, ensured that electoral results reflected overwhelming popular support for the regime. So successful was this combination of functions that for nearly three-quarters of a century, the PRI was essentially fused with the government, and the two were often considered one and the same.

By the late 1990s, however, the PRI confronted a much more competitive electoral environment. The reality of the situation hit the party hard and fueled its preexisting internal divisions. The reformers who believed that the party's future depended on its ability to adopt more democratic practices (internally and externally) found themselves at odds with the more retrograde "dinosaurs," or *prinosaurios*, who favored traditional PRI practices such as electoral alchemy. Such divisions contributed to the PRI's defeat in the 2000 and 2006 presidential elections, but they did not prevent the party from flourishing at the state and local level. Even in the immediate aftermath of the 2000 presidential elections, the PRI continued to control the largest portion of seats in the federal legislature, half of the country's governorships, and the overwhelming majority of city governments. However, in the absence of a single dominant figure calling the shots from Los Pinos, the presidential residence, political power became more decentralized among the party leaders and prominent federal and state *priísta* officials. In many states, the PRI even opened itself to greater internal competition, producing candidates who proved that the party could win without the need for patronage, electoral fraud, or illicit government assistance.

Moreover, after its disastrous electoral performance in 2006, the PRI also began working to renew its national leadership by selecting Beatriz Paredes as its party chairwoman. Paredes was the first woman ever elected as governor of her home state of Tlaxcala, in 1987, and she was the third woman to head the PRI. Under Paredes's leadership in the July 2009 federal midterm elections, the PRI succeeded in winning 37 percent of the vote overall and capturing 240 seats in the Chamber of Deputies (48 percent). In the six states where elections took place that year, the PRI held on to three governorships and took away two from the PAN in Querétaro and San Luís Potosí. The PRI's only major loss was in the state of Sonora, where the PAN gubernatorial candidate won after he capitalized on a daycare fire in which more than forty small children died as a result of poor government regulation of the facility.

Thus, while support for the PRI declined significantly in the late 1990s and early 2000s, by 2009 the party had rebounded, and it looked poised to recapture the presidency in 2012. Strong national support from organized labor, rural voters, and party loyalists, together with a young, handsome, politically savvy candidate, may simply be too much for the other parties to defeat. Indeed, in public opinion polls leading up to the elections, Enrique Peña Nieto, the former governor of the state of Mexico and the PRI's heir apparent, consistently emerged as the party's frontrunner. The only other viable candidate within the PRI, Manlio Fabio Beltrones, had less than 10 percent party support and garnered only 7 percent of the independent vote, while Peña Nieto captured nearly 70 percent of independents.[2]

The PAN

Without a doubt, the strongest opposition party during the twentieth century was the National Action Party (PAN).[3] Formed in 1939 by a group of disenchanted entrepreneurs, professionals, and activist Catholics, the PAN was meant to provide a conservative and institutionalized alternative to the official party. Its founder, Manuel Gómez Morin, represented a group that believed that the PRI's hierarchical organization and corporatist practices violated the democratic ideals of the revolution and the principle of separation of powers set forth in the constitution. Instead PAN members, or *panistas*, favored a government that promoted the common good through democracy, compassion, and protection of private property. Moreover, the left-leaning economic policies enacted by Lázaro Cárdenas in the mid-1930s were objectionable to many in the PAN because they required a high level of state intervention in the economy. For example, *panistas* objected to the creation of *ejidos*, or collective farms, which were anathema to private property and economic efficiency, and served to dampen entrepreneurial drive in the countryside.

Another important group within the PAN was made up of Catholic activists who staunchly opposed the regime's secular character and its enforcement of the constitutional provisions that prohibited Church involvement in politics. Their mentor was Efraín González Luna, an ardent Catholic and an advocate of political humanism, a doctrine advanced by Catholic thinkers like Thomas Aquinas and Thomas More, which articulated the belief that a perfect society is possible if humans are able to maximize their true potential. The social doctrine of the Catholic Church served as the moral foundation for many of the party's social policies, chief among them the importance of family and compassion for the poor. In practice this meant that the state should not intervene in areas best left to the individual, family, or local community—or rather, "As much society as possible, as much government as necessary."[4] According to *panistas*, the role of government

was to help people help themselves by providing educational and economic opportunities for self-realization.

From 1940 until the mid-1970s, the party organization's primary preoc-
cupation was not so much ideology as it was what strategy would provide
the most effective challenge to the regime. While all *panistas* opposed the
PRI's methods and ideology, they disagreed on whether to participate in
the electoral process. Some believed that it was necessary for the party to
field candidates in order to openly challenge the PRI. Others favored non-
participation rather than tacit approval of what were invariably fraudulent
electoral contests. Disagreement on the issue together with small size and
lack of resources meant that the PAN was either unable or disinclined to
field candidates in all elections. Yet by the mid-1940s, the PAN consistently
won a handful of federal deputy positions and at least one mayoral post.[5]
Nevertheless, these electoral victories did not resolve the party's internal
dispute over electoral participation. Disagreement over the issue was so
severe that it prevented the party from agreeing on a candidate for the 1976
presidential election and pushed the party to the brink of extinction.

The PAN could have disappeared, had it not been for several important
developments. First, economic instability beginning in the 1970s led to the
disenchantment of some businessmen and industrialists, particularly in the
north, who perceived the crisis to be the result of the PRI's incompetence
and corruption, and they channeled their disgust with the regime into support for the PAN. With a renewed injection of entrepreneurs within the
party and expanded support from urban, middle-class voters also suffering
from the economic downturn, the PAN was poised to make solid electoral
gains throughout the late 1980s and 1990s. The party's success was also a
product of its strategy of focusing, at least initially, on local and state elections where the party had a good chance of winning, particularly in major
metropolitan areas. To provide an idea of the party's dramatic reversal of
fortune, in 1985 there were 26 mayors, 51 state legislators, and no governors from the PAN. By 2000 those numbers had increased to 329, 299,
and 9, respectively, and the PAN's governors and mayors together governed
almost 42 percent of Mexico's population.

Despite its electoral successes, the PAN continues to have significant internal factions that are sometimes at odds with one another. The PAN is a
right-of-center party that advocates social conservatism (e.g., opposes abortion and homosexuality and supports traditional morality and religious education) and free-market economic policies (e.g., supports private property
and self-sufficiency and opposes state intervention in the economy). Its socially conservative base is comprised of devout Catholics who, in the spirit
of González Luna, believe that the purpose of the party (and government)
is to defend society's moral norms and enable individuals to realize their
true material and spiritual potential. Its pro-business members are drawn

from businessmen and professionals, often described as *neopanistas*, or new *panistas*, who entered the party during the 1980s and tended to place greater emphasis on winning elections than on strong ideological principles.

Regionally, the PAN enjoys its strongest support in the business-friendly northern states (e.g., Baja California, Chihuahua, Nuevo León) and traditionally conservative central western states (e.g., Guanajuato, Aguascalientes, Querétaro). The party's core base of support comes primarily from those middle- and upper-class urban dwellers who are relatively better educated and more likely to identify themselves as Catholic than most Mexicans. Yet one of the keys to the party's success in 2000 was its ability to reach beyond its traditional base of support and appeal to another type of voter: one who wanted regime change.[6] In a clear triumph of the *neopanistas* over the traditionalists, the party's strategy was to tap into popular disgust with the corruption and lack of transparency associated with the status quo. This, together with the charisma and colorfulness of Vicente Fox, convinced many voters that the PAN represented the best avenue for change. The party's hard-won gains were relatively short-lived, however. Fox's *sexenio* was characterized by congressional gridlock and few policy successes, and the party bore the brunt of the public's disenchantment with change. In the 2003 midterm elections, the PAN's share of seats in the Chamber of Deputies declined from 207 to 153.

The PAN's prospects for winning the 2006 presidential election did not seem much better. Given disappointment with the Fox administration's limited accomplishments and strong support for the PRD in public opinion polls, many observers expected the PAN to lose the 2006 election. In a competitive primary, the party selected as its candidate a longtime party bureaucrat named Felipe Calderón. While his selection was somewhat of a surprise to outside observers, Calderón's experience in the party established his credentials as an ideologically committed *panista*, and his ties to party leaders and staunch partisans were quite strong. However, his appeal to voters in the general electorate was weaker. Until December 2006, Calderón was a consistent third-place contender behind his PRI and PRD rivals in the general election.

From January through March 2006, Calderón gained sufficient recognition and support to rival PRI candidate Roberto Madrazo, but remained about ten points behind PRD candidate Andrés Manuel López Obrador. Then, in the last several weeks before the election, PAN candidate Felipe Calderón gained significant ground. By election day on July 2, the resulting dead heat contributed to one of the most contentious presidential elections in modern history, and by far the greatest test of Mexico's independent federal electoral authorities to date.

Calderón emerged victorious in the legal challenges that followed the contested election, but he faced the unenviable task of governing with a fractionalized and significantly polarized legislature. This meant that on issues where the PRI and the PRD chose to unite, they combined their strength in both houses of Congress to hinder the president's program and block PAN legislation. Perhaps it is not surprising then, that a number of Calderón's initiatives fell short of expectations, and his failure to unequivocally improve Mexico's public security situation led disappointed voters to withdraw their support of the party in the 2009 midterm elections.

Ironically, twelve years after Vicente Fox championed the idea of political change in Mexico, the PAN has lost substantial popular support, and many voters now appear to believe that the best path to change is to restore the old ruling party to office. Some of this shift in opinion clearly derives from Fox's and Calderón's mixed records of success, but the party's weak popular support heading into the 2012 election also stems from the fact that the PAN does not have a clearly identified candidate to unify the party membership. One year before the election, the field is wide open, with at least seven possibilities: Santiago Creel, Josefina Vázquez Mota, Ernesto Cordero, Alonso Lujambio, Javier Lozano Alarcón, Emilio González, and Heriberto Félix. Polling data consistently show Creel and Vázquez Mota as the most popular among *panistas*, but neither captured a significant number of independent voters, and both suffered from negative evaluations by the population at large. Early in the summer of 2011, Ernesto Cordero, Calderón's finance minister, announced his interest in running for president and was immediately supported by a group of 134 influential *panistas*.[7] Up to that point, Cordero was considered a dark horse with limited name recognition. However, his cabinet-level position led many to suspect that he was the president's unspoken choice. Even if this is the case, it remains to be seen how much influence Calderón will be able to wield in a system without a *dedazo*.

The PRD

In many ways the Party of the Democratic Revolution (PRD) is the antithesis of the PAN. It is a relatively young party with a decidedly left-of-center ideology, and it comprises a significant number of ex-*priístas*.[8] While the PAN has a strong base of support in northern Mexico, the PRD's strength lies in the center and southern part of the country, primarily Mexico City and poorer states like Michoacán, Guerrero, and Chiapas. Unlike the PAN, women in the PRD have held important leadership posts, including Amalia García, who served as PRD party chairperson (2000–2002) and as governor of Zacatecas (2004–2010). Still, one similarity between the PRD and the PAN is that both parties were formed as a result of disenchantment and dissatisfaction with the ways of Mexico's ruling party.

The PRD began as an electoral alliance of former *priístas* with several small leftist parties and nonpartisan social movements for the purpose of supporting Cuauhtémoc Cárdenas in his bid for the presidency in 1988. Until 1987, Cárdenas, son of Lázaro Cárdenas, one of Mexico's most beloved presidents, was a prominent member of the PRI. In 1986, Cárdenas and other members of the party's left flank formed the Democratic Current (Corriente Democrática, CD) and openly criticized the de la Madrid administration's adoption of free-market economic policies as a betrayal of the revolution. The CD also called for the PRI to use democratic primaries, rather than the *dedazo*, to select the party's candidates—a move that presumably would have prevented the selection of another technocrat as the party's presidential candidate. When the party rejected the proposed internal reform, Cárdenas and others in the CD left the PRI and began to forge the National Democratic Front (Frente Democrático Nacional, FDN), a leftist coalition that brought together parastatal parties like the now-defunct Authentic Party of the Mexican Revolution (Partido Auténtico de la Revolución Mexicana, PARM) with popular movements in order to mount what would be the most serious electoral challenge to the PRI to that point.

Garnering 31 percent of the vote, the FDN fared much better than anyone, especially the PRI, expected.[9] With Cárdenas at the helm, it attracted voters who yearned for a return to a past when the ideals of the revolution were supposedly alive and well. Furthermore, the FDN was able to capitalize on growing dissatisfaction with the PRI. Mexico was just beginning to emerge from its most serious financial crisis, and their recent economic hardship weighed heavily on many voters' minds. The PRI's candidate, Carlos Salinas de Gortari, was sure to deepen the technocratic approach introduced by his predecessor, and Cárdenas and the FDN represented an alternative for voters who wanted to send a message to the PRI.

Almost immediately after the election, some members of the FDN, led again by Cárdenas, began the process of transforming the movement into a bona fide political party. But the newly formed PRD did not fare well in subsequent elections. Its vote share in the 1991 midterm elections plummeted to a mere 8 percent, and by 1994, when Cárdenas again ran for president, it recovered only some of its former popularity in garnering 17 percent of the vote. The PRD's decline in the early 1990s was caused by several factors.[10] First, the party comprised a number of disparate groups with different ideals and goals. While this heterogeneity was key to the FDN's success in 1988, it hindered the consolidation of the party as an organization because it complicated tasks that should have been relatively straightforward. So, for example, defining the party's platform and choosing candidates and leaders were hotly contested issues that often created further division rather than uniting competing factions. Moreover, these divisions also had adverse effects on the PRD's internal democracy, because the losers often claimed that the winners had triumphed through fraud. In the end, the real loser was the PRD as a whole, because internal charges of

fraud and corruption damaged the party's external image as a serious pro-
ponent of democracy and a viable electoral alternative.

As a young organization the PRD also suffered from a lack of institutionalization. Initially, many of the party's internal rules and procedures were
decided on an ad hoc basis, and the arbiter of last resort was the party's
leader, Cuauhtémoc Cárdenas. This method of operation, while perhaps
suitable for a temporary political movement, was inadequate for a consolidated political party because, at the very least, it made enforcing rules
difficult and promoted overreliance on a charismatic leader.

The internal weaknesses of the PRD were compounded by external efforts to hinder its success. Most notable of these was the PRI's campaign
to undermine its leftist challenger. The PRI's bitterness toward the PRD
stemmed from what many *priístas* considered Cárdenas's unforgivable
betrayal of leaving, openly criticizing, and then challenging the PRI in
the late 1980s. Additionally, the PRI felt threatened by the PRD's popular
appeal and its attempts to woo the party's progressive elements and traditional base of support with calls for economic nationalism and attention
to the poor. As a result, the PRI used state resources to harass or even
harm PRD activists and gleefully publicized the PRD's internal scandals.
It also used its control of the media to portray the PRD as a radical party
prone to violence. For example, in the 1994 presidential campaign, a PRI
television advertisement showed mob violence with burning and looting
while a solemn voice suggested that a vote for change would be a vote for
insecurity and instability. Finally, the PRI routinely stole elections, forcing *perredistas* to mount postelectoral challenges that further branded the
party as confrontational and incapable of playing by democratic rules.
Adding to the PRD's negative image was its reputation for intransigence.
The party's refusal to negotiate with other parties was as much a result of
the PRD's internal divisions as it was a principled stance. Regardless of the
reasons, this attitude also reinforced the notion that the PRD was a bunch
of wild-eyed radicals more intent on using its power in Congress to stand
in the way of, rather than promote, reform and progress.

These difficulties notwithstanding, the PRD enjoyed a revival of sorts in
1997 when Cárdenas was decisively elected mayor of Mexico City with 44
percent of the vote, and it nearly doubled its share of seats in Congress.
Undoubtedly, the PRD's gains in the late 1990s were due, at least in part, to
the mobilization of its core base of support: the rural poor in the southern
states and voters in Mexico City. But this mobilization and the party's appeal
to others probably would not have occurred were it not for the fact that the
1997 elections were the first to take place after the calamitous peso devaluation of 1994. Unfortunately for the PRD, it was not able to parlay its 1997
gains into a similar showing in 2000, when Cárdenas was again the party's
presidential candidate. His mediocre performance as Mexico City's mayor

and lackluster presidential campaign, together with the party's damaged reputation and the popularity of Vicente Fox, meant that the PRD did not make many inroads with voters; it garnered only 16.6 percent of the national vote.

More notable was the party's showing in 2003, when, in relatively good economic times, its share of seats in the Chamber almost doubled from fifty-two to ninety-five. Indeed, this appeared to be a sign of the party's good political fortunes to come. As early as 2002, political observers had begun to note strong support for Mexico City mayor Andrés Manuel López Obrador, known by his initials as AMLO. AMLO's ascendancy was remarkable because it marked the first time that someone other than three-time PRD presidential candidate and party founder Cuauhtémoc Cárdenas might represent the party in a presidential election. AMLO was a former member of the PRI who left the party with Cárdenas. He ran unsuccessfully for governor of his home state of Tabasco in 1994, in an election that evidenced widespread electoral fraud favoring the eventual winner, PRI candidate Roberto Madrazo. Thereafter, AMLO went on to become state party president, national party president, and finally mayor of Mexico City, all the while building a reputation for his commitment to the poor and his ability to use popular mobilization as leverage in negotiations.

Until March 2006, AMLO enjoyed a comfortable five- to ten-point lead over his rivals, with a high of nearly 45 percent public support in late 2005. However, a series of negative attacks on AMLO—as well as a number of campaign blunders, such as choosing not to appear at the first of two live televised debates—ultimately changed the course of the election. Thereafter, the candidates were in a dead heat in the race for the presidency.

On election day, Calderón obtained 35.8 percent of the vote, just slightly above AMLO's 35.3 percent. Given the close result, AMLO refused to recognize Calderón's victory and demanded a vote-by-vote recount of all ballots; he alleged that nearly 3 million votes had been deliberately omitted from the count. However, Mexican electoral regulations did not allow for a full recount and instead required that legal challenges be made through specific charges in districts where alleged violations of electoral law had occurred. The IFE did conduct a recount of the more than 11,000 precincts where there was evidence of error or inconsistency, but it ruled against a full recount. In the end, the Federal Electoral Tribunal (TRIFE) did not identify sufficient votes to overturn the results of the election.

Rather than accept this decision, AMLO took the unusual step of holding a public vote among supporters assembled at the Zócalo in Mexico City, based upon which he declared himself Mexico's legitimate president. In September, members of the PRD staged dramatic protests in Congress, successfully blocking President Fox from giving his annual report to the legislature. Later, in December 2006, the PRD unsuccessfully tried to prevent Calderón entering the legislature to be sworn in as president. President

Calderón therefore took office in a context of considerable controversy, raising questions about whether, in the eyes of many citizens, he would be able to achieve sufficient legitimacy to lead the country. For several months thereafter, some of AMLO's most dogged supporters set up permanent street demonstrations and encampments in Mexico City.

Still, public attention to and support for AMLO gradually diminished, partly because of the recalcitrant position he adopted after losing the presidential election. Even within his own party, some PRD leaders preferred a more pragmatic stance, and still others overtly criticized him for being a sore loser. Indeed, by 2007, a majority of PRD leaders broke sharply with AMLO by voting to officially recognize Calderón's government and, in 2008, by supporting Jesús Ortega as party chairman in a highly contentious internal election marred by accusations of fraud. As party chairman, Ortega adopted a much more conciliatory policy toward the PAN, including negotiations to consider strategic alliances in state-level elections in Oaxaca, Puebla, and Sinaloa. Ortega's leadership helped the PRD gain newfound political influence and restored the party to a more centrist position. However, Ortega also seriously alienated AMLO and many within the PRD. As a result, he did not emerge as a serious contender for the party's 2012 presidential nomination. Instead it became a contest between AMLO, who still enjoyed considerable support from his party, and Marcelo Ebrard, the highly popular mayor of Mexico City. Both candidates enjoyed high name recognition; however, public opinion surrounding AMLO and his platform tended to be overwhelmingly negative, and polls taken in the summer of 2011 suggested that he was unlikely to win more than 20 percent of the vote in a contest against the PRI's Peña Nieto. While public opinion of Ebrard was more positive, the same polls showed him unlikely to fare any better than AMLO in a national election.[11]

Other Parties

In addition to Mexico's three major political parties, there are a number of smaller parties that rarely win a majority of votes in district-level contests for executive or legislative office. However, because Mexico's federal and state legislatures and city councils allow for a certain degree of proportional representation, these small parties nevertheless are able to obtain a place in government. Also, because there is substantial public funding available for all registered political parties in Mexico, small parties have access to resources that enable them to attract followers and promote their agendas in the media. As electoral competition has intensified in recent years, the importance of small parties has increased because the larger parties see them as useful strategic partners in building electoral and governmental alliances.

The most successful of Mexico's smaller parties is the Mexican Green Ecological Party (Partido Verde Ecologista de México, PVEM), also known as the Mexican Green Party. The PVEM has obtained a significant share of the vote—between 3 percent and 7 percent—in federal elections since 1994, and has been an important coalition partner for each of the three major parties in federal and state elections (see textbox 6.1). Most recently, the PVEM has become an important partner of the PRI in elections.

Other parties that have found representation in the federal legislature are the New Alliance Party (Partido Nueva Alianza, PANAL), Convergence for Democracy, now Convergence (Convergencia), and the Labor Party (Partido del Trabajo, PT). The PANAL was founded in 2005 with the support of Mexico's teachers' union, the National Union of Education Workers (Sindicato Nacional de Trabajadores de la Educación, SNTE). The PANAL's creation appeared to be the result of the estrangement of SNTE leaders from the PRI. Aside from a general commitment to workers' rights, the PANAL does not have a well-articulated political agenda. In contrast to both the PVEM and the PANAL, the PT and Convergencia do have relatively clear ideological principles and policy agendas. Indeed, both of these parties have a leftist orientation that supports the redistribution of resources to the poorest sectors of society and calls for social justice and the respect of basic human rights. The PT is reminiscent of a Cold War–era socialist party in its commitment to economic nationalism and rejection of free-market economic policies, but it was not founded until 1990, after the fall of the Berlin Wall. Convergencia was founded in 1999 and, in contrast to the PT, favors neoliberal economic strategies as long as they are tempered with some government intervention. Their ideological leanings make both Convergencia and the PT "natural" allies of the PRD; in fact, they nominated the PRD's presidential candidates in both the 2000 and 2006 national elections, and they formed alliances with the PAN and the PRD to win the governorship of Oaxaca in 2010. Convergencia also joined the PAN-PRD-PANAL alliance that won in Puebla and the PAN-PRD alliance that won Sinaloa that same year.

Generally speaking, though, small parties in Mexico tend to have limited influence and, in some cases, a relatively short lifespan. For example, despite the prominence of its presidential candidate, Patricia Mercado, the leftist Social Democratic and Agrarian Alternative Party (Partido Alternativa Sociodemócrata y Campesino, PASC) joined the graveyard of party history in Mexico after failing to meet the necessary voter threshold in the 2009 midterm election. If President Calderón's reform proposal to reduce proportional representation and access to public funds gains traction in the coming years, it is possible that other small parties could follow the example of the PASC and other defunct third parties.

Textbox 6.1. MEXICO'S UNUSUAL GREEN PARTY

Despite its origins as a community-based nongovernmental organization and its stated commitment to preserving the environment and promoting sustainable development, the Mexican Green Ecological Party (Partido Verde Ecologista de México, PVEM) has very weak green credentials. Indeed, the party's greater claim to fame is its involvement in corruption scandals, some of which potentially threaten rather than protect the environment. For example, in 2004, Senator Jorge Emilio González Martínez, president of the PVEM, was caught on videotape negotiating the exchange of $2 million for government permits to develop land in Cancún. The party also gained notoriety for being fined $16 million by the IFE for violating campaign spending laws in the 2000 election.

Notwithstanding the PVEM's questionable commitment to environmental causes and its dubious accounting skills, as a party organization it has demonstrated a shrewd ability to obtain power by making itself available as a coalition partner. In 2000, its partnership with PAN candidate Vicente Fox in the Alliance for Change was mutually beneficial in that it provided the PVEM with a springboard to an unprecedented number of legislative offices, and it gave the PAN a 5 percent boost that helped to win the presidency. When the alliance fell apart in 2001, the PVEM wasted no time in pairing up with the PRI for the 2003 midterm and 2006 presidential elections. Again, this strategy paid off for both parties by increasing the former's seat share in the Chamber of Deputies and strengthening the latter's legislative plurality. Currently the party has six senators and twenty-one deputies.

The PVEM's involvement in the scandals mentioned above undoubtedly hurt its credibility as a coalition partner and its popularity among voters. Equally serious is the fact that the party has no discernable platform beyond protecting the environment and supporting the death penalty, and even this lacks clearly articulated goals or strategies. On the one hand, an ideological void no doubt provides important flexibility when it comes to making alliances with larger parties, as it is sure to do again in 2012. On the other hand, the party runs the risk of losing popular support if voters do not feel that it stands for some coherent ideological or policy agenda. So far the party's lack of a coherent ideological platform has not prevented it from achieving some measure of success, but these factors make the PVEM's long-term prospects uncertain.

THE MEXICAN ELECTORAL SYSTEM

For most of the twentieth century, the PRI achieved a dominant position within Mexico thanks in part to an internal organization that facilitated power sharing among competing groups, the monopolization and clientelistic distribution of state resources, and the occasional use of electoral fraud and political repression. However, equally important was its ability to manipulate the electoral system in its favor, while coopting opposition parties to participate in and legitimate the political process. For several decades, the official party used a combination of biased electoral rules and fraud to ensure that it would win elections.[12] The evolution of laws governing party formation and participation in the electoral arena almost always favored the PRI and ensured that it would be consistently overrepresented in the legislature. This was a key component of *presidencialismo* and essential for the party to single-handedly amend the constitution and stay in power. Yet, at the same time that the manipulation of electoral institutions helped that ruling party maintain its hegemony, it also allowed sufficient competition to encourage the formation and participation of minor opposition parties. Indeed, in hindsight, the evolution of rules such as the requirement that parties demonstrate a national following actually forced opposition parties to broaden their appeal and garner the popular support that eventually undermined PRI dominance and gave way to multiparty democracy. Below we outline the major evolutionary phases of the Mexican electoral system since the revolution, including reforms that established periods with particularly distinctive arrangements in 1946, 1963, 1976, 1990, and 2007.

The Postrevolutionary Electoral System

The foundations of the Mexican electoral system were established by the 1917 Mexican constitution and the 1918 Federal Electoral Law. At the outset, the postrevolutionary electoral system was relatively decentralized, since voter registration processes and district boundaries were determined by state-level councils (*consejos de listas electorales*) and the conducting of elections was overseen by municipal authorities. Moreover, the electoral law of 1918 allowed independent candidates to run for office and created a very low threshold for party registration, since new parties could be registered with the support of just one hundred citizens (see table 6.2).

The 1918 Federal Electoral Law was more restrictive in one important way: the possibility of reelection. As noted in chapter 3, the 1917 constitution included an absolute prohibition on presidential reelection. In January 1927, Plutarco Calles and the supporters of Álvaro Obregón removed this restriction by amending Article 83 of the constitution to

Table 6.2. The 1917 Postrevolutionary Electoral System

Relevant Areas	Key Features
Electoral Regulation	• National legislature confirms presidential and congressional elections. • Supreme Court resolves electoral disputes. • Elections overseen by municipal authorities. • State level *consejos de listas electorales* compile voter registration and determine district boundaries.
Party Formation / Eligibility	• Parties must have support of 100 citizens and publish governing rules. • Political parties prohibited from religious affiliations. • Independent candidates allowed.
Representation / Terms of Office	• No reelection. • Four-year presidential term. • Senators are elected by plurality vote from single-member districts for four-year terms. • Deputies are elected by plurality from single member districts for two-year terms. • One deputy per 60,000 inhabitants, with at least two per state and one per territory/DF. A 1928 constitutional reform later modified the representative formula to be one deputy per 100,000 inhabitants.

permit reelection for up to one nonconsecutive term. In addition, a few days after this reform, the constitution was further amended to increase the presidential term from four to six years. However, although Obregón was reelected in 1928, he was assassinated shortly after his victory, and thereafter no Mexican president was ever again reelected. Indeed, in April 1933, restrictions on presidential reelection were restored by constitutional amendment, and, additionally, new prohibitions were added regarding the reelection of governors and the consecutive reelection of federal legislators (see textbox 6.2).[13]

The 1946 Federal Electoral System

After several challenges posed by opposition parties and independent presidential candidates during the 1930s and 1940s, the regime enacted the Federal Electoral Law of 1946 to insulate the ruling party. The reform outlawed independent candidacies and required political parties to demonstrate a minimum level of national support in order to be officially recognized and participate in elections. In 1954, the threshold for party registration was raised from 30,000 to 75,000, with a minimum of 2,500 members in each of two-thirds of the states. In the early 1970s, the

---

Textbox 6.2. "NO REELECTION"

"Effective suffrage, no reelection," the slogan adopted by Francisco I. Madero in the uprising against Porfirio Díaz, led to the long-term institutionalization of single-term limits in Mexico. Ironically, though, this very commitment to "no reelection" appears to severely hamper the related principle of "effective suffrage." Although votes count more today than in any previous era of Mexican history, the prohibition of reelection limits the effectiveness of voters' decisions by making it impossible for them to either reward or punish the individuals they elect. Yet despite these problems, and the fact that eliminating the ban would almost surely increase the quality and accountability of politicians, attempts to introduce consecutive reelection for national legislative and local offices have not elicited widespread support.

As an institutionalized feature of the Mexican political system, "no reelection" has given rise to powerful beneficiaries with a vested interest in maintaining the status quo. Chief among its supporters are members of the old guard within the PRI, who argue that introducing reelection would weaken the party by creating incentives for politicians to pay more attention to their constituents, on whom they will depend for career advancement, than to the party organization. These vested interests help explain why it has been difficult to bring about change, even with widespread recognition among scholars and politicians that eliminating the ban would represent a step forward in Mexico's transition to democracy. Therefore, when Calderón introduced the possibility of eliminating the ban on reelection at the subnational level and in the national legislature, it failed to garner widespread support even though it was seen by many to be a progressive measure designed to increase the power of Mexican voters.

---

requirement was relaxed slightly to 65,000, in an effort to promote greater pluralism and hence legitimacy for the political system.[14] (See table 6.3.) Of course, relatively few parties were able to meet these requirements, and even fewer were able to consistently maintain their financial and political independence and thus behave as a true rather than a loyal opposition.

The 1946 electoral system established the foundations for a system in which the PRI would dominate politics for the rest of the century. In 1954, revisions to the Federal Electoral Law also gave the Federal Electoral Commission (Comisión Federal Electoral, CFE), or its state and district counterparts (formed in 1951), the responsibility of settling electoral disputes. With the 1954 Federal Electoral Law, the National Electoral Registry was created and empowered to define district boundaries and maintain voter lists.

Table 6.3. The 1946 Federal Electoral System Reforms

Relevant Areas	Key Features
Electoral Regulation	• Established the Federal Electoral Oversight Commission, headed by minister of the interior (*gobernación*) to organize and oversee elections. • Established National Voter Registration Agency to define districts and develop voter lists.
Party Formation / Eligibility	• Candidates must have support of a political party. • Parties must be national with at least 30,000 supporters: 1,000 in each of two-thirds of the states and territories.
Representation / Terms of Office	• No major changes to the terms of federal electoral system until introduction of party deputies in 1963, and the modification of the electoral threshold for these deputies from 2.5 to 1.5 percent of the national vote in 1973.

The 1963 Party Deputy System

In 1963 President Adolfo López Mateos introduced a form of limited proportional representation (PR) in the Chamber of Deputies, through what were known as party deputies (*diputados plurinominales*). These seats were reserved for parties that received at least 2.5 percent of the national vote. Each party that met this threshold was granted one seat for each .5 percentage of the vote that they received, up to a maximum of 20 seats. Any party that received more than 20 percent of the national vote was ineligible to receive party deputy seats; therefore these seats were essentially off limits to the PRI.

Yet while party deputy seats appeared to be a generous gift to the opposition, the 20 percent limit also represented a glass ceiling for the National Action Party, which was beginning to garner greater national support beginning in the 1960s. Ironically, if the PAN was too successful (gaining more than 20 percent of the vote nationwide), it could lose representation in the legislature by becoming ineligible to receive party deputy seats. Meanwhile, small parties blossomed under this system, since they could get access to legislative positions relatively easily. Thus, the addition of party deputy seats was a novel way to allow the opposition representation, all the while preserving the PRI's majority by fragmenting the opposition into small fringe parties and punishing any opposition parties that managed to receive more than 20 percent of the national vote.[15] In the aftermath of the social unrest of 1968, a new Federal Electoral Law in 1973 lowered the minimum threshold for party deputy seats from 2.5 percent to 1.5 percent, increased the maximum threshold to 25 percent, and increased the maximum number of seats to 25.

The 1976 LFOPPE Reform

The charade of electoral competition was exposed in the 1976 presidential election when the PRI candidate, José López Portillo, ran unopposed and Mexico could not credibly claim to be democratic. As noted in chapter 4, in 1977 López Portillo introduced the Federal Law of Political Organizations and Electoral Processes (LFOPPE), which sought to increase the access of smaller opposition parties by creating two methods of obtaining official registration. Organizations could apply for conditional registration, and hence participate in national elections, if they could demonstrate four years of continuous political activity. Conditional parties could obtain permanent registration if they received 1.5 percent of the national vote.[16] To accommodate minority parties, one hundred seats in the Chamber of Deputies were set aside specifically for the proportional representation of those parties that met this threshold but won fewer than sixty of the three hundred single-member district seats (see table 6.4).

Table 6.4. 1977 Federal Law of Political Organizations and Electoral Processes (LFOPPE)

Relevant Areas	Key Features
Electoral Regulation	• Composition of Federal Electoral Commission (CFE) changed to include a representative from each party, one senator, one deputy, and a notary public. • CFE given the authority to register, deny, or withdraw party registration. • CFE responsible for choosing the number and composition of PR districts. • Free monthly radio and TV access for all registered parties.
Party Formation / Eligibility	• Any party that fails to take its seats loses its registration and vote. • Parties required to have at least 65,000 supporters nationwide, with at least 2,000 residing in two-thirds of states and territories. • Established two methods of party registration: 1) *Conditional registration* given to organizations with four continuous years of political activity. In order to obtain permanent registration, must obtain 1.5% of vote in national election; 2) *Definitive registration* given to parties that submit party statutes and evidence of 65,000 members: 3,000 in one-half plus one of states, or 300 in one-half plus one of all federal districts.
Representation / Terms of Office	• Number of seats in Chamber of Deputies is increased to 400, 300 SMD, 100 PR seats for parties that win fewer than 60 SMD, and at least 1.5% of vote. • In 1986, the number of seats in Chamber increased to 500, 300 SMD and 200 PR, and a governability clause gives party with highest vote (even if less than 51%) a majority in Chamber.

A subsequent constitutional amendment in 1986 further increased the size of the Chamber of Deputies to five hundred, with the addition of one hundred more plurinominal seats. While this appeared to create more space for the opposition, in fact changes to the allocation formula gave the PRI access to the proportional representation seats for the first time. Furthermore, the reform was more beneficial to the PRI than to the opposition because the so-called governability clause discussed in chapter 4 also guaranteed the party with the highest vote a majority in the Chamber, even if it won less than 51 percent of the national vote. In fact, this is what occurred in the 1988 congressional elections, when the PRI won only 239 of 500 seats (47.8 percent).

The LFOPPE reform also established new regulations that sought to address long-standing media bias favoring the ruling party. In the past, close connections between government officials and owners of media outlets, combined with the widespread practice of paying kickbacks to reporters, made it next to impossible for the Mexican press to have an objective or independent voice. To be sure, in the aftermath of the Tlatelolco massacre and several government crackdowns in the early 1970s, many newspaper journalists began to reexamine their previous complicity and take on a more independent and critical stance vis-à-vis the government.[17] The LFOPPE also facilitated a greater degree of media access by including provisions to grant all registered political parties free monthly television and radio time. Like many reforms of the time, this provision was more symbolic than substantial: the government, in concert with the media outlets, determined which time slots were given to the opposition, and it became common practice to relegate the opposition's ads to times when audiences were smallest.

In short, the 1977 reform and the 1986 constitutional amendment made it easier for smaller parties to participate in elections, gain a nominal level of representation, and even increase their access to voters though mass media outlets. Yet the overall effect of the reform was to enhance the legitimacy of the Mexican political system by making it appear more competitive than it really was. At the same time, the cap on minority representation ensured that opposition parties with larger followings would never pose a serious threat to the PRI. Therefore, at least initially, the primary beneficiary of the 1977 law was the PRI, whose hegemonic position was preserved.

COFIPE and Other Electoral Reforms of the 1990s

In the aftermath of the controversial, fraud-ridden presidential election of 1988, when several opposition parties formed a coalition to support Cuauhtémoc Cárdenas against PRI candidate Carlos Salinas, electoral reform took on renewed urgency in Mexico. In response, the PRI, together with the support of the PAN, passed the Federal Code of Electoral Institutions and

Procedures (COFIPE), which dramatically changed the rules for candidate registration, electoral regulation, and seat allocation (see table 6.5). First, in a clear response to Cárdenas's National Democratic Front, COFIPE required that joint candidates be supported by an official coalition, and that coalitions nominate common candidates for more positions than just the presidency. This new law was a specific attempt to prevent another Cárdenas-like figure from challenging the PRI. The PAN agreed to support the measure because it feared that Cárdenas and other leftist candidates would seek to win elections using the FDN's strategy.

The 1990 COFIPE reform also transformed electoral oversight. Before 1990, the government tightly controlled electoral process through a variety of mechanisms. For example, the minister of the interior, who was always closely linked to the president, headed the CFE, the body in charge of organizing and ruling on elections. This arrangement allowed the standing government and the ruling party to intervene directly in electoral matters, including the settlement of electoral disputes and charges of fraud. It is therefore unsurprising that the PRI was able to use fraud with impunity to ensure favorable electoral results. However, in the 1988 presidential election, the crash of the vote-tabulating system on election night severely delegitimized the PRI and gave the opposition greater leverage to negotiate the replacement of the CFE with the Federal Electoral Institute (Instituto Federal Electoral, IFE) as the country's chief electoral authority. Initially, the minister of the interior remained head of the IFE, and the PRI was over-represented on the governing board; however, over time, the IFE became an independent institution.

The COFIPE also eliminated the governability clause but replaced it with a similar arrangement in which a majority of Chamber seats was automatically awarded to the party with the most victories in single-member districts.[18] In doing so, the new law established more specific thresholds for seat allocation: if a party won less than 35 percent or between 60 and 70 percent of the national vote, its seat share was proportional to its vote share. If it won more than 70 percent, it would automatically receive 350 seats, or a two-thirds majority. But a party that won between 35 and 60 percent of the national vote was awarded 50 percent plus one, or 251 seats, and two additional seats for each percentage point above 35 percent. This was the scenario most likely to apply to the PRI, and it ensured that the PRI would always have an absolute majority.

In a second round of reforms in 1993 and 1994, the Salinas administration conceded more space to the opposition by doubling the size of the Senate to 128 members, and it made Senate elections concurrent with presidential elections. However, Salinas again altered electoral rules for the Chamber to favor the ruling party.[19] Thus, while the opposition benefited from the addition of 32 Senate seats to be awarded to the second-place

Table 6.5. 1990 Federal Code of Electoral Institutions and Procedures (COFIPE)

Relevant Areas	Key Features
Electoral Regulation	• Federal Electoral Institute (IFE) replaces CFE as chief electoral authority.
	• Led by Consejo General, which is comprised of minister of the interior (*gobernación*), four representatives of the majority party, one senator and one deputy from majority party, one member of Congress from the opposition, and six independent members, nominated by president and confirmed by two-thirds majority in Chamber of Deputies.
	• Consejo General adjudicates electoral disputes.
	• All parties choose precinct observers.
	• New voter registration list with photo identification card.
	• New formula for public funding of political parties; limits on campaign spending; new procedures for reporting and monitoring party finances.
	• In 1993, the IFE was granted power to certify congressional elections.
Party Formation / Eligibility	• Coalitions must be formed well in advance of elections.
	• No two parties can nominate a single candidate unless they form a coalition for all elected offices.
	• Coalition candidates do not count toward parties' total for PR seats.
Representation / Terms of Office	• Eliminates first governability clause in favor of a formula that overrepresents the party with the most victories in SMD in the Chamber, so that if winning party gets 35% of vote, it automatically gets 250 SMD seats plus one PR seat, for a simple majority.
	• In 1993, the second governability clause was eliminated, and a new law established that no single party can hold more than 63% of total seats in Chamber.
	• In 1993, the number of Senate seats increased to four from each state, for a total of 128. First-place party wins three seats, and the second-place party, one seat.

party in each state and the Federal District, and from the elimination of the provision that prevented a party from holding more than 315 seats in the Chamber, it was nevertheless disadvantaged by a new provision that allocated the 200 plurinominal seats on the basis of each party's share of the overall vote—a move that made it easier for the PRI to protect its majority in the lower house of the legislature.[20]

Since the above-mentioned reforms appeared to be successful in protecting the PRI's advantages while lending the appearance of greater democratic legitimacy, it is possible that no further reforms would have occurred thereafter. However, the guerrilla uprising in Chiapas on January 1, 1994, and the political assassinations leading up to the presidential elections that same year led to hurried negotiations on a new set of reforms to bolster the legitimacy of electoral results. Specifically, the new Federal Electoral Law changed the governing board of the IFE so that its six independent councilors would be chosen by consensus of the major political parties (rather than nominated by the president) and approved by a two-thirds majority of the Chamber. In addition, the new 1994 law required parties to submit a report of campaign revenue and spending to the IFE and established new campaign contribution and spending limits for individuals, labor unions, and anonymous donors (contributions from businesses, churches, and foreign organizations were expressly forbidden). The 1994 reform also established the Federal Electoral Tribunal (Tribunal Federal Electoral, TRIFE). The TRIFE was composed of the Chief Justice and four other Supreme Court justices—appointed with two-thirds congressional approval—whose purpose is to examine disputes relating to congressional elections.

After he took office in 1994, President Ernesto Zedillo called for more reforms to strengthen the legitimacy of the electoral process. First, an electoral reform in 1996 made the IFE truly independent by requiring that its president be an independent citizen chosen by the Chamber of Deputies (see table 6.6). The reform also established the Supreme Court as the final arbiter of electoral disputes and integrated the TRIFE into the Supreme Court bureaucracy. The 1996 reform also gave the IFE the right to buy the time slots for party advertising and charged it with monitoring the media for signs of bias. More than previous reforms, the 1996 electoral laws paved the way for all political parties in Mexico to compete on an equal footing in local and national elections. For example, during the presidential campaign of 2006, the IFE forced the PAN to discontinue advertisements that it deemed undue personal attacks on the PRD's López Obrador.

The Zedillo administration's reforms also made it impossible for the majority party's share of seats to exceed its share of the vote by more than 8 percent and capped its seats in the Chamber at 300 seats, significantly less than the 350 needed to unilaterally amend the constitution. New proportional representation allocation formulas in the Senate also made it easier for the opposition to win seats. Without a doubt, the new laws played an important role in giving the opposition greater access to positions in the national legislature. Thus, it is not coincidental that the PRI lost its majority in the Chamber of Deputies in 1997, the first year that the reforms were in effect. Moreover, since 1997, no party has won more than a plurality in either house of the national legislature.

The 2007 Federal Electoral Reform

In the political crisis that followed the controversial 2006 presidential election, several new laws were introduced that constituted the first

Table 6.6. 1996 Electoral Law Reforms

Relevant Areas	Key Features
Electoral Regulation	• Federal District: Introduces direct election of mayor/governor of DF.
	• Allocates public campaign funds to all political parties: 30% are distributed equally among parties, 70% based on share of vote in previous election.
	• Establishes sanctions for violating spending laws.
	• Parties must submit annual reports on revenue and spending.
	• Permanent commission established to oversee campaign spending and party expenditures.
	• Establishes independent audit of voter registration list.
	• Legalizes participation of international election observers.
	• IFE president is an independent citizen (rather than minister of the interior) chosen by consensus and with two-thirds approval of Chamber.
	• Voting rights within IFE limited to its president and eight independent electoral councilors chosen by consensus with two-thirds approval of Chamber, to serve six-year terms.
	• Establishes Supreme Court as final arbiter of electoral results.
	• Integrates Federal Electoral Tribunal (TRIFE) into Supreme Court bureaucracy.
	• IFE given right to buy time slots for political party advertising.
	• IFE monitors media for signs of bias.
Representation / Terms of Office	• Changes Senate seat allocation to two per state (64), 32 to second-place parties, and 32 on the basis of PR.
	• Majority party in Chamber can have no more than 300 seats and number of seats cannot exceed share by more than 8%.

major electoral reform since the end of the era of PRI hegemony. The new reforms granted the IFE expanded regulatory oversight of the media, the message, and the money employed in electoral campaigns. First, the 2007 reforms established new restrictions on the purchase of media air time (radio and television) for campaign purposes, limiting its use to political parties and forbidding individuals and private interest groups from advertising or campaigning on a candidate's behalf. Part of the intent of this reform was to ensure that candidates and their parties, and not shadowy, deep-pocketed interest groups, are the ones responsible for the messages conveyed in a campaign. A second aspect of the 2007 reform was to introduce new restrictions on the content of campaign messages to prevent the use of negative campaigning against individuals, parties, and institutions. In the wake of the very negative campaign messages targeting AMLO, this reform was intended to restore civility to political campaigns in Mexico.

Finally, a third component of the 2007 reform set limits on the amount of public funds distributed to political parties, as well as new restrictions on campaign contributions from private individuals to political parties. In 1987, the Federal Electoral Code established that parties would receive public funds in proportion to their electoral returns and percentage of seats held in the Chamber.[21] Shortly thereafter, in 1990, COFIPE altered the allocation formula and introduced electoral spending limits. However, the latter were so high that they made no practical difference in the way the PRI funded its electoral campaigns. COFIPE also established procedures for reporting and monitoring campaign spending, yet in practice these rules were widely ignored. Further reform occurred in 1996 when parties were obligated to submit annual revenue and spending reports, and Congress established that public, rather than private funds would be the most important source of campaign financing.[22] Even with the limits on private contributions enacted in 2007, Mexican elections are among the most expensive in the world, and many argue that further reform is needed to ensure that competition among the parties remains fair.

Each of these reforms at least nominally strengthened the role of the IFE in the regulation of campaigns and elections. What remains to be seen, of course, is whether the IFE can in fact enforce the letter and spirit of the 2007 electoral reforms. With regard to the first component of the reform, interpreting what counts as political advertising can be difficult, since indirect advocacy or issue advertising can be developed to favor or harm a particular candidate or party without overtly political language. For example, an interest group could presumably still seek to subtly sway the electorate by using an advertisement about abortion in a district where a candidate expresses strong views on that topic. Likewise, determining when the content of campaign messages is negative is a highly subjective exercise that could make it difficult for the IFE to maintain the appearance of objectivity. Moreover, trying to restrict negative campaigning could even be harmful if it prevents voters from being well informed about candidates' bad behavior or the unfulfilled promises of an incumbent political party. Lastly, effectively capping campaign expenditures has proved to be a notoriously difficult task in many democratic systems.

Electoral Trends in Mexico

The long-term prospects for all of Mexico's political parties have been significantly determined by the evolving configuration of Mexico's electoral institutions. For seven decades, the design of Mexico's electoral system was one of the major factors that kept the PRI in power. However, over the last three decades of the twentieth century, a series of gradual electoral reforms, like the introduction of proportional representation, also helped dramatically transform the Mexican political system, as opposition parties grew both in electoral support and representation in public office. This dramatic reshaping of the Mexican party system illustrates the changing preferences of voters over time, but it also offers a testament to the power of institutions as a means to convey those preferences into tangible political outcomes. The leaders of the PRI understood that power and used institutions very carefully to preserve the position of the ruling party, but because opposition groups were successful in renegotiating the rules of the game, they were ultimately able to shift the results in their favor.

Over the last thirty years, the party that most clearly benefited from the declining power of the PRI was the PAN. In part, this reflected the PAN's institutional strength as Mexico's long-established and second largest political party, as well as its ability to attract and field strong candidates to oppose the ruling party, particularly when the economic crises that started in the 1970s drove many businessmen and women into politics. However, the PAN's ability to advance politically also reflected its ability to negotiate specific reforms, such as giving a portion of senate seats to the second largest party in a given state. As a result of such reforms, the PAN was able to establish a strong foothold at the local and state level and ultimately to succeed in developing a dominant position over the PRI in the national political arena.

After twelve years of continuous rule and declining political fortunes in local and midterm elections, it is not clear the PAN will maintain its position as Mexico's new ruling party. One measure it has taken to stave off a return of the PRI has been to negotiate with its traditional rivals in the PRD and other opposition parties to form electoral coalitions. While coalitions tend to be more common in parliamentary systems of government, Mexico's use of proportional representation creates incentives for parties to pool their respective shares of the vote into a plurality or even a majority winning coalition. This tactic proved successful for various multiparty coalitions in the states of Chiapas in 2006 and Oaxaca in 2010. While certain parties—such as the PRI and the PVEM—have found it relatively easy to strike up regular, mutually beneficial alliances, constructing broad coalitions across parties with opposing ideological points of view has proven more difficult.

In the case of the PAN and the PRD, for example, the parties joined forces in 2010 to oust the PRI for the first time in Oaxaca, Puebla, and Sinaloa by supporting gubernatorial candidates Gambino Cue, Rafael Moreno, and Mario López Valdez, respectively. But PAN-PRD alliances have not always been successful, and more often than not, both the PAN and the PRD have opted not to join forces. Indeed, after their successful run in 2010, the PAN went so far as to sign a secret pact with the PRI affirming its commitment not to enter into alliances with the PRD in the 2011 elections in the state of Mexico, with President Calderón using this agreement as leverage to negotiate a new federal tax reform package. When the PRI-PAN "anti-alliance" pact fell apart, members of the state party organizations of both the PAN and the PRD began working to establish a coalition, until the national leaders of the PRD finally voted to oppose the agreement in April 2011. In the absence of a PAN-PRD coalition, the PRI was able to maintain control of the governorship of the state of Mexico, an important stronghold for the PRI and a strong predictor of the outcome of the 2012 presidential election.

To be sure, by the later part of the Calderón administration, most pundits had already begun to speculate that PRI candidate Enrique Peña Nieto would have the advantage in the 2012 presidential election. A young, attractive candidate, Peña Nieto had important advantages heading into the general election, but the most important was the ability of the PRI to unite behind a single candidate for the first time in over fifteen years. Indeed, from mid-2009 onward, the PRI consistently outperformed its rivals in public opinion polls, regardless of which candidates the other parties selected (see figure 6.1). Furthermore, a series of Mitofsky polls in the spring and summer of 2011 indicated that Enrique Peña Nieto had 87 percent support among PRI voters and consistently garnered about 47 percent support among voters who expressed a preference. Meanwhile, although the PAN's Santiago Creel enjoyed 65 percent name recognition, voters had an unfavorable opinion of him and his platform. Moreover, no PAN candidate received more than 19 percent support among voters asked whom they would choose if the election were held that day. Similarly, while the PRD's top candidates, AMLO and Marcelo Ebrard, enjoyed high name recognition, many voters held strongly negative opinions (in the case of AMLO) or only mildly positive opinions (in the case of Ebrard). All of these results reinforced the notion that Enrique Peña Nieto is the man to beat in 2012.

CONCLUSION

Although the PRI dominated the Mexican political arena for seven decades, in the late 1980s the opposition began to organize and compete effectively for power. By the mid-1990s, Mexico had a multiparty system and a competitive electoral system. In 2000, the PAN's victory in the presidential election opened a new era in which electoral competition and uncertainty became the new norm. Indeed, intense competition in the 2006 presidential election provoked perhaps the greatest test of Mexico's democratic electoral system to date, given the PRD's initial refusal to recognize the results. However, changes within the PRD softened its position and even led to important collaboration with the PAN in certain state

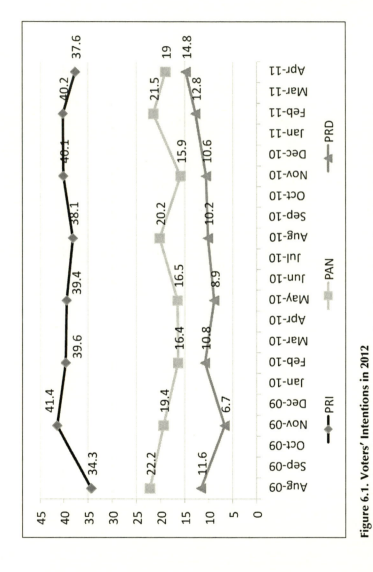

Figure 6.1. Voters' Intentions in 2012

Source: Consulta Mitofsky, *Preferencia electoral para la presidencia de México (sin candidatos),* February 2011.

elections, as a check against the resurgence of the PRI. Despite these efforts, however, in the 2009 midterm election and in the lead up to the 2012 elections, the PRI had returned to a strong position to retake the presidency. There is much speculation about what a return of the PRI to Los Pinos could mean for Mexican democracy. However, given all of the changes to Mexico's political parties and electoral institutions we have highlighted in this chapter, it seems unlikely that the PRI would be able to recapture its dominant position of the past: the opposition is much stronger and more deeply rooted in Mexican society, and Mexico's electoral institutions have been reformed to prevent the excesses of single-party hegemony. For these reasons it appears quite certain that competitive party politics will continue to be an important feature of contemporary Mexican politics for the foreseeable future.

7

Mexican Political Culture

After hundreds of years of authoritarian or semi-authoritarian rule in Mexico, are Mexicans ready for democracy? Many scholars believe that certain political values, civic attitudes, and participatory behaviors are necessary to consolidate and sustain democratic governance. Yet some have suggested that Mexican society lacks these attributes and instead exhibits a customary adherence to hierarchical leadership structures, patronage networks, and political subservience, dating as far back as the conquest. Such assertions dramatically oversimplify a very complex problem and must be viewed with caution. In the worst cases, claims that Mexicans are naturally inclined to authoritarianism result from stereotypes, ethnocentric biases, or other inappropriately subjective standards. Nevertheless, it is important to explore the dimensions of Mexico's widely shared political orientations and evaluate their relevance in explaining contemporary political outcomes. For example, in a country where four in five people identify themselves as Catholics, it makes sense to ask how religious beliefs factor into Mexicans' political considerations. Likewise, since many scholars feel that certain political behaviors—such as high rates of voter turnout—can positively reinforce democratic governance, what can we make of current trends in Mexico? Or, to the extent that people have strong positive opinions or expectations regarding Mexican political institutions, what does this say about the quality of democracy? This chapter explores the multiple facets of Mexican political culture, first by defining the concept and discussing its importance for stable democracy. The focus then turns to two important indicators of the country's democratic health: Mexicans' attitudes toward politics and their political behavior.

STUDYING POLITICAL CULTURE IN MEXICO

Political culture is an overarching concept used to describe a collective set of values and beliefs, norms and behaviors, and attitudes and feelings about politics. Individuals acquire these orientations toward the political system through a prolonged process of socialization—beginning in their families and communities—and through the day-to-day accumulation of information and experiences through education (which varies by level and type); media; and social, professional, and ethnic group affiliations. Naturally, historical context and events may factor heavily into people's political attitudes. We saw in previous chapters, for example, how key events like the Mexican Revolution, the 1968 student massacre, the 1985 earthquakes, and multiple crises in 1994 shaped the political viewpoints of millions of Mexicans. For many political scientists, the influences of political socialization and shared historical experiences on a society's political culture must be carefully studied through comparative analysis to understand the differences among countries.

Gabriel Almond and Sidney Verba conducted the first major comparative study of Mexican political culture in 1963. *The Civic Culture* compared the political culture of five countries: the United States, the United Kingdom, Germany, Italy, and Mexico. Through analysis of cross-national survey data, the authors attempted to identify and categorize different types of political culture and how they contributed to specific regime types.[1] In general, Almond and Verba's findings supported those of previous, smaller studies: they found that Mexicans were largely parochial and narrowly self-interested in their political attitudes, and therefore tended to be apathetic or distrustful toward politicians and public institutions. In this regard, Mexico was found to be similar to Italy and different from the United States and the United Kingdom, whose citizens were more politically aware and engaged. The major conclusion of this study was that having a civic culture in which citizens were active and involved in politics helped promote democratic governance, while the lack thereof contributed to authoritarianism. Based on these findings, the authors claimed that stable democracy was much more viable in the United States, the United Kingdom, and to a lesser extent Germany, than in Italy or Mexico.

Almond and Verba's study was a landmark for understanding political culture because it was the first systematic, comparative study to employ large cross-national surveys. Indeed, subsequent empirical studies were often modeled on this seminal piece. Like *The Civic Culture*, many of these studies found that Mexicans held values and attitudes that demonstrated political apathy and alienation, and actively contributed to support for authoritarian leaders, single-party hegemony, and centralized political control. Such studies tended to support the notion that the Mexican personality was predisposed to paternalism, subservience, and subordination, which caused them to accept authoritarianism and not challenge the status quo.

Yet the notion of political culture involves highly amorphous and intangible concepts and requires observers to generalize across many individual perspectives. Social scientific research in this area is therefore fraught with serious methodological and analytical concerns (see textbox 7.1). For example, given that people's thoughts about politics are often very complex—and may even have internal contradictions—can we truly measure and analyze their viewpoints with any degree of certainty? Given Mexico's regional diversity and social disparities, can we talk realistically about a single Mexican political culture? For many scholars such questions make it difficult and even controversial to conduct social scientific research about political culture. Indeed, critics frequently argue that studies of political culture are too imprecise, too methodologically flawed, and often too biased to be of much analytical value. Even when well designed, studies of political culture may be subject to overgeneralization or false causal connections. Hence, such studies may lead to stereotyping or to exaggerated claims about the salience of beliefs, attitudes, and norms in determining political outcomes.

Many early studies of Mexican political culture had significant shortcomings that cast doubt on the validity of their findings and brought

---

Textbox 7.1. STUDYING POLITICAL CULTURE: CHICKEN OR EGG?

One of the main problems associated with the study of political culture stems from the fact that it is very difficult to ascertain whether political culture (e.g., propensity to vote, party affiliation, policy preferences, support for democracy) is what drives political behavior and outcomes, or whether political culture is instead shaped by social norms and values, socioeconomic characteristics, and institutions (e.g., belief in equality, education levels, political parties). Assuming Mexicans do indeed hold authoritarian values, is this the cause or effect of centuries of nondemocratic governance? When people are subject to repression, they tend to act obsequiously or face the real possibility of persecution. It is also difficult to believe that political culture is a determining factor precisely because values and belief systems are very slow to change. Hence if culture has causal relevance, how can we explain relatively sudden changes in political outcomes, such as Mexico's democratization in the 1980s and 1990s? Many critics of political cultural analysis feel that beliefs, norms, and attitudes, while they should not be ignored, cannot be assigned sole—or even primary—causal significance for macrolevel political outcomes like the ultimate success or failure of democracy.

well-deserved criticisms. For example, in some cases, early survey question-naires administered by foreign researchers contained translation errors that probably affected the way Mexicans responded to the questions they posed.[2] Another problem is that the effort to generalize findings about political culture beyond a sample population can lead to erroneous con-clusions about the overall population, particularly in large national and cross-national surveys.[3] For instance, in past studies, researchers frequently tended to underrepresent Mexico's rural population and focus instead on urban areas that were easier to reach.[4] Understandably, in order to fully assess a country's political culture, researchers must make an effort to care-fully identify the key cleavages and differences that distinguish various sec-tors of the population.

Contemporary studies continue to struggle with the methodological challenges of systematically gauging political culture.[5] Still, when done properly, such studies can help us better understand how people think about politics, what their preferences are with regard to political outcomes, and how they behave and express themselves politically. For example, one finding that has been fairly consistent across different studies is that education levels and gender are important determinants of political atti-tudes: males and educated Mexicans are more likely to be interested in and actively participate in political activities.[6] Other studies have substantiated early findings that most Mexicans distrust politicians and politics and that low-income citizens are less likely to expect fair treatment by government officials and institutions (e.g., local bureaucracy, law enforcement).[7] How-ever, we must be careful about how we interpret such results. Below, we consider these issues as we evaluate three major aspects of political culture in Mexico: values and belief systems, norms and behaviors, and attitudes and feelings. In the process, we consider the major trends found in Mexico, and how they are relevant to the country's political development and con-temporary democratic politics.

MEXICAN VALUES AND BELIEF SYSTEMS

Many social scientists interested in political culture focus on how values and belief systems can shape political and economic outcomes.[8] Values and beliefs are perhaps best understood as the philosophical frameworks or worldviews that determine people's priorities, goals, and notions about how things should be. In politics, people often interpret and act on ideas, information, and events depending on how these conform to relatively well-established principles or systems of understanding of the world, such as those established by a religion or an ideology. While some people may also act entirely without regard to preestablished principles, even such pragmatism might be considered a belief system in itself. What is important is that, to the extent that they are measurable, widely shared values and belief systems can have political significance since they help observers determine (and perhaps even predict) what people think is important and how they may behave. In what way, then, do values and beliefs seem to play a role in Mexican political culture? Below, we examine the historical origins of Mexican values and belief systems, as derived from the country's Spanish colonial heritage. Subsequently, we consider the emergence of democratic values in contemporary Mexico.

The Legacies of Spanish Colonialism and the Mexican Revolution

Some observers believe that democracy has been slow to develop and is relatively weak in Latin America because of the cultural legacies of Spanish colonialism. According to this view, Spanish colonizers introduced political, social, and economic institutions (e.g., viceroyalty, the Catholic Church, and mercantilism) that reified hierarchy within the bureaucracy and society, institutionalized social and political inequality and absolutism, and instilled inherently authoritarian values and beliefs in the population.[9] However, while there is no doubt that Spanish colonialism had deep and lasting influences in Mexico, it is more difficult to explain exactly how it continues to affect Mexican politics today, more than five hundred years later.

How, for example, could Mexico transition from autocratic rule to democracy in just a few decades if the legacy of colonialism were so strong? It is likely that Mexican attitudes in the twentieth century were more directly affected by education (or lack thereof), and by the ability of the PRI and the government to politically socialize citizens with the use of mass media and by manipulating symbols of the revolution.[10] The PRI sought to embody the revolution and, in the process, greatly shaped popular attitudes about the system. In its rhetoric, faithfully transmitted through the public education system and mass media outlets, the government consistently emphasized that the PRI embodied national unity.[11]

This strategy worked well for much of the twentieth century. For reasons discussed in earlier chapters, however, the regime's legitimacy began to falter in the late 1960s and subsequent decades. It is no coincidence, then, that Mexican political attitudes began to change during the same time period: levels of political interest and participation increased, as did commitment to democratic values.[12] By the late 1980s, for example, the number of Mexicans with an interest in politics was on a par with that of countries like Germany and the United Kingdom, and there was a much greater willingness among all Mexicans to discuss politics. Furthermore, Mexicans of all ages and socioeconomic circumstances expressed pride in their country and were more likely than in the past to favor the rule of law over strong leadership.[13] Most important, as education levels grew and as the PRI's ability to monopolize sources of information diminished, Mexicans illustrated increasingly democratic impulses by voting for candidates of the opposition.

Democratic Values in Contemporary Mexico

In trying to evaluate the strengths and prospects for democratic governance, one approach is to simply ask people whether they believe democracy is the best form of government. According to the Latinobarómetro survey, an annual study on public opinion in eighteen Latin American countries, regional support for democracy grew from 47 percent in 2001 to 61 percent in 2010.[14] However, in Mexico, the percentage of respondents voicing support for democracy proved more varied, jumping from 46 percent at the start of the Fox administration to 63 percent in his second year, but closing at 49 percent support by the end of the decade (see figure 7.1). Hence, despite the growing support for democracy that we observed in the first edition of this book, compared to the rest of the region, Mexico now falls below average in terms of popular support for democracy. On the bright side, respondents' agreement that authoritarian government is preferable in certain circumstances fell fairly steadily during the same period,

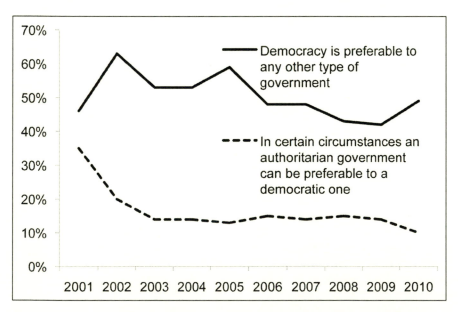

Figure 7.1. Mexican Views on Democracy in Latinobarómetro Survey, 2001–2010
Source: Latinobarómetro poll, published in the *Economist*, December 2, 2010: http://www.economist.com/node/17627929.

dropping from a high of 35 percent in 2001 to a low of 10 percent in 2010. If most Mexicans are not yet quite happy with their democracy, neither do they seem to feel inclined to support authoritarian rule.

What is especially notable about these trends is the flexibility of attitudes. This seems to suggest that the antidemocratic tendencies observed among Mexicans in the past may have been more a symptom of authoritarian rule than the result of deeply held beliefs. At the very least, they have proved sufficiently malleable to change significantly during Mexico's larger process of democratization. Thus, assuming that values and beliefs are also causally relevant—that is, significant in facilitating or undermining democracy—what might help strengthen current trends in Mexican support for democratic governance? One hypothesis is that the regionwide shift to democratic rule in Latin America might positively reinforce domestic support for democracy in Mexico. This assumes, however, that the current wave of democratic rule will endure for the foreseeable future, and that Mexican values and beliefs about democracy are somehow shaped by these international trends. Neither assumption appears to be borne out in the data described above. Perhaps a stronger hypothesis is that the performance of democratic governance, as well as Mexicans' own sense of political efficacy, will be the primary determinants of continued Mexican support for democracy over the longer term. In this sense, Mexicans' longer-term support for democracy may depend critically on the emerging political norms and attitudes about politics, to which we turn in the next two sections.

POLITICAL NORMS AND BEHAVIORS IN MEXICO: FROM CLIENTS TO CONSTITUENTS

Is it customary in your community, as it was during the heyday of New York City's Tammany Hall, to vote "early and often"? Or, more likely, do nearly half of the people in your community prefer to spend their time doing other things, rather than turn out to vote at all? Do you participate actively in sport teams, civic organizations, and neighborhood groups that help weave a tight social fabric in your community? Or do you spend most of your time isolated from your neighbors, whose names you barely know? Many scholars think that your answers to such questions may reveal a great deal about the political dynamics of your community, since they provide information about norms and behaviors that may encourage or detract from democratic political life. Norms and behaviors constitute regular but informal standards or patterns of conduct. Like formal political institutions, norms may represent widely acknowledged standards or social rules. Yet norms are informal in the sense that they are not codified, and in some cases may not be openly discussed or even consciously recognized. Norms may reflect deeply held values and beliefs such as those noted above, as well as opinions and attitudes about what constitutes acceptable social conduct.

For much of the twentieth century, Mexican political culture was strongly influenced by norms and behaviors that reinforced autocratic rule of the PRI. As we have noted in earlier chapters, the corporatist arrangement that coordinated and controlled disparate societal interests under auspices of the revolutionary party deeply influenced political behavior. By designating official labor, peasant, and middle-class interest groups and hand-selecting their leaders, the PRI was able to become highly inclusive, while at the same time maintaining a paternalistic orientation toward society. This institutional arrangement was successful at uniting the revolutionary family, and it provided access and representation to groups that otherwise might have remained outside the system. However, the corporatist system worked against the development of independent interest groups and the principle of political equality because it wholly excluded groups and individuals that were not officially sanctioned by the government. Thus corporatism was instrumental in shaping Mexican political behaviors because citizens quickly learned that there were few benefits to challenging the system, and that the only way to obtain access to government resources was to play by the PRI's rules.

Recurring economic crises and mismanagement undermined the PRI's corporatist and clientelistic system by severely reducing its ability to dole out public resources. As a result, people began looking for new methods of accessing the system. Although today only minor vestiges of the former corporatist system remain, patron-client relationships are still ubiquitous. Many Mexicans have been socialized to believe that personal relationships with people in positions of power are the most effective means of accessing the political system. So, although outright voter fraud and blatant intimidation are now rare, it is still common for both politicians and citizens to eschew political institutions and government bureaucracy in favor of private clientelistic relationships.

Civic Behavior in Contemporary Mexico

What has fundamentally changed in Mexico is the degree of influence that clients now have vis-à-vis their patrons. The advent of political competition through free and fair elections has dramatically increased the relative power of voters as "clients" and exposed their "patrons" to greater political vulnerability. Whereas the PRI's political clients once gladly traded votes and it shows signs of support for minor offerings from the ruling party's political candidates, today's candidates must clamor to attract the support of more discerning voters who have many choices—and perhaps better offers—before them.

Indeed, for most of the twentieth century Mexican voters did not have a real choice when they went to the polls because the PRI was assured victory in nearly every election, and voting was rarely a free enterprise. Under these circumstances, voters often went to the polls out of fear that failure to vote for the PRI would restrict their access to important resources (e.g., union jobs, agricultural credit, basic services)—or conversely, voters supported the PRI because they received something tangible in return (e.g., food, clothing, attention to a local problem). For these and other reasons, PRI supporters tended to be very loyal to their party, faithfully supporting all of its candidates, election after election. To the extent that Mexicans supported the opposition, it was almost always an effort to express dissatisfaction with the ruling party by casting a protest vote. However, as the PRI's legitimacy faltered during the 1980s, partisan loyalty declined and voters began to support candidates who could defeat the PRI and to focus on policy issues such as free trade and foreign investment. This was particularly true of the 2006 election, which was centered on two starkly different candidates and their opposing policy platforms.

Although the absence of reliable electoral data makes it difficult to generalize about Mexican voting behavior before 1988, it is clear that in the short span of a single generation, Mexican voters embraced democratic participation and learned to be highly informed and sophisticated voters. For example, in the 1988 election, which marked the first opportunity for voters to make a meaningful choice at the polls, it was mainly the PRI faithful who cast their votes for Salinas.[15] In general, these people tended to be less-educated females who lived in rural areas. Those who opted to oppose the PRI then had to make a choice between the PAN and Cuauhtémoc Cárdenas. Supporters of the former were more likely to be from urban areas in the north, to support neoliberal economic policies, and to attend church regularly, while Cárdenas supporters were both rural dwellers and members of the urban working class, and particularly inhabitants of Mexico City. The common denominator in this eclectic group appears to have been opposition to free trade and foreign investment.

In the 1994 presidential election, party loyalty was again very important: 65 percent of those who voted for the PRI said they always voted for the same party, and 75 percent of those who voted for Salinas also voted for Zedillo. Loyalty was also important for the opposition: more than two-thirds of all voters supported the same parties in 1988 and 1994.[16] Yet while the PRI appeared to be relatively secure among its base before 1994, the growing popularity of the opposition and the devastating effects of the 1995 peso crisis drastically eroded the size of its loyal base. Yet, the PRI was not the only party to see a decline in voter loyalty. After 1997, voters became increasingly undecided, and in 2000 fewer than half of all Mexican voters identified with any party. Party identification hit a low in 2004, when only 28.3 percent claimed that they belonged to a specific party and always voted for that party, before rebounding.[17] By 2010, only a slight majority (52 percent) claimed to identify with a particular party, while 34 percent identified themselves as independent.[18] Furthermore, it remains difficult for parties to make assumptions about who their supporters are, because traditional socioeconomic and demographic characteristics such as levels of education, gender, occupation, income level, and even region are no longer reliable predictors of partisan support.[19]

Thus, it appears that by the late 1990s a significant portion of the Mexican electorate was willing to support different parties from one election to the next, and this makes electoral outcomes much more uncertain than in the past. Uncertainty is a positive development for Mexico. Combined with an impartial and transparent electoral process, it creates incentives for citizens to pay more attention to politics, and for politicians to pay more attention to citizens. Competitiveness also lends itself to greater participation and voter turnout, since the choices on election day may be more consequential. Indeed, Mexico has seen relatively high rates of voter turnout since the onset of democratization in the late 1980s. Unlike the past when the perception of electoral fraud damaged the credibility of the system and increased abstentions, most eligible voters now eagerly participate in presidential elections (see figure 7.2).

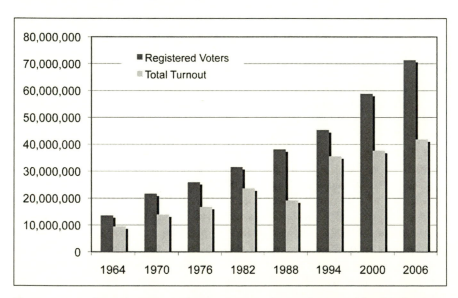

Figure 7.2. Registered Voters and Voter Turnout in Mexican Presidential Elections, 1964–2006

Source: International Institute for Democracy and Electoral Assistance. http://www.idea.int/vt/country_view.cfm?CountryCode=MX (accessed April 1, 2011).

This new dynamic has heightened the importance of campaigns and personality-based politics. Given smaller loyal party bases, candidates' personal characteristics and media outreach had a significant influence on Mexican voting behavior in the 2000 and 2006 elections. For example, in 2000, the PRI's base was smaller and the number of undecided voters was higher than it had been in the past. Moreover, the availability of more unbiased news coverage and the nationally televised debates worked in Fox's favor because they allowed him to project a positive image of a straight-talking, no-nonsense professional with the gumption to promote change. Meanwhile, Fox's negative advertisements highlighted Labastida's political and personal shortcomings and thereby helped convince undecided voters to support the PAN. Candidates and media campaigns were also at the forefront of the 2006 presidential campaign. However, unlike previous elections, policy issues were more important in the 2006 presidential election. The two frontrunners, Calderón and López Obrador, presented opposing economic platforms, and voters cast their ballots based on which plan they felt was best for Mexico's future. Also, using negative campaign tactics to smear his opponent, Calderón was ultimately more successful in convincing a slim margin of voters that a vote for López Obrador would produce undesirable consequences. As this book goes to press, the 2012 campaign has already become similarly candidate-centered, with much attention focusing on the most prominent candidate, Enrique Peña Nieto, seen by many as the young, handsome face of the new PRI.

While some Mexican voters might be bothered by the shift to flashy campaigns and smooth-talking candidates, the choice ultimately resides with them. As scholar Jonathan Fox has observed, Mexicans began making the transition from clientelism to citizenship in the 1990s, and the kind of governments that they will have from here on hinges on voters' levels of political awareness and involvement.[20] By 2002, a UN Development Programme survey provided important evidence that Mexicans were becoming much more politically engaged than in the past. For example, 81 percent of the sample reported voting in the 2000 election, 59 percent reported contributing to or actively engaging in civic or religious organizations, 40 percent participated in at least one collective demonstration, and 22 percent had contacted a government representative. Just under 30 percent reported doing all of the above.[21] Mexicans' attitudes toward the voting process have also improved. Of the small number of respondents who did not vote (19 percent), nearly 9 percent of them tried to but were unable to cast votes because they lacked the proper documents, had expired documents, or did not appear on the rolls. Seventy-three percent were either in agreement or very much in agreement that elections offer real options to choose among parties, and two-thirds agreed or very much agreed that voting allows citizens to influence political events. Less than 3 percent of respondents claimed that voting offers no option, is a farce, or makes no difference.[22] This was a significant change from the past, when the vast majority of Mexicans felt that elections were a sham.

The dual challenge the country faces is to consolidate these gains while simultaneously protecting them from erosion in the face of increased violence and intimidation by drug-trafficking organizations trying to influence the outcome of elections. The potential for such organizations to undermine the democratic electoral process was made clear in the midterm and subnational elections of 2009 and 2010, with the high number of political assassinations of candidates and officeholders in the north of Mexico. The overall climate of fear served not only as a warning to those who would use positions of power to counter the drug war, but also to voters who might support such initiatives. Whether this was a temporary setback or will become a more permanent feature of the political process, and hence Mexican political culture, remains to be seen.

MEXICAN ATTITUDES AND PUBLIC OPINION

Political attitudes and public opinion reflect individuals' current views and feelings—their psychological or emotional orientations—in relation to political phenomena, actors, and events. People's political attitudes may also include specific policy preferences regarding such things as capital punishment, gay rights, or universal health care. Or they may have to do with a person's gut feeling about a politician or idea. While an individual's political perspective can be shaped by deeply held values and beliefs that evolve over longer periods of time, attitudes and opinions can often change quite rapidly in response to experiences, circumstances, and the revelation of new information. For example, adherents to the Catholic faith have fairly predictable attitudes on abortion, as a result of beliefs formed by the position and teachings of the Church. At the same time, a voter's opinion about a given candidate depends not just on agreement or disagreement with the candidate's philosophical positions—often derived from well-entrenched values and beliefs—but also on feelings toward that candidate based on daily observations: how the candidate responds to a verbal attack, whether the candidate makes a witty and timely remark, and to what degree a candidate makes a fool of himself or herself on television.

Like all people, Mexicans have strong opinions about policies, politicians, and the political process in general. With democratization, citizens have become more forthcoming about their political attitudes, and public opinion polls and surveys are now prevalent. Virtually every day, it seems, a newspaper or polling firm has released the results of its latest survey: about the names Mexicans most prefer for their children, about their feelings regarding relationships, or who is their favorite musician or *cantante*. So too it is with regard to questions about Mexican politics. Growing interest and technical capability among academics, newspaper companies, private polling firms, and even political parties have produced some interesting findings about Mexican views and feelings about politics and political issues.

So how do Mexicans feel about politics and their political leaders? What do Mexicans care about in terms of public policy, and what do they expect from democratic governance? How do their attitudes and opinions change over time? These are questions of critical importance in any democratic political system, or at least for policy makers who wish to gauge and respond effectively to public concerns. In recent years, a plethora of data and information has become available to evaluate contemporary Mexican attitudes about politics. We may try to glean something about Mexico's political culture, for instance, by looking at attitudes toward the government. As mentioned earlier, surveys and polls suggest that while many Mexicans express support for democracy, they remain fairly skeptical of contemporary government institutions and political leaders. Indeed, when asked in July 2006—in the immediate aftermath of the presidential election—how much confidence they had in the president, the national Congress, the judicial system, and other key institutions, in several cases, barely half of the respondents expressed confidence in these institutions.[23] (See figure 7.3.)

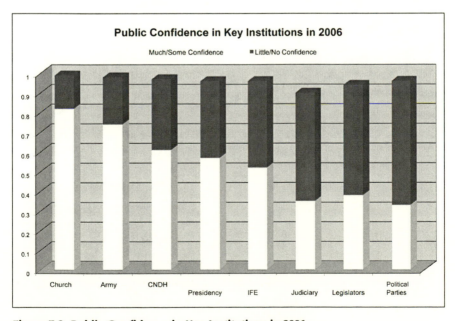

Figure 7.3. Public Confidence in Key Institutions in 2006
Source: Parametría, www. parametria.com (acccessed September 2007).

Still, it is difficult to say that Mexican skepticism about contemporary political leaders and institutions is tantamount to a lack of support for democracy. We need only look at similar polls in the United States to see that public support for Congress is generally low; people may love their own legislative representative, but they tend to despise the legislature. Moreover, it is also important to note that public opinion can be fickle, and that polls generally provide only a snapshot of respondents' sentiments at a given point in time. Indeed, if we look at approval and disapproval ratings of four key institutions in figure 7.3, we see that in 2006 the public was skeptical of political parties, lawmakers, and judges, but a majority had confidence in the IEF and the presidency. Importantly, Mexicans expressed the highest confidence in the Church and the army.

As in many countries, Mexicans' feelings about many different aspects of politics are often projected—rightly or wrongly—on the head of government. Hence, presidential approval ratings may also provide an indicator of public opinion about the political, social, and economic direction of the country. Given the social unrest and lingering divisions from his controversial election in 2006, many doubted Felipe Calderón's ability to govern effectively. However, he enjoyed relatively high approval ratings almost continuously during his first three years in office, thanks in large part to widespread support for his involving the military in Mexico's drug war (see figure 7.4). Beginning in late 2009, his support diminished somewhat due to Mexico's prolonged

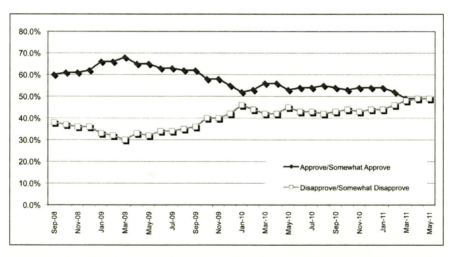

Figure 7.4. Public Approval and Disapproval Ratings for President Felipe Calderón, 2006–2011

Source: Mitofsky data for December 2006–2007 from Mitofsky-Roy Campos Tracking Poll, "Evaluación de gobierno," March and June 2007. Data for December 2006–May 2011 from Consulta Mitofsky, "Aprobación de Gobierno."

economic slowdown and the growing perception that the government was losing the war against the drug traffickers. Public opinion polls of this kind provide important feedback to politicians about the preferences and priorities of voters. In an increasingly democratic society, the president and other elected officials in Mexico have realized the importance of considering and prudently responding to such shifts in public opinion.

Indeed, Mexico's elected leaders need to take into careful consideration the issues that Mexicans feel are most important and the policy preferences that they express. In this regard, Mexicans tend to express some clear and consistent priorities and concerns in surveys and public opinion polls. For the past ten years, Mexicans have regularly identified "economic crisis" and "public insecurity" as their top two concerns (see figure 7.5). Combined economic problems (hardship, unemployment, poverty, low salaries, and inflation) have been the top concern for a majority of Mexicans for most of the last decade, while the issue of public security (crime, drug trafficking, and corruption) has become more worrisome over the same time period.

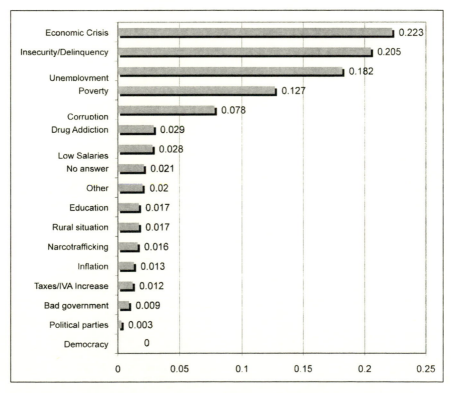

Figure 7.5. Public Opinion: Principal Problems in Mexico, Average 2000–2006
Source: Consulta Mitofsky, "Evaluación final de gobierno," November 2006.

These results are hardly surprising, since economic difficulties have been a major challenge in Mexico over the last few decades, while the country's war on drugs is a relatively recent phenomenon. Still, given that Mexico enjoyed modest economic gains from 2000 to 2005, it is notable that many Mexicans continued to feel concerns about the effects or prospects of economic crisis, more so than any other pressing policy problem, even drug trafficking. While concerns about economic hardship remained relatively constant between 2001 and 2008, they spiked in 2009 and continue to remain high, reflecting the economic difficulties that Mexico has experienced during the global recession that began in 2008.

Concerns about crime and violence increased noticeably in 2005, due largely to the outbreak of significant levels of drug-related violence. In spite of President Calderón's efforts to stop drug trafficking, public perception of problems related to public insecurity remain higher than they did during the Fox administration. In both 2005 and 2006, more than 25 percent of Mexicans polled identified crime and public insecurity as their top concern, more than any other single policy problem. This helps explain why the Calderón administration embraced a law-and-order policy agenda from the outset and earned high marks as a result, at least initially. However, as the drug war dragged on and became more violent, victory proved elusive, and public support declined. Not surprisingly, Mexicans are now more concerned with crime and violence than ever before.

CONCLUSION

Not surprisingly, Mexicans distrusted a system that, at least until recently, was overwhelmingly associated with fraud, corruption, and impunity. After decades of living in the PRI-dominated system in which election rigging, raiding public coffers, and manipulating voters was common and even expected, how could Mexicans trust or embrace their political system? Yet as we have seen, attitudes and consequently political behavior have changed significantly since the late 1980s. Generally speaking, Mexicans are now more willing to talk about and participate in the political process. They are also more inclined to believe in the value and superiority of democracy. The electorate is more sophisticated in its ability to use elections to reward and punish politicians and parties, and thereby to hold them accountable for their actions.

Undoubtedly, these changes are the result of the confluence of a number of different factors. The role of education is likely to be key. On the whole, Mexicans are better educated than they ever were in the past. Basic education and higher literacy rates have increased people's understanding of the political system and of their rights and responsibilities in a democracy.

Another important factor is access to information. While print media are still relatively expensive and have small circulations, access to political information is widely available on television—which is by far the preferred medium in Mexico.[24] Moreover, although in the past all press coverage was notoriously biased in favor of the PRI and government, many mass media outlets and Internet sources are much more independent. Therefore, citizens have access to alternative viewpoints and sources of information. Finally, the increased transparency and competitiveness of the political system have fostered greater confidence that citizen participation has a real impact. Political reform and the creation of the impartial Federal Electoral Institute have gone a long way toward convincing voters that they have meaningful choices and that votes will be counted accurately.

Like citizens in many countries, Mexicans remain distrustful of public institutions, democracy, and politicians, and they adhere to clientelistic practices. But as we have shown in this chapter, Mexicans have also become significantly more democratic in their orientation. As long as they continue to demand transparency and accountability and continue to assume the responsibilities of democratic citizenship, there is little reason to believe that authoritarian attitudes and behavior will return to past levels. Nor is it necessary for such attitudes to disappear entirely in order for Mexico to continue on its road to democracy: even in long-standing democracies there are citizens who distrust and even reject their governments. What is most important is that the majority of Mexicans come to accept that democracy is the only game in town.

8

Mexican Civil Society

If the sole measure of the vibrancy of democracy were the number of social movements and civic organizations present in a society, Mexico would likely pass muster: a recent survey estimated that there are currently more than 10,000 civic organizations in the country, almost five times more than the 2,364 that existed in 1994.[1] Yet the sheer number and exponential increase over the past thirty years, while impressive, are not by themselves evidence of a vibrant democratic society. As many scholars have pointed out, civic organizations and grassroots social movements are a key component of democracy only in so far as they provide a counterweight to the state; disseminate democratic norms like political equality, reciprocity, and trust; and disseminate democratic practices, such as organized participation and articulation of political demands.[2] Therefore, the nature of the organizations and movements also has an impact on the overall quality of a democracy. While some nongovernmental organizations in Mexico have unambiguously contributed to the democratization process by disseminating democratic norms and practices, others continue to perpetuate authoritarian and clientelistic norms and practices and therefore have a much more questionable impact.

THE EMERGENCE OF MEXICAN CIVIL SOCIETY

The conditions that led to the proliferation of civic organizations in Mexico beginning in the 1970s parallel the factors that paved the way for the rise of opposition political parties discussed in chapter 4. Yet while the rise of the political opposition unequivocally contributed to the process of democratization by introducing electoral competition, there are two reasons why the impact of societal organizations on the democratization process has been mixed. First, the ability of civil society to provide an effective counterweight to the state is hindered by the fact that many aspects of policy formation and decision making remain centralized in the executive branch. Although this dynamic began to change somewhat under the Fox administration, its persistence, combined with the prohibition on reelection and lack of territorial representation, means that interest groups and civic organizations have limited opportunities to influence policy and few incentives to lobby the legislature for policy action. Instead they must navigate the narrow and treacherous path that leads to influence with the president, governor, or mayor. Not surprisingly, those groups that have the most reliable access are those that are well established and have existing, often quasi-corporatist links to the state. As discussed in greater detail below, organized labor, one of the largest and most powerful interest groups in Mexico, while much weaker than in the past, has managed to maintain links to the state and therefore continues to exercise powerful influence over policy in sectors such as education and the petroleum industry.

Second, although there is little doubt that greater pluralism has bolstered democracy in Mexico, its overall impact on democracy is mixed. To illustrate, in 1999, Poder Ciudadano (Citizen Power), a national coalition of six hundred NGOs (nongovernmental organizations), came together to draft a national agenda that called for reforms to economic policy, recognition of indigenous rights, protection of human rights, and democratic reform, to be presented to the country's political candidates. Both President Fox and Mexico City Mayor Andrés Manuel López Obrador went on to incorporate ideas and actors from this coalition into their administrations.[3] Thus, the presence and activities of Poder Ciudadano appear to have bolstered the democratic process in Mexico. At the same time, several scholars have shown that civic organizations, especially those with few resources operating in a hierarchical environment, tend to adopt similar practices rather than promoting democratic principles. Recent survey data comparing democratic values held by members of civic organizations compared to those held by society at large have shown that the former were actually less likely to value principles such as freedom of expression and organization over economic stability, and they were only slightly more likely to believe that their opinion mattered to public officials. On a more heartening note, members of civic organizations were more likely than nonmembers to be interested in politics, participate in informal political activities (e.g., protests, sit-ins, etc.), and vote in elections.[4] It is clear, then, that the character and influence of civic organizations in Mexico is still in flux. The remainder of the chapter examines some of the most prominent groups and social movements that make up civil society, and offers some reflections on their impact on democracy in Mexico.

ORGANIZED LABOR

Although labor technically had the autonomy to organize and articulate its own demands during the period of PRI hegemony, the Mexican government exercised a considerable amount of control over this group. The executive, together with the Ministry of Labor, established the legal terms for forming unions, enacting strikes, and negotiating with employers. So while workers could form unions at any time, they were not eligible to strike or negotiate unless they met basic organizational requirements, could convince the government of the legitimacy of their demands, and were officially recognized by the government. Even officially recognized unions had to follow government-regulated procedures for contract negotiations and strikes. Thus the government's ability to grant a union official recognition—and to establish the rules of the game—formed the basis of the corporatist arrangement with organized labor and allowed the state to assert considerable political control over workers.

Why would workers and labor unions acquiesce to such government control? Some might argue that they had little choice, since the government repressed "independent" unions and any who rejected the government's corporatist arrangement. This claim accurately captures reality, but over the longer term two conditions were critical to sustaining worker support of government control. First was the postrevolutionary regime's ability to deliver important general benefits for labor, including a commitment to an economic model that provided low inflation, protection for domestic industries, and continuous growth from the 1940s through the 1960s. Members of officially recognized labor unions benefited not just from the job opportunities created by a vibrant and growing economy, but also from access to government-subsidized housing, health care, and basic consumer goods.

Labor's loyalty to the PRI during hard times can be explained by the second important element of its corporatist arrangement with organized labor: the cooptation of union leaders and organizations. The government granted union leaders tangible benefits, including government positions, political influence, and state subsidies to sustain their organizations. In return, they were expected to deliver the consistent support of labor for the PRI at the polls and at political rallies, and a compliant workforce for progovernment businesses. A worker who wanted access to scarce jobs, promotions, or perks associated with a particular job or industry had to demonstrate loyalty to the union's leadership. Individuals who rejected this arrangement were ousted from unions, and unions who refused to play by the government's rules were denied access to jobs, wage increases, and even protections afforded by the constitution and federal labor code.[5]

Despite the close relationship between labor leaders and the PRI, the economic position of organized labor steadily declined during the 1980s and 1990s. In the aftermath of serious economic crises during those decades, the government often adopted economic policies that were detrimental to the interests of the working class. For example, drastic reductions in government spending led to job cuts, wage freezes, price increases, and reduced benefits even for those belonging to sanctioned labor unions. Another reason for the change was that the neoliberal approach to economic development adopted in the mid-1980s called for cutting tariffs on imports, reducing government subsidies in most areas, and privatizing state-owned enterprises. As Middlebrook points out, "The closing or privatization of state-owned enterprises eroded what had long been the principal advantage of some of Mexico's largest and most influential unions: the ability to use their political leverage to win concessions from state managers in negotiations over wage and fringe benefit levels and contract terms."[6] Thus, organized labor lost on two counts: the economic crisis meant that the government had fewer resources to hand out, and the new economic development strategy expressly reduced both the state's role in regulating the economy and diminished the privileged position of Mexico's labor unions in the revolutionary family.

Labor's gradual decline was also facilitated by President Salinas (1988–1994), who made a concerted effort to reform state-labor relations. The relationship between Salinas and labor was strained from the beginning by the fact that the Confederation of Mexican Workers (Confederación de Trabajadores de México, CTM), the most powerful labor confederation in the country, had refused to support Salinas and his neoliberal economic agenda. Once in office, Salinas shrewdly bestowed favor on those labor leaders willing to accept his policy changes and ruthlessly purged those who did not. For example, he had the leader of the petroleum workers union arrested, and he forced the resignation of the long-standing leader of the National Union of Education Workers (Sindicato Nacional de Trabajadores de la Educación, SNTE) to make way for a new leader more receptive to decentralizing the public education system. Additionally, despite his belief that the market should be the determining force for wages, employment levels, and working conditions, Salinas used the government's power to limit strikes, intervene in negotiations between workers and employers, and minimize wage increases. Still, Salinas could not afford to completely alienate labor, since this sector's support was still essential for political stability—especially in the face of neoliberal reform. While labor's influence and privileges clearly declined during the Salinas *sexenio*, some unions were able to maintain their influence as long as they were willing to accept the new rules of the game.

With labor's gradual decline during the 1980s and 1990s, unions lost members and mobilization strength. Years of economic crisis and restructuring led to declining real wages and job losses that made union membership much less attractive than it had been in previous decades. For example, by the early 1990s there was virtually no difference in the average wages earned by union and nonunion workers, and the modest wage increases that unions did manage to secure were still well below the rate of inflation.[7] Furthermore, economic crises led to hundreds of thousands of job losses, which reduced the opportunities for labor organizations. Even after the country began its economic recovery in the late 1990s, most of the union jobs created lacked security and benefits—reinforcing the notion that union membership no longer guaranteed the perks of the past.

Meanwhile, the PRI's electoral losses and the rise of the PAN in contemporary Mexico ensured that organized labor would not regain its former privileged position. Like many members of the PAN, Vicente Fox was highly critical of traditional state-labor relations, not only because of his ideological conviction that the state should play a very limited role in negotiations between labor and management, but also for the obvious political reason that organized labor's support was essential to the PRI's hegemony. Therefore, comprehensive reform of the labor code became one of his policy priorities. Ultimately, Fox did relatively little to alter state-labor relations because the PRI maintained such a strong presence in Congress, and because it was clear even to Fox that for the country to enjoy political stability and attract foreign investment, harmonious relations with organized labor were essential.

Like Fox, President Calderón attempted to introduce several initiatives aimed at challenging the power of organized labor. These initiatives met with mixed success. For example, PEMEX's notoriously powerful union remained largely untouched, and succeeded in securing a 21 percent pay increase for its members in 2009 even as the company saw a 20 percent drop in production and a 40 percent drop in exports.[8] Still, Calderón did manage to strike a blow to a powerful government union by closing Central Light and Power (Luz y Fuerza del Centro, LFC) in November 2009, citing the parastatal energy company's corruption and inefficiency. In 2008, the company's service to 25 million people had lost twice as much money as it took in from energy sales. The closure resulted in the dismissal of the forty-four thousand members of the company's sole union, the Mexican Syndicate of Electricians (Sindicato Mexicano de Electricistas, SME), with two-and-a-half years of severance pay. Calderón's decision was criticized by thousands of protesters, but it also drew support from customers who suffered from high prices, poor service, and even extortion rackets by company officials.[9]

Ironically, another of Calderón's most notable accomplishments vis-à-vis labor was to forge a strong working relationship with the SNTE, Mexico's largest teachers' union. The SNTE was founded in 1943 from the various regional teachers' confederations then in existence. Although it has experienced internal factional splintering in recent years, the SNTE maintains an impressive 1.5 million members and remains the largest teachers' union in Latin America. The union's leader, Esther Elba Gordillo, formerly secretary general of the PRI and now a prominent member of PANAL, maintains significant influence over the union and established important ties to the Calderón administration that netted important gains for both sides. For example, without Gordillo's support, Calderón would have found it impossible to privatize the state workers' pension fund.[10] For Gordillo's part, the number of teaching jobs remained high, even during the economic downturn, and the Calderón administration provided millions of pesos for teacher training and other programs. Perhaps the most high-profile concession made to Gordillo was the appointment of her son-in-law to the position of undersecretary of public education.

Dissidents within the SNTE have criticized Gordillo's alliance with the Calderón administration and efforts to privatize the pension and other measures as selling out her rank and file. Several times since 2006, members have taken to the streets to protest the government's policy initiatives and attempts to reform different aspects of the education system. Nevertheless, Gordillo's power remains strong, and already there are signs that she will parlay it for further gains by establishing ties to Enrique Peña Nieto, the PRI's front-runner for the 2012 presidential election.[11]

Others have argued that Gordillo has prevented the government from implementing desperately needed education reform.[12] Indeed, under her leadership, the SNTE has remained a hierarchical organization where jobs and career advancement are based on clientelism and personalism, or corruption, rather than on ability, merit, and democratic elections. Furthermore, the union blocked attempts at reform by rejecting teacher evaluations and accountability proposed by the Calderón administration.[13] Additionally, internal divisions within the union have had a negative impact on the overall quality of basic education in Mexico.[14] Given this reality, it is difficult to say that the SNTE has contributed to the democratization process in Mexico. Nevertheless, the union's internal shortcomings have not prevented it from performing the important function of aggregating and representing the interests of its members—an essential feature of any democracy.

THE PRIVATE SECTOR

Private business was not formally organized and recognized within the corporatist system that supported the PRI, in large part because the rhetoric of the revolution was focused on the rights of those excluded by the Porfirian economic and political models. Yet unlike other groups excluded from the revolutionary family, the private sector depended on and benefited from the state for a number of reasons. First, there were often close family ties between the private sector and the ruling elite. Indeed, while it was an un-written rule that entrepreneurs were not to seek public office, it was quite common for politicians to be closely related to businessmen by blood or marriage. Second, Mexico's industrialization strategy and macroeconomic philosophy of state-led development (discussed in chapter 9) were highly beneficial to domestic industrialists, who enjoyed protectionist measures and "Mexicanization laws" that provided significant economic benefits and insulated them from foreign competition.[15] Finally, the private sector exerted important influence on economic policy because it was organized in a number of independent business associations that were not shy about expressing their views or pressing the government when necessary.

During the era of PRI hegemony, businesses were required to belong to at least one voluntary association. This legal stipulation had the effect of organizing the private sector in ways that it otherwise might have eschewed, and it gave rise to a number of associations that played an important role in the political process. Because the PRI did not allow entrepreneurs formal access within the party via elected or appointed offices, voluntary business associations in Mexico became the most important channel for the private sector's political influence when it perceived a threat of undesired state intervention into the economy (e.g., new labor laws, establishment of new state-owned enterprises, land expropriations).[16] By far the most influential association was, and continues to be, the Mexican Council of Business Executives (Consejo Mexicano de Hombres de Negocios, CMHN), a highly selective group of approximately forty owners and executives of Mexico's largest, most important firms (e.g., Telmex, Cemex, Modelo, Banamex, etc.), which gathers monthly to discuss common issues and, importantly, to meet with cabinet-level government officials for an informal exchange of ideas on timely economic issues. Despite the PRI's lock on power, this group was commonly consulted by government officials before substantial policy changes were implemented. In cases where this failed to happen (changes to tax policy in the 1970s, bank nationalization in 1982), the CMHN and other associations vociferously and publicly denounced the government. The CMHN also helped support and fund other important business associations such as the Business Coordinating Council (Consejo Coordinador Empresarial, CCE), an organization that originally brought together industry, commerce, agriculture, finance, and employers in a com-mon effort to counter President Echeverría's leftist reforms. As a united force, the CCE was able to challenge the government and gain concessions in ways that single organizations acting unilaterally could not and dared not for fear of reprisals. Thus, because of their size (both in financial and numerical terms), sophisticated organization, and independence, business organizations exercised a level of clout uncommon to groups not formally included in the PRI's corporatist system.

Not surprisingly, the introduction of the neoliberal economic model and electoral competition changed the dynamics of state-business relations in Mexico. These changes coincided with a desire on the part of the private sector to play a more active political role. President López Portillo's unilateral nationalization of the banks in 1982, coupled with the country's devastating debt crisis, shattered the private sector's confidence in the existing system and prompted many to seek alternate forms of pressing their interests.[17] In this sense it is not a coincidence that members of the business community (e.g., Manuel Clouthier and Vicente Fox) began to increasingly support opposition parties, particularly the PAN, and run for office themselves.[18]

New opportunities to influence and participate in the electoral process, combined with the repeal in 1996 of the legal requirement that business maintain membership in a voluntary association, reduced the size and importance of some business associations. However, others played a pivotal role in the economic transition to a more market-driven model when the government created an opportunity to play a formal political role in the negotiation of the North American Free Trade Agreement (NAFTA). The Salinas administration endorsed the CCE's creation of a trade advisory group, the Coordinating Body of Foreign Trade Business Associations (Coordinadora de Organismos Empresariales de Comercio Exterior, COECE), whose purpose was to collect and organize information that would help shape Mexico's proposed trade agreement. This group was the business sector's only representative and, interestingly, the administration refused to entertain individual or personal overtures from outside the COECE to influence the negotiations.[19] While the invitation to participate in the NAFTA negotiation process was in many ways unprecedented and reflected respect for the clout and insight of the group, the creation and activities of the COECE also laid bare important internal divisions within the private sector. The first was between big business, which was already active in the international market and looked forward to increased access to the U.S. and Canadian markets, and smaller firms that produced primarily for domestic consumers and stood to suffer from foreign competition in the Mexican market. The second was between agriculture and industry, which would have to adapt to the new free trade regime, and banks, which would remain protected from foreign competition. These divisions made it difficult for the COECE to speak with one voice and created an opportunity for the opposition parties to court small and medium-size businesses and others marginalized in the negotiation process. Ironically, for many of these groups, increased electoral competition did not bring better representation of their interests because their business associations no longer had the internal coherence, resources, and membership to lobby effectively. Yet subsequent legislation and actions by President Zedillo and his successors helped address some of the unmet needs of those who felt that NAFTA in its original form disproportionately favored big business and financial institutions. [20]

One element of the neoliberal economic model that benefited Mexican entrepreneurs tremendously was the move to privatize state-owned enterprises. The sell-off of companies such as the telecommunications firm Telmex allowed highly capitalized businessmen (e.g., members of the CMHN) to use their strong connection to the government to buy these firms on advantageous terms and to develop monopolies, which have made them billionaires but are now widely recognized to stymie competition and economic growth. The ability of these groups to maintain their monopolies in the face of strong foreign and domestic criticism attests to the continued strength of the business community and its influence on policy makers, and it suggests that while big business has done an excellent job of promoting its own interests, the group has done little to promote democracy more broadly.

THE MEDIA

As we saw in previous chapters, the Mexican media played an important role in supporting the PRI government during its era of electoral hegemony. Although there was a fair amount of private ownership in broadcast and print media, both types of outlet developed symbiotic and, in some cases, dependent relationships with the government, in which the press provided selective, generally favorable coverage of the regime in exchange for generous subsidies, outright payoffs, and lucrative broadcast concessions. As Lawson argues, it was the combination of government control of the media's agenda, silence on delicate issues, and partisan bias in favor of the PRI that created a relatively docile and dependent press for much of the twentieth century. [21] While media owners continue to have ties to government, the press in Mexico is today much more independent and plays an important role in supporting democracy by providing alternative sources of information and serving as a government watchdog. The transition of print and broadcast media from virtual arms of the government to independent components of civil society occurred at different times for slightly different reasons. We discuss each of these below.

Print Media

Mexico has always had a large number of periodicals, yet until the early 1970s, virtually all newspaper coverage of political matters favored the ruling party and provided no meaningful outlet for the opposition. Like the corporatist system, the PRI constructed a top-down, mutually beneficial arrangement in which newspapers received generous government support in exchange for favorable coverage of the regime. Those media owners, editors, or journalists who refused to play by the rules were alternately bought off, harassed, or coerced so that they did not pose a threat to the regime. This system was facilitated by the fact that reporters were poorly paid and exercised low journalistic standards because they often lacked advanced education and training in investigative techniques. As a result, they were susceptible to the *embutes*, or bribes, offered by government officials that regularly amounted to more than their official salaries. The government used other types of payments as well. For example, newspaper owners benefited from newsprint and advertising heavily subsidized by the government. The distribution of newsprint was controlled and funded solely by Paper Products and Imports (Productora e Importada de Papel, Sociedad Anónima, PIPSA), a state-owned company. PIPSA not only had the ability to dramatically reduce the costs of production (by issuing cheap credit, paying shipping costs, or selling newsprint at reduced prices), it also gave the government a handy form of leverage when individual publications refused to play by the government's rules.

Another type of payment was government advertising, particularly by government-owned or -supported banks and firms, which made up the vast majority of newspapers' revenue and, like access to newsprint, could be withheld in order to force compliance with the government's rules. One of the most blatant forms of government propaganda was the *gacetilla*, a story prepared by government officials to promote a particular policy or individual, but disguised as a real news article. Newspapers were paid generously for including the *gacetillas* in their publications, and this type of paid advertising made up a significant portion of income for both journalists and newspapers.

While this system worked well for several decades, the same political and economic events that prompted the decline of the PRI also fundamentally altered the state's relationship with the print media. After the Tlatelolco massacre and several government crackdowns in the early 1970s, many newspaper journalists began to reexamine their previous complicity and take a more critical stance vis-à-vis the government. During this time many new and independent publications, including *Proceso, unomásuno, La Jornada, El Financiero, Siglo 21, El Diario de Yucatán* and *El Norte/Reforma* emerged and founded the beginnings of Mexico's truly independent press. The transition of Mexico's press was not without consequences. In order to forestall the change, the government stepped up its repressive tactics, and between 1980 and 1996 approximately sixty journalists were murdered.[22]

In addition to the political causes of change, recurrent economic crises made it increasingly difficult for the government to pay off the press, and this reduced the incentives for reporters to provide favorable coverage of the PRI. Additionally, the adoption of neoliberalism made it more difficult to justify such high state support of the media. In the early 1990s, President Salinas altered the old system by eliminating bribes from Los Pinos; drastically reducing government advertising, credit, and subsidies on newsprint; and forcing newpapers to pay their taxes. Together these factors forced newspapers to become more economically independent, and when combined with the new, more professional practices adopted by journalists, created the conditions for a more capable and independent press. Today, the quality of Mexico's print news is among the strongest in Latin America and offers Mexican citizens investigative reporting and a wide variety of viewpoints on political actors and issues.

Broadcast Media

If the relationship between the state and print media was cozy during the era of PRI hegemony, the relationship between the state and broadcast media was an even clearer form of collusion, in which the state allowed a single network to control virtually all television broadcasting. From the early 1970s to the early 1990s, Televisa enjoyed a near monopoly on television broadcasting in Mexico: it held 80 percent of the audience, the first cable television license, a majority of the country's satellite capturing stations (built by the government), and virtually all of the television frequencies. Given such generous concessions, it is not surprising that Televisa's coverage of the ruling party was always favorable and almost never overt in its criticism, even in the wake of clear government failures like its inept response to the 1985 earthquakes and its shenanigans surrounding the 1988 presidential election.

At least three factors led to the gradual opening of Mexico's broadcast media in the 1990s. First was the government's decision to privatize some channels, which led to the creation of several stations with independent voices, including channels 40 and 22. The heaviest hitter among them was TV Azteca, which became Televisa's biggest rival; over time, competition between the two led both to adopt more independent reporting. Second was the increased demand from civil society for new and independent media voices willing to represent and discuss the myriad issues associated with Mexico's democratic opening. By the early 1990s, it was increasingly clear that Televisa was out of touch with political reality, when it insisted on supporting the party even in the face of calamitous economic and political failures. Finally, the death of Televisa's owner, Emilio Azcárraga Jr., who was sometimes "more pro-PRI than the PRI itself," paved the way for the network to find a new strategy and attitude toward democracy.[23]

Together these and other factors helped shift Mexico's broadcast media system from a noncompetitive, monolithic extension of the state to one with multiple players and viewpoints. Nowhere was this shift more noticeable than in televised election coverage. Whereas the PRI received 80 percent of all television coverage leading up to the 1988 election, in 1994 its coverage had declined to approximately 50 percent, and by 1997 the PRI was featured in only 34 percent of television airtime. Equally important was the shift in the tone of reporting. While the PRI was presented as the only viable choice in 1988 and 1994, by 1997 the opposition's candidates were treated as serious contenders, and coverage of the PRI was not always positive.[24] This trend continued into the 2000s and indeed is one of the reasons why Mexicans chose non-PRI candidates in the first two presidential elections of the twenty-first century.

Today Mexicans continue to enjoy relatively balanced broadcast and print media coverage, and they have had roundly positive effects on the development of Mexico's democracy. Whereas the press once helped legitimize and reinforce the dominance of the PRI, print and broadcast media now provide alternative sources of information and monitor government officials' behavior so that citizens are much better informed about political matters (see table 8.1). Nevertheless, challenges remain. Broadcast media are still dominated by a few powerful actors that often take pro-government, if not pro-PRI, stances and use their influence to protect their oligopoly, often

Table 8.1. The Political Effects of Mexico's Media

Media under PRI Regime (1930–1980s)	*Media during Transition to Democracy (early 1990s)*	*Political Effects of a More Independent Media (mid-1990s–early 2000s)*
Government controls the media's agenda	Media exercises more independence on what it will cover	Coverage of civil society legitimizes and fosters collaboration
Media remains silent on issues that might hurt the government	Begins to investigate issues previously omitted from coverage	Coverage of scandals provokes further rejection of PRI
Media blatantly favored the PRI in its coverage of policies and elections	More balanced coverage of campaigns and public officials	Balanced campaign coverage increases support for opposition

Source: Chappell Lawson, *Building the Fourth Estate: Democratization and the Rise of a Free Press in Mexico* (Berkeley: University of California Press, 2002), 180.

at the expense of consumers' economic interests. Furthermore, freedom of the press is incomplete in Mexico, since journalists are still commonly harassed, threatened, and even killed for reporting on delicate matters such as human rights violations and drug trafficking. Indeed, reporters and editors from small regional newspapers who have sought to publicize the nature and effects of the drug war have been targeted by drug-trafficking organizations, making Mexico one of the most dangerous countries in the world for journalists.[25] Furthermore, while journalists now openly criticize public officials, they are often subject to both self-censorship and outside censorship when they cover important groups and actors such as the Catholic Church, influential individuals (e.g., Carlos Slim), advertisers, and drug traffickers.[26] So while Mexico's press has done much to strengthen civil society and promote democracy, societal and political conditions continue to put limits on the media's freedom and independence.

THE ROMAN CATHOLIC CHURCH

Despite the fact that the vast majority of Mexicans (88 percent) are Roman Catholic and consider themselves religious, the relationship between the Roman Catholic Church and the government was tense until the mid-1990s. As discussed in chapters 1 and 2, during the postindependence and revolutionary periods the government sought to limit the role of the Church in state affairs, and in the 1917 constitution went so far as to deny it (and other religious organizations) legal standing. The rift between church and state widened during and in the aftermath of the Cristero rebellion in the late 1920s, and it settled into a modus vivendi in which the Church refrained from participating in political matters and the state did not interfere in religious matters. In general, this arrangement was stable, although bishops would sometimes comment on government policies, such as family planning, that were thought to contradict the teachings of the Church. This activity was, strictly speaking, illegal and often met with criticism from the government and those who argued for the clear separation of church and state. During this time, the political influence of religious organizations was also limited by the fact that they were legally excluded from the corporatist arrangement and therefore had minimal access to decision makers.

The established modus vivendi was abruptly upended in 1986, when Church officials suspended church services and issued public condemnations to protest the PRI's use of electoral fraud in state elections.[27] In 1992, after several years of animosity, tension between the Church and the state eased when the Salinas administration backed a constitutional amendment that granted the Church (and other religious organizations) legal status; restored their right to own property and capital; and reinstated the right of the clergy to comment on political issues as long as they did not endorse or condemn candidates for public office or run for office themselves.[28]

Since that time, the Church has not shied away from criticizing government policies that contradict its teachings, such as family planning, the introduction of sex education in schools, and laws permitting abortion and gay marriage. Furthermore, some individual members of the clergy have embraced the invitation to participate more publicly in political life. For example, many have issued their views on the importance of democracy in pastoral letters and organized democracy workshops to encourage parishioners to vote and participate in other forms of political expression, both to support the democratization process and to ensure that the politicians elected represent their political views. [29] Perhaps the most high-profile instance of a clergy member advocating political action was the bishop of San Cristóbal de las Casas, Samuel Ruíz, who throughout the 1990s openly sided with indigenous groups against the government in their quest for democracy, autonomy, and redress. His efforts to mediate the conflict were largely praised inside Mexico, despite the discomfort they caused the Mexican Roman Catholic Church and the Vatican.

The Church has also had an important, if more indirect, influence on politics through the many nongovernmental organizations that it sponsors or informs. Beginning in the mid-1980s, a number of Catholic religious orders began to sponsor or influence NGOs that focused on the protection of human rights in Mexico and Central America. Currently, two-thirds of all NGOs in Mexico have a religious affiliation or origin (though not all are Catholic), and many have actively promoted issues such as electoral transparency, social justice, the alleviation of poverty, and the protection of human rights.[30]

While most Mexicans feel that religion plays an important role in their lives, the majority also believe in the importance of a clear distinction between church and state, and they do not believe that politicians should pass laws according to their religious beliefs.[31] As in the United States, there are geographic areas where religious conservatives make up the majority of the voting population, and public policies often reflect their views. For example, in the state of Guanajuato, abortion is illegal under virtually all circumstances, including pregnancies that occur as a result of rape and incest. Meanwhile, in Mexico City, where the population is much more secular, abortion and gay marriage are both legal. The juxtaposition of such different laws reflects not only the heterogeneity of Mexican religious values but also the varied influence that religious groups have on the policy-making process.

WOMEN

In many ways, the Mexican revolutionaries were ahead of their time when it came to gender relations: divorce and remarriage were legalized in 1914, and the 1917 Law of Family Relations gave women the right to own property and equal rights in marriage, including the right to receive alimony and equal custody of children.[32] However, the 1917 constitution did not grant women the right to vote. Claiming that they lacked the capacity to participate in politics, the framers of the constitution refused to extend voting rights to women. Universal suffrage was not present in Mexico until 1953, when women were granted the right to vote in national elections. Yet long before that time, Mexican women were politically active. As noted in chapter 2, women actively participated in the revolution as spies, arms smugglers, and *soldaderas* (a combination of companion, cook, laundress, nurse, and soldier) for the rebel armies.[33] Women from the upper social classes formed clubs and organizations to support leading figures in the revolution, like Francisco I. Madero and Venustiano Carranza.

According to scholar Victoria Rodríguez, a unified women's movement first emerged in 1935 through the Sole Front for Women's Rights (Frente Unico Pro Derechos de la Mujer, FUPDM), an organization that brought together women and women's organizations from a variety of ideological and socioeconomic backgrounds and lobbied for equal voting rights and a variety of other social reforms concerning children and indigenous women.[34] After some notable victories in these areas in the early 1950s, the women's movement essentially went dormant until the late 1960s, when it reemerged and, like many other social movements, worked to raise awareness about social and economic discrimination as well as inequality in Mexico.

During the 1970s and 1980s, feminists were active in a number of areas, pressing for new laws to protect women's reproductive rights and establishing publications, academic programs, and support organizations (e.g., shelters, rape crisis centers). Much of this activity, especially in the aftermath of the economic crisis of 1982 and the devastating earthquakes in Mexico City in 1985, was incorporated into a larger movement to protest the government's neglect of the poor, lower, and middle classes. In other words, women's political activism broadened its focus to include issues that often had a disproportionate effect on women, rather than remain narrowly focused on what are often considered women's issues. This trend continued into the 1990s, and the women's movement continued to encompass a variety of goals, including more government attention to poverty, crime, and violence; better access to education; legislation to promote social and economic equality in the workplace; and efforts to promote greater female participation in politics.

During the Fox administration, Congress created the National Women's Institute (Instituto Nacional de las Mujeres, INMujeres) for the purpose of advancing the status of women in society. The Calderón administration bolstered this effort by giving the institute added power and a budget of 7 billion pesos, and by setting the goal of full gender equality in Mexico by 2012.[35] Yet perhaps the truest testament to women's progress in the Mexican political sphere is the fact that many so-called gender issues are now incorporated into mainstream politics.[36] For example, in 2007 the Mexico City Assembly passed a law making abortion legal and free in Mexico City for women over the age of eighteen during the first twelve weeks of pregnancy. While the measure remains highly controversial and has led to some political backlash, it passed due to the efforts of a broad array of women's organizations and because it enjoyed support from both the general population in the capital and male city assembly members.[37]

Women have significantly increased their role in Mexican politics by joining the ranks of political parties. All political parties in Mexico count on women as members, activists, and loyalists, yet until the mid-1990s, it was uncommon for women to hold positions of power within party organizations and rare for women to represent their parties as candidates for public office. This situation has changed somewhat, thanks in part to the recognition that women have long played an important role in party activities and in many cases are as well suited as their male counterparts for public office. But women have also been given a boost by an electoral law passed by the IFE in 2000, which requires that women constitute a minimum of 30 percent of candidates from each party. Without a doubt, this gender quota has contributed to an increased number of women running for political office in Mexico. Whereas in 1997 women accounted for only 25 percent of all national-level candidates, in 2000 they accounted for 34 percent. In the 2000 elections for the Chamber of Deputies, women accounted for 38 percent of all candidates.[38] However, initially there was no provision to specify where women should be positioned on a party's electoral list. As a result, it was common for parties to name female candidates as substitutes or place them at the bottom of the electoral lists to reduce their chances of winning a seat.[39] This practice has declined since 2003, when a new law specified that female candidates must run as regular candidates in order to meet the quota and that they cannot be relegated to the bottom of the list.[40]

The gender quota law notwithstanding, the three major parties in Mexico have differed significantly in their willingness to nominate female candidates and allow women to serve as party leaders. The PRD adopted a 20 percent quota in 1990, long before the IFE made it mandatory for all parties, and stipulated that every third candidate (on the party list) should be female.[41] Moreover, the PRD's quota required that women have at least 30 percent representation in the party's executive committee, and it is common for women to serve in that party's highest positions of power. For example, Amalia García was the party's president from 1999 to 2002, followed by Rosario Robles. Robles also represented her party as Mexico City's mayor in 1999.[42]

Within the PRI, women have also had success in obtaining leadership positions. María de los Ángeles Moreno and Dulce María Sauri both served as the party's president, and Socorro Díaz Palacios and Esther Elba Gordillo served in PRI's second highest position of secretary-general. However, in general, women face significant obstacles to advancement within the party. For example, despite having adopted a 30 percent quota in 1993, the PRI regularly ignored the quota or relegated women to inferior positions on electoral lists, or chose women as candidates for districts and cities of little importance to the party.

Of the three major parties, the PAN is the only one that did not adopt a gender quota before 2000 and in fact challenged Coahuila's state gender quota law in the Supreme Court. Despite the party's reticence to use quotas to increase female representation, women have come to play a more important role in the PAN's membership in the past decade. After the 2009 midterm elections, one-third of the PAN's federal deputies were women, and Josefina Vázquez Mota was a leading contender for the party's 2012 presidential nomination. Thus on the whole, women appear to have fared about as well (or as poorly) in the PAN as their counterparts in other parties.[43] Clearly, all three parties can do much more to promote women within their organizations, since none has consistently upheld the 30 percent rule when it comes to women in leadership positions within the party. In this sense, the parties' outward support for women belies the stronger belief that women are inferior political candidates. While some women may indeed be weaker because they lack the experience or training of their male counterparts, this is not always the case.

Given that women face such serious obstacles to advancement in their own parties, it is hardly a surprise that they are also underrepresented in government. Figure 8.1 demonstrates that the number of women in the Mexican legislature has increased at a steady rate. By 2010, the percentage of female legislators reached an all-time high at 133 deputies (26 percent) and 27 senators (21.1 percent). While these numbers are significant and compare favorably to most other countries in the Americas, including the United States, they still fall short of the IFE's goal of 30 percent and are a far cry from 51 percent, the share of women in Mexico's population. Moreover, women who are elected to the legislature tend to sit on less influential committees that have traditionally been deemed more appropriate for women (e.g., Gender and Equity, Culture, Civil Protection, Health, and Social Development).

In contrast to the other areas of government, women have a long and impressive history of representation in the Mexican judiciary. The first woman

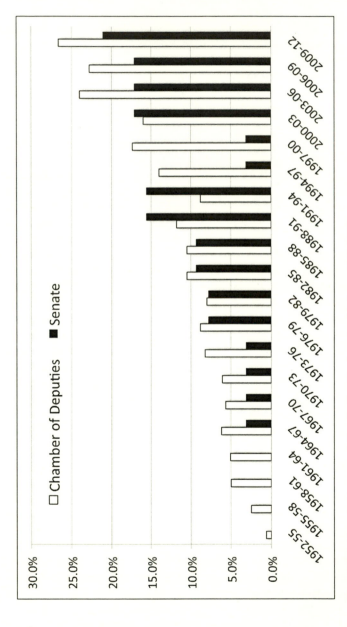

Figure 8.1. Female Representation in the Mexican Legislature, 1952–2012

Source: Victoria E. Rodríguez, *Women in Contemporary Mexican Politics* (Austin: University of Texas Press, 2003), table 4.1 and www. camaradediputados.gob.mx, www.senado.gob.mx.

was appointed to the Supreme Court in 1961, and by the late 1980s, women comprised roughly 10 percent of the judicial branch's top officials. These numbers continued to increase in the 1990s, when women accounted for 19 percent of Supreme Court justices, 15 percent of federal magistrates, and 24 percent of judges.[44] The number of women declined somewhat after the reorganization of the judiciary in 1995. In 2010, only two of eleven members of the Supreme Court were female: Justice Olga María del Carmen Sánchez Cordero, and Justice Margarita Beatríz Luna Ramos.

Like most countries, Mexico has never elected a female head of state, and only a few women from minor parties have ever run for president. Their relatively poor showing suggests that the women who have run for president were not strong candidates and/or that many Mexicans were reluctant to elect a woman as their leader. It will be interesting to see whether the PAN's Vázquez Mota can overcome these obstacles, should she be chosen to represent her party in the upcoming election. While Mexico has never had a female president, women have held appointed posts within the executive branch: between 1976 and 2010, ten women served as cabinet ministers. The first major appointment was made in 1998, when Ernesto Zedillo chose Rosario Green as Mexico's first female secretary of foreign relations. Vicente Fox appointed three women to his cabinet, but only one occupied a top-tier position (as the head of social development). Felipe Calderón's cabinet improved on this slightly with four female cabinet appointees, including those in two top positions: Georgina Kessel (energy secretary) and Patricia Espinosa Castellano (foreign secretary); in the second half of his term he appointed Marisela Morales to the post of attorney general.

If women have been underrepresented at the national level, the problem is more severe in state and local governments. Only a handful of women have been governors, and nationally, women rarely comprise more than 15 to 20 percent of state legislators.[45] Female representation at the municipal level is even more disappointing. Between 2000 and 2005, only 3.5 percent of mayors and less than 20 percent of city council members were women. One small recent advance for women is that whereas in 1995, female mayors tended to govern smaller, more impoverished municipalities, by 2004, they were equally likely to be found in larger municipalities with higher average levels of income and living standards.[46] Yet because women continue to be so severely underrepresented at the subnational levels, states have increasingly begun to adopt gender quota laws for state and local elections.

The incorporation of women as political equals is essential for democracy; however, the fact that women have become more active in the political sphere should not by itself be taken as proof that Mexico is more democratic. In fact, women may be just as inclined as men to use undemocratic tactics and to reinforce hierarchical patterns of behavior if they have incentives to do so. Like all citizens, the women interested in promoting democracy must adopt appropriate norms and practices. Many times they encounter these incentives and opportunities less through formal political institutions than through informal ones such as grassroots organizations, which we discuss below. Women's community activism has been important in Mexico's democratic transition not only because, in many cases, it led the government to address key citizen demands, but also because it gave women valuable political experience and likely facilitated their entry into the formal political arena.

GRASSROOTS ORGANIZATIONS

From the 1980s to the present, a tremendous number of grassroots organizations have emerged on the political landscape in Mexico. Grassroots social mobilization has taken a variety of forms, but all have expressed dissatisfaction with the status quo and sought to influence policy and government decisions from outside the formal political system. In this section, we examine the role of three different methods of activism: social protest movements, civic organizations, and armed rebellion. Each represents a different method of interaction with the state, and together they provide a snapshot of the dynamism and importance of grassroots organizations and, simultaneously, a clearer understanding of the failures of the Mexican political system to address the needs of different groups in society.

Social Protest

Social protests tend to arise when communities come together to demand government attention to a specific issue or problem that they feel has been inadequately addressed. In Mexico, years of economic crisis and corruption created a legacy of government inaction and ineptitude (e.g., failure to provide housing or basic public services such as water, electricity, trash removal, etc.) that gave rise to a plethora of urban social movements and protests. Some of the most successful movements were organized and orchestrated by neighborhood associations, student activists, and other groups that coordinated protest strategies and marshaled supporters in great numbers to put pressure on officials to provide greater access to land as well as more and better housing. These urban popular movements were highly successful, not only at securing more housing for the dispossessed but also at planning and negotiating the formation of new urban neighborhoods. And while their tactics often involved breaking the law (by illegally settling on appropriated land and tapping into water and electricity services), it can also be said that these movements contributed to the development of Mexican civil society by providing an avenue for mass participation and adopting internal institutions that allowed citizens to express their opinions and to be involved in decision making. In this way, urban popular movements led to a number of notable accomplishments, such as successful petitions for health clinics, waste disposal, paved streets, and new bus routes, as well as greater access to land and housing.

As in many countries, social protest in Mexico occurred when formal political channels either did not work or were not accessible to citizens. In most cases, the movements represented impoverished and uneducated people who initially viewed their options for producing change as very limited. Furthermore, many of the leaders of these social protests did not start out with the idea that they were engaging in political activism. Rather, they decided to take action only because they had no other way of resolving their problems. Women were often at the heart of urban protest movements, because problems associated with public service provision disproportionately affected their ability to carry out their everyday responsibilities as homemakers and breadwinners.

One particularly high-profile social protest occurred in the city of Monterrey in the early 1980s, when women from different levels of income and education came together to put pressure on local and state governments to extend basic water services to the many areas of the city with inadequate access to water service.[47] As Vivienne Bennett explains, women in this protest movement used several tactics to force the government's hand, including large-scale rallies in front of public officials' offices, washing their laundry and bathing their children in public fountains, and staging sit-ins in government buildings. They also used more radical and disruptive methods such as roadblocks that effectively stopped all vehicular traffic in downtown Monterrey, and seizing "water authority vehicles and . . . holding vehicle and driver hostage until water service was improved."[48] Various neighborhoods in Monterrey used these tactics repeatedly over a five-year period and then disappeared abruptly when the government finally resolved the problems with water service provision.

Today, Mexicans continue to use mass mobilization to express their dissatisfaction with the government. For example, in late 2006 a teachers' strike in the state capital of Oaxaca quickly grew into a large amalgamation of disenchanted groups intent on demonstrating their anger over the dire living conditions and the dearth of education and employment opportunities in the state of Oaxaca. Together these groups formed the Popular Assembly of Oaxacan Peoples (Asamblea Popular de los Pueblos de Oaxaca, APPO) and carried out blockades of important toll roads, sit-ins and vandalism of government offices, the takeover of local radio and TV stations, and violent clashes with the police.[49] Later that year, losing presidential candidate Andrés Manuel López Obrador mobilized tens of thousands to march through Mexico City to protest the election results, and in the summer of 2008, hundreds of thousands of people fed up with crime and insecurity took to the streets of all thirty-two states to demand a more effective response from the Calderón administration.[50]

More recently, in May 2011, relatives of victims of drug violence and various civic organizations participated in a march from Cuernavaca to Mexico City to express their rejection of the government's military strategy against drug-trafficking organizations, which claimed roughly forty thousand lives between 2006 and 2011. At its apogee, the March for Peace with Justice and Dignity included tens of thousands of supporters and a citizens' pact that called for identifying the victims of drug violence and solving the crimes that led to their deaths; a new, nonmilitary strategy; a stepped-up effort to combat corruption and impunity; a focused attack on money laundering; immediate attention to societal problems that contribute to broken societies (e.g., education, health, employment); and participatory democracy.[51] Given that Calderón's response was to reaffirm the importance and effectiveness of the military strategy, it is not clear that the March for Peace will succeed in bringing about changes in the short term. However, there is little doubt that mass mobilizations such as these are an important part of the democratic process because they provide opportunities for citizens to freely organize, participate, and express their views on issues they believe are important. Moreover, mass demonstrations and social movements tend to create voters out of citizens who previously felt left out of the political process, a phenomenon that may not bode well for policy makers who choose to downplay their importance.

Civic Organizations: Alianza Cívica

While social movements tend to arise to address a specific problem and then disappear, civic organizations are institutionalized groups with greater permanence. One of the most notable civic organizations in Mexico is Civic Alliance (Alianza Cívica, AC), a collection of approximately four hundred NGOs and civic groups that joined forces in the aftermath of the fraud-ridden presidential election of 1988 for the purpose of ensuring fairness and transparency in elections. Very active throughout the 1990s, with chapters in twenty-nine of the country's thirty-one states, AC regularly monitored elections (deploying nearly forty thousand poll watchers for the 1994 presidential election), evaluated media coverage of elections for signs of bias, and worked to promote greater awareness of voters' rights and responsibilities. In these efforts, AC became an effective citizen watchdog that served as a check on the government's power to influence electoral outcomes: for example, its efforts regularly turned up instances of fraud, such as vote buying and efforts by the government to use social programs to influence voters.[52] In this way, the organization performed the important function of promoting electoral fairness and transparency at a time when Mexico's electoral institutions had yet to become fully independent and effective.

Moreover, AC was one of the first independent, nonpartisan organizations to stress the importance of civic engagement for the transition to democracy.[53] While the common belief that free, fair, and transparent elections would result in the defeat of the PRI was what originally brought the group together, members held a wide range of political views, and state-level chapters had the autonomy to operate independently. This gave the organization the flexibility to respond to local characteristics and political conditions, and to find creative ways to promote civic engagement. Interestingly, AC did best in areas where state-society relations remained authoritarian. According to Alberto Olvera, in states like Coahuila, Sonora, and Yucatán, AC helped strengthen local groups and forge new space for civic activism, while it had less success in places like Guadalajara and Mexico City because preestablished NGOs did not embrace or necessarily welcome the arrival of AC in what they perceived to be their realm of activity.[54]

Alianza Cívica's high visibility and solid reputation made it attractive to other groups in society seeking greater political engagement. For example, in 1995, the Zapatistas (discussed below) asked AC to organize and implement a referendum in order to gauge popular support for indigenous rights in Mexico. The so-called National Consultation for Peace and Democracy elicited over a million responses and sent a clear message to the Zedillo administration that many Mexicans were sympathetic to the plight of the country's indigenous population. Other public consultations of this kind also helped put a number of economic issues on the public agenda and served as referenda on the Zedillo administration's commitment to the neoliberal economic model.

Ironically, now that the electoral process and the Federal Electoral Institute are more transparent and autonomous, the AC's role has been diminished. Consequently, it has begun to focus less on elections and increased its attention to civic education (especially of young people), monitoring public finance, and accountability. Additionally, under the Calderón administration, AC began to mobilize civil society to pressure the government to change its military approach to combating drug-trafficking organizations.[55] Although Alianza Cívica's activities have been limited in scope, the organization has played an important role in coordinating other grassroots groups and in demonstrating how civil society can work together to promote change and to strengthen Mexican democracy.

Revolutionary Movements: The EZLN

Unlike social movements and civic organizations, revolutionary movements seek to change the status quo through the use of force. Leftist guerrilla movements have a long history in Latin American politics, but in the postrevolutionary period, Mexico seemed relatively immune to armed rebellions.[56] This changed on January 1, 1994, when the Zapatista Army of National Liberation (Ejército Zapatista de Liberación Nacional, EZLN) rang in the new year by taking over several towns and attacking an army base in the southeastern state of Chiapas.[57] The EZLN forces numbered approximately two thousand indigenous people, led by disaffected intellectuals from Mexico City who together sought to spark radical social and political change in Mexico. The Zapatistas released a declaration stating the rationale for the uprising and identifying their goals as "work, land, housing, food, education, independence, liberty, democracy, justice, and peace."[58] (See textbox 8.1.) President Salinas responded by sending in twelve thousand troops, and with the help of armored vehicles and air strikes, the Mexican military forced the Zapatistas to retreat into eastern tropical forests and lowlands. In all, approximately 150 people were killed, and on January 12, President Salinas proposed a cease-fire and agreed to negotiate with the EZLN if they laid down their arms.

The peace talks between the government's Commission for Concordance and Peace (Comisión de Concordia y Pacificación, COCOPA) and the EZLN's leadership, the Committee of the Clandestine Indigenous

---

Textbox 8.1. FIRST DECLARATION FROM THE LACANDON FOREST

¡Hoy decimos basta! Today we say enough is enough! To the people of Mexico: Mexican brothers and sisters: We are a product of 500 years of struggle: first against slavery, then during the war of independence against Spain led by insurgents, then to promulgate our constitution and expel the French empire from our soil, and later [when] the dictatorship of Porfirio Díaz denied us the just application of the Reform laws and the people rebelled and leaders like Villa and Zapata emerged, poor men just like us. We have been denied the most elemental education so that others can use us as cannon fodder and pillage the wealth of our country. They don't care that we have nothing, absolutely nothing, not even a roof over our heads, no land, no work, no health care, no food, and no education. Nor are we able freely and democratically to elect our political representatives, nor is there independence from foreigners, nor is there peace nor justice for ourselves and our children.

Source: Excerpt cited in George Collier and Elizabeth Lowery Quaratiello, *Basta! Land and the Zapatista Rebellion in Chiapas* (Oakland, Calif.: Institute for Food and Development Policy, 1994), 2.

Revolution (Comité Clandestino Revolucionario Indígena, CCRI) began in February under the aegis of Bishop Samuel Ruíz, the noted advocate of indigenous rights; Manuel Camacho Solís, a well-respected negotiator representing the government; and an EZLN spokesperson operating under the alias of Subcomandante Marcos. In just two weeks, the two sides drew up thirty-two tentative accords. Each side then took the agreement to their respective constituencies for approval, but Zapatista supporters rejected the accords, and talks did not resume again until September 1995.

After five months of negotiations, the two sides agreed to the San Andrés Accord on Indigenous Culture and Rights, an agreement that acknowledged the need for the right of self-determination, territorial autonomy, and recognition of customary laws of indigenous peoples. In December 1996, the COCOPA, together with a congressional commission, drafted a bill to incorporate key elements of the San Andrés Accord into new legislation. Initially, the Zapatistas agreed to the new drafts, but they became disillusioned when Congress dragged its feet on recognizing indigenous autonomy and customary laws and insisted on amending the proposal. The EZLN rejected the subsequent draft and broke off all negotiations with the government. Neither side appeared willing to back down from its demands or reinitiate the peace process until December 1997, when government-supported paramilitary forces killed forty-five Zapatista supporters at a prayer meeting in the village of Acteal. Domestic and international pressure forced the resignations of the governor and the minister of the interior and compelled the Zedillo administration to introduce a watered-down version of the COCOPA legislation in the Senate in March 1998, which ultimately went nowhere.

In early 2001, Vicente Fox extended an olive branch by removing some military installations in Chiapas and reintroducing the original (1996) COCOPA bill in the Senate. For their part, the Zapatistas organized a march to Mexico City to rally popular support and demonstrate their willingness to negotiate with the new administration. Subsequent negotiations produced a constitutional amendment that recognized the rights of indigenous peoples but did not ensure protection for self-government, collective land rights, control of natural resources, customary law, or collective legal rights.[59] Therefore, although the Fox administration claimed that it had successfully solved the Chiapas "problem," the Zapatistas and many indigenous peoples felt that the new legislation was largely symbolic.

Since 2001, the Zapatistas have remained largely silent. Their followers, about twenty thousand people, live in self-governed communities in Chiapas. They do not allow police or government officials to enter the land, but they are closely monitored by the Mexican army. Periodically the Zapatista leadership issues statements, usually to condemn local and national politicians and the political process more generally. In January 2006, the Zapatistas emerged unarmed in order to launch a six-month peaceful tour of the country. The purpose of the campaign was to design a new political order from the ground up by meeting with ordinary people and leftists who were similarly disillusioned with the formal political system.

To date, this movement has not offered a clear political alternative, and many argue that the Zapatistas represent a failed revolutionary movement. While it is true that the EZLN's efforts have not led to an overhaul of Mexico's social and political systems, it is probably their influence that explains why every president since Ernesto Zedillo has increased public works spending in the country's indigenous regions. Moreover, although national legislative reform has been slow and difficult, the EZLN did provide impetus for a number of state-level reforms since the mid-1990s. For example, the state of Oaxaca now has laws that guarantee the ability of indigenous communities to govern themselves using "customary practices," or *usos y costumbres*, which have their roots in pre-Hispanic and colonial times and allow communities to choose their leaders in an assembly and to use common-law judicial norms for conflict resolution.[60]

Thus although the Zapatista's initial methods were indubitably antidemocratic, their longer-term effect has contributed to democracy by prompting the Mexican government to be more responsive to indigenous demands for basic services and for more meaningful inclusion in the political process.

CONCLUSION

There can be little doubt that Mexican civil society has changed remarkably in the past twenty-five years. Once controlled by a top-down organizational structure and presided over by the PRI, it is now more plural and autonomous than at any other time in its history. Spurred by a number of economic and political factors in the 1980s and 1990s, diverse groups began to organize for the express purpose of pressing their demands and gaining access to the political system on their own terms, rather than seeking incorporation into the PRI or official corporatist sectors.

Although the emergence of Mexican civil society has provided some important and influential outlets for political organization and activism that have enhanced the quality of Mexico's democracy, the persistence of quasi-corporatist relationships between the state and some organizations, as well as authoritarian, clientelistic practices within some organizations, has contributed little to democracy. If Mexico is to deepen its democracy, the state must continue to make it possible for citizens to freely organize for the purpose of pressing their political demands. At the same time, the organizations themselves must also work harder to adopt and disseminate democratic values and practices.

Part III

KEY DOMESTIC POLICY ISSUES

9

Mexico's Political Economy

MEXICAN ECONOMIC DEVELOPMENT

Many people in the United States are unaware that Mexico's economy is the twelfth largest in the world, with a GDP of nearly $1.5 trillion in purchasing-power parity, larger than South Korea or Canada. Nor do people typically realize that Mexico has long been considered among the strongest and most successful economies in the developing world. Indeed, Mexico benefits from tremendous natural wealth, major manufacturing zones, and cosmopolitan cities with highly sophisticated centers of art and culture. Yet paradoxically, for all of its success, Mexico's progress was impeded by deep and recurring economic crises in the 1970s, 1980s, and 1990s, further exacerbating long-standing problems such as poverty and severe income inequality. One of Mexico's greatest contradictions is that economic modernity and widespread endemic poverty coexist, often within the space of a single city block. Understandably, such inconsistencies contribute to frequent misperceptions of Mexico as an economically backward country. Most important, these issues raise the question of why Mexico's periods of economic success have not been sustainable, and why prosperity has failed to penetrate all segments of society.

In this chapter, we address these issues first by examining the various models used to promote economic growth and development in Mexico. We emphasize that these economic models' inherent characteristics often contributed as much to income inequality as they did to raising living standards. We will also explain why Mexico has repeatedly enjoyed periods of incredible economic growth only to be followed by devastating crises, and we will comment on the challenges the country faces in pursuing a sound economic future.

MODELS OF DEVELOPMENT

In a broad sense, Mexico's economic development followed the global shifts occurring in the nineteenth and twentieth centuries (see figure 9.1). Thus, Mexico's economic development is similar to that of many Western countries, especially those in Latin America. At different times between independence and the current era, Mexico has embraced varied levels of state involvement in the national economy. From the colonial period until the late 1870s, Mexico's economy was, like most of Europe's, mercantilist in orientation, in which first the Crown and later the Mexican government had a high level of involvement in economic transactions. During the Porfiriato, the country again followed Europe's lead and embraced a liberal economic approach that emphasized free trade and foreign direct investment. In the 1940s, Mexico, like many developing countries, adopted

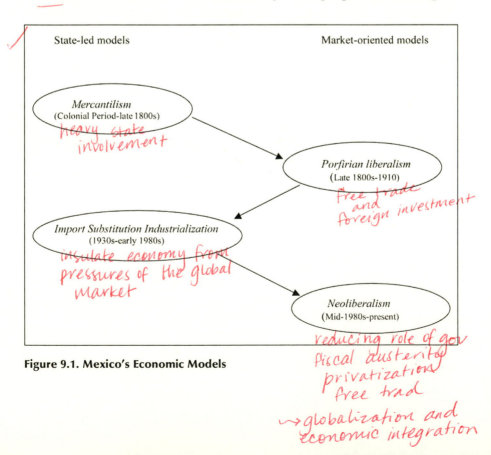

Figure 9.1. Mexico's Economic Models

import substitution industrialization (ISI), an inwardly focused state-led plan designed to insulate the national economy from the pressures of the global market during the Great Depression. In the wake of the debt crisis of the 1980s, Mexico later adopted a neoliberal approach that once again called for reducing the role of the government in the economy by promoting fiscal austerity, privatization, and free trade. Mexico's shift toward neoliberalism coincided with the worldwide trend toward greater globalization and economic integration. Hence today, as in the past, Mexico's economic model is as much a product of global incentives and pressures as it is reflective of an independent choice made by its leaders.

EARLY HISTORICAL DEVELOPMENT: MERCANTILISM AND PORFIRIAN LIBERALISM

Mexico's early economic history was dramatically shaped by the legacies of colonial mercantilism. Mercantilism was characterized by the extraction of natural resources for the benefit of the Spanish Crown, severe restrictions on trade, and the resulting development of a dependent relationship in relation to the mother country. After independence in 1821, Mexico suffered the withdrawal symptoms of its political and economic separation from Spain. In this context, economic and political instability became mutually reinforcing, as government budget deficits, enormous foreign debt burdens, and severe currency instability contributed to half a century of political conflict, foreign military interventions, and armed uprisings. In this context, the lack of political stability and government funds made it difficult to invest in the infrastructure needed to develop the Mexican economy.

The long period of political stability generated by the dictatorship of Porfirio Díaz (1876–1910) finally enabled Mexico to achieve significant economic progress. Díaz's undisputed political authority and ability to impose order allowed his regime to employ a multipronged strategy that combined protectionism with massive amounts of foreign investment and the development of critical infrastructure to promote economic development in Mexico. At the same time, the export-oriented economic model that was in place at the turn of the century reified and exacerbated income inequality, and thereby helped sow many of the seeds that would erupt in Mexico's revolution in 1910. Mexico's export-oriented model of economic development was based primarily on the domestic production of agricultural goods (e.g., henequen, wood, hides, coffee, cattle, cotton, sugar, vanilla) and precious and industrial metals (e.g., gold, silver, copper, zinc, graphite, lead, antimony) for export to other countries.[1]

The Díaz regime introduced the export-oriented model using a combination of economic policy tools. First, it imposed high protective tariffs (ranging from 50 to 200 percent of product value) on foreign goods entering the country. This made imports more expensive and therefore less attractive to Mexican consumers. He also adopted the silver standard, pegging the peso to silver, which helped stabilize the Mexican currency (at least in the short term). Together these measures—tariffs and a stable currency—gave domestic entrepreneurs incentives to offer competitively priced, locally produced goods and therefore encouraged the formation of domestic industries. Although Mexicans began to invest more in the domestic economy, their role in promoting economic growth and development paled in comparison to that played by foreigners. Díaz encouraged a flood of foreign investment into the Mexican economy by eliminating obstacles (e.g., taxes, extraction fees, export duties) and creating incentives for foreigners to finance Mexico's economic growth.[2] In less than twenty years, Mexico watched foreign investment increase from 100 million pesos in 1884 to 3.4 billion in 1911.[3]

However, the Porfirian economic model presented several important problems for Mexican society. First, although the Mexican economy was much larger and more productive in 1910 than it had been thirty years earlier, it was still highly dependent on the ebbs and flows of the international economy. Since foreign capital played such an integral role in the country's economy, it was extremely vulnerable to events that would prompt foreign investors to remove their money. While much of the foreign investment was fixed and therefore could not easily be removed (e.g., real estate and infrastructure), it was nevertheless possible and relatively easy for foreigners to withdraw or withhold their investments with little or no warning. Additionally, as an export-based economy, Mexico was highly sensitive to the drop in prices of its goods. This reinforced the country's vulnerability to economic downturns, which often happened virtually overnight. Mexico learned firsthand the extent of its vulnerability when a worldwide economic downturn that began in 1907 reduced demand for Mexican products. The problem was exacerbated by a related drop in the price of important commodities like silver, and soon Mexico found its export earnings drastically reduced.

As a result of these trends and heavy infrastructure investment, Mexico's foreign debt grew tremendously during the Porfiriato, more than doubling from 193 million pesos in 1896 to nearly 590 million pesos in 1911.[4] Reduced export earnings and impending loan payments to foreign banks put an enormous amount of pressure on the Díaz regime to find an alternative source of revenue. The solution was to raise taxes on the middle class—a measure that was met with considerable dissatisfaction and did relatively little to resolve the country's financial problems.

inflation

Further complicating Mexico's economic situation was the fact that the influx of foreign capital had an inflationary effect on the domestic economy. Indeed, the cost of living steadily increased, but wages and economic opportunities did not keep pace with inflation. Despite record economic growth, overall real wages in Mexico therefore actually fell 25 percent between 1898 and 1911. The drop in real wages was steepest for agricultural workers, who made up two-thirds of the workforce. Additionally, by 1910 fewer Mexicans had access to private or communal property than at any other time in the country's history. Instead, most of the peasantry was forced into debt peonage on large haciendas that produced mainly for export rather than domestic agricultural consumption.[5] Thus, despite all of the contributions that the export-oriented economic model of the Porfiriato made toward Mexican economic development, it also had a deleterious effect on the quality of life of the average Mexican, maintaining and exacerbating poverty, high rates of illiteracy, widespread malnourishment, and low life expectancies. Without a doubt, the severe economic inequality of the Porfirian system contributed to the discontent that fueled the Mexican revolution, which ultimately gave way to an entirely different approach to managing the economy.

negative impact on agriculture

severe economic inequality
↓
1910 Revolution.

ECONOMIC NATIONALISM AND STATE-LED GROWTH

The Mexican revolution slowed growth and development for almost thirty years. The country's capacity for production was severely hampered by the reduction in the size of the population (about one of every fifteen Mexicans died during the war), and many of the nation's industries and much of its infrastructure were largely destroyed during the multiyear conflict. Political unrest also frightened foreign investors and therefore significantly reduced Mexico's most substantial source of capital. Therefore, the first two decades following the Mexican revolution presented serious economic difficulties for the country. As political stability began to develop in the late 1920s, the Great Depression hit. The global economic crisis had dramatic effects on Mexico: exports decreased drastically as demand for Mexican goods dropped; foreign capital (which had started to return) once again dried up; and as a result, Mexico's GDP declined to its lowest levels in twenty years. Of course, these events had serious consequences for the lives of ordinary Mexicans. Lack of capital meant that job opportunities were scarce, government services were virtually nonexistent, and labor and social unrest were rampant. Therefore, when Lázaro Cárdenas assumed the presidency in 1934, he faced several formidable economic as well as political challenges.

Great Depression

Many of Cárdenas's most significant economic policies (e.g., redistribution of land, expropriation of petroleum) were inextricably linked to

Lázaro Cárdenas.

his efforts to bring about greater distribution of resources and economic nationalism at the expense of foreign investors and the domestic private sector. But Mexico's shift to a more inwardly oriented economic model was also the result of external factors over which it had no control. More specifically, with the outbreak of World War II in 1939 and subsequent U.S. involvement in 1941, Mexico began to experience a "natural" shift in trade patterns. As Europe and the United States focused on war making, they had fewer economic and human resources for the production of food, textiles, and consumer goods. Consequently, the demand for Mexican exports increased substantially and helped revive levels of economic growth not seen since the Porfiriato. At the same time, Mexico had to find a way to acquire the vast array of finished manufactured goods that it normally imported from countries that were at war. This necessity prompted the development of domestic industries to produce Mexican substitutes for value-added manufactured products as diverse as industrial metals, machinery, consumer goods, and furniture. This practice of substituting domestically produced products for goods that were formerly imported is known as import substitution industrialization (ISI). ISI became Mexico's principal economic development strategy—one that would be used for roughly forty years and produce both astounding economic growth and devastating economic and social failures.[6]

As mentioned earlier, between 1940 and 1970 Mexico enjoyed an average increase in GDP of more than 6 percent. This period of incredible growth and development was known as the Mexican Miracle and is even today an enviable accomplishment for any country. How was Mexico able to produce such miraculous economic success? Without a doubt, much of the explanation lies in a decision by the Mexican government to reinforce its new economic approach and promote industrialization. The adoption of ISI in the 1940s marked the beginning of Mexico's industrialization process. Before that time, the economy was almost exclusively based on the extraction and production of raw materials. The ISI model required a significant amount of involvement by the state, which provided much of the necessary investment capital for developing domestic industries from scratch. President Manuel Ávila Camacho (1940–1946) and his successors made a concerted effort to promote industrialization using these policy tools—not just because this represented a promising strategy for Mexican economic growth and development, but also because it gave the regime performance legitimacy (see textbox 9.1).

The implementation of ISI faced some early challenges when, for example, World War II ended and the demand for Mexico's exports dropped, while the demand for imports rose simultaneously—often to supplement domestic industries with foreign intermediate goods. In response to this problem, the presidential administration of Miguel Alemán Valdés (1946–1952)

Textbox 9.1. IMPORT SUBSTITUTION INDUSTRIALIZATION (ISI): A CURE FOR UNDERDEVELOPMENT?

Mexico's decision to deepen ISI in the 1950s and 1960s was influenced by prevailing wisdom in the region about the nature of Latin American "underdevelopment." A number of Latin American economists and intellectuals advocated ISI as a method of promoting consistent development—an outcome that had never materialized with export-oriented economic models. They argued that only by establishing domestic industries capable of producing manufactured goods demanded by local consumers and diversifying their economies, would developing countries be able to break out of their dependency on industrialized countries.

These dependency theorists claimed Latin America's lack of development was the direct result of being exploited by "the core"—industrialized countries like the United States, which purchased raw materials at relatively low prices and used them to manufacture finished goods that they then sold back at a premium to countries like Mexico. Thus a dual dependency was created: the developing country depended on the industrialized country as a market for its raw materials, but it similarly depended on it for value-added imports that it could not produce at home. If Latin American countries developed their own industries, they would diversify their economies, become more productive, reduce their vulnerability, and be less dependent on the core for their economic survival.

ISI helped many developing countries achieve many of these goals for a time. However, the model required the use of expensive technology, high trade barriers (e.g., tariffs, export subsidies, industrial incentives), loose monetary policy, and tax breaks (for domestic producers), all of which required an extraordinary amount of capital from the government. Had the model sustained the momentum it produced in the early phase of its implementation, the resulting economic growth might have offset the dislocations that occur after prolonged use of such expensive policy tools. Unfortunately for Mexico and much of Latin America, the model became exhausted once the relatively small domestic markets were saturated with manufactured goods, and economic growth was no longer sufficient to underwrite further investment in the enterprise. Yet rather than switch macroeconomic models, most countries in the region chose to deepen ISI—to focus on the production of different, generally more durable industrial goods. This move produced economic growth for some, but it required even more capital and led to a frenzy of borrowing from international lending institutions. Although debt financing can be a good strategy for promoting economic growth and development, in the end, the inherent flaws of ISI combined with high levels of government spending on wages, social programs, and public services, as well as several external factors such as the oil shocks and the global recession of the 1970s that brought with it higher interest rates, came together to undermine many of the economic gains that ISI had brought to Latin America.

worked to sustain the new formula for economic development by developing policies to ensure continued ISI. This involved several related elements: the development of state-owned enterprises in heavy industry (e.g., oil and petrochemicals, steel, automobiles); increased governmental expenditures on much-needed infrastructure (e.g., roads, communications, ports, dams, irrigation) to further promote domestic development; higher import restrictions (e.g., tariffs, quotas) on finished consumer goods to make them less competitive with domestically produced alternatives; reduced import restrictions on intermediate and capital goods to supplement domestic industrial production; and foreign direct investment (FDI) in important economic sectors.

Investment was a critically important aspect of Mexico's ISI model because it introduced much-needed capital and made available cutting-edge technology and professional training that otherwise would have been absent. However, unlike FDI in the Porfirian era, investment encouraged under ISI was highly regulated by the state. For example, the government required that transnational companies operating in Mexico use locally produced inputs, train workers and managers, and transfer critical technologies to local industries. Moreover, foreign firms were prohibited from wholly owning production facilities and operations in Mexico. This policy, described as Mexicanization, required a majority of local ownership. Despite such unfavorable terms, many foreign companies continued to invest in Mexico because it was the only way to have access to the domestic market without the high tariffs placed on imported goods. Furthermore, there were a number of loopholes for getting around local ownership requirements.[7] Another form of FDI that was unique to Mexico's version of ISI was the establishment of the *maquiladora*, or assembly plant, industry along the border with the United States.

Another challenge for the ISI model was that by the 1950s, rapid economic growth and investment, increased government spending, and loose monetary policy combined to produce high levels of inflation, as the increased availability of money caused prices to rise dramatically. In response, the administration of President Adolfo Ruiz Cortines (1952–1958) moved to stabilize economic development, first by devaluing the peso in 1954 (and pegging the value of the Mexican currency to the U.S. dollar at a rate of 12.5 pesos to the dollar), and then by carefully managing the money supply and government expenditures to maintain that exchange rate. The managed exchange rate required Mexico to significantly tighten its monetary policy, which helped curb inflation. At the same time, devaluing the peso also spurred tourism and exports, since Mexican goods and services were now more attractive to foreigners. In this way, the government's policy of stabilizing development bolstered the ISI model and enabled Mexico to take advantage of a worldwide period of postwar economic growth and prosperity during the 1950s and 1960s.

However, for all of its success at producing economic growth, Mexico's economic formula had important limitations.[8] For example, while ISI brought benefits—specialized training, better job opportunities, higher wages, better access to services like health care and education, and improved standards of living—such benefits were generally limited to specific sectors, individuals, and groups (e.g., industrialists, managers, and officially recognized labor unions). In an effort to improve the lot of the masses, the government of Adolfo López Mateos (1958–1964) made a concerted effort to more widely redistribute the proceeds of the miracle. Indeed, the strength of the economy during López Mateos's *sexenio* allowed him to expand the national social security system, initiate health and immunization campaigns, create public housing facilities, improve educational opportunities, and redistribute 30 million acres of land—more than any other president since Lázaro Cárdenas. López Mateos was also the first president to seriously enforce the policy of Mexicanization, either nationalizing or requiring Mexican ownership in several key sectors (including telecommunications, petrochemicals, mining, and automotive inputs). As discussed in chapter 13, in 1964 Mexico also began to foster growth in its northern border region with targeted investments and special policies. For his efforts to broaden the positive effects of Mexico's economic growth and for his nationalist policies, López Mateos is fondly remembered in the country's political memory.

Still, during this period, the significant gap between rich and poor continued to grow dramatically, and sluggish growth for middle-income sectors left many dissatisfied with the Mexican Miracle. This underlying dissatisfaction, which became manifest during President Gustavo Díaz Ordaz's term (1964–1970), fueled strikes and demonstrations by doctors, insurgent labor unions, and the 1968 student movement, and was ultimately attributable to the shortcomings of Mexico's economic strategy.[9] By the 1960s, Mexico had passed the supposedly easy phase of ISI, which focused on fostering high-value-added manufactured and consumer goods, using protective tariffs that prevented foreign competition and government subsidies that gave domestic producers a boost. During this phase, however, Mexico's domestic production of industrial and commercial inputs—the backward linkages that support manufacturing—was only weakly developed. Instead, the government encouraged large domestic manufacturers to obtain inputs from abroad, by lowering tariffs on those imports (while protecting finished products). By moving to the more difficult second stage of ISI, Mexico might have developed more midlevel and semiskilled jobs.[10] However, without such opportunities, the Mexican economy was unable to meet the rising expectations of the generation of the 1960s.

At the same time, like the U.S. dollar, Mexico's currency was becoming overvalued—unduly expensive in relation to other currencies—constraining the

purchase of Mexican exports abroad. An overvalued currency is a common oc-
currence and can be corrected by floating or devaluing the currency to reflect
its true value. As noted above, however, from 1954 on Mexico maintained a
fixed rate of exchange relative to the dollar, which was itself fixed at a rate of
$35 to an ounce of gold. By the 1960s, the strength of the dollar was being
undermined by large U.S. trade and fiscal deficits; with more dollars circulat-
ing in the international economy, the real demand for U.S. currency was lower
than the fixed rate of exchange.[11] To address this problem, the United States
would need to adjust the value of the dollar to actual levels of demand or
dramatically improve its balance of payments by spending less money abroad.
That happened in 1971, when the United States opted to do both, breaking
from the gold standard and imposing a hefty 10 percent tariff on all U.S. imports.[12] The result was a significant slowdown in the international economy
and a serious blow to Mexico. On the one hand, without the gold standard as
an anchor, the initial fluctuations of the dollar affected currencies that were
pegged to it (like the peso), creating broader instability and inflation that
disproportionately hurt the lower and middle classes. On the other hand,
the new tariff on U.S. imports further deteriorated the demand for Mexico's
products in the United States, its most important trading partner.

Thus, Luis Echeverría's administration (1970–1976) faced the difficult
task of restabilizing the economy and finding new ways to promote growth
and development. Echeverría's approach supplemented ISI policies with
what he called "shared development" policies, such as higher wages for
workers and price controls on basic food items like tortillas, beans, and
milk; investment in public works like schools, health clinics, a credit program for small farmers, and rural infrastructure; and nationalization of certain industries, including telecommunications and tobacco. Increased government spending to finance these projects had to come from somewhere,
and in the wake of an economic downturn, Echeverría had little choice
but to borrow capital from abroad. In the short term, his strategy paid off
and economic output nearly matched the heady days of the miracle. However, the president's move to increase the role of the state in the economy,
while also eliminating some of the subsidies and other privileges formerly
extended to industrialists, alienated the business class and caused capital
flight that undermined Mexico's prospects for economic recovery.

When Echeverría left office in 1976, the Mexican economy was in crisis.
Federal and trade deficits created a severe imbalance in the budget, two
devaluations left the peso at only half its previous value, and inflation was
up 30 percent. The International Monetary Fund (IMF) had placed stringent
restrictions on Mexico, virtually eliminating international loans as a source
of much-needed capital. Rational investors, both foreign and domestic, had
taken their money elsewhere, and ordinary Mexicans were facing extraordinary hardship. Even food was in short supply: agricultural production was

depressed and Mexico was forced to import basic food products, which further exacerbated its balance of trade problems. Hence it was clear by the mid-1970s that the miracle was over.

When Echeverría's successor, José López Portillo, took office, he initially adopted a conservative economic outlook. López Portillo's strategy for economic recovery was in line with IMF strictures, including drastic cuts in government spending, floating the peso until it reached a stable rate of exchange, and guarantees to entice investors back to Mexico. Yet, Mexico was soon able to break with such austerity measures when the discovery of vast new petroleum reserves was announced in early 1977. Now Mexico had a chance not only to escape financial crisis but, in López Portillo's terms, chart a new and promising course for the future by "administering abundance." Indeed, with 60 billion barrels in proven reserves and 250 billion in potential reserves, oil paved the way for economic growth that far outstripped levels attained even during the 1950s and 1960s: petroleum exports increased exponentially, from $500 million in 1976 to a whopping $13 billion in 1981, and the Mexican economy grew 8 percent annually.[13]

Determined to avoid the inflationary and dislocating effects of petrolization of the economy, the López Portillo administration implemented a gradual approach that called for a moderated pace of extraction and export. The intention was to use oil proceeds to finance further industrialization—a move that would simultaneously ensure that Mexico did not become overly dependent on oil exports and provide a solid industrial foundation and diverse economy capable of fueling long-term development. To that end, the Industrial Development Plan was launched in 1979. Continuing the ISI model, its aim was to use tax breaks, subsidies, and energy discounts to encourage the creation of eleven new industrial zones that concentrated on the production of expensive inputs such as steel, petrochemicals, machinery, and capital goods and thus eliminate the need to import them from abroad. It was believed that the industrialization project would also allow the government to address some of the country's most pressing social issues by producing enough jobs to absorb Mexico's burgeoning population and providing resources to be used in promoting rural development.

Given the ambitiousness of these goals, Mexico required more capital than the country actually had on hand.[14] Yet this was not a problem thanks to the high price of oil, Mexico's seemingly endless supply of petroleum reserves, and the eagerness of private banks and international lending agencies such as the World Bank to make loans guaranteed by future oil earnings. For its part, Mexico was eager to borrow because interest rates were very low and it had valuable collateral with which to guarantee its debts.

An unfortunate confluence of national and international factors turned Mexico's dreams of oil wealth into an economic nightmare. Domestically, the oil boom brought millions of new jobs and investment, but rapid economic growth also increased the rate of inflation, which undermined the already limited effects of price controls. Subsidies on basic food items and other cost of living expenses (e.g., housing and public services) increased substantially.[15] Additionally, rampant corruption and mismanagement at all levels of government and the bureaucracy hindered the success of the López Portillo administration's development project, as massive amounts of resources were siphoned off by politicians and bureaucrats or diverted to important political actors lining their own pockets.

Meanwhile, Mexico's balance of payments deficit grew exponentially during the same period because it had borrowed so heavily to jump-start oil and other industries as well as to increase investment in development. This situation ultimately led to two significant problems: debt and devaluation. First, Mexico's foreign debt almost tripled, from approximately $30 billion to $80 billion in 1982, or 18 percent of the country's GDP, earning Mexico the dubious distinction of being the world's second-most-indebted country (after Brazil). When world interest rates rose and oil prices plummeted in 1981–1982, Mexico's export earnings fell far short of government expectations, and the government was forced to borrow even more money abroad to cover the shortfall.[16]

Second, by the early 1980s, the peso had become overvalued as a result of the imbalance of payments. As Mexico attempted to cope with its sudden debt crisis, further borrowing and increased capital flight exacerbated that imbalance. With rapidly dwindling foreign reserves and mushrooming debt, López Portillo initially refused to devalue the peso, vowing that he would defend Mexico's national currency "like a dog." Yet the administration ultimately had little choice but to devalue the currency (twice), causing the peso to lose nearly three-quarters of its value. This severely decreased the already declining purchasing power of ordinary Mexicans, who found it even more difficult to make ends meet.

The devaluations also prompted even greater capital flight as investors, foreign and domestic alike, sought to protect the value of their capital by moving it out of the country. To control the mass exodus of capital, the government froze foreign currency accounts and put strict controls on the amount of currency that could be exchanged, angering the business community. Finally, the devaluations had the effect of increasing the amount owed to foreign creditors, who had made most of the loans in dollars. With such a severe economic downturn in a short period of time, it was not long before Mexico simply ran out of dollars. The debt crisis officially began on August 15, 1982, when the Mexican government publicly announced that it would no longer be able to make payments on its debt. That sent shock waves through the international financial community, which was faced not just with the prospect of an $80 billion default, but with the much larger threat of a $700 billion mass default if other countries in similar conditions followed suit.[17] Just two weeks later, in his final national address, President López Portillo stated that capital flight was the primary culprit in the crisis and, to eliminate the threat it posed to the future of the country, announced that all private banks would be nationalized. While the bank nationalization was popular among the middle and lower classes, who believed that the business class should share responsibility for the crisis, it created a serious rift between the PRI regime and members of the private sector.

NEOLIBERAL REFORM AND ECONOMIC RESTRUCTURING

When López Portillo assumed the presidency in 1976, he was hailed as the pragmatic and sober influence that was needed to resolve the serious crisis left behind by Luis Echeverría. Yet in 1982, Mexico's economic situation was drastically worse than it had been six years earlier. Economic growth had dropped to zero, inflation was running in the triple digits, and Mexico had no way to begin to repay its multibillion-dollar foreign debt. Thus Mexico ushered in what became known as the "lost decade," nearly ten years of economic stagnation. López Portillo's successor, Miguel de la Madrid Hurtado (1982–1988), had to find a way out of the mire that left Mexico, once an international darling, now a virtual pariah. De la Madrid's response to the crisis demonstrated his belief in the superiority of a free-market or neoliberal economic model for bringing about stability and growth.

The neoliberal economic model, which emphasized a laissez-faire approach, was also known as the "Chicago School" economic model or the "Washington Consensus" (see textbox 9.2). De la Madrid's first move was to accept the terms of a rescue package put together by the IMF, which included new loans to enable Mexico to resume payments on its debt. However, the package simply bought the country more time to pay the interest on its previous loans; it did not reduce the total amount that Mexico owed to foreign creditors. In exchange, de la Madrid agreed to implement a series of economic reforms that would first stabilize the economy and then restructure its orientation to promote higher levels of growth.

Chief among the reforms was cutting back on public spending to reduce the budget deficit and control inflation. This required the government to lower or even eliminate "unproductive" expenditures such as food subsidies, pensions, and public services. In all, de la Madrid managed to cut government spending by a third, but the budget cuts disproportionately affected the poor and working classes who most relied on public programs. After another devaluation in 1986, the peso again lost nearly half its value, and Mexicans had even less purchasing power than before. Equally devastating was the introduction of a new 15 percent value-added tax (VAT) tacked on to nearly all goods. This sales tax, together with increased income

Textbox 9.2. NEOLIBERALISM

Neoliberalism refers to an economic perspective that advocates a free market approach to economic development, and it was believed by some to be a way to promote the emergence of democratic politics. Because it was strongly advocated by economists from the University of Chicago and policy makers in Washington, D.C., it is also known as the Chicago School model or the Washington Consensus approach. Unlike ISI, which requires high levels of state investment and involvement in the economy, the neoliberal strategy reflects the belief that the government should play a minimal role in the economy. The cornerstones of the neoliberal approach are stabilization, structural adjustment, and trade liberalization.

Stabilization refers overall to tightening the money supply in order to create the conditions necessary for the other two components of neoliberalism. This generally requires devaluing currency, freezing wages, reducing government spending on wages (i.e., laying off workers) and public services (e.g., health care, education, infrastructure), and making it difficult and expensive to borrow money by tightening credit and raising interest rates. The overall effect is to improve in the balance of trade by making exports cheaper and imports more expensive.

Structural adjustment is the next step and is aimed at reducing the government's role in the economy. In particular, structural adjustment is meant to shift a wide array of economic activities, such as the distribution of goods and services, from the public to the private sector. In practice it requires that government "privatize," or sell to private investors, services (e.g., health care, education, and utilities) and industries (e.g., energy, banking, telecommunications) that it once controlled. The logic here is that the private sector in an open market economy is more efficient and more productive because it must respond to the pressures of competition (both domestic and international). The end result is therefore posited to be more efficient production methods, higher-quality outputs, lower prices for consumers, and greater overall economic stability, since the government no longer has the responsibility to provide services or underwrite industrial development.

Trade liberalization is the final component; it means shifting away from protectionism in order to promote trade and attract foreign investment. By reducing (and ideally eliminating) tariffs, subsidies, quotas, and bureaucratic restrictions, governments again curtail their involvement and instead allow the international market to determine the allocation of resources. Countries achieve greater gains from trade by basing the production of exports on their comparative advantage and importing the goods they cannot produce efficiently. Thus exports and foreign investment become the engines of economic growth.

taxes, was supposed to add $10 billion to government coffers, but as a flat tax, it marked an additional way that the lower classes were forced to bear the brunt of the crisis. Another of the IMF's conditions for providing emergency loans was that Mexico become more open to international trade. During the ISI era, tariffs and other trade barriers were used with alacrity to insulate domestic producers from the effects of foreign competition. While these protectionist measures fostered the development of domestic industries, they ultimately resulted in inefficient production methods and goods that had difficulty competing on the world market. The new approach called for the Mexican government to reduce trade barriers in order to introduce competition that would result in higher quality goods and greater world demand for Mexican manufactured goods.

The reforms helped bring inflation under control, at least temporarily, but they also led to a recession, as real wages and income fell; unemployment rose; the cost of basic food items like tortillas, beans, milk, eggs, and cooking oil increased by roughly 25 percent; and living standards generally declined. Moreover, even when inflation was in check, Mexico was still unable to achieve economic growth. Another drop in oil prices depressed export earnings, and domestic industrialists faced difficult and sometimes insurmountable obstacles to competing on the world market, thus leading to a decline in productivity and general economic stagnation. Meanwhile, the government had pledged to spend 53 percent of the federal budget to repay the debt, leaving very little with which to stimulate economic investment and growth. Hence, in contrast to the success of the miracle years, the Mexican economy shrank by an average of 6 percent every year between 1982 and the early 1990s.[18]

Rather than reverse course, the de la Madrid administration deepened the use of austerity in an effort to further stabilize the economy and reduced the role of the state in the economy in order to spur economic growth. In addition to larger cuts in public spending, de la Madrid began to sell off many state-owned enterprises to private interests, arguing that the private sector was much better suited to efficient production. He also signed on to the General Agreement on Tariffs and Trade (GATT) in 1986 in order to commit Mexico to reducing its trade barriers and leveling the playing field for foreign imports. Nevertheless, for all of the economic restructuring that had taken place and the sacrifices made by ordinary Mexicans, it appeared that Mexico had made very little progress by the end of de la Madrid's term: public debt remained high at 19 percent of GDP; inflation was up again, to 143 percent; and the Mexican stock market nearly collapsed in 1987.[19]

As de la Madrid's term came to a close in 1988, the memory of severe economic hardship was still fresh in the minds of most Mexicans, who were appreciably worse off than they had been six years before. Under the circumstances, it would not have been surprising if de la Madrid's successor chose to abandon the neoliberal approach in favor of a radically different alternative. However, because the country was still beholden to international loans and their conditions, and because the incoming president, Carlos Salinas de Gortari, was equally committed to neoliberalism, Mexico stayed the course. As de la Madrid's minister of budget and planning, Salinas had masterminded much of the administration's economic policies and had no intention of deviating from this approach when he became president. Instead, he implemented a strategy designed to encourage long-term investment in Mexico—a key component of the neoliberal economic model. His first step in this direction was to initiate talks with commercial banks to make Mexico's debt burden more manageable. By July 1989, Salinas had succeeded in lowering the country's annual payments and reducing Mexico's debt by $48.5 billion.[20] This achievement, combined with Salinas's reprivatization of the banks and other industries, went a long way toward restoring confidence in the private sector.[21] Hence, in the short term these measures spurred capital repatriation, and in the long term they made it less likely that the country would again be undermined by massive capital flight.

Meanwhile, on the domestic front, Mexico's Economic Solidarity Pact (Pacto de Solidaridad Económica, PSE) was beginning to bear fruit. The pact was an agreement made by government, labor, agriculture, and business to work together to promote economic stabilization. The government pledged to further tighten monetary policy and reduce protectionism but to keep wages fixed. For their part, labor agreed not to strike for higher wages, and agriculture and business agreed not to raise prices on their goods and services. The economic pact produced quick and positive results, as inflation declined and GDP began to grow. Soon inflation was under control, domestic interest rates had decreased, foreign reserves were higher, and GDP was growing steadily. To most observers, it appeared that Mexico had returned from the brink of collapse and achieved the impossible: a stable, healthy, and growing economy.

In this context, in August 1990, Salinas announced his intention to pursue what became the most renowned component of his neoliberal project: a free trade agreement with the United States and Canada, known as the North American Free Trade Agreement (NAFTA).[22] The details surrounding NAFTA are discussed in chapter 13; here we note that the treaty was important not only because it gave Mexico the means to attract foreign investment and pursue export-driven growth, but also because it committed the country to the neoliberal approach, since an international treaty would be very difficult for future administrations to overturn. This institutionalization of free-market reforms served to deepen both domestic and international confidence in Mexico, so much so that between 1990 and 1994, Mexico became the second largest recipient of private investment in the world.

Unfortunately, beginning in 1994, the inflow of foreign capital began to reverse, and by the time Salinas left office later that year, the peso had become grossly overvalued, leading to yet another major devaluation and economic crisis. How could this have happened if presidents de la Madrid and Salinas had taken all the prescribed steps to bring Mexico the stability and growth attributed to the market-based economic reform? The answer is that, in some senses, the neoliberal policies worked too well and were not properly managed. That is, Salinas's confidence-boosting measures encouraged a huge influx of foreign capital investment, which offset once persistent trade imbalances, increased Mexico's foreign reserves, and helped curb inflation. The government tried to sustain that investment, and the peso's value, by selling short-term, dollar-denominated treasury bonds called *tesobonos*, which paid a high rate of interest to investors. The drawback was that keeping investment in Mexico became more difficult over time, especially as a series of domestic and international events led to the gradual withdrawal of foreign capital over the course of 1994. That year, an increase in U.S. interest rates, the Zapatista uprising, and several high-profile political assassinations led investors to pull their money out of Mexico. The withdrawal of foreign capital caused Mexico's foreign reserves to dwindle, naturally contributing to an overvalued peso and pressure to adjust the value of the currency to actual market demand. Ironically, Salinas had refused to devalue the peso because he was afraid it would spark further capital flight and destroy all of the confidence in Mexico's economy that he had worked so hard to build. These were unacceptable risks in 1994, since the U.S. Congress was heatedly debating whether or not to ratify NAFTA—Salinas's crowning achievement. Also, devaluation would bring about more economic hardship for Mexicans, something Salinas found unacceptable in an election year. Therefore, the Salinas administration refused to accept the economic and political risks of devaluation, and in so doing, virtually guaranteed that Mexico's next economic crisis would be worse than those that had come before.

As a result, less than three weeks after assuming the presidency, Ernesto Zedillo was forced to devalue the peso or face economic collapse. In just two weeks, the peso lost 30 percent of its value, and the value of the Mexican stock market was cut in half. Foreign reserves dropped by $4 billion, and Mexico once again found itself on the verge of economic collapse. The Zedillo administration, still wet behind the ears, exacerbated the situation by not sending clear signals about the course of action it intended to pursue, thus creating even greater instability. Much of this was precipitated by the circumstances surrounding Zedillo's selection as Salinas's successor: as a distant second choice, and indeed the only viable choice after the assassination of Luis Donaldo Colosio, Zedillo was widely perceived as a weak leader with neither the authority nor political acumen to govern. This led all influential groups both within and outside the PRI to try to apply pressure to the administration for specific policies that would protect their interests.

However, Zedillo chose to stick with the neoliberal approach of his predecessors, not just because he too was a U.S.-trained technocrat but also because this assured Mexico assistance from the United States. The Clinton administration, together with the IMF, orchestrated a $47 billion bailout that used future earnings from the export of oil as collateral. In exchange, Zedillo agreed to reintroduce Mexico to the harsh realities of fiscal austerity. The results were predictable: Mexico avoided economic collapse but began a deep recession that saw GDP decline by 6 percent and real wages drop by more than 10 percent. What was less predictable was that the recession was relatively short-lived, lasting only eighteen months, and that Mexico, to the surprise of many, demonstrated not only that it was able to repay the loans, but also that it was able to do so ahead of schedule. Yet serious problems remained, most notably in the banking sector.

In the aftermath of the peso crisis, interest rates shot up, effectively increasing the amount of outstanding debt owed to Mexican banks. Already finding it difficult to adjust to the increased cost of living, debtors were now faced with interest rates as high as 100 percent on their outstanding loans. Further complicating matters from the banks' perspective was the fact that Mexico lacked the legal mechanisms to force debtors to repay their loans. The result was an impending catastrophe that threatened to bring down the banking sector, and the Zedillo administration was forced to orchestrate a bailout. The solution was the creation of the Savings Protection Banking Fund (Fondo Bancario de Protección al Ahorro, FOBAPROA), a government agency that bought out many of the banks' bad loans for a total of $65 billion. While FOBAPROA helped breathe new life into the Mexican banking sector, the decision to bail out the banks raised the hackles of many, who viewed it as a thinly veiled attempt to save the nation's largest lending institutions, who had lent too much and taken too many risks during the Salinas administration.[23] Critics were also enraged by the Zedillo administration's decision (and Congress's approval) to convert the outstanding loans, equivalent to 15 percent of GDP, into public debt.[24]

Persistent weaknesses in the banking sector notwithstanding, Zedillo achieved what few thought was possible: he stabilized the Mexican economy. By the end of his *sexenio*, the current account was more balanced, inflation was under control, the exchange rate had stabilized, government spending was in check, foreign debt was shrinking, and macroeconomic growth was restored. In the final year of Zedillo's term, GDP grew by 6.6 percent, and Mexico had managed to recapture some of its former economic glory. Thus, Zedillo became the unlikeliest of heroes, not only bringing Mexico back from the brink but also charting a course toward macroeconomic stability and growth.

When Vicente Fox took office in late 2000, he had an unprecedented opportunity in Mexico's recent experience—namely, to begin his term without the need to address impending economic collapse.[25] Accordingly, Fox arrived with ambitious plans for promoting economic development, including greater investment in infrastructure and education, and support for small businesses. Moreover, he promised annual GDP increases of 7 percent. Yet curiously, these auspicious circumstances were not sufficient to ensure Fox's success. Why not? This question is particularly relevant because much of Fox's political success was attributed to his experience as an executive at Coca-Cola, one of the world's most successful multinational firms. The answer has at least three components. First, Mexico and the world suffered a serious economic downturn in the aftermath of September 11, 2001. Second, even without this event, Fox was not particularly shrewd in the way he pursued many of his economic goals. Third, many of his proposed plans were so sweeping in their design that they were bound to encounter resistance in the legislature. *largely unsuccessful*

Overall, the Fox administration worked hard to maintain Mexico's economic stability, and these efforts largely paid off. At the end of Fox's term, Mexico enjoyed a balanced budget, mild inflation, a healthier banking sector, a stable peso, and a growing stock market. However, these accomplishments were overshadowed by sluggish growth (GDP averaged less than 2 percent annually between 2001 and 2006); very low job creation; and Mexico's drop to become the third largest source of U.S. imports, after Canada and China.[26] Therefore, while Felipe Calderón's government inherited a fundamentally sound economy, it was left to address the shortcomings of the Fox administration in order promote further economic growth and development.

In his first years in office, Calderón managed to steer a steady course, with the Mexican economy doing relatively well even in the face of a U.S. recession, a falling dollar, inflationary pressures, and a global financial crisis. However, with the deepening global recession, it became increasingly difficult for Mexico to maintain strong rates of growth. For example, in 2007 Mexico's economy grew at a rate of 3.3 percent, but in 2008 it contracted 1.3 percent. And in 2009, Mexico suffered its worst economic downturn in thirty years, suffering 6.5 percent decline in GDP.[27] The economy's dismal showing in 2009 was due to the unfortunate confluence of several factors, including the steep decline in oil prices and dwindling petroleum reserves; the H1N1 flu epidemic, which drastically reduced tourism (Mexico's second most important source of foreign capital); and the Calderón administration's military strategy to counter drug trafficking, which has cost millions and precipitated extreme increases in violence that have further reduced tourism. Luckily, it appears that the worst of the worst is over. In 2010, Mexico's economy grew 5.4 percent as demand for its exports (e.g., automobiles, agricultural products, and oil) rebounded. Forecasts for 2011 and 2012 predict that GDP will expand by more than 4 percent each year. These predictions provide solid reasons for optimism; however, the country still faces important challenges and these gains serve to highlight how sharply Mexico's economy declined during the crisis.

MEXICO'S FUTURE ECONOMIC CHALLENGES

After Mexico's miraculous economic recovery from the peso crisis and its ability to weather the severe economic downturn that happened after 9/11, many proponents of neoliberalism claimed that ten-plus years of economic restructuring had made the Mexican economy much more stable and resilient. While there is little doubt that Mexico is now better able to bounce back from deep economic shocks, the country still faces several important economic challenges in the twenty-first century. First, as with any export-based model, the Mexican economy is vulnerable to exogenous shocks that reduce the price or demand for its exports. This is particularly true for Mexico, since the vast majority of its exports are sold to one country: the United States (see table 9.1). Mexico is also vulnerable because it relies so heavily on oil for its revenue—roughly 37 percent of the government's revenue comes from the export of petroleum. While a significant drop in oil prices on a par with those of the 1980s does not seem likely, prices have fluctuated greatly in recent years, and Mexico's reserves are quickly dwindling. Not surprisingly, Mexico's oil output and therefore its oil export income have declined significantly. If Mexico is going to avoid another catastrophe precipitated by its dependence on petroleum, it must take action now.

There are at least two potential solutions to this problem. The first is the highly controversial (and unpopular) option of privatizing the petroleum industry. PEMEX, the national petroleum company, is a bloated and corrupt bureaucracy sorely in need of rationalization and modernization. Some argue that privatizing the industry and welcoming foreign investment

Table 9.1. Mexico's Most Important Trade Partners, 2009

Exports (% by destination)	Imports (% by origin)
1. United States (80.7)	1. United States (48.1)
2. European Union (5.1)	2. China (13.9)
3. Canada (3.6)	3. European Union (11.6)
4. Colombia (1.1)	4. Japan (4.9)
5. Brazil (1.1)	5. South Korea (4.7)

Source: World Trade Organization. http://stat.wto.org/.

is the only way to rapidly update Mexico's production facilities so as to be able to more quickly and efficiently tap into the country's 12.9 billion barrels of proven reserves, much of which is located in inaccessible areas such as the deep waters of the Gulf of Mexico. Yet privatizing an industry that is widely considered to be integral to Mexico's independence and sovereignty will be no small task. In accord with the majority of the population, the PRD and many members of the PRI have consistently opposed privatization and foreign control of the petroleum industry. Indeed, in 2008, the PRD led the charge against Calderón's energy reform proposals to partially privatize the petroleum industry, with the goal of injecting new capital and increasing competition in the energy sector. The Mexican government could also invest more in the development of other economic sectors to offset the decline in oil revenue and to diversify Mexico's export earnings. But this too is difficult, expensive, and only likely to produce results in the medium and long term. Therefore, it is probably in Mexico's best interest to promote industry reform (even if privatization is not forthcoming) and diversification of exports in order to ensure a steady stream of revenue in the future. Just how to accomplish this is unlikely to be straightforward or easy.

A second possible way to reduce oil dependence and promote economic development is to increase tax revenue. Of the twenty-nine members of the Organisation for Economic Co-operation and Development (OECD), Mexico ranks last in the amount of revenue it collects from businesses and private citizens. While most OECD states collect roughly 30 percent of GDP from tax receipts, Mexico's tax revenue hovered around 10 percent in the late 1990s and has increased to only 17.5 percent. The recent increases are laudable but are barely over the 15 percent that is considered necessary for a government to provide basic public services and infrastructure. Therefore, if Mexico is going to reduce its dependence on oil and maintain macroeconomic stability, it must find a way to increase its tax revenues—no small task given that, at least until recently, there was no taxpaying culture in Mexico. Indeed, businesses and citizens alike had few incentives to contribute to coffers they knew were used to enrich politicians rather than to promote the public good. Calderón has worked to succeed where Fox failed, designing a set of reforms to increase tax receipts and working with the multiparty Congress to achieve a consensus on fiscal reform. The fiscal reform package approved in September 2007 achieved this goal, resulting in significant increases in new revenue to allow government spending on infrastructure, energy subsidies, and education.

A related challenge for Mexico is the emergence of the informal economy, particularly in the aftermath of the crises of the 1980s and 1990s. As formal employment opportunities disappeared and the cost of living increased, Mexicans were forced to find new economic survival strategies. For many this meant emigrating to the United States. Many of those who stayed became self-employed, setting up taco stands, selling wares in areas with high pedestrian traffic or at makeshift marketplaces, working as domestic servants and day laborers, and so on. These kinds of economic activities allow millions to make a living or cover periodic budget shortfalls. However, they take place as personal arrangements among citizens and as such are not taxed or regulated by the government. The result is that the government loses out in valuable revenue generated by the informal economy, and, as we discuss further in chapter 10, citizens are vulnerable to exploitation and economic instability.

Further plaguing Mexico's economic future is the presence of several highly influential domestic monopolies and oligopolies. In theory, privatization of firms leads to greater efficiency and competitiveness, since entrepreneurs, unlike government bureaucrats, must respond to market forces in order to stay in business. However, in Mexico the sale of industries previously owned by the state led to the creation of private monopolies (most notably in telecommunications and broadcasting) and oligopolies (cement, airlines, financial sector). This creates a number of problems. First, Mexican consumers suffer from the absence of competition. As an example, Mexicans pay some of the highest telecom rates in the world because Carlos Slim's companies Telmex and Telcel control 80 percent of Mexico's landlines and 70 percent of all cell phone service, respectively. Additionally, domestic monopolies have the overall effect of making the country less competitive on the international market. Notorious for using domestic legal loopholes to protect their market dominance, Mexican monopolies have been able to keep out both foreign and domestic competitors, and this has the potential to undermine investment and growth.

While nearly everyone acknowledges the problem that monopolies and oligopolies pose to the economy, it has been difficult to muster the political will to challenge their power. However, in the spring of 2011, there were some positive signs of change. In April, Congress passed a new antimonopoly law that punishes those convicted of anticompetitive practices with high fines and jail time. Shortly thereafter, the Supreme Court ruled that Telcel must abide by new regulations preventing exorbitant connection fees, and Mexico's antitrust regulator levied a $1 billion fine against the company for monopolistic practices.[28] Of course, whether these efforts will begin to limit the influence of the country's largest monopoly remains to be seen, but the new laws are clearly a step in the right direction.

Also pressing is the dire need to create higher-paying jobs. Like many of his predecessors, Fox pledged to create a million jobs a year during his *sexenio*—equal to the number of Mexicans entering the workforce. Yet Fox was unable to keep his promise, only coming close to one million jobs in the last year of his administration. For his part, Calderón proclaimed himself the "jobs president" before taking office, but until 2010, his efforts were not enough to counteract more powerful economic trends that led to mass job loss. The good news is that in 2010, Mexico netted over 700,000 jobs, mainly in manufacturing, services, and retail.[29] Importantly, 70 percent of the new jobs are permanent, a crucial requirement not only for workers to earn enough to live on but also to provide steady sources of income that further contribute to economic growth and create incentives for citizens to stay home rather than look for better opportunities in places like the United States. While the 2010 figures are promising, they are but drops in the bucket relative to the country's needs: Mexico must continue to create permanent jobs in order to sustain its economic growth and productivity.

Finally, Mexico must also find a way to maintain its competitive edge in trade and industry. For many years, Mexico was the prime destination for multinational firms that wanted access to lower labor wages and lower transportation costs on goods destined for the U.S. market. Today, wages in many parts of Central America and Asia, particularly China, are far lower than those paid in Mexico. In many cases, the wage differentials are large enough to offset increased shipping costs that are invariably incurred when goods are transported from more remote locations. Moreover, national governments all over the world are much more savvy at attracting the attention of multinationals looking for new locations for their production facilities. Without its traditional comparative advantages, Mexico must find other ways to remain competitive. Of particular concern is Mexico's relatively low levels of investment in science and technology; it ranks last among OECD countries in this category. Without sufficient resources in these areas, it will be impossible for Mexico to increase its productivity, promote innovation, and otherwise remain competitive in the global economy. Clearly there needs to be a greater focus on promoting industries and products for which there is high demand in emerging markets like China, if Mexico is going to redefine its economic niche and maintain its comparative advantage. Countries that can tap into a market as large and with as much potential as China's are much more likely to be successful in the future than those that remain overly focused on traditional markets like the United States.

All of these issues present significant challenges for Mexico's economic growth and stability. There is little doubt that Mexico must work more aggressively to chart its course for the future. Unless it develops a sound and coherent strategy for promoting economic development, the gains of the past two decades are sure to erode over time. Yet perhaps the biggest challenge that Mexico currently faces is how to distribute economic gains more equitably.

CONCLUSION

As we have noted throughout this chapter, Mexico has enjoyed periods of impressive growth, yet much of the population has failed to benefit from the country's economic success. The miracle years of ISI favored the domestic business class but left behind many in the working class and the countryside. The neoliberal economic model appears to have taken no less a toll on ordinary Mexicans: stabilization, structural adjustment, and trade liberalization required the government to enact policies that made life very difficult for most Mexicans. The combined effects of high unemployment, stagnant wages, reduced government services, and higher prices made economic survival a constant struggle. This hardship, difficult in the best of times, was dramatically worsened by the peso crisis of the mid-1990s and the global recession of the late 2000s. If Mexico hopes to achieve true economic development and reinforce its democratic gains, it must address its severe income inequality and myriad problems associated with widespread poverty. It is to these issues that we turn in chapter 10.

10

Poverty, Inequality, and Social Welfare Policy

First-time visitors to Mexico are often struck by images of economic hardship that confirm their preconceptions about Mexico as a poor country, such as street children selling gum and ramshackle shanty housing. Yet what many visitors find, often to their surprise, is that Mexico is also a country of tremendous wealth. For example, the country is home to Carlos Slim, the telecommunications magnate who was ranked in March 2010 as the world's richest man (a position he has held alternately in recent years with Bill Gates and Warren Buffett). Mexico's cosmopolitan cities—Mexico City, Monterrey, Guadalajara—boast fabulous hotels, chic restaurants, high-priced shopping districts, and luxury automobile dealerships. Wealthy Mexicans travel to Disney World and Europe for vacation and send their children to expensive private schools. Because of this disparity, visitors often come to the simple, not completely inaccurate conclusion that Mexico's poverty and inequality are the result of government corruption and unfair privileges in Mexican society. But the dimensions and causes of poverty and income inequality in Mexico, as elsewhere, are complex and require careful analysis in order to better understand and address them.

In this chapter, we consider the nature of poverty and inequality in Mexico and their implications for the country's overall economic development. In the first part of this chapter, we will try to understand what factors have contributed to the persistence of poverty and income inequality during an era of expanding international trade and economic productivity. In the second part of this chapter, we will examine the different approaches to promoting social welfare in Mexico and how they have changed over the last two decades. In the process, we will discuss the major contemporary

227

Mexican government programs and policies that have been developed to deal with poverty and inequality. What emerges from this discussion is a clear indication of the enormity and complexity of Mexico's greatest challenge and a look at the ways in which its leaders have responded. Throughout, we also consider the implications for Mexico's long-term process of democratic consolidation.

UNDERSTANDING POVERTY AND INEQUALITY

What does it mean to be poor in Mexico? This is a difficult question because the concept of poverty is relative. What one person considers to be poor economic conditions in a particular country (or even in a given community) may actually be relatively better than those considered poor in another. For example, a poor person living in the United States may have access to services that are not available to many of the world's poorest citizens: clean running water, electricity, medical vaccinations, public housing, and cable television. At the same time, the relative cost of goods may vary significantly from one region or country to another. Thus, poor people living in Mexico—who earn much less money than their counterparts in the United States (where the poverty line in 2009 was about $22,050 annual income for a family of four)—may also find it far less expensive to meet their basic needs for food, housing, medicine, and so on.

How then can we begin to analyze poverty and inequality in Mexico? When is a person considered poor? How is inequality manifested in Mexico's economy, and with what implications? In Mexico, as in the United States, poverty is often defined according to household income from wages and other income-based measures, such as GDP per capita. Yet such measures capture only part of what it means to be poor. Economists therefore also evaluate other factors that indicate the quality of life and degree of inequality for people who are economically disadvantaged. As we discuss below, both income-based and qualitative measures show a relatively high rate of poverty and inequality in Mexico compared to the United States and other developed countries.

Additionally, income distribution in Mexico approaches the most unequal in the world: while the wealthiest quintile (20 percent) of the population owns roughly 60 percent of the country's resources, the poorest quintile claims a paltry 3 percent of the national income. Nowhere is the disparity more evident than in a comparison of Carlos Slim with an ordinary Mexican citizen. Slim, a Mexican tycoon, owns a broad array of Mexican companies, including telecom, retail and department stores, restaurants, a banking and insurance firm, and an airline. The Slim fortune was estimated in 2010 to be $53.5 billion, up 7 percent from the 2008 edition of this book. In contrast, an ordinary Mexican earns approximately $10 a day, has no health insurance, does not own a car, and is unable to finish high school, let alone college. Therefore, when considering Mexicans' economic well-being, it is essential to take into account the distribution of wealth in the country.

Income-Based Measures of Poverty and Inequality

One common income-based definition of poverty in Mexico is centered on the country's daily minimum wage, which is set at about double the cost of a minimum basket of goods, or about US$4.50 per day.[1] Any Mexican household that survives on less than the minimum wage is generally considered to be poor or marginalized (*marginalizado*). Those Mexican households earning incomes less than the cost of a minimum basket of goods—or roughly half the poverty line—are often described as living in extreme poverty.[2] According to these definitions, approximately 40 percent of Mexicans live in poverty, while roughly 28 percent live in extreme poverty.[3]

Since the cost of living can vary significantly from place to place, it is common for income to be adjusted for purchasing power parity (PPP).[4] Controlling for PPP in GDP per capita, we can see that Mexican citizens earn far less (about US$13,800 annually) than U.S. citizens (about US$47,400 annually). Indeed, despite Mexico's ranking as having the twelfth highest GDP, relative to its population Mexico ranked eighty-fifth in terms of GDP/PPP per capita in 2010.[5] While income-based measures give us an approximation of how much money people have at their disposal, they tell us less about the circumstances in which people live. For this reason, some economists have suggested trying to find other ways to measure poverty that include other dimensions that impact a person's basic quality of life. One of the most influential measures, developed by the UN Development Programme, is the Human Development Index (HDI), which combines indicators of life expectancy, educational attainment, and income levels to provide a relative measure of development that takes into account quality-of-life issues associated with poverty. The highest level of development is 1 and the lowest is zero.[6] Using this index, we can see in table 10.1 that Mexico, considered a country with "high human development," is ranked 56 out of 169 countries, yet its level of human development lags behind several other Latin American countries with far smaller economies.

Qualitative Measures of Poverty and Inequality

Indicators such as the HDI capture the reality that poverty is both relative and multidimensional. In other words, being poor also implies additional circumstances, largely as a result of having restricted access to basic

Table 10.1. Human Development Index (HDI) Rankings for the United States and Key Latin American and Caribbean Countries, 2010

Country	HDI Value	World Ranking (out of 169 Countries)
United States	.799	4
Chile	.783	45
Argentina	.775	46
Uruguay	.765	52
Panama	.755	54
Mexico	**.750**	**56**
Costa Rica	.725	62
Peru	.723	63
Brazil	.699	73
Venezuela	.696	75
Ecuador	.695	77
Colombia	.689	79
Dominican Republic	.663	88
El Salvador	.659	90
Bolivia	.643	95
Paraguay	.640	96
Honduras	.604	106
Nicaragua	.565	115
Guatemala	.560	116

Source: UN Development Programme International Human Development Indicators. http://hdr.undp.org/en/statistics/.

services relative to most other people in an economy. Poor people are often deprived of proper prenatal care, vaccinations, adequate shelter, nutritious food, education, regular medical attention, and access to lifesaving medicines. As a result, the impoverished often have a much lower quality of life—and a shorter life. In fact, in the words of one economist, "poverty kills."[7] For this reason, it is important to draw on a wider range of qualitative indicators—the actual living circumstances of people—that help us understand the dimensions of poverty and inequality in Mexico.

Economists in the Fox administration sought to further elucidate the problem of poverty by developing a more complex scale of indicators that incorporated both income-based and qualitative measures. The poverty index developed by Fox's Technical Committee for Poverty Measurement identified three distinct categories or levels of poverty: inadequate nutrition (*alimentaria*), inadequate access to health and education (*capacidades*), and inadequate material resources (*patrimonio*).[8] Using these measures, the Fox administration achieved a somewhat more nuanced—and disturbing—assessment of poverty in Mexico than that based solely on the minimum wage. One alarming finding was that a much higher proportion of Mexico's rural population had a lack of access to basic nutrition (34 percent), health care (41 percent), and material resources (60 percent) than urban dwellers. Indeed, people living in urban areas were one-third as likely to lack basic nutrition, less than half as likely to lack access to health care, and just over half as likely to be lacking in basic material needs as the 25 percent of Mexicans living in rural areas.

Regardless of whether a quantitative or qualitative measure of poverty is used, it is clear that the proportion of Mexico's population living in poverty is about average for Latin America. At the same time, the percentage of poor people living in Mexico is significantly higher than in the United States, where poverty rates have remained close to 12.5 percent—or about 1 in 8 persons—over the last two decades. Why, given its relative economic strength, does Mexico have such high poverty levels and such tremendous inequality? Below, we consider in greater detail the factors that have contributed to poverty and inequality in Mexico, which helps shed light on some of the possible policy solutions for improving the quality of life in Mexico.

EMPIRICAL TRENDS IN POVERTY AND INEQUALITY IN CONTEMPORARY MEXICO

Over the course of the twentieth century, the quality of life for most Mexicans improved. This was particularly true during the early years of the economic miracle, when unemployment declined, wages increased, and the levels of inequality diminished. Yet even in this era of economic prosperity, poverty was not eliminated because many of the improvements in income brought by economic growth were accompanied by other changes. For example, like many developing countries, Mexican development has been accompanied by steady population growth throughout the twentieth century. By 2010, Mexico's population, estimated to be over 112 million, was more than eight times larger than its population of 13.6 million in 1900. Much of the population explosion occurred during the middle part of the century, in the heyday of the economic miracle and throughout the 1970s. Thus, although the economy was expanding during this period, so was the size of the population. Therefore, greater national wealth did not necessarily mean better conditions for everyone.

Currently, the vast majority of the population (65 percent) is between fifteen and sixty-four years of age. Although this age group will continue to make up the bulk of the population in the short term, the country is expected to undergo a demographic shift, as decreased family size reduces the number of youngsters and the percentage of seniors age sixty-five and older increases to roughly 23 percent (up from its current level of 6 percent) of the population by midcentury. This shift will undoubtedly place a greater strain on Mexico's economy and government services as its baby boom generation moves into retirement. Indeed, as we discuss below, Mexico has already begun to brace for this challenge by significantly reforming its pension system.

Another critical aspect of Mexico's economic development and social transformation over the twentieth century has been the rapid rate of urbanization in the postwar era and the greater demands that this has placed on Mexico's urban infrastructure, educational institutions, and social welfare services. In 1950, 57.4 percent of the population lived in rural areas; this number declined to 34 percent by 1980, and then to 25 percent in 2000. New urban dwellers were drawn to jobs and higher wages in major metropolitan areas, or otherwise compelled to move by the decline of Mexico's traditional agricultural sector.[9]

This metropolitan demographic shift helped improve living standards for many Mexicans by providing greater employment opportunities and access to basic services that may have proved scarce in the countryside. This, in turn, provided a high degree of legitimacy to the PRI government for much of the mid-twentieth century. However, with the series of economic crises and devaluations that Mexico experienced beginning in the 1970s, the living conditions and relative wealth of many Mexicans deteriorated significantly.[10]

During the lost decade of the 1980s, unemployment soared and inflation drove prices up while wages stagnated. Mexico's subsequent economic restructuring brought further job losses in uncompetitive industries, notably agriculture. Those who remained employed saw the steady deterioration of their wages due to soaring inflation over the course of the decade. Subsequent currency volatility further diminished the buying power of Mexican wages. In sum, during the 1980s and 1990s, real wages declined nearly 40 percent, while the minimum wage lost nearly 70 percent of its purchasing power. Although middle incomes improved significantly in Mexico over the 1990s (especially in northern Mexico), by the end of the decade the buying power of Mexico's poor was still less than a third of what it had been in 1980.

For many people in contemporary Mexico, poverty is a chronic, systemic, and multigenerational condition related to a lack of access to basic economic opportunities. As noted above, poor people often lack access to basic health care and nutrition, decent housing, adequate education, formal employment, and capital or credit for investments that would significantly improve their quality of life *and* enable them to participate more effectively in the economy. In terms of demographic patterns and geographic distribution, chronic poverty has particular characteristics in Mexico. For example, rural and indigenous people have been consistently overrepresented as a share of Mexico's impoverished population over many generations. In addition, women and children are especially prominent among the chronically poor; this is in part because women have significantly lower earning potential than men, and because poor people are likely to have more children than average. Hence, on the whole, Mexicans who are ethnically indigenous, rural, young, and female are more likely to find themselves living in chronic poverty.

In addition to chronic poverty, some economists refer to the problem of transitional poverty, which is the result of a sudden and significant macroeconomic shift.[11] In other words, individuals who were previously not considered poor may suddenly experience a worsening in their economic situation due to a sudden crisis: unemployment, rising prices, or the death of the family breadwinner. While the effects of transitional poverty can be less discriminating than those of chronic poverty, people already at the lower end of the economic spectrum are certainly more vulnerable than others. For example, the purchasing power of the minimum-wage earners may not rise consistently with the rate of inflation. Similarly, when the peso is devalued relative to other national currencies (like the dollar), the rising cost of imported goods can quickly spiral out of reach. In such cases, people who might be considered above Mexico's nominal poverty line may suddenly have less purchasing power than they once did.

Both chronic and transitional poverty raise important questions about democracy in Mexico. First, we must consider how poverty—whether chronic or transitional—played a role in Mexico's long period of single-party hegemony under the PRI, and whether changes in the economic conditions contributed to its prolonged process of democratization. As we have argued in earlier chapters, the PRI actively catered to Mexico's chronically poor population throughout its long period of political dominance. In fact, the ruling party dramatically improved the living conditions of poor people during Mexico's midcentury economic miracle, earning important performance legitimacy for the PRI regime as a result. Not surprisingly, the PRI tended to draw significant support at polls from poor voters.

Why did the poor continue to support the PRI even as Mexico's economic situation worsened during the 1980s and 1990s, when the PRI's performance legitimacy appeared to dissipate? It may be that the poor—especially the chronically poor—could be easily enticed to report to PRI rallies and even sell their votes in exchange for various forms of political patronage and direct material benefits, such as sandwiches, T-shirts, hats, and even washing machines. At the same time, as Vivienne Bennett argues, the relative decline in economic conditions for persons living in extreme and chronic poverty—such as a *campesino* living off the land—might have been very different than for urban middle class and moderately poor Mexicans suddenly thrust into transitional poverty by economic shocks.[12] If so, those who experienced transitional poverty may have been more likely to mobilize in support of the political opposition, whether voting for PAN mayors and governors in the mid-1980s or for Cuauhtémoc Cárdenas in 1988. In this way, poverty and economic hardship may have had simultaneously divergent effects on the PRI's support base, and on the process of democratization.

A second and related question regarding the politics of poverty—and especially inequality—in Mexico is how it may bear on the future of democratic governance, as well as the policies of democratic governments. Advocates of modernization theory argue that a large middle-class population is beneficial to democratic governance, because middle-class voters tend to have characteristics that promote active political participation, such as higher levels of education and a larger stake in the outcome of government policies. If this is the case, then Mexico's large poor population could be a barrier to democratic governance, insofar as they may be vulnerable to political manipulation and lack commitment to democratic participation. At the same time, even if the millions of poor Mexicans prove to be highly democratic in their orientation, the country's extreme levels of inequality skew political outcomes in favor of the few extremely wealthy Mexicans, who can buy access to power and thereby corrupt the political system. What is clear for now, as we saw in the 2006 elections and during the global economic downturn that followed two years later, is that policy makers can ill afford to ignore the issue of poverty and inequality.

As they design Mexico's future social welfare policies, it will be necessary for Mexican politicians to consider the nature and causes of poverty. As we have discussed, addressing both chronic and transitional poverty will likely require policy makers to develop different approaches to improve the overall macroeconomic situation and to provide assistance to alleviate the effects of a temporary crisis. Tackling complex, ingrained patterns of poverty may require longer-term, multifaceted strategies. For example, some policy makers seeking to alleviate the symptoms of multigenerational poverty may focus on programs providing access to basic services, such as food assistance and medical care. Others may develop programs to increase the accessibility of grants and loans for making investments (e.g., new businesses and housing). Still others may emphasize the need for targeted programs to increase educational quality and access for the children of poor families. Below we consider the policy prescriptions employed in recent decades and their implications for combating poverty and reducing inequalities in Mexico.

REFORMING SOCIAL WELFARE POLICY IN MEXICO

Social welfare policies are government programs that seek to provide assistance to members of society who cannot meet their own basic needs. Governments provide this safety net because they seek to maximize the overall welfare of society. Effective social welfare policies accomplish this goal by making sure that fewer members of society suffer undue hardship and more individuals can make positive contributions to the whole of society. To accomplish these goals, most social welfare programs seek to provide assistance that helps level the economic playing field. Such policies often provide food, health care, housing, education, and job training to those who need assistance.

In effect, social welfare programs are the manifestation of what many political scientists and policy analysts refer to as the welfare state. The notion of the welfare state emerged during the early and mid-twentieth century, as governments in industrializing societies wrestled with the political demands of newly empowered workers, as well as the challenges of economic crises in a much more complex and interconnected global economy. As we have seen in earlier chapters, Mexico's revolutionary government was, in fact, one of the first to formally embrace a strong caretaker role for the state. Numerous provisions of the 1917 constitution commit the state to the provision of overall societal welfare, such as education and health care. However, it was not until the 1930s, during the administration of Lázaro Cárdenas, that the Mexican government adopted policies seriously committed to the protection of social welfare; even then, progress toward meeting the basic needs of society was limited over the coming decades.

One explanation of why Mexico's welfare state has been ineffective in reducing poverty may be the significant lack of policy continuity across administrations, or political manipulation by the ruling party for many years. There has been a tendency in Mexico for each new presidential administration to eliminate or reconfigure the social welfare programs of its predecessors. In most cases, each president endeavored to place his own stamp on Mexican social welfare policy by introducing a new program, scope, or emphasis in order to create mechanisms for clientelistic distribution of resources to consolidate his political power.

The frequent alterations to Mexico's social welfare policy can be seen in the historical development of the two main cabinet-level agencies that address these issues: the Ministry of Social Development (Secretaría de Desarollo Social, SEDESOL) and the Ministry of Health (Secretaría de Salud, or Salud). Today, the secretaries of both agencies report to the president and oversee a large bureaucratic organization with a wide variety of programs. The names, functions, and significance of many of these programs have varied over time, as nearly every new president renamed or otherwise attempted to redefine the direction of Mexican social welfare policy. The Ministry of Development was originally created under another title in 1959 to oversee public works projects. The agency continued to deal with housing, public works, and ecological projects under various titles until 1992, when it was again renamed to SEDESOL and made generally responsible for dealing with poverty alleviation and social assistance.[13] The Ministry of Social Assistance (Secretaría de Asistencia Social, SAS) was created in 1938 to provide general social welfare assistance. However, by the 1980s, the social welfare functions of the agency became more specialized in public health, and in 1992 the agency was renamed the Ministry of Health, with that as its sole mission, and other social welfare programs were gradually transferred to SEDESOL.[14]

Alterations to Mexican social welfare policy have not been solely based on reorienting political and societal loyalties. In recent decades there have been important differences in the design and the underlying philosophical approaches of social welfare programs in Mexico. In the process, recent modifications to social welfare policy in contemporary Mexico have begun to significantly reshape the state's relationship to society, and expectations about the role of government in providing for individual well-being. Below we consider traditional state-centered approaches to social welfare policy in Mexico, as well as recent innovations emphasizing a greater role for public-private partnerships in the provision of social welfare. In particular, we focus on the key antipoverty programs that exemplify this shift in approaches in Mexico.

Traditional Social Welfare Programs

Beginning in the early and mid-twentieth century, Mexican social welfare programs sought to provide universally accessible redistributive benefits to the needy through intensive government involvement. The Mexican government established a wide range of programs—administered by SEDESOL and other agencies—to provide food assistance, universal medical care (for formally employed workers), and pensions for the elderly. The Mexican government's social welfare programs reflected the progressive orientation of the revolution, with universally accessible benefits for the poor. In Mexico, some critics viewed such social welfare programs as wasteful forms of patronage intended to build support for the PRI regime (highly susceptible to official corruption). Often such programs merely alleviated the symptoms of poverty and proved ineffective as long-term solutions to the problem.

Mexico's National Company for Popular Subsistence (Compañía Nacional de Subsistencias Populares, CONASUPO) provides a useful example. Founded in the 1960s, CONASUPO provided public subsidies for the production and distribution of staple foods like beans, rice, wheat, and corn (including tortillas). The fiscal crisis of the early 1980s led the government to gradually scale back support for CONASUPO, and by the 1990s it had significantly reduced its subsidies for most food products except beans and corn. The urgency to dismantle the food subsistence program increased in the fall of 1998, due to a major scandal involving former CONASUPO official Raúl Salinas, brother of former president Carlos Salinas. A U.S. Department of Justice investigation alleged his possible involvement in money laundering activities through the program. By the end of the year, the Mexican Congress decided on the total liquidation of this program.

CONASUPO was essentially replaced by two separate programs operated by the Ministry of Agriculture, Livestock, Rural Development, Fishing, and Food (Secretaría de Agricultura, Ganadería, Desarrollo Rural, Pesca y Alimentación, SAGARPA) to help subsidize agricultural production. The first program was called Alianza (the name was later modified by the Fox administration to be Alianza Contigo) and provides subsidies and financial assistance for the purchase of farm implements and irrigation. The second program is called Program for Direct Assistance in Agriculture (Programa de Apoyo Directo al Campo, PROCAMPO) and provides direct subsidies to protect farmers to offset international competition from foreign agribusinesses that receive subsidies from their governments, particularly those from the United States.[15] Thus the Mexican government essentially continues to provide subsidies for farmers and Mexican consumers—especially for corn and widely consumed corn-derived products like tortillas—which creates ample political support for these programs. President Calderón learned how strongly such subsidies are supported during his first few months in office, when he initially refused to offset agricultural price increases in early 2007 (see textbox 10.1).

Moreover, in addition to food subsidies, the Mexican government provides an array of other broadly accessible social assistance, such as the National Workers' Housing Fund Institute (Instituto del Fondo Nacional de la Vivienda para los Trabajadores, INFONAVIT), which assists workers in saving and obtaining loans to buy a home, and the health care and pension system described later in this chapter. Such programs fit the model of traditional social welfare programs, but they have increasingly seen important modifications that reduce or otherwise significantly alter the government's role in welfare service provision. To understand this shift, we now turn to look at the new trend toward market-oriented social welfare programs.

Government-Community Partnership Programs

Beginning in the late 1980s, Mexican policy makers gradually began to shift away from the use of traditional social welfare programs. Faced with

---

Textbox 10.1. PRESIDENT CALDERÓN AND THE TORTILLA CONFLICT

The issue of food subsidies became a contentious one for President Felipe Calderón, who attempted to reduce the deep divisions following the 2006 election by pledging to make fighting poverty his first priority. Yet when Calderón initially refused to offset the increase in the price of corn—the principal ingredient in tortillas, an indispensable staple of the Mexican diet—during his first few months in office, his pledge to help the poor seemed disingenuous. Calderón later negotiated a voluntary price cap on corn in which producers and retailers agreed not to allow corn to be sold above 45 cents a pound. Still, while Calderón supporters widely viewed this pact to be in keeping with his promise, his critics were incensed by the fact that the cap still allowed the price of corn to increase. Moreover, the higher price of tortillas was just one of many signs of inflation: between January 2006 and January 2007, the price of tortillas increased 40 percent, eggs were up 46 percent, sugar had increased by 26 percent, and rice cost 15 percent more. In response, a broad coalition of groups, including members of Congress from the PRD and the PT, as well as peasant organizations, civic groups, and unions, organized a series of public demonstrations, the largest attracting tens of thousands of supporters, to call for the systematic reintroduction of price controls on basic food items. Notably marginalized from the demonstrations was Andrés Manuel López Obrador, who was forced to speak after the main event had ended rather than taking center stage. Still, while López Obrador's support seemed seriously diminished, Calderón's ability to address the needs of Mexico's poorest citizens remained a critical challenge throughout his term.

---

enormous fiscal deficits, massive foreign debt, and spiraling inflation, Mexican policy makers sought to dramatically reduce public sector spending as part of the country's neoliberal economic restructuring. As we saw in the previous chapter, the shift toward fiscal austerity was partly the result of the pressure from the United States and international organizations like the World Bank and the International Monetary Fund, as well as the ascendancy of neoliberal economic policies that focused on market-driven policies and reduced state intervention.

In this context, reducing or eliminating government social welfare programs was one way that Mexican policy makers believed they could effectively respond to these multiple pressures. Yet, reducing public sector spending on social welfare policy also presented potential domestic political risks. As we saw above, throughout the decade, ordinary Mexicans were adversely affected by economic crisis, and—with the PAN gaining ground and new opposition forming on the left—the PRI government hoped to avoid losing political support for the regime. Hence, at the outset of his term, President Carlos Salinas introduced a new plan to address Mexico's social welfare needs, while also steering the country toward a different sort of public assistance.

In 1989, Salinas introduced the National Solidarity Program (Programa Nacional de Solidaridad, PRONASOL), also known simply as Solidaridad, as a complement to his aggressive neoliberal economic agenda. PRONASOL provided direct government funds or transfers to be used for the development of public works projects and social welfare programs, which had important political implications for building PRI support. Moreover, the type of projects—which included the construction of roads, water filtration plants, hospitals, clinics, recreational facilities, classrooms, and schools—was not particularly unique or distinct from populist or traditional social programs. However, it was the nature of its implementation that made PRONASOL emblematic of a new emphasis in social welfare policy programs emerging not only in Mexico, but also worldwide. Such programs placed greater emphasis on individual and community participation as the state's partners in the provision of social welfare, both as a way to reduce costs and to ensure a greater sense of personal responsibility among beneficiaries. Rather than providing universal benefits—such as access to health care or old-age pensions, even for those who can afford to pay their own way—this new brand of social welfare policy sought to ensure greater efficiency through the targeting of benefits. In the case of PRONASOL, the Salinas administration required local communities and stakeholders to form project committees, and it required that the beneficiaries of public works projects contribute their own labor, materials, or money to each project. In many ways, PRONASOL was considered an important innovation in government social welfare programs, and it marked an important shift in the underlying philosophical approach toward social policy in Mexico.

PRONASOL emphasized the decentralization of social welfare distribution, more efficient targeting of individual communities, and greater civic participation and social responsibility in its programs. Yet, at the same time, critics charged that PRONASOL in fact perpetuated strong central control, since in many cases its resources went directly to local communities, bypassing state and local governments. The program was also widely criticized because some projects were perceived as wasteful or blatant evidence of corruption. While the program led to the construction of many important infrastructure projects, PRONASOL funds were famously used to construct impractical projects in communities that had more obvious social needs; many poor indigenous communities, for example, received regulation-size basketball courts through the program. Finally, substantial amounts of money were misappropriated or went into lucrative contracts for government cronies who produced inadequately constructed projects. Not surprisingly, members of the political opposition claimed that Solidarity committees were thinly veiled extensions of the PRI, intended to bolster the party's lagging support in an era of economic crisis.

When President Ernesto Zedillo took office in December 1994, his administration was particularly sensitive to the charges of political manipulation that had been applied to PRONASOL and hoped to develop an alternative program that would again reshape Mexican social policy. However, key constituencies continued to support the program and, more importantly, the monetary crisis Zedillo faced at the outset of his term delayed major innovations until August 1997, when he introduced a new program called Progresa and began gradually dismantling PRONASOL. Progresa was a $155 million program intended to address the problem of extreme poverty through education, health care, and nutritional supplements. One of the main features of the program was direct cash stipends or scholarships (ranging from around US$10 to US$100 per month) made to low-income families—especially in carefully selected indigenous and rural communities—to keep their children in school. The program had a special emphasis on providing education for females, whose families were awarded higher stipends for keeping their daughters in the program. Tested initially in nine states during the previous year, the program was expanded to serve 1.9 million families at the national level over the course of 1997–1998; by the end of Zedillo's term, the program grew to reach 2.4 million families.[16]

Critics of Progresa—including then presidential candidate Vicente Fox—pointed to its failure to address the challenge of economic development, its perpetuation of a dependent state-society relationship, and the potential for political manipulation. That is, such critics viewed Progresa as a poor substitute for promoting economic growth and development. They also suggested that the Zedillo administration was able to use the program to manipulate public opinion in poor rural communities in favor of the PRI. Progresa reached approximately 40 percent of rural Mexican households by the end of Zedillo's term, and some recipients feared the program would be abolished if the PRI lost the 2000 elections.[17] In response to such criticisms, the Zedillo administration could point to Mexico's significant economic recovery and a restoration of growth by the end of his term. Also, Progresa was meticulously designed to ensure that participants were selected on the basis of need and not by political considerations.

In the end, Progresa proved extremely popular, given its impact in such a large number of households (reaching over 13 percent of the population in 53,000 communities by the end of Zedillo's term).[18] The program also enjoyed substantial legitimacy and support from international organizations like the World Bank and the Inter-American Development Bank, which lauded its efforts to break the cycle of multigenerational chronic poverty through education. In fact, in 2002, the Inter-American Development Bank announced the approval of its largest loan ever to Mexico: US$5 billion for the multiphase, six-year expansion of Progresa to cover urban areas and increase coverage of previously ineligible families. Hence, whatever criticisms Fox made of the program during the presidential campaign, his administration had strong incentives to continue and expand Progresa. Fox did choose to rename the program, which was now called Oportunidades, and gave more of the population access to its benefits. By the end of 2006, coverage extended to 5 million families—double the participation under Zedillo—from 2,441 municipalities in all thirty-one Mexican states and the Federal District.[19]

The Calderón administration opted to continue the Oportunidades program, which has continued to receive ample international recognition; indeed, in April 2007, New York Mayor Michael Bloomberg made headlines when he announced that he would implement a local program modeled on Oportunidades. Again, in the grand scheme, Oportunidades represents an interesting hybrid program of the two contrasting models of social welfare provision that have predominated in recent years. Like most traditional social welfare programs, Oportunidades emphasizes universal accessibility and the provision of handouts in the form of transfers and direct welfare benefits to people in need. Yet, like PRONASOL and the other community-based programs that have emerged in recent decades, Oportunidades seeks to help beneficiaries help themselves by establishing specific obligations to participate in the program. Policy analysts will likely need more time to evaluate the staying power and effectiveness of this model, and whether it can ultimately help break the cycle of multigenerational poverty.

MARKET-BASED SOCIAL WELFARE PROGRAMS

Our discussion of social welfare policy has so far focused primarily on social assistance programs that alleviate poverty. While such programs are an important part of the social welfare function of the modern state, they are not the only means—or necessarily the best way—to reduce poverty and promote overall social well-being. In most countries, the state's role in facilitating economic development, as well as providing other universal services—such as education, health care, retirement pensions for the elderly—arguably provides much greater overall social welfare than a reliance solely on direct assistance to the poor. With this in mind, President Fox emphasized the need for government programs that promote long-term economic development as a solution to poverty and inequality in Mexico.

One of the flagship programs that the Fox administration tried to launch was the Plan Puebla-Panamá, a regional development project that was intended to expand infrastructure and improve the connectivity of poor regions to domestic and world markets.[20] To implement the plan, Fox sought to work with his counterparts in Central America, and—importantly—to attract matching funding from private sector and international financial institutions. Yet, the Plan Puebla-Panamá faced significant criticism, especially by the Zapatista rebel movement, charging that it would facilitate the exploitation of indigenous peoples by further exposing them to the global economy. Perhaps more important, the failure of Fox's fiscal reform efforts made it difficult to secure the necessary revenue and private sector matching funds to follow through with the plan. In succeeding Fox, President Felipe Calderón expressed his interest in continuing efforts to implement the Plan Puebla-Panamá, but by the midpoint of his *sexenio* it became clear that the plan would receive no additional funding or lip service.

In recent years, a second policy innovation intended to create jobs for the working poor has been the use of microcredit lending. Limited access to capital presents a serious obstacle to economic advancement for poor people. While the wealthy can reinvest their accumulated wealth to make financial gains, the poor must often scrape by to survive. Without access to loans and credit, the poor are unable to initiate their own microenterprises (such as a local taco business) or make larger personal investments that build equity and improve their quality of life (such as purchasing a home). In developing countries like Mexico, obtaining such loans is difficult because banks lack assurances that the loans will be properly repaid. For these reasons, many economists and international organizations have increasingly advocated programs that assist poor people by providing access to credit, often with loans as small as fifty to a few hundred dollars provided on a very short-term basis. Such programs not only help people address short-term emergencies but can serve as a means to jump-start new business ventures.

President Fox was the first to introduce such a program, titled the National Small Business Financing Program (Programa Nacional de Financiamiento al Microempresario, PRONAFIM). By August 2006, PRONAFIM had distributed approximately $660 million in microcredit loans.[21] Although the program did not reach all would-be borrowers and some borrowers had difficulty repaying the loans, those households that participated in the program had measurable gains in spending on education, health, and recreational activities by loan recipients. These results seem to indicate at least preliminary benefits from participating in the program.[22] However, whether microlending constitutes a serious strategy to combat poverty remains to be seen. Recently critics of the practice have called attention to the fact that while microloans may keep impoverished people afloat, they often do little to facilitate the accumulation of wealth—a key component of reducing poverty. Furthermore, the largest private microlending enterprise in Mexico, Compartamos, is a for-profit bank that is criticized not only for the appearance that it is profiting from others' misfortune by accumulating profits, but also by charging exorbitant interest rates (sometimes more than 100 percent).[23] Therefore, further studies of PRONAFIM and other microcredit programs will be needed to evaluate their broad and long-term impact on poverty reduction in Mexico.

Finally, another recent approach to promoting economic development for the poor has centered on microregions, where Fox hoped to create special economic development zones, especially in poor areas. Under the slogan "With You: Hands at Work" (*Contigo, manos a la obra*)—the Fox administration sought to coordinate public-private partnerships between private businesses, universities, and communities to stimulate economic opportunities in 250 development zones in seventeen states and 476 poor municipalities throughout Mexico. The program succeeded in attracting participation from Cemex (Mexico's largest cement company), which provided concrete at reduced cost for paving dirt floors, as well as from the prestigious Monterrey Technological Institute and Microsoft, which donated computing equipment and training in these development zones. Yet the Contigo program also directed resources to other forms of poverty alleviation, health care, and education, such as access to basic nutrition, vaccinations, and Spanish-language lessons in indigenous communities.

Perhaps the best-known Contigo initiative was the 3-for-1 migrant remittance program (Programa 3x1 para Migrantes), which the Fox administration initiated in 2002 in an effort to leverage the billions of dollars sent back by migrants to their home communities in Mexico each year. Most money sent back to Mexico by migrants is intended to help their families back home, putting food on the table, assisting with home improvements, sending children to school, and the like. But some experts have noted that the economic development effects of such cash transfers are limited, since they are not channeled into long-term economic development projects. The 3-for-1 program tries to address this issue. For every peso migrants contributed to the 3-for-1 program, the federal, state, and local governments invested one peso each in matching funds for projects that to help improve those communities. By 2005, the government estimated that the program had benefited over 4 million people, distributing nearly $20 billion in investments to migrant-sending communities. Projects included social assistance programs, highway and street paving projects, electrification, and other local improvement projects, with 76 percent of federal funds for the program concentrated in five moderately poor migrant-sending states: Jalisco, Zacatecas, Guanajuato, Michoacán, and San Luís Potosí (in order of spending).[24] It is not clear that these projects will have long-lasting effects;

some may be mere white elephant projects that do relatively little to promote economic development. For another, most migrant remittances are directed by individuals to support their families; getting migrants to contribute to public goods is more difficult, since it does not provide a direct personal benefit. Hence, experts still disagree as to whether migrant remittances truly can (or should) be harnessed for economic development purposes.

What is clear is that in recent years, policy makers have increasingly emphasized innovative approaches to solving poverty through strategies that emphasize economic development. This shift may be particularly representative of Mexico's larger political transformation in that the country's new governing party—the PAN—has a strong business orientation, or it could simply reflect broader global policy trends such as the now widespread practice of paying single mothers to send their children to school and take them to regular medical check-ups. In the longer term, critics are sure to raise questions about the effectiveness of these strategies and whether they are politically motivated.[25] Yet to turn such criticisms into a political advantage, PRI and PRD opponents of the PAN will need to develop an alternative set of policies that successfully engages the poor and, ideally, helps improve their conditions.

REFORMING EDUCATION, HEALTH CARE, AND SOCIAL SECURITY

In addition to strategies that improve economic development opportunities as a means of combating poverty, policy makers and experts have also increasingly pointed to the need for reforms in Mexican education. At the same time, the Mexican government has recently tried to expand and modernize the provision of health care and retirement pensions, to better address the basic needs of society. Below we briefly outline the current systems in place, the areas for improvement, and recent or pending reforms in these areas.

Education

Mexico's constitution guarantees all citizens access to a basic education. Like the United States, Mexico has multiple levels of education, including primary school, secondary or middle school, and preparatory or high school. Unlike in the United States, however, two-thirds of Mexican children age three to five also attend preschool, which generally consists of three grades, corresponding to the child's age.[26]

All told, approximately 91 percent of students enrolled at these levels attend public schools. Mexico has a number of alternative programs to provide access to primary education, including adult education programs and bilingual-bicultural programs for many of Mexico's numerous indigenous dialects and cultures. Since 1993, a secondary education—the equivalent of U.S. middle school—has been obligatory for all persons aged twelve to sixteen who have completed primary education. Students over age sixteen are eligible to study in facilities designed for vocational studies or in adult-oriented secondary education programs. Together, preschool, primary, and secondary education constitute what Mexican officials describe as the basic education required by the constitution; approximately 25 million students (77 percent of all students) are enrolled at this level, with approximately 1.1 million (67 percent) of Mexican teachers working in basic education.

Preparatory (*preparatoria*) education is the Mexican equivalent of U.S. high school.[27] While preparatory school is typically required for entrance to university and professional schools, it is neither obligatory nor guaranteed. Approximately 3.6 million Mexicans attended preparatory schools in 2005–2006, though this represented a relatively small proportion (only about 11 percent) of total student enrollment in the Mexican education system (see figure 10.1). Since 1990, however, there has been a modest increase in the proportion of students attending early childhood education and higher levels beyond basic or middle school education. The largest increases can be seen in the proportion of students going to preschool (up from 10.9 percent in 1990 to 13.8 percent of total student enrollment in 2005) and preparatory school (up from 8.4 percent in 1990 to 11.3 percent of all student enrollment in 2005). These trends are especially promising because of the perceived long-term benefits of preschool—including better student retention, performance, and socialization—and the potential for increased advancement to higher education. However, meeting the obligatory requirements of preschool established by law while ensuring a high level of quality is likely to prove challenging; in 2007, the Ministry of Education reported difficulties in ensuring full preschool enrollment for all Mexican children, due to a lack of adequate teachers and facilities.[28]

Mexican higher education (*educación superior*) is provided by university, vocational, and other specialized educational programs. The objective of higher education is to promote the development of professionals in various areas of science, technology, culture, and other specialized fields. While higher education programs may be either public or private, the vast majority of students at this level attend public universities. This reflects the fact that public universities tend to be much more affordable than private universities. For example, for many years there was virtually no cost—students paid a few U.S. cents per year—to attend the National Autonomous University of Mexico (Universidad Nacional Autónoma de México, UNAM), the largest university in Mexico, with more than two hundred thousand

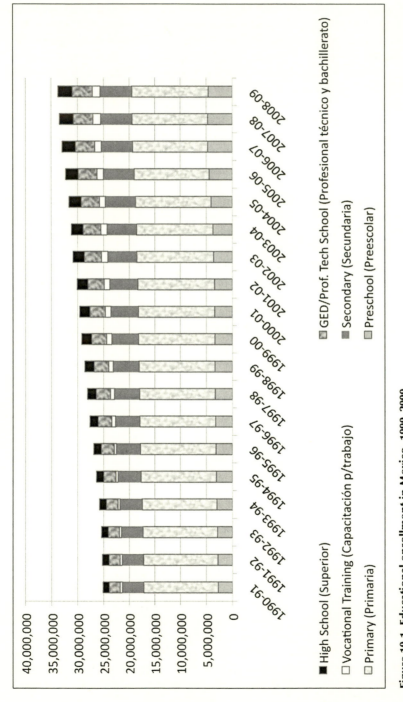

Figure 10.1. Educational enrollment in Mexico, 1990–2009

Source: Secretaría de Educación Pública, "Sistema educativo de los Estados Unidos Mexicanos: Principales cifras ciclo escolar, 2008–2009" (Mexico City: Mexican Secretary of Education, 2009), 23.

students. In fact, when university officials tried to introduce higher fees in 2000, students and faculty waged a massive 291-day strike to protest, essentially shutting down classes. Government troops reclaimed the campus on February 6, 2000, arresting about seven hundred people and drawing accusations of minor abuses. The campus was reopened the following week, but authorities declined to follow through on their plan to significantly increase fees; today, UNAM's annual tuition rates typically amount to several U.S. dollars, depending on the student's major. By comparison, college tuition and fees range between US$11,000 and US$12,000 annually to attend the privately run Monterrey Technological Institute (Instituto Tecnológico y de Estudios Superiores de Monterrey, ITESM) or the Eastern Technological Institute for Higher Studies (Instituto Tecnológico de Estudios Superiores del Oriente, ITESO) in Guadalajara.[29] Since Mexican universities typically do not have on-campus dormitories, these rates do not include room and board.

Mexico's total budget for education represented about 5.7 percent of GDP, which was about average for OECD countries.[30] However, much remains to be done to improve the quality of Mexico's education system, which ranks last among OECD countries with an average Programme for International Student Assessment (PISA) score that indicates its students lag more than two years behind their peers in the highest-performing country.[31] There are also disturbing patterns of unequal access to education in Mexico. While the national illiteracy rate was about 8 percent in 2006, many northern and urban states enjoyed much lower rates than average: Baja California (1.4 percent), the Federal District (2.7 percent), and Nuevo León (2.8 percent). At the same time, poor southern states suffered the worst rates of illiteracy in the country: Guerrero (18.2 percent), Oaxaca (18.3 percent), and Chiapas (19.4 percent). Many experts believe that addressing such inequities is critical as a means of alleviating poverty and promoting economic development. Still, important questions must be asked about the kind of educational reforms that are needed, and specifically how improved educational opportunities will be translated into opportunities for better employment and compensation.

How these questions are addressed will have important implications for contemporary democratic politics in Mexico. First, one obvious implication for Mexican democracy is that an educated populace may foster a more politically active and responsible electorate. Educated voters are usually more likely to turn out at the polls, and they are often more in tune with political issues; uneducated voters are sometimes left out or easily misled—which some fear is even worse. Improvements in education may therefore make for better and more participatory democratic politics overall. Second, over the next decade, the state of education in Mexico will likely have corresponding implications for Mexico's political parties as they compete for votes. Indeed, advances in education arguably may have favored the PAN's gradual rise to power, especially in the well-educated north, while the PRI long depended on its ability to draw support from (or exploit) poor and uneducated voters. The PRI has learned how to compete for the support of Mexico's educationally advanced northern voters, but at the same time there appears to be significant competition between the PRI and the PRD for the voters in Mexico's underprivileged southern states. The implications of this dynamic are unclear. It remains to be seen whether improved rates of education in these states—combined with better economic opportunities—might lead more southern voters to consider supporting the PAN.

Health Care and Social Security

Health care is an important policy area that has major social welfare implications and bears significantly on any discussion of poverty and inequality in Mexico. The Mexican government has long played an integral role in the provision of social security services, including health care, disability, life insurance, and retirement benefits, and today provides coverage of some sort to approximately 80 percent of the population. Most public medical and retirement services are provided through the Ministry of Health, which was created in 1943, when the Mexican government was beginning to embrace a much greater role in the provision of social welfare. The main public health-care services overseen by the Ministry of Health are distinguished by whether recipients are public or private employees. Government employees and their families are covered by either federal- or state-subsidized health-care programs. Federal employees pay approximately 8.5 percent of their salary to the social security insurance program of the Institute of Security and Social Services for Government Employees (Instituto de Seguridad y Servicios Sociales de los Trabajadores del Estado, or ISSSTE), while state and municipal employees are covered by state-level programs. All other formally employed Mexicans similarly pay into the Mexican Social Security Institute (Instituto Mexicano del Seguro Social, or IMSS) insurance program.[32]

IMSS is a much larger program than ISSSTE, since coverage extends to all affiliated private sector employees, their spouses, children, and parents of the primary affiliate. Both IMSS and ISSSTE also play a much broader role than the U.S. social security system, delivering a variety of health-care services, unemployment insurance, pensions for retired and disabled persons, life insurance, and programs for day care, recreation, culture, and the arts.[33] Finally, in addition to the 47 percent of the population covered by the programs mentioned above, there are a variety of other public and private health-care services available in Mexico. Thanks to a major health system reform in 2003, the Ministry of Health provides some direct services to the other half of Mexico's population who are self-employed, unemployed, or not employed in the formal sector.[34] In addition, the Comprehensive Family Development Program (Desarrollo Integral de la Familia, DIF), for example, is a decentralized government agency operated at the federal, state, and local levels to provide a wide array of services for families. At the same time, there are a variety of private and nonprofit medical care programs in Mexico. For those who are self-employed or can afford private health coverage or attention, private prepay insurance programs and fee-for-service medical care are available; indeed, this roughly 3 percent of Mexicans (mostly with relatively high socioeconomic status) has access to some of the most skilled medical professionals in the world. Generally speaking, both public and private medical services, as well as prescription drugs, are comparably more affordable than in many developed countries. Indeed, it is common along the U.S.-Mexican border, for example, for U.S. citizens to travel south to Mexico to obtain cheaper health services and medicines.

Despite this seemingly extensive infrastructure and accessibility for health care and social security, there are important limitations to Mexico's system that are germane to any discussion of poverty and inequality. First, as noted above, there can be a significant distinction in the quality of care provided by public and private medical services. While this is generally true in many public health-care systems, the degree of inequality in Mexico makes the gap in the quality of private-public medical services particularly severe. Indeed, as Knaul and Frenk note, the World Health Organization ranked Mexican health care 51st out of 191 countries in 2000, but scored Mexico much lower (144th) on the issue of financial equity in the health-care system.[35]

Second, the Mexican health-care system is not easily accessible to many Mexicans. While the system theoretically provides universal coverage to all public and private sector employees, the reality is quite different. Because a large number of Mexicans—possibly as many as 40 percent—are employed in the informal sector, their wages are not typically reported to the government, and employers do not pay into Mexican social security. Because these individuals are not eligible for ISSSTE or IMSS social security coverage, the Ministry of Health operates a variety of programs—including the Popular Insurance Program (Seguro Popular, SP) and IMSS–Oportunidades—that endeavor to provide support for this significant portion of the population.

To make matters worse, it became increasingly apparent during the 1990s that the IMSS pension system for formal employees was headed toward bankruptcy. Like other pension programs, IMSS relied on payroll deductions from employee wages to ensure that they will continue to receive income during their retirement. Like the United States, Mexico is in the midst of a major generational change that will significantly impact the functioning of its pension programs over the next two decades. Population growth and mortality rates in both countries have fallen significantly since World War II and the number of people paying in to the system has declined, while the number of people needing its benefits has increased. Furthermore, increased life expectancy, which is now over seventy, also means that pension recipients now require benefits for a longer period of time.[36] Adding to this urgent demographic reality is the fact that significant problems, including evasion in payroll contributions, weakened the financial structure of the pension program.[37]

In this context, Mexican public officials have attempted to make several major reforms, beginning with a series of modifications to the pension system and, more recently, with significant reforms to the public health-care system. First, beginning in the early 1990s, the Mexican government attempted to address the pension problem by increasing the amount of workers' IMSS contributions, and by introducing in 1992 a new program for worker pensions, known as an employer-defined contribution plan. This employer contribution program, known as the Retirement Savings System (Sistema de Ahorro para el Retiro, SAR), required that employers contribute 2 percent of a worker's salary to an individual retirement account (IRA) managed by Mexican banks for the employee.[38] Drawing on these investments, SAR was intended to help supplement IMSS pension contributions and bolster an individual contributor's retirement income. However, the SAR program experienced significant problems, including poor regulation, confusion, and excessive concentration in the management of accounts.[39] In 1997, reforms to the SAR introduced a new employee-defined contribution program in which not only employers but all formally employed workers were now required to make mandatory fixed payroll allocations into privately operated pension fund plans. The perceived advantage of the 1997 reforms was the potential for private financial institutions—also known as Retirement Funds Administrators (Administradoras de Fondos para el Retiro, AFORES)—to generate significantly greater returns and better service for pensioners.[40] Indeed, based on experiences in other Latin American countries, the AFORES program was viewed by many observers as a successful model for retirement pension management and a way to boost Mexico's domestic savings rate.[41]

During the Fox administration, however, Mexico's public health-care and social security system continued to suffer from a lack of coverage for uninsured persons. In 2003, an estimated 20 percent of the Mexican population did not have access to health and social security coverage of any kind.[42] By comparison, an estimated 15 percent of the U.S. population—including 30 percent of all people living in poverty (and one in nine children)—did not have any health-care insurance at that time, and depended primarily on pay-as-you-go care or emergency medical coverage. Moreover, Mexico's pension system also evidenced some problems in the administration of AFORES (including high operating costs, commissions, and fees), the relatively low amount of contributions to retirement accounts, and—perhaps more significantly—a lack of portability for workers wishing to transfer their pension funds from one employer to another. In 2003 a major reform was passed that expanded health-care coverage from the 47 percent covered by IMSS and ISSSTE to an additional 11 million uninsured families, or roughly 50 million Mexicans. This reform created the National System for Social Protection in Health (Sistema Nacional de Protección Social en Salud, SNPSS) and its centerpiece, the Popular Insurance Program, with the goal of expanding universal coverage to all uninsured Mexicans by 2010.[43]

Upon taking office, President Calderón declared public health and social security to be a continuing priority for his administration, with a special emphasis on increasing overall coverage and equity within the existing system. At the start of his term, Calderón significantly increased the budget for health-care programs and announced a major initiative to provide universal access to all Mexicans born at the start of his administration on December 1, 2006. In addition, his administration announced plans to significantly expand the functions of the Popular Insurance Program to better and more rapidly expand coverage to those currently uninsured. Calderón also rolled out new mobile health programs to provide medical services in poor and remote rural areas, and a series of new hospitals and clinics was to be opened throughout the country during his term. Finally, in his 2006–2012 National Development Plan, Calderón specifically targeted the 100 poorest municipalities of the country for special efforts to improve access to social welfare programs, as well as for improved opportunities for economic development.[44]

Later, in March 2007, the administration proposed significant reforms to the government pension program, ISSSTE, that were approved the next month. The ISSSTE reform signaled the Calderón administration's ability to negotiate with the opposition-dominated legislature, as well as vital support that Calderón enjoyed from some labor allies who favored the benefits that the reform would bring to government employee teachers.[45] The ISSSTE reform was the first part of Calderón's plan to expand changes to other areas of the social security system, by expanding coverage available to independent workers (including those employed in the informal sector), increasing the required contributions to pension programs, and by allowing the possibility to roll over or move pension plans between different employers. His legislative success in passing the reform appeared to boost Calderón's overall public approval ratings, and brought very favorable responses from the private sector and the international community.[46] Still, whether Calderón's efforts result in long-term improvements to Mexico's health-care and retirement benefit system will require further evaluation.

CONCLUSION

Despite Mexico's economic strengths—and even tremendous prosperity—the country's continued development depends on improving the lot of poor Mexicans. Better distribution of wealth and opportunities would enable them to make a greater contribution to the overall economy. To some degree, Mexico has made progress toward this end, particularly as the economic turmoil of the 1980s and 1990s has subsided in recent years. Indeed, recent Mexican government strategies to promote social welfare have focused significantly on promoting economic development, both at the regional and grassroots level. This emphasis appears to be yet another reflection of the new emphasis on the state's role as a facilitator—and not the direct caretaker—of both the economy and social welfare.

At the same time, there has been an important shift away from traditional government policies for promoting social welfare, toward new market-oriented policies that promote greater individual responsibility and opportunity. For some, this shift in the Mexican approach to poverty represents a positive transition away from cumbersome, state-centered programs that encouraged clientelistic abuse and welfare dependency. But the shift away from traditional social welfare policies has fierce critics. For them, the new orientation of social welfare programs in Mexico and the dismantling of the social safety net places the actual burden of poverty alleviation on Mexico's poor and remains unproven as a means to promote long-term economic development. Indeed, whether economic times are good or bad, large numbers of Mexican people feel dissatisfied with the government's ability to deliver economic prosperity.

The debate over how best to address poverty and inequality in Mexico is far from over, particularly in the wake of the most recent recession. In broad terms, the PRD and other leftist parties, as well as many within the PRI, emphasize redistribution and assistance to the poor, while conservatives in the PAN and some in the PRI favor promoting market-driven opportunities. Just as it shaped the presidential election of 2006, this issue is sure to play a prominent role in 2012. Improving the quality of life for all Mexicans will remain a challenge for some time to come. How these issues are handled will undoubtedly also hold major implications for contemporary Mexican democracy, both in terms of future political outcomes and the ability of the country's millions of poor voters to participate as full and active democratic citizens.

11

The Rule of Law in Mexico

Over the last two decades, elevated levels of crime and violence, pervasive governmental corruption, and inadequate access to justice have contributed to a severe security crisis in Mexico. Foremost among Mexico's recent security challenges has been the conflict among powerful organized crime groups that have killed tens of thousands of people in their efforts to profit from the illicit U.S. drug market. The most pessimistic assessments suggest that this crisis will prove too great for Mexico's new democracy.[1] After a sharp increase in violence in 2008, a worst-case assessment by the U.S. Joint Forces Command pointed to Mexico as one of two countries worldwide—along with Pakistan—that could suffer a sudden collapse into a failed state.[2] In 2010, comments by U.S. Secretary of State Hillary Clinton suggested that Mexico's security woes are a sign of domestic insurgency.

Despite these dire appraisals, Mexico's problems are not even remotely similar to those found in so-called failed states, like Afghanistan, Congo, and Somalia.[3] With the exception of very limited geographic areas, the Mexican state maintains a monopoly in controlling its defined territory. Also, while the tactics of Mexico's drug-trafficking organizations may *resemble* those of insurgents or even terrorists, they generally lack the kind of political agendas associated with such threats.[4] Moreover, severe security challenges are not unique to Mexico; other emerging democracies—such as Colombia, Brazil, Russia, and South Africa—have struggled with severe problems of crime, violence, and corruption that detract from democratic governance. Indeed, violence elsewhere in the Western Hemisphere is actually far worse than in Mexico. Compared to most of its neighbors, Mexico's overall rate of homicide over the last several years has been relatively low (see table 11.1).

Still, there is no doubt that current levels of crime and violence severely challenge the Mexican government and undermine the confidence of its citizens. Mexico suffers from the chronic inadequacies of its criminal justice and judicial system, including limited training, insufficient resources, and outright corruption. In part, these inadequacies have to do with Mexico's incomplete transition to democratic governance, which requires a

Table 11.1. Homicides per 100,000 Inhabitants in the Americas, 2003–2008

Country	Data Source	2003	2004	2005	2006	2007	2008
Jamaica	National Police	37.1	55.5	62.8	49.9	58.7	59.5
El Salvador	Observatorio	58.8	64.5	62.4	64.6	57.3	51.8
Honduras	Observatorio	33.6	31.9	35.1	42.9	50.0	60.9
Venezuela	NGO	47.5	43.2	36.4	36.4	44.2	47.2
Colombia	National Statistics Office	61.4	52.8	43.8	41.2	40.1	–
Belize	National Police	24.8	28.6	28.7	31.9	32.9	34.3
St. Kitts & Nevis	National Police	20.9	22.7	16.3	34.2	31.7	35.2
Anguilla	National Statistics Office	15.8	7.6	7.3	28.4	27.6	–
Dom. Republic	Attorney General	17.8	24.1	25.2	22.2	21.5	–
Brazil	Ministry of Justice	–	–	–	–	20.4	22.0
Puerto Rico	National Police	20.3	20.5	19.7	19.0	18.5	20.4
Guyana	National Statistics Office	27.1	17.2	18.6	21.3	15.1	20.7
Nicaragua	National Police	11.9	12.0	13.4	13.1	12.8	13.0
Paraguay	National Statistics Office	17.1	17.4	15.0	12.3	12.2	–
Bolivia	National Statistics Office	29.0	41.6	9.5	29.1	10.6	–
Mexico	NGO	12.4	11.2	10.7	10.9	9.6	11.6
Costa Rica	National Police	9.5	6.6	7.8	8.0	8.3	–
Chile	UN Survey	12.5	9.8	8.2	19.2	6.6	8.1
Uruguay	Ministry of Interior	5.9	6.0	5.7	6.1	5.8	–
United States	UN Survey	5.6	5.4	5.5	5.6	5.5	5.2
Argentina	Ministry of Justice	7.6	5.9	5.5	5.2	5.2	–
Canada	UN Survey	1.5	1.7	1.8	1.7	1.6	1.7

Source: Countries selected based on available data from the UN Office on Drugs and Crime, table titled "Homicide Statistics, Criminal Justice and Public Health Sources—Trends (2003–2008)." Observatorio refers to the Observatorio Centroamericano sobre Violencia.

major transformation of the state's coercive institutions to ensure that law enforcement agencies are accountable, that the judicial system is autonomous and impartial, and that other institutions can reasonably ensure citizens' access to justice. Unfortunately, progress on these changes has been slow. Judicial reforms passed in 2008 will not take full effect throughout the country until 2016, and police reform is a long-term challenge that will require years of investment and experimentation. In the meantime, President Felipe Calderón has turned to the military to help secure areas troubled by crime and violence, raising concerns about military corruption and human rights violations that could seriously undermine public support for the military.[5]

This chapter addresses the problems of crime and violence in contemporary Mexico in this still-evolving context. The first half discusses the importance of the rule of law for a healthy democracy and the inability of Mexico's judicial system to deal adequately with the recent public security crisis. We then address Mexico's most pressing rule of law challenges and its prospects for justice sector reform. Throughout this chapter, we try to illustrate the important relationship between democracy and the rule of law, since they provide mutually reinforcing support for one another.

DEMOCRACY AND THE RULE OF LAW IN MEXICO

Does the rule of law exist if some actors in society regularly and flagrantly violate the law—that is, when there is a high rate of crime? Can there be rule of law in authoritarian regimes, where dictators and soldiers can violate the law with impunity? Is there rule of law when the law itself is blatantly unjust, as when discriminatory laws were enforced by the government under Nazi Germany, South African apartheid, or U.S. Jim Crow legislation? Answers to these questions vary widely, since societal standards and evaluations of the rule of law differ over time and from country to country. Still, it is clear that these questions touch on fundamental aspects of the rule of law, as it is commonly understood in scholarly literature on the topic.

The rule of law incorporates several key presumptions: that actors in society are mostly held accountable to the law (e.g., individual crimes are prevented or punished), that representatives of the state are also generally held accountable under the law (e.g., punished for corruption), and that there is typically access to justice under the law (e.g., equal treatment under the law, due process, and human rights protections).[6] Yet, while our analysis focuses primarily on criminal justice, on the legal responsibilities of the state, and on the legal rights of citizens, it is important to note that the rule of law is not limited to these issues. Nor is the provision of the rule of law solely a function and reflection of state power. Governmental regulation and civil legal protections in Mexico—such as corporate oversight, contract enforcement, and property rights—also contribute to the enforcement of law and order. At the same time, civil society and individual communities play a major role in promoting the rule of law.

However it is conceptualized, essential elements of the rule of law were effectively absent for much of the twentieth century during PRI rule. Criminals could act with a degree of impunity because of ineffective law enforcement, or because they could negotiate agreements with corrupt public officials. The hegemonic and clientelistic nature of PRI rule also meant that there were few checks against abuses of state power, and a tendency to utilize public positions and resources for personal advantage. Rare but sometimes severe instances of repression—as well as systematic violations of due process and human rights—further compromised access to justice in Mexico during the PRI regime. Yet at the same time, the PRI also achieved a certain degree of equilibrium and control, effectively contributing to a relative degree of order. Indeed, the country appeared to experience a continuous net decrease in criminal activity—as measured by the number of suspects charged with certain crimes—from the 1940s well into the 1970s (see figure 11.1).[7]

MEXICO'S PUBLIC INSECURITY CRISIS

In the 1980s and 1990s, Mexico experienced a sharp increase in certain forms of crime, especially robbery and theft.[8] For example, in Mexico City, many citizens became victims of armed assailants who forced them to withdraw the maximum daily amount allowed at automatic teller machines (typically equivalent to a few hundred dollars), sometimes holding the victims until after midnight in order to make a second withdrawal. This became known as an express kidnapping (*secuestro express*), since assailants typically held their prisoners for only a few hours.[9] What factors have contributed to Mexico's dramatic increase in violent crime? The country's economic difficulties are perhaps the most obvious factor. Beginning as early as the 1976 peso devaluation and spiking in the mid-1980s during the debt crisis and again after the 1994 peso devaluation, certain rates of crime have risen along with increases in unemployment, inflation, inequality, and instability. As jobs were lost in the formal sector in the 1970s and 1980s, Mexico's informal sector expanded dramatically—by some estimates accounting for 40 percent of all employment and economic activity—with the proliferation of street vendors, pirate taxis, and a burgeoning market for secondhand goods.[10]

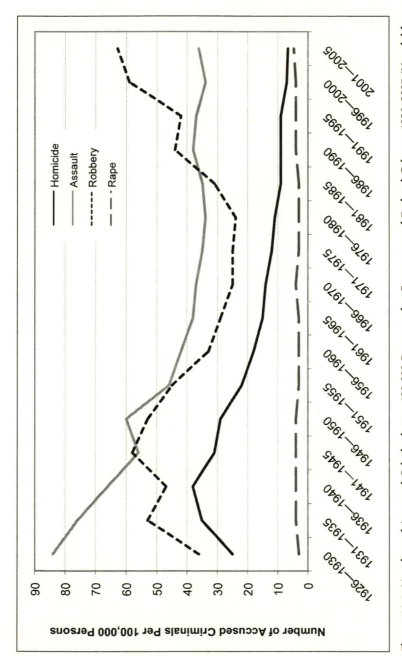

Figure 11.1. Number of Accused Criminals per 100,000 Persons, for Common and Federal Crimes, 1926–2005 (Homicide, Assault, Robbery, and Rape)

Source: Data on accused criminals (*presuntos delincuentes*) compiled from INEGI by Pablo Piccato from 1926–2001 and by David Shirk and Rommel Rico from 2001–2005.

However, Mexico's security problems ran deeper than economic crisis and petty crime. During the 1990s, unsolved plots led to the high-profile assassinations of PRI party president Francisco Ruiz Massieu and PRI presidential candidate Luis Donaldo Colosio. In addition, there were hundreds of femicides (*femicidios*) in Ciudad Juárez, Mexico's largest border city (located just across from El Paso, Texas). At the same time, elevated numbers of homicides in some states resulted from labor and land tenure disputes that provoked protests and violent conflicts in places like Chiapas and Oaxaca. As a result of such instances of violent crime, Mexicans have been barraged by gruesome, full-color images of violence—alarming crime stories of rape, assault, and murder—in the so-called red page (*nota roja*) journalism of daily newspapers and media broadcasts.

Still, the worst violence in Mexico has arisen from conflicts among drug-trafficking organizations. Mexican drug traffickers rose to prominence in the 1980s, as trafficking routes shifted from the Caribbean to Mexico. By the 1990s, the downfall of Colombia's major drug-trafficking organizations gave organized crime groups in Mexico the upper hand. Today, perhaps 450,000 people in Mexico rely in some significant way on drug trafficking as a source of income, and official estimates suggest that drug-trafficking activities now account for 3 to 4 percent of Mexico's more than $1 trillion GDP.[11] Whatever economic opportunities it has created, the rise of Mexico's illicit drug-trafficking industry has also exacted a terrible social cost. In 2009 alone, a weekly tally compiled by *Reforma* documented 6,587 drug trafficking–related killings, an increase of about 20 percent over the previous year.[12] By late 2010, the annual count had surpassed 10,000 killings. All told, the number of homicides resulting from organized crime during the Calderón administration is estimated at more than 45,000 deaths.

INADEQUACIES OF MEXICO'S JUDICIAL SYSTEM

In the face of growing crime and violence, the inability of the Mexican justice system to adequately respond to escalating crime and violence constitutes a second major contributing factor to Mexico's security crisis. Mexico's law enforcement, judicial, and security institutions face systemic resource limitations, inadequate professional training, procedural and organizational inefficiencies, and corruption—serious problems that seriously compromise the rule of law. Mexican crime experts like Guillermo Zepeda, author of the book *Crime without Punishment* (*Crimen sin castigo*), point to the abysmal performance of the criminal justice system in obtaining reports of criminal activity, investigating those crimes, and prosecuting cases efficiently with due process of law. Indeed, according to crime victimization surveys at the start of the Fox administration, only about 25 of 100 crimes were reported because of the intense distrust and lack of confidence Mexicans felt toward police and other public authorities. Of those 25 reported crimes, only 4.6 were actually investigated; and of those crimes, only 1.6 (35 percent) resulted in the filing of criminal charges against a suspected criminal (*presunto delincuente*).[13]

As discussed in chapter 5, civil law systems like Mexico's frequently draw on Roman law and an inquisitorial model of criminal justice, which derive from historical and cultural factors in civil law systems that placed the judiciary in the position of gathering evidence and making determinations of guilt or innocence on behalf of the state. In Mexico, public prosecutors (*ministerio público*) and the judicial police (*policía judicial*) have oversight over criminal investigations and an active role in levying charges against the accused before the court. As in other civil law systems, the court requires compelling indications of guilt in advance of trial and sentencing. Once accused, a suspect is often held in detention prior to sentencing, since voluntary pretrial release of the accused (e.g., through bail bonding) is rare in Mexico. As a result, due to enormous case backlogs, defendants awaiting a sentence account for roughly 40 percent of all prisoners in Mexico. Moreover, because Mexican court procedures rely more on written than oral presentation of information—and do not currently use jury trials—criminal procedure lacks the degree of transparency and public scrutiny found in other systems. Ultimately, with or without a sentence, many prisoners complain of severe overcrowding, poor conditions, corruption, and abuses within Mexican prisons.[14]

Thus, while many civil law systems theoretically maintain a presumption of innocence prior to the verdict of the court, defendants are commonly viewed as guilty until proven innocent. Given the ineffectiveness of the criminal justice system, many victims of crime and their communities are dissatisfied. In one survey, less than 20 percent of Mexicans said that they would expect the justice system to provide a fair trial and due process. Of those who *had* used the justice system (only 25 percent of the sample), half felt that they received neither a fair trial nor a prompt resolution, and 33 percent reported major problems with the process or being asked for a bribe.[15] Furthermore, many Mexicans do not feel that civil rights are widely respected or perceive equality before the law to be the norm. While 55 percent of respondents believed that women always or nearly always have their rights respected, fewer than 10 percent felt that poor and indigenous people are treated fairly.[16]

In some cases, crime victims experience a double victimization when they attempt to report crimes, since police investigators are often ill trained to deal with the posttraumatic stress of victimization and—in the worst cases—may even ask victims to pay a bribe for a speedier investigation of their case. However common such scenarios may be, they contribute to the general sense that crime victims have little access to justice in Mexico, and they suggest that there are pervasive and systemic problems that must be addressed by comprehensive rule of law reforms. To better understand these problems of access to justice, as well as the related challenges of maintaining order and governmental accountability, we examine next some of the major rule of law challenges in Mexico that have come to symbolize the failures of the Mexican criminal justice system.

MAJOR RULE OF LAW CHALLENGES IN MEXICO

Below we discuss three major rule of law challenges that illustrate the difficulty of providing order, accountability, and access to justice in contemporary Mexico. Our examination of drug trafficking addresses perhaps the most violent and visible evidence of the absence of order in Mexico, and it provides a foundation for understanding related bilateral issues discussed in chapter 13. We then discuss corruption, which is often rational and self-perpetuating—and perhaps the best illustration of how the system fails to require accountability and further compromises the rule of law. The serial murders in Ciudad Juárez mentioned above are explored in greater detail here to provide a case study in problems that most citizens face in attaining access to justice in Mexico.

Drug Trafficking

Since the 1990s, ordinary Mexicans have been beleaguered by daily media accounts of killings and assaults committed by drug traffickers and gangs involved in producing and transporting cocaine, methamphetamine, and other narcotics primarily for consumption in the United States. In 2010 alone Mexico had, on average, at least thirty drug-related murders per day. Clearly the illegal drug trade reinforces the weakness of Mexican authorities and the judicial system more generally. Drug trafficking yields such enormous profits—with estimated proceeds back to Mexico of at least $6 billion to $7 billion annually—that drug cartels are often better equipped than the law enforcement agencies that combat them. Drug-trafficking organizations frequently take advantage of the relatively low salaries and low levels of professionalism among police and public officials, offering a combination of bribes and threats—"silver or lead" (*plata o plomo*)—which undermines effective law enforcement.

Understanding how Mexico came to be a major producer and the primary transit point for drugs imported to the United States requires some consideration of the long-term evolution of the so-called war on drugs. It is easy to forget that consumption of narcotics was largely unregulated at the start of the twentieth century. Indeed, drugs like heroin, cocaine, and marijuana were consumed regularly not only for recreation but as "snake oil" remedies for a wide variety of illnesses. Immigrants to the United States played an integral part in establishing the linkages and networks of transport and distribution for narcotics, both before and after drugs were criminalized in the United States in the 1920s and 1930s. Late-nineteenth-century production and distribution of narcotics to the United States originated largely from Asia (particularly China) but later shifted to Europe and the Middle East. By the mid-twentieth century, drug-trafficking operations—primarily for heroin—were largely controlled by the Cosa Nostra, Italian mobsters with ties stretching from Turkish producers to French refiners and ultimately into U.S. markets.

This so-called French Connection was broken in the late 1960s, thanks to successful law enforcement efforts and to the relocation of drug production and flows. By the 1970s and into the 1980s, shifting preferences made cocaine the drug of choice among U.S. consumers. This led to the development of highly sophisticated trafficking networks to the United States from the Andean region, where coca grows naturally (primarily in Bolivia and Peru) and is consumed liberally as an herbal remedy for altitude sickness. Colombian cartels based in the cities of Medellín and Cali achieved a level of remarkable influence, audacity, and even social prestige. Indeed, the notorious cartel drug lord Pablo Escobar effectively bought a seat in Congress and cultivated a reputation as a folk hero for Colombia's poor. Over a year and half after escaping from jail in July 1992, Escobar was killed in a U.S.-aided operation by Colombian law enforcement. Although the Medellín cartel was briefly succeeded by the Cali cartel, Escobar's death signaled the decline of the Colombian cartels.

Historically, Mexico had been an important but low-level supplier of drugs to the United States, notably sending homegrown products like marijuana and opium from the Golden Triangle of Chihuahua, Durango, and Sinaloa, as well as other major drug-producing states like Michoacán and Guerrero. During the heyday of the Colombian cartels, most Andean product was moved into the United States via the Gulf of Mexico to Miami. However, as U.S. interdiction efforts in the Gulf gained ground, the Colombians increasingly relied on Mexican supply networks into the United States. With the disintegration of Colombia's major cartels in the late 1980s and early 1990s, there was a shift in control as Mexican organized-crime groups took over the transport and distribution of drugs. Moreover, thanks to the corrupt government officials who allowed Mexican organized-crime groups to operate with impunity, there was little significant intergroup conflict or violence, since their territories and markets were clearly demarcated and even agreed upon. Because of their territorial segmentation, high degree of coordination, and oligopolistic control over the drug trade, these organized crime groups became known as drug cartels.[17]

During the 1980s, the dominant Mexican drug-trafficking organization was known as the Guadalajara cartel, headed by Miguel Angel Félix Gallardo from the Pacific coastal state of Sinaloa. Félix Gallardo was a former police officer, who—thanks to close ties to political figures at the state and national level—developed an extensive trafficking empire and became one of Mexico's wealthiest drug barons. The well-protected network that Félix Gallardo cultivated included many of Mexico's most notorious contemporary drug traffickers, most of them also hailing from Sinaloa.[18] While this network operated freely thanks to the complicity of government officials, its downfall began when, in late 1984, a Mexican army raid seized thousands of tons of marijuana at the El Búfalo ranch in the northern state of Chihuahua.

After the fall of the Guadalajara cartel, its remaining members went on to consolidate their own separate trafficking organizations in the 1990s, each named after their bases of operations in Tijuana, Sinaloa, and Ciudad Juárez. The Tijuana cartel was operated by the seven brothers, four sisters, and other relatives of the Arellano Félix family, all of whom were believed to be family members of Miguel Angel Félix Gallardo. The Sinaloa cartel was headed by Ismael "El Mayo" Zambada and Joaquín "El Chapo" Guzman. The Juárez cartel was operated by Amado Carrillo Fuentes until his demise on the operating table while undergoing plastic surgery in 1997, after which his brother Vicente Carrillo Fuentes took over the organization. In addition to these groups, the Gulf cartel in the northeastern portion of the country had operated independently from the Guadalajara cartel for many years, and in the late 1990s was taken over by a trafficker named Osiel Cárdenas.

It is worth noting that, until the 1990s, drug-trafficking organizations operated with tremendous impunity and with relatively little violent conflict among them. However, after the splintering of the Guadalajara cartel, competitive pressure, personal rivalries, and vendettas over business deals gone wrong led increasingly to high-profile violence among these groups. The Arellano Félix Organization (AFO) achieved infamy for its alleged murder of Cardinal Posadas Ocampo in Guadalajara in 1994, in a reported case of mistaken identity. The incident also provoked rumors of connections between the Church and drug traffickers that were further fueled by the film *El crimen del Padre Amaro*. In 2002, the killing and arrest of Ramón and Benjamín Arellano Félix, respectively, and the arrest of Osiel Cárdenas significantly deteriorated the Tijuana and Gulf cartels. Meanwhile, the Juárez and Sinaloa cartels, which formed an alliance known as the Federation or the Golden Triangle Alliance, which incorporated a large network of traffickers, began to encroach on the territories of the Tijuana and Gulf cartels.[19]

Violence among the cartels began to increase significantly in 2005, with a noticeable rise in the number of drug-related killings in major drug-producing and trafficking areas. Levels of violence grew most dramatically starting in January 2008, when the Sinaloa cartel suffered an internal schism that led to the breakaway of their long-time collaborators from the Beltrán Leyva family, as well as the breakdown of its alliance with the Juárez cartel. In that year, the rate of violence in Ciudad Juárez increased more than tenfold, as the Sinaloa cartel attempted to take over trafficking operations in one of the most important trade corridors between the United States and Mexico. Violence also increased in Baja California in 2008, as an AFO lieutenant named Teodoro "El Teo" Guzman joined forces with the Sinaloa cartel and allegedly killed hundreds of people and dissolved their bodies in industrial chemicals in his attempt to take over the Tijuana cartel. Further violence resulted when a naval commando raid in Cuernavaca killed Arturo "El Jefe de Jefes" Beltrán Leyva in December 2009, and his lieutenants battled for control of the organization in the state of Morelos. In 2010, after the sentencing of Osiel Cárdenas on drug charges in the United States, the Gulf cartel suffered yet another blow when the group known as Los Zetas—elite military defectors who had been recruited to serve as the cartel's enforcer group—attempted to take control over drug-trafficking operations in northeastern Mexico.

In short, clashes between major trafficking organizations and government efforts to capture their top leadership have resulted in significant eruptions of violence in recent years. In this sense, law enforcement successes have actually increased violence by fueling the intense competition among organized crime groups. We will return to this issue later in this chapter and again in chapter 13, but for now it is important to emphasize the negative impact that the drug trade has on the state's ability to effectively enforce the law. Although Mexico's drug trafficking and violence have remained relatively contained, in some states (e.g., Baja California, Chihuahua, Nuevo León, Tamaulipas, and Michoacán) drug-related violence has reached extremely high levels and creates a sense of fear for ordinary citizens. Much of this violence has become more localized, as the fragmentation of major cartels has given way to crime and violence by small-time thugs and street-level dealers. At the same time, as noted above, the pervasive influence of organized crime syndicates contributes to the continued corruption of Mexican law enforcement—including both the military and civilian police—even at the highest levels. Hence, it is appropriate that we now turn to the problem of corruption in Mexico.

Corruption

Corruption is a prominent aspect of U.S. citizens' perceptions of Mexico. But what do we mean by corruption? Experts often distinguish political or official corruption (abuse of public office for private gain) from other forms of illegal or dishonest conduct that may occur in society, such as white-collar crime, money laundering, or cheating on college exams. Transparency International's Corruption Perceptions Index (CPI) measures corruption among public officials by rating a given country's "perceived levels of corruption, as determined by expert assessments and opinion surveys." With a CPI score of 3.1 in 2010 (where 0 is "highly corrupt" and 10 is "highly clean"), Mexico's score ranks about average for Latin America, but well below countries like Iceland (8.5), Germany (7.9), Japan (7.8), the United Kingdom (7.6), Chile (7.2), or the United States (7.1).[20] It is also important to note that ongoing corruption, both official and otherwise, negatively impacts average Mexicans and Mexico's overall economic development.[21] Indeed, the high economic costs of corruption, impunity from the law, and a general lack of transparency are substantiated by research on other countries in Latin America and the rest of the developing world and have increasingly concerned experts focused on the question of development.[22]

Why is corruption detrimental to society? This is a complicated question, but for our purposes there are at least three elements to the explanation. First, in the context of the rule of law, corruption makes it possible for some to live outside the scope of the law. Once this precedent is set, everyone has an incentive to bypass or simply ignore the law, making rules irrelevant and society chaotic. Second, corruption has the potential to limit a country's overall economic development because it functions as an arbitrary tax that benefits a few at the expense of society as a whole. Compromised economic development, in turn, prevents the state from addressing important societal needs and taking measures that might reduce corruption (e.g., improve training, raise salaries). Finally, corruption undermines the principle of equality and directly hinders transparency and accountability, all elements that are essential for a well-functioning democracy. Where corruption is rampant, people are much less likely to trust government and official institutions, and state officials (e.g., politicians, bureaucrats, law enforcement officers) are less likely to be held accountable for unethical or unlawful behavior. The result is that not everyone is equal before the law. Those who can pay bribes or otherwise exercise influence are less likely to be punished, and society is unable to hold the state accountable for actions that violate the law.

How can we explain why corruption is so pervasive in Mexico? Many analysts give credence to the idea that cultural factors—the core values, attitudes, belief systems, and behavioral norms of Mexican society—contribute significantly to corruption. According to this view, Mexicans developed ingrained patterns of corruption because of norms and behaviors derived from the legacies of Spanish colonialism—in which corrupt personal enrichment was widely practiced at the expense of the Crown. These patterns of behavior are said to contribute to a lack of socially responsible values, leading Mexicans to be more prone to the shortsighted pursuit of self-interest than respect for the interests of society at large.

No doubt there are Mexicans—and people of all nationalities—who fit this description, but this is not an intrinsic characteristic of Mexican political culture. If these values are present in Mexican society, it is rather a result of informal systems (such as clientelistic networks) or formal institutional failures (such as no reelection) that lead to rational, albeit undesirable, incentive systems and patterns of behavior. The pattern and practice of official corruption in Mexico was linked to practices institutionalized under the PRI and earlier authoritarian governments.[23] In such a context, it is often difficult for even the most well-intentioned person to avoid participating in corrupt practices. As we noted above, the politicians and police who accept bribes from drug traffickers often take the more logical of two choices: silver over lead. On the other hand, most Mexicans abide by the law and do not try to bribe police when they go to other countries like Spain and the United States, which have lower rates of corruption. Meanwhile, some U.S. citizens have been known to engage in corrupt practices (like bribing police) when they go to Mexico. This suggests that corruption may be driven by larger, systemic factors, rather than by intrinsically held beliefs and value systems. In other words, motorists are more likely to acquiesce to corrupt practices—like fixing a speeding ticket by bribing a traffic cop—if that will prove significantly less burdensome than surrendering their driver's license, appearing in court, or paying a fine. Also, police officers or judges are likely to be much more susceptible to corruption if they have received little training or vetting before obtaining the job, if they are poorly paid, and if there is little likelihood of being caught. Indeed, in some cases, politicians and police may themselves be victims in a larger chain of corruption, in which their supervisors require them to generate a quota by collecting bribes, and ultimately no one is held accountable for unlawful actions.

For this reason, except in rare instances, it is often difficult to build a case to implicate high-level officials for drug-related corruption. Moreover, even when there is political will, corruption charges are notoriously hard to prosecute, as illustrated by the case of dozens of Michoacán mayors and high-level officials arrested in a May 2009 federal operation commonly described as *El Michoacanazo* (the "big blow" in Michoacán). The fact that these officials were arrested several weeks prior to the federal and local elections that year and all but one were acquitted and released in the ensuing months provoked accusations that the operation was politically motivated.[24] Similar accusations resulted in 2010, when federal forces arrested former Tijuana mayor and aspiring PRI gubernatorial candidate Jorge Hank Rhon in Baja California on charges of illegal possession of firearms.[25] Still, Mexico has achieved some success in prosecuting other high-profile corruption cases in recent years, as illustrated by the 2010 arrest and extradition of the former

PRI governor of Quintana Roo (1993–1999) Mario Villanueva.[26] In the long run, Mexico's ability to combat corruption will no doubt depend on its ability to increase the relative costs for those seeking to subvert the law, both by better compensating public officials and by increasing the probability of punishment for those who make or take bribes. Requiring accountability will have positive reinforcing effects on both the maintenance of order and economic development. But in order to improve accountability, Mexico's citizens must demand greater access to justice.

Victims' Rights

In October 1992, the ravaged body of a fifteen-year-old girl named Gloria Rivas was found abandoned in the desert, one of the first to be discovered in an apparent wave of killings of women and girls that today numbers approximately four hundred in the Mexican border metropolis of Ciudad Juárez. Most of the victims in the so-called Ciudad Juárez femicides shared common characteristics with Gloria. That is, most victims tended to be young and attractive, with dark skin and dark hair; and most were poor or working class (many of whom worked in assembly plants or *maquiladoras*). When families and activists first began to report and denounce the murders, they were often shocked to find that government officials reacted lethargically or even with hostility. Activists alleged that police sought to cover up their own incompetence or even possible involvement in the murders, and that government officials along with the business community tried to downplay the number of murder victims in order to prevent a negative image for the city.

Meanwhile, the patterns of violence, sexual assault, mutilation, and discarded bodies found in many of the murders generated a wide range of theories. Some believed that the murders were the result of a lone psychopathic killer, while others pointed to underground pornography rings, human trafficking/sexual slavery, organ harvesting, recreational killing by young men from wealthy families looking for an adrenaline rush, victory celebrations by drug traffickers, and satanic cult rituals. Several factors contributed to the murders and to the failure to resolve the situation. The fact that many of the victims came from poor backgrounds meant that they and their families did not have adequate education, information, or other basic necessities (transportation and telephones) to fully access the justice system. The very fact that the victims were poor also contributed to the initial lack of official attention to the problem. Meanwhile, the political manipulation of the investigation into the murders by officials from the major political parties in the state of Chihuahua (the PAN governed the city, while the PRI governed the state) clouded the lines of accountability and the extent of the problem.

Of particular concern, however, were the lack of professionalism and also the ineffectiveness of Mexican law enforcement in solving these crimes. On the one hand, insufficient training, inaccurate identification of victims and suspects, the lack of DNA testing facilities, and the excessive caseloads of investigators point to pervasive problems of police training and resource capacity; on the other hand, the covering up of evidence and the lack of political will proved illustrative of the widespread problems of corruption and impunity in Mexico. Feminist activists and scholars like Irasema Coronado and Kathleen Staudt at the University of Texas–El Paso also pointed to the deprecation of women in general as a contributing factor to the Juárez femicides and other violence against women along the border. Negative and misogynistic portrayals of women in popular and traditional culture in both Mexico and the United States, they argue, sometimes perpetuate the idea that the women are victims of their own choices. Indeed, some police and city officials suggested to families of victims that the women dressed inappropriately or were prone to promiscuous behavior and therefore somehow invited the attacks. However, such attitudes gradually gave way because families, community activists, and nongovernmental organizations pressured the government to do something. International pressure, thanks in part to news coverage and documentary films like *Señorita extraviada*, also helped promote greater attention to the issue.[27] In 2009, the Inter-American Court of Human Rights issued a decision that the Mexican government should be held accountable for specific killings identified in 2001, a decision backed by the European Parliament in 2010.

Meanwhile, prolonged political pressure led the Chihuahua state legislature to approve a massive justice sector reform introduced in 2006 by Governor José Reyes Baeza Terrazas. This reform introduced new legal innovations— like oral trials to provide greater transparency, efficiency, and swiftness—to help make the administration of justice more transparent and efficient (see textbox 11.1). At the same time, national and international crime experts have begun to introduce training and modern forensics procedures to help authorities more effectively investigate and prosecute crimes. Still, with so many unresolved cases, it will likely take many years to sort out the botched investigations and achieve some resolution for the victims' families. This effort will no doubt be further complicated by the fact that Chihuahua has become the epicenter of violence in Mexico as a result of conflict among drug-trafficking organizations.

In the meantime, Chihuahua serves as an unfortunate illustration of the problem of access to justice in Mexico and demonstrates the urgent need for modernizing and improving its justice system. The initial unwillingness of authorities to respond to the demands of victims shows that achieving the rule of law will require a certain degree of public pressure and mobilization. In this sense, democracy shares yet another important link to the

---

Textbox 11.1. CHIHUAHUA'S FIRST ORAL TRIAL

In June 2007, the state of Chihuahua held its first oral trial, with the case of Anselmo Chávez Rivero, a man charged with the rape of two minors. Chávez was of indigenous descent and required courtroom interpreters during the trial, as he and other witnesses testified in their native Tarahumara language. Chávez was originally arrested before Chihuahua introduced its new criminal code and trial procedures in 2006. Those reforms significantly modified Chihuahua's inquisitorial system, introducing elements from the accusatorial system—such as oral trials—used in common law systems like that of the United States. When Chávez was given the option of a trial under the new procedures, he agreed. Ironically, his conviction under the reforms reportedly resulted in a longer sentence—twenty years—than if he had been prosecuted under the old system (which would have resulted in an eight-year sentence). The Chávez trial marked a new era not only for Chihuahua's justice system, but also for the rest of Mexico. Many legal experts hope that similar criminal justice and trial procedure reforms introduced in other states throughout the country will significantly enhance the rule of law in Mexico over the coming decades.

Source: Luis Alonso Fierro, "Dictan primera sentencia en juicio oral," *El Diario de Chihuahua*, July 18, 2007.

---

rule of law. Whether protecting the rights of victims or the accused, both democracy and the rule of law require active vigilance and participation from civil society. Fortunately, Mexicans have begun working toward these ends. Ordinary citizens and nongovernmental organizations like Mexico United against Crime (Mexico Unido contra la Delincuencia, MUCD) have organized hundreds of thousands of people to march in the streets, demanding better public security and a new culture of lawfulness. Public and nongovernmental watchdog agencies—like the National Human Rights Commission (*Comisión Nacional de Derechos Humanos*, CNDH) and the Citizens' Institute for the Study of Public Insecurity (*Instituto Ciudadano de Estudios Sobre la Inseguridad*, ICESI)—have held authorities to account for their failures and transgressions. Mexican lawyers have taken up the causes of the indigent and the wrongfully accused, and raised public awareness of the need for due process through popular documentary films like *The Tunnel* and *Presumed Guilty*, which help chronicle the penal system's labyrinths of injustice.[28] The country's Catholic leaders have increasingly spoken out against the evils of drug trafficking, amid concerns that the clergy itself has been targeted for violence, extortion, and even corruption by organized crime.[29] Moreover, in a climate of extraordinary transparency and openness, intrepid Mexican journalists have courageously documented government corruption, abuses, and ineptitude. If anything, even in the face of great turmoil, there is hope for Mexico in the strength and perseverance of its people as they demand justice from their authorities. In recent years there have been significant efforts to pressure Mexican authorities to address these demands, including several high-profile nationwide protests in 2004, 2008, and 2011 led by prominent family members of crime victims, such as María Elena Morera, Alejandro Martí, and Javier Sicilia. Below we consider how authorities have responded to these demands by working to promote the rule of law in Mexico.

RULE OF LAW REFORM EFFORTS IN MEXICO

What is the prognosis for the short and long term to improve the rule of law in Mexico, and what are the possible strategies to address ongoing challenges? At first blush it would appear that the prospects for meaningful reform are dim because there are so many entrenched interests, including police, lawyers, and judges, who often prefer to maintain the status quo. Thus, although President Zedillo's reforms of the late 1990s did manage to insulate the Supreme Court from political influence and to introduce new merit criteria and oversight for other federal judicial appointments, they stopped short of addressing general concerns regarding systemic backlogs, delays, and ineffectiveness in the justice system. President Fox was successful in gaining legislative support for an access to information law (akin to the Freedom of Information Act in the United States), as well as civil service reforms intended to decrease corruption and improve the quality and effectiveness of governance. However, Fox was unsuccessful in passing a 2004 judicial reform that would have produced a major overhaul of the Mexican criminal justice system, including the unification of federal police forces, the autonomy of prosecutors from executive power, the creation of a separate criminal justice system for minors, and major reforms to criminal procedure, including police investigation of crimes, a stronger presumption of innocence, the use of oral argument in trial proceedings, and the possibility of plea bargaining.[30]

Nonetheless, under President Calderón, progress was made on several of these items thanks to a judicial reform package that came into effect on June 18, 2008. The 2008 judicial sector reform introduced three major sets of changes to the Mexican criminal justice system: first are new criminal procedures (oral adversarial trials, alternative sentencing, and alternative dispute resolution mechanisms); second are stronger due process protections for the accused; and finally, police and prosecutorial reforms to strengthen public security, criminal investigations, and efforts to combat organized crime. The reforms provide a timeframe of up to eight years for the revision of federal and state legal codes and procedures; the physical modification of courtrooms, the development of police investigative capacity, and the construction of jails for crime suspects; and the retraining of judges, court staffs, lawyers, and police. Advocates hope the reform will bring about greater transparency, efficiency, and fairness, though there are serious concerns among critics that there are inadequate resources and too little time to properly implement the reforms. The reforms are already being tested in states like Chihuahua, Coahuila, Oaxaca, and Nuevo León, which had previously experimented with similar changes prior to 2008 (see table 11.2).

As difficult as it is, reforming the justice system may actually be less challenging than combating organized crime and drug trafficking. Antidrug efforts that seek to dismantle and eliminate organized crime syndicates are sometimes successful. For example, in December 2006, when President Felipe Calderón took office, he cracked down on drug-trafficking organizations by sending seven thousand troops to the Pacific states of Michoacán and Guerrero, as well as three thousand troops to the city of Tijuana. The presence of the army led to a number of important arrests and the confiscation of millions of dollars' worth of illegal drugs. Moreover, Calderón took the unprecedented step of extraditing to the United States high-level narco-traffickers, including Gulf cartel leader Osiel Cárdenas in 2007 and Benjamín Arellano Félix in 2010, both of whom were wanted in the United States on drug charges.

[margin annotation: Operation Michoacán]

Table 11.2. Progress on State-Level Judicial Reforms through December 2010

Tier 1	Advanced stages of implementation	Nuevo León, Chihuahua, Oaxaca, Morelos, Zacatecas, Durango, México State, Baja California
Tier 2	Legislation recently approved or under debate, but implementation pending	Aguascalientes, Yucatán, Campeche, Veracruz, Guanajuato, Sonora
Tier 3	Some progress, but pending debate and approval of reforms	Chiapas, Distrito Federal, Colima, Tamaulipas, Tabasco, Jalisco, Michoacán, San Luis Potosí, Hidalgo, Nayarit, Querétaro, Quintana Roo, Coahuila
Tier 4	Few signs of significant effort	Puebla, Baja California Sur, Tlaxcala, Guerrero, Sinaloa

Source: Matthew C. Ingram and David A. Shirk, "Judicial Reform in Mexico: Toward a New Criminal Justice System," Special Report (May 2010), Trans-Border Institute, University of San Diego. http://justiceinmexico.org/publications/justice-in-mexico-project.

Despite the overwhelming popularity and success of these efforts, many Mexicans remain wary. Other major law enforcement efforts against narco-trafficking organizations occurred with similar fanfare at the start of previous presidential administrations, only to taper off and demonstrate transience of their benefits. Indeed, if historical trends are any guide, the elimination or even serious reduction of drug trafficking is not on the intermediate horizon. Instead, it is much more likely that the arrest and extradition of key leaders during the past few years has encouraged aspirants from the major cartels to engage in violent battles to establish their dominance and a new balance of power. Once a new balance is reached, society may see a decline in violence, but this hardly means that the problem will be solved.

Another problem stems from President Calderón's decision to mobilize federal troops for the purpose of combating narco-trafficking. The militarization of Mexico's anti-drug initiatives has been a decades-long phenomenon, a "permanent campaign" that stretches back to the deployment of troops in counter-drug initiatives as early as the 1930s.[31] That said, this phenomenon accelerated greatly under recent administrations. By the mid-1990s, more than half of Mexico's thirty-two states had military officers assigned to police command positions, and hundreds of military personnel were incorporated into rank and file positions in other civilian police agencies.[32] This increased reliance on the military represents a significant hazard. Presently, the military is one of the most respected institutions in Mexico. Yet, the military lacks the proper legal mandate and training for law enforcement activities and criminal investigations, and has been charged with significant violations of basic human rights. Between December 2006 and July 2011 there were nearly five thousand complaints of human rights violations to the National Human Rights Commission.[33] Another risk is that corruption of the military by organized crime groups could seriously diminish its prestige in the public eye, leaving Mexico without any reliable weapons in the fight against drug traffickers.[34]

It is virtually certain that the Calderón administration and future governments in both Mexico and the United States will continue to face the challenge of how to eliminate the drug trade in the foreseeable future, while Mexico will continue to struggle with the externalities of the drug trade on society and on its justice system. Any solutions are likely to be long term, economically costly, politically difficult, and fraught with unforeseen problems. For example, promoting the rule of law in Mexico will require a deep, sustained commitment to ensuring due process; yet many citizens and victims may find it difficult to accept the presumption of innocence for individuals accused of ties to organized crime. Moreover, better law enforcement might help Mexico, but it could also push organized crime into neighboring countries in Central America and the Caribbean. Meanwhile, seemingly simple solutions like legalizing illicit drugs—as 46 percent of California voters (nearly

3.3 million people) favored doing for marijuana in the November 2010 election—will not likely eliminate organized crime in Mexico entirely but would surely lead to greater social and health problems in the United States. Finally, decreasing consumer demand in the United States would effectively undermine the drug trade, but achieving this goal has so far been elusive.

CONCLUSION

Clearly there is no silver bullet that will strengthen the rule of law in Mexico. This is because promoting the rule of law—especially in the area of governmental accountability and responsiveness—is not merely about reducing crime. It is not a policy output but rather a process that must be continually refined in any democratic system. In the United States and elsewhere, political competition and the alternation of political parties in elected office proved essential to reform over the last century. It is reasonable, therefore, to expect that democratic competition will be a driving force for justice sector reform in Mexico, even though the absence of reelection is a serious impediment to both accountability and responsiveness. Yet so long as the serious rule of law challenges discussed above persist, justice sector reform will undoubtedly remain among voters' top priorities. Politicians will be under pressure to make changes that reflect the public will.

In the short term, confronted with overwhelming and immediate challenges, it is easy to fall prey to self-fulfilling pessimism. A longer-term view, though, offers the advantage of an obtainable horizon and reachable goals. What is certain is that Mexico's domestic efforts cannot result in rapid improvements in the rule of law and reductions in transnational organized crime without cooperation, support, and constructive engagement from the United States. Indeed, while keeping in mind nationalist concerns about the protection of sovereignty, addressing Mexico's crime and drug challenges cannot be considered a solely Mexican concern. The negative externalities of Mexico's "unrule" of law have clear and direct effects on U.S. citizens and interests, including U.S. tourists who travel to Mexico each year, U.S. nationals residing in Mexico, and the billions in annual business conducted with Mexico. Moreover, the pervasiveness and strength of transnational organized crime networks in Mexico—and the lack of integrity in the Mexican law enforcement and security apparatus—has raised serious concerns that Mexico could become a transit point for terrorists and weapons to enter the United States. U.S. collaboration with Mexico to address these problems is both essential and in the direct national and strategic interest of the United States. The following chapters will address these issues.

Part IV

MEXICAN FOREIGN RELATIONS

12

Mexican Foreign Policy

The nature and evolution of Mexico's state formation and governance has had a profound effect on its relationships with other countries and its position on the world stage. Emerging as an independent nation in the early nineteenth century, Mexico found itself caught between the imperialist designs of well-established nations in Europe and the expansionist ambitions of the United States. Indeed, in addition to fending off two invasions by France, Mexico lost more than a third of its national territory to its northern neighbor. Not surprisingly, this harsh introduction to international politics helped make Mexico a cautious player on the world stage. During the Porfirian era Mexico actively sought to build stronger relations with both Europe and the United States to a degree that some Mexicans felt undermined national sovereignty. Yet, after the 1910 revolution, Mexico began to articulate a vision of foreign policy that reflected at least a nominal commitment to self-determination, nonintervention, and peaceful conflict resolution, both in the protection of its own interests and in its treatment of foreign powers.

In this chapter, we examine contemporary Mexican foreign policy, with an emphasis on its general principles, priorities, structure, and process. We discuss the specific considerations that have shaped foreign policy approaches and decisions in modern Mexico, particularly with regard to its multilateral relations and increasing role on the world stage. In the next chapter, we will explore Mexico's special bilateral connection to the United States and the specific policy issues that define that relationship.

MEXICAN FOREIGN POLICY:
FOUNDATIONS, STRUCTURE, AND PROCESS

As a medium-size regional power, Mexico's options in the international arena are significantly affected by the balance of power in the world system. Mexican foreign policy reflects the opportunities and constraints that result from this context. At the same time, foreign policy making in Mexico also responds to particular national interests and domestic concerns that have to do with internal political dynamics. In this sense, like those of most countries, Mexico's foreign policy is what international relations specialists refer to as "intermestic." That is, it reflects both international and domestic concerns. This is especially true in an era of globalization, as Mexico's secretary of the exterior, Patricia Espinosa, underscored in remarks to the London School of Economics in 2008: "No longer do we live in a world in which 'foreign' refers to everything but ourselves. Our everyday lives are effectively and constantly influenced by ideas and actions, trends and values originating beyond our borders. They become so rapidly familiar that it would now be odd to call them foreign."[1]

Mexico came into existence as a sovereign country in the nineteenth century. Domestically, this was an era of state formation and perpetual re-formation, during which Mexico's sovereignty and territorial integrity were highly vulnerable to the threat of foreign incursion. During its first century of independence, Mexico experienced clashes over its foreign debts, incursions by would-be emperors and filibusters, and territorial invasions and interventions. The intrastate competition of this period dramatically impacted Mexico's perceptions of its role and prospects in the Westphalian system. Concerns about the preservation of its national sovereignty made Mexico a cautious player on the world stage, often reluctant to take on political or military commitments beyond its borders. More often than not, encroachments on Mexican sovereignty triggered deep nationalist sentiments that have subsequently shaped the outlook of Mexican foreign policy makers in important ways ever since. In particular, Mexico's geographic position next to the United States has factored heavily into its worldview.

The Structure and Process of Mexican Foreign Policy

As in other presidential systems, Mexico's foreign policy is generated and conducted principally by the executive branch, though the constitution maintains a significant role for the Senate. The foreign policy role of the president is primarily outlined with other powers of the executive branch in Article 89 of the constitution. This article grants executive authority—with ratification by the Senate—both to declare war and enter into treaties, as well as the general power to direct foreign policy. Article 73 of the constitution affirms congressional authority to regulate the status of foreigners within Mexico's national territory, as well as its power to declare war based on reports by the executive branch. Congressional oversight of foreign policy is more clearly articulated in Article 76, which enumerates the Senate's powers to ratify treaties and diplomatic accords, as well as its power to authorize the deployment of Mexican troops abroad and to permit foreign forces within Mexican territory. Within the executive branch, foreign policy is overseen primarily by the secretary of foreign relations, who is appointed directly by the president and often referred to as the chancellor (*canciller*). The secretary of foreign relations is responsible for reporting to the president on matters of foreign policy and for managing the country's diplomatic missions and activities abroad. Mexico's diplomatic efforts are largely targeted to places and topics where the country has strong national interests. (See textbox 12.1.)

Generally speaking, Mexican foreign policy is structured in terms of bilateral efforts to work directly with other countries, and involvement in international organizations and other multilateral initiatives. Historically much of its attention was focused on the United States. However, in the past three decades Mexico has dramatically increased its outreach to other countries. For example, it has established direct bilateral free trade agreements with a number of countries, including Bolivia, Chile, Colombia, Costa Rica, Israel, Nicaragua, and Uruguay. As of 2011, Mexico had representation in seventy-three embassies and seventy-one consulates and consulates general around the world, as well as representation in Ramallah and Taiwan.[2] These entities help promote Mexico's interests abroad by negotiating matters of state, monitoring developments in other countries, promoting the nation's culture and standing around the world, advancing Mexican economic interests, and providing assistance to Mexican nationals living or traveling outside of their home country. Mexican nationals work with their embassy or consulate to obtain official paperwork, such as government-issued identification and certificates (e.g., consular identification cards and marriage licenses). Mexico's embassies and consulates also provide services to foreign nationals and companies, such as visas, contacts, and other assistance.

Within the Ministry of Exterior Relations (Secretaría de Relaciones Exteriores, SRE), Mexican Foreign Service (Servicio Exterior Mexicano, SEM) personnel are charged with a duty to "promote and safeguard Mexico's national interests vis-à-vis foreign nations and within the international organizations and meetings in which Mexico participates." They are divided into diplomatic or consular personnel and technical or administrative support staff. All diplomatic personnel are expected to be fluent in English and one other official language of the United Nations. SEM personnel also take specialized classes and gain access to a diplomatic career through the Instituto Matías Romero, the Mexican foreign service school founded in 1974

Textbox 12.1. MEXICO'S FOREIGN MINISTER

Patricia Espinosa Cantellano was appointed minister of the exterior at the start of the administration of President Felipe Calderón in December 2006. A career diplomat, Secretary Espinosa joined Mexico's foreign service in 1981 and went on to serve as part of Mexico's Permanent Mission to the United Nations, chief of staff to the under-secretary of foreign affairs, director of international organizations, director general of American regional organizations and mechanisms, national coordinator for the Río group, and ambassador to Germany and Austria.

As foreign minister, Secretary Espinosa regularly reports not only to the president, but also to the Mexican Senate's Foreign Relations Committee. In her 2010 report to this committee, the foreign minister emphasized the country's increasing prominence on the world stage. Her words below illustrate Mexico's accomplishments in this regard, as well as the recognition that her agency depends on the legislature's continued support for these activities:

> We are a country renowned for its many contributions to peace, security and development in the world, as evidenced by our work in forums such as the G20 or the United Nations Security Council, and by our participation in international forums such as APEC or the World Economic Forum in Davos; and by Mexico's position in favor of strengthening the rule of law and the observance of human rights, and in fighting climate change and transnational organized crime, in which we play an active and constructive role. That we are hosting major international meetings in Mexico such as the COP 16, the Global Forum on Migration and Development, and the International Telecommunication Union Conference is also proof of that recognition. . . . Mexico maintains diplomatic relations with virtually all countries of the world and has strengthened its ties of cooperation and exchange with them through 80 diplomatic offices. We have also developed a large consular presence: an important network made up of 70 offices around the world that provides services and protection to Mexicans abroad and that has become stronger through the strong support of Congress.

Source: Mexidata, "Mexican Minister Presents Annual Report on Foreign Policy," Mexidata.Info, Monday, October 4, 2010. http://mexidata.info/id2827.html (accessed June 13, 2011).

in honor of Mexico's first ambassador to the United States. All Mexican ambassadors and consular authorities are named by SRE and approved by the Senate, though they are not necessarily required to have professional standing as career diplomats. Indeed, as in other countries, ambassadors are often political appointees with close ties to the sitting president or his party. One example is Arturo Sarukán, Mexico's ambassador to the United States from 2006 to 2012, who was Felipe Calderón's top foreign policy adviser during his campaign for the presidency. Ambassador Sarukán is a Mexican of Russian-Armenian and Spanish descent, whose family fled Europe to escape both Bolshevik and fascist governments. Prior to his appointment, Sarukán had previously been a member of Mexico's foreign service and was appointed consul general in New York City.

Still, while diplomatic appointees are often highly qualified, they sometimes generate controversy. In March 2011, there were disagreements in the Senate over the appointment of four of Mexico's most important consuls general: Manuel Sada Solana in New York, Eduardo Arnal Palomera in Chicago, David Figueroa Ortega in Los Angeles, and Andrés Chao Ebergenyi in Denver.[3] Opposition parties accused President Calderón of designating political appointees rather than career diplomats to these very important posts, which together serve millions of Mexicans living abroad. In particular, some senators raised concerns that the political appointment of consular authorities could be a means to manipulate the vote of Mexicans living abroad. Absentee voting was permitted in 2005, though turnout in the 2006 elections was quite low. In 2010, the IFE extended the window for absentee voting to 75 days prior to an election in an effort to increase turnout abroad.[4] Ultimately, the Senate approved all four consular nominees.[5]

In addition to its bilateral diplomatic efforts, Mexico also maintains permanent missions in a number of international organizations, including the Agency for the Prohibition of Nuclear Weapons in Latin America and the Caribbean, the European Union, and the Organisation of Economic Cooperation and Development (OECD). Mexico has also played a prominent role in the Organization of American States (OAS), a regional organization established in 1948 to promote cooperation, peace, and security in the Western Hemisphere, and has consistently supported the United Nations as one of its top ten financial contributors. Mexican diplomatic representatives regularly serve in the UN's various committees and agencies, and Mexico has served four terms as a nonpermanent member of the UN Security Council.[6] As we discuss in more detail below, Mexico's increased recent participation on the Security Council is a significant shift from its traditional aversion to participation in this particular body, especially in comparison to several other Latin American countries (see table 12.1).

Table 12.1. Representation of Latin American Countries as Nonpermanent Members of the UN Security Council

Country	Years
Argentina	1948–1949; 1959–1960; 1966–1967; 1971–1972; 1987–1988; 1994–1995; 1999–2000; 2005–2006
Bolivia	1964–1965; 1978–1979
Brazil	1946–1947; 1951–1952; 1954–1955; 1963–1964; 1967–1968; 1988–1989; 1993–1994; 1998–1999; 2004–2005; 2010–2011
Chile	1952–1953; 1961–1962; 1996–1997; 2003–2004
Colombia	1947–1948; 1953–1954; 1957–1958; 1969–1970; 1989–1990; 2001–2002; 2011–2012
Costa Rica	1974–1975; 1997–1998; 2008–2009
Cuba	1949–1950; 1956–1957; 1990–1991
Ecuador	1950–1951; 1960–1961; 1991–1992
Honduras	1995–1996
Mexico	1946; 1980–1981; 2002–2003; 2009–10
Nicaragua	1970–1971; 1983–1984
Panama	1958–1959; 1972–1973; 1976–1977; 1981–1982; 2007–2008
Paraguay	1968–1969
Peru	1955–1956; 1973–1974; 1984–1985; 2006–2007
Uruguay	1965–1966
Venezuela	1962–1963; 1977–1978; 1986–1987; 1992–1993

Source: http://www.un.org/sc/members.asp.

Over the last two decades, Mexico has also significantly increased its participation in international affairs through numerous multilateral treaties and conventions. As we noted in chapter 9, in addition to entering GATT in 1986 and signing NAFTA in 1994, Mexico has entered into several other multilateral economic and trade agreements, notably the Asia Pacific Economic Cooperation (APEC) organization in 1993; Group of Three Trade Agreement (G3) with Colombia and, initially, Venezuela, in 1994; the Mexico–European Union (EU) Free Trade Agreement in 2000; the Mexico–Northern Triangle Agreement with Guatemala, El Salvador, and Honduras in 2000; and the Mexico-European Free Trade Association (EFTA) with Iceland, Liechtenstein, Norway, and Switzerland in 2001. These agreements provide Mexico with favorable terms of trade in more than forty countries, which especially benefit Mexico's domestic production by lowering the cost of intermediate and capital goods, many of which are important for its export sector. These associations also provide Mexico with an opportunity to exercise leadership in the international arena, as when Mexico hosted the APEC conference in 2002, the Fifth World Trade Organization (WTO) Ministerial Conference in 2003, and the 2010 United Nations Climate Change Conference. (See textbox 12.2.)

Textbox 12.2. THE CANCÚN SUMMIT

In December 2010, Mexico played an active role in global efforts to address environmental issues by hosting the United Nations Framework Convention on Climate Change in the resort city of Cancún, along the Caribbean coast. Mexico has an important stake in the issue of climate change. In per capita terms, Mexico is one of the top twenty largest greenhouse-gas-emitting countries, though its emissions are much lower than those of most developed countries. According to a 2009 report by the World Bank, Mexico is also one of the countries most likely to suffer from the negative effects of climate change, with 70 percent of its GDP in areas at risk to natural disasters.[1] The Cancún Summit followed talks hosted in Copenhagen in late 2009, which were largely seen as a disappointment because of the failure to establish a strong international accord to combat climate change. By contrast, the Cancún Summit was seen as a modest success, partly because of the foundation provided in Copenhagen but also because of Mexico's careful planning and diplomatic efforts during the talks. Unlike the Copenhagen Summit, which included highly publicized participation by heads of state, the gathering hosted in Cancún brought together cabinet and other high-ranking officials with policy expertise on climate change. In her role as host and president of the summit, Mexico's foreign minister, Patricia Espinosa, also made a concerted effort to minimize objections to the negotiation of a consensus from countries like Venezuela, Bolivia, Cuba, and Saudi Arabia.[2]

---

1. Global Facility for Disaster Reduction and Recovery, "Integrating Disaster Risk Reduction into the Fight against Poverty," World Bank. http://www.gfdrr.org/gfdrr/sites/gfdrr.org/files/publication/GFDRR_Annual_Report_2009.pdf.

2. David Bosco, "Foreign Policy: How Mexico Mastered Multilateralism," National Public Radio. http://www.npr.org/2010/12/15/132076505/foreign-policy-how-mexico-mastered-multilateralism.

Mexico on the World Stage: Principles and Priorities of Mexican Diplomacy

In addition to outlining the structure and administrative process of foreign policy making, Part X of Article 89 of the Mexican constitution identifies five distinct normative principles that guide the executive branch's conduct in world affairs: national sovereignty, nonintervention, legal equality of states, international cooperation, and the nonviolent resolution of international conflicts. Specifically, the constitution states:

Third Title, Chapter III, Article 89, The powers and obligations of the President shall be the following . . .

Part X: To direct foreign policy and make international treaties, as well as
terminate, denounce, suspend, modify, amend, withdraw reservations, and
formulate interpretive declarations about them, submitting these for the approval of the Senate. In the conduct of this policy, the head of the Executive
Power will observe the following normative principles: the self determination
of peoples; the [principle of] non-intervention; the peaceful resolution of conflicts; the proscription of the threat or use of force in international relations;
the legal equality of states; international cooperation for development; and the
struggle for international peace and security.[7]

The first clause of the passage above affirms long-standing powers attributed to the executive branch since Mexico gained its independence.
However, neither the 1824 constitution nor the liberal constitution of 1854
articulated specific normative principles to guide Mexico's foreign relations,
as outlined in the second clause. These normative principles were introduced in the 1917 constitution, and they reflect the concerns that grew out
of Mexico's experiences in the international arena during the nineteenth
century. Understanding these principles and how they affect Mexico's foreign policy priorities requires some review of the country's historical development and international experiences.

From the beginning, Mexico's strategic position in the international
arena was disadvantaged by its relatively late emergence as an independent
state after breaking from Spain in 1821 after an eleven-year war of separation. Mexico's independence was quickly recognized by Spain's rivals, beginning with England, but the next two decades produced internal disorder
and infighting that hampered Mexico's ability to thrive in the international
system.[8] Notably, as a result of this internal turmoil, Mexico had difficulty
maintaining its territorial integrity, as portions of its northern regions
seceded to form an independent Texas in 1836. Moreover, in an era of
expansionism and competition, Mexico's domestic disarray gave both European powers and the United States relative advantages to pursue their own
interests, often at Mexico's expense. This foreign competition dramatically
shaped Mexico's political development and its overall outlook on international relations well into the modern era.

Among the earliest foreign interventions in Mexico was the Pastry War of
1838–1839, the first of two French military invasions.[9] Determined to support debts claimed by French nationals, France imposed a naval blockade
on Mexico, leading to the escalation of hostilities and the successful invasion of the port of Veracruz. Great Britain supported Mexico, but France
succeeded in capturing Veracruz and forced Mexico to pay reparations.
Second, as a result of this defeat and the domestic turmoil that followed,
Mexico was in an even more disadvantaged position when tensions developed over the U.S. annexation of Texas in 1845. The ensuing hostilities
resulted in the U.S.-Mexican war of 1846–1848, which we discuss in greater

detail in the next chapter. Suffice it to say that, although the conflict lasted little more than a year, it forever altered the fate of both countries. Under the 1848 Treaty of Guadalupe Hidalgo, Mexico ceded roughly half of its territory, which contributed in no small part to the subsequent emergence of the United States as a dominant world power. Meanwhile, Mexico maintained a long-standing resentment of the conflict, viewed primarily as a war of U.S. aggression and intrusion. Also, in terms of its domestic politics, the war led to the ouster of the conservative political factions that had largely dominated Mexico since independence, leading to greater support for liberal political forces.

That political shift led to continued internal conflict and yet another consequential foreign intrusion in the second French intervention in Mexico, from 1861 to 1867. As a result of tensions over lingering debts to France, Britain, Spain, and the United States, the liberal government of President Benito Juárez suspended payments to Mexico's foreign creditors. As tensions rose, discontented conservatives appealed to France's Napoleon Bonaparte III to help install a new emperor, Maximilian von Hapsburg. Meanwhile, Mexican diplomats like Matías Romero Avendaño lobbied heavily for support from Washington, which was embroiled in the U.S. Civil War, and other neighboring countries. By 1867 the forces of ousted President Benito Juárez drove Maximilian out of Mexico City, thereby reestablishing Mexican sovereignty and bringing an end to European intrusion on its soil. After Porfirio Díaz seized power in 1876, the great dictator succeeded in making Mexico "safe" for foreign investors, helping attract a flood of foreign capital and reversing the pattern of debt and underdevelopment that characterized Mexico's first five decades of independence. In this context, Mexico finally found a semblance of peace, prosperity, and even prestige in the international arena, albeit through the domestic repression and severe economic inequality that accompanied the Díaz regime.

The 1910 revolution interrupted the Porfiriato's sanguine relationship with the world's dominant foreign powers, as these countries watched and in some instances sought to influence the events unfolding in the clash between Mexico's insurgent and counterrevolutionary forces. While the government was preoccupied first with the revolution and later with national consolidation, Mexico's international role was relatively limited. The final outcome of the revolution significantly shifted the country's position on the issues of self-determination and nonintervention. The introduction of normative policy prescriptions into the constitution, in regard to both foreign intrusion at home and Mexico's role abroad, fundamentally reshaped the country's international orientation for most of the twentieth century.

Following from the principle of national sovereignty and nonintervention, Mexico adopted a foreign policy position known as the Estrada Doctrine, which was first articulated by Genaro Estrada, secretary of foreign relations under interim president Pascual Ortiz Rubio. The Estrada Doctrine asserted that Mexico and other states should not make evaluations or judgments regarding other governments, out of respect for the sovereign right to self-determination of all peoples. Mexico put this doctrine into practice throughout the twentieth century by avoiding normative proclamations about the actions or character of other states and, perhaps most notably, by offering prompt formal recognition of new governments. Mexico's position largely reflected the frustration that resulted from the difficulties it faced in gaining recognition for new governments after independence and after the 1910 revolution. As a result of the Estrada Doctrine, Mexico moved quickly to become the first country to recognize the new governments of Russia, China, and Cuba. That said, there have been some exceptions to the Estrada Doctrine, notably Mexico's initial refusal to recognize Franco's government in Spain in the 1930s and its refusal to recognize the government of Taiwan.[10]

In addition to the Estrada Doctrine, the effort to put revolutionary ideals into practice also influenced Mexico's standing and outlook in international politics. This was particularly noticeable with regard to oil. After Venustiano Carranza's ouster by Álvaro Obregón, the Bucareli Agreement converted oil into a bargaining chip in Mexico's efforts to ensure recognition and political support from the United States. However, as George Grayson argues, the nationalization of oil under Lázaro Cárdenas, which placed the country's oil holdings off limits to foreigners, fundamentally altered Mexico's understanding of its international position. In addition to the initial tensions that this created with Great Britain and the United States, the conversion of oil from a mere commodity into a patriotic symbol significantly constrained Mexico's options in a critical aspect of international trade and geopolitics.[11]

Meanwhile, world events placed pressure on Mexico to reevaluate one of the core principles of its foreign policy doctrine. Specifically, Mexico found itself forced to choose between the Allied and Axis powers in World War II. In the late 1930s, Germany made a concerted effort to develop strong trade and political relationships in Latin America and provided military training to most countries in the region.[12] Mexico ultimately opted to provide political, economic, and military support to the Allied forces. In the lead up to the war, Mexico had condemned Mussolini's invasion of Ethiopia in the League of Nations during the Abyssinia Crisis of 1935–1936, based on the principle of respect for national sovereignty.[13] However, President Cárdenas sought to maintain neutrality in the brewing conflict among the world's major powers. In 1941, his successor, Manuel Ávila Camacho, fully broke off relations with the Axis powers as a result of the attack on Pearl Harbor. Then, in 1942, the sinking of a Mexican oil tanker by German forces led Mexico to declare war, which led to the deployment of thirty-one P-47 Thunderbolt fighter pilots and 150 ground crew members of Squadron

201, known as the "Aztec Eagles." Squadron 201 supported U.S. and Filipino forces in the Pacific Theater and were decorated by all three countries for their service, including posthumous honors for five servicemen who died in combat.[14] Still, Mexico's participation in World War II arguably violated both the Estrada Doctrine and the principle of nonviolent resolution of international conflicts, and provoked significant internal disagreements among supporters of the Axis powers and others who opposed Mexico's participation in the war.

The end of World War II ushered in a new global distribution of power that pitted the United States against the Soviet Union in the Cold War, which featured a bipolar international system characterized by two dominant actors of roughly equal strength and diametrically opposed ideologies. The shift from several dominant actors to just two with competing ideologies narrowed the foreign policy choices for countries like Mexico, which lacked the power to challenge the status quo. In effect, all states were forced to choose between the United States and its belief in the superiority of capitalism, and the Soviet Union and its commitment to communism. Tepid support for one was generally seen as an endorsement of the other, and this mind-set made it virtually impossible for a country like Mexico, with its geographic proximity to the United States, to maintain an independent foreign policy agenda. Yet in spite of these constraints, or maybe even because of them, Mexico managed to assert its independence without ever posing a true threat to U.S. hegemony or national interests.

In the aftermath of World War II, Mexico joined the Rio Pact, a collective security agreement signed in 1947 by most countries in the Americas, pledging to come to one another's aid in the event of foreign aggression. The terms of the agreement are somewhat vague with regard to the nature of the assistance; participation is not automatic and countries are not necessarily obligated to provide military support to one another. The agreement theoretically functioned as a bulwark against further communist intrusion in the region, and it was therefore viewed as a U.S.-friendly institution.[15] At the same time, Mexico used international forums such as the Organization of American States (OAS) and the United Nations to express its opinion on international matters, which more often than not amounted to criticizing U.S. efforts to keep the hemisphere free of communist influence.[16] It was not until the 1970s under President Luis Echeverría that Mexico actively sought a higher profile in the international arena. For example, when Chile's president, Salvador Allende, was removed from office by a military coup in 1973, the Echeverría administration immediately broke off diplomatic ties with his successor, the leader of the coup, Augusto Pinochet. This change in approach was the result of the confluence of several domestic and external factors, including greater self-confidence and loftier ambitions that came along with the discovery of massive new oil deposits. Also important was Mexico's desire to have greater weight in multilateral negotiations on various international economic issues. Mexico and other developing countries sought greater equality in the areas of trade, investment, foreign aid, and technology transfers.[17]

The Echeverría administration, buoyed by the new clout bestowed on Mexico by huge oil reserves, reached out to form alliances with other developing countries with similar goals. Central to this effort was Mexico's active participation in the establishment of a New International Economic Order (NIEO), a multilateral agreement that sought the redistribution of global resources so as to promote greater equality among nations and create a new option for countries tired of operating within the constraints of the Cold War.[18] More specifically, the NIEO's goals included obtaining higher profits for Third World exports, greater access to international capital, lenient debt renegotiations, more foreign aid, the promotion of technology transfers, and a greater role in managing the international monetary system. To the dismay of many, the NIEO achieved very little. Ultimately, the diversity of the signatories was too great to overcome, and consensus on goals and strategies proved elusive. Yet Echeverría did position Mexico at the forefront of the movement and thereby broadened the country's international profile and aspirations.

Another aspect of Mexico's emerging international role was its willingness to publicly choose sides and later help broker peace agreements in Central America's civil wars. In the 1970s and 1980s, both Nicaragua and El Salvador experienced intense civil wars that pitted pro-Marxist guerrilla forces against U.S.-backed, staunchly anticommunist authoritarian dictators accustomed to using repression to squelch opposition. Ironically, Mexico's decision to actively support the leftist rebels in Central America was an effort to uphold the sanctity of national sovereignty by countering U.S. intervention in the region. In 1979, President José López Portillo made it clear that Mexico would support leftist rebels in their efforts to challenge the status quo. In support of the Sandinistas in Nicaragua, he ordered his foreign minister to block a U.S. proposal in the OAS that would have paved the way for a cease-fire and a democratic transition, but notably stopped short of ensuring that the Sandinistas would take power. The López Portillo administration then provided much diplomatic and economic aid to the Sandinistas in their war against the contras, an anticommunist paramilitary force aided by the Reagan administration. Although Mexico did not provide as much support to the Marxist Farabundo Martí National Liberation Front (Frente Farabundo Martí para la Liberación Nacional, FMLN) in El Salvador, it openly showed its support by making a joint declaration with France that recognized the leftist rebels as a legitimate "representative political force" and called for negotiations with the military regime that enjoyed support from the United States. Not coincidentally, it was during this same period that the López Portillo administration renewed its ties with Cuba, inviting Castro to Mexico for his first visit since 1956.

The 1982 inauguration of Miguel de la Madrid as Mexico's president ushered in a new foreign policy approach to Central America. The new administration drastically reduced aid to the Sandinistas and distanced itself from Cuba.[19] It also promoted the peace process as a member of the Contadora Group, a group comprised of the foreign ministers of Mexico, Venezuela, Colombia, and Panama, and, notably, excluded the United States. The resulting Contadora Initiative called for talks between warring parties and included "a comprehensive series of negotiating points, trade-offs, and mechanisms for verification and enforcement." It also stated that foreign intervention was forbidden and rejected the idea that the underlying causes for the problem were rooted in Soviet and Cuban subversion.[20] Initially, the final draft of the Contadora Act for Peace and Cooperation in Central America received broad support from key actors in the region, including El Salvador and Nicaragua. Thus, its prospects looked good when it was taken to the UN General Assembly for review. However, Contadora ultimately failed to bring about peace because the United States was displeased by the plan's failure to explicitly remove the Sandinistas from power in Nicaragua.[21] Despite the failure of Contadora, Mexico and the other countries were internationally praised for their efforts and rightly so, since the initiative served as the basis for a different plan drafted by Costa Rican President Óscar Arias in 1987 that succeeded in moving the Central American peace process forward.

The breakup of the Soviet Union in the early 1990s ended the Cold War. Without an ideological rival or a military equal, the United States became the world's only superpower. However, late in the twentieth century, strong economic challenges from the European Union, Japan, and eventually China made it necessary for the United States to strengthen its ties to other countries in the Western Hemisphere and to appreciate Mexico's economic importance. The end of the Cold War made it possible for many countries to recast their foreign relationships and ushered in the era of neoliberal economics. Accordingly, during the 1990s, Mexico strengthened its economic ties to the United States and Canada, and it also renewed its effort to broaden its trade relationships outside of North America.[22] Although the United States remains the country's most important trading partner, Mexico has significantly diversified its trade partnerships, as indicated earlier.

Although one might assume that Mexico would naturally have strong economic ties with other Latin American countries, historically this was not always the case because of the geographic proximity and economic importance of the United States for Mexico. Indeed, many in South and Central America have long regarded Mexico as an extension of U.S. economic dominance rather than as a kindred spirit, much less an economic regional leader. These feelings were heightened with the implementation of NAFTA, which led to the characterization of Mexico as "culturally Latin, financially NAFTA" and to the widespread belief in the region that when push comes to shove, Mexico will inevitably side with the United States on economic issues.[23] Evidence of this truth is said to have emerged in 2003 during negotiations over the creation of a Free Trade Area of the Americas (FTAA) and in WTO meetings that same year. In these meetings, Brazil and Argentina insisted that both regional and global free trade agreements could not move forward until dominant economies like those of the United States and the European Union began to eliminate agricultural subsidies that protect their domestic producers at the expense of unsubsidized foreign competitors. While Mexico could benefit from more free trade in Latin America, it was understandably reluctant to support measures that would infringe on its privileged access to the U.S. market. This is particularly true when it comes to Brazil, Argentina, and to a lesser extent, Chile, its most serious regional competitors.

Meanwhile, Mexico has long looked to Europe as its best option for diversifying its foreign economic relationships. In the 1970s and 1980s there were several halfhearted attempts to pursue this objective, with little success: European investment in Mexico was always very low compared to their investment in other countries in the region.[24] However, by the late 1990s, both sides had a clear interest in strengthening their ties to one another. Mexico dearly wanted access to the large European market to help boost its export earnings and reduce its dependence on the United States. The European Union wanted to enjoy Mexico's low production costs and ideal location as an exporter to the United States. Mutual benefit led to the ratification of a free trade agreement between Mexico and the European Union in 2000. After that, trade volume and earnings, as well as investment, increased in fits and starts. Between 1999 and 2001, trade increased more than 20 percent and European investment in Mexico more than tripled to $6.7 billion. Meanwhile, Mexican foreign direct investment in Europe nearly doubled to $329 million.[25] In the economic downturn that followed September 11, 2001, trade and investment between the two sides followed global trends and declined, but it still showed gains relative to the pre–free trade agreement era. With the subsequent rebound of Mexico's economy, most expect that Mexican-EU trade will increase significantly in the coming years. And while it is highly doubtful that the transatlantic relationship will ever seriously rival that of Mexico and the United States, it does represent a growing counterweight to U.S. economic dominance in the region.

Mexico's economic ties with several countries in Asia have also grown significantly in recent years. Japanese and South Korean firms have long had a presence in Mexico, with billions invested in the *maquiladora* industry along the U.S.-Mexican border.[26] Moreover, in 2006, Japan supplied 6 percent of Mexico's imports, while South Korea supplied slightly less at 4.1 percent.

That year, Mexico and Japan also signed a free trade agreement that led to a 23 percent increase in trade between the two countries. Yet while Japanese and Korean firms were attracted to Mexico because of its competitive wages and close proximity to the U.S. market, this is not true of the newest Asian actor on the scene.

Many in Mexico see China as their most formidable international rival, given the latter's ability to offer rock-bottom production costs. These fears are well founded: more than two-thirds of *maquiladoras* that closed by 2003 had relocated to China, where the average daily wage per worker is $2 to $6 less than the average wage in Mexico. Additionally, while foreign direct investment (FDI) in Mexico has declined over the past few years, China receives the world's largest share of FDI.[27] China also gained trade share at Mexico's expense by keeping its currency undervalued—a strategy that makes Chinese products comparatively cheap on foreign markets, including Mexico's. In contrast, Mexico's experience with financial crises led it to maintain large capital reserves, leading to an overvalued peso. The result is that Mexico's exports are more expensive and less attractive to consumers, especially relative to Chinese exports. Finally, China will soon make inroads in the Mexican automobile market, given current plans for Chinese firms to begin assembling small, affordable cars in Mexico.

There is little doubt that China and, to a lesser extent, other emerging economies like India, as well as lower-cost *maquiladoras* in Central America, challenge Mexico's ability to stay globally competitive. As we saw in chapter 9, this pressure has forced Mexico and other countries with mid-size economies to recognize that in order to become more competitive, they must improve education, job training, and infrastructure if they are to maintain and attract new industries. Less attention has been paid to an equally important point: the Chinese and other emerging markets also offer important opportunities for those countries and industries that are poised to meet the growing demand for energy, natural resources, and investment. Therefore, it would benefit Mexico to focus at least as much attention on this aspect of the relationship as it does on lamenting the economic prowess of the country it considers to be among its most formidable rivals.

Meanwhile, Mexico's connections to countries in Africa and the Middle East are less well developed than those noted above. Ties to Africa have been historically limited, partly because of a lack of trade compatibility. Mexico has embassies in just seven out of fifty-three African countries.[28] Of these, its most substantial relationship in the region is with South Africa, which quickly became Mexico's largest African trading partner after the removal of trade restrictions placed on the apartheid regime in the 1990s. However, in 2010, overall trade volumes were a modest $3.5 billion, and Mexico remained South Africa's third largest Latin American trading partner, after Argentina and Brazil.[29]

In the case of the Middle East, in addition to limited gains from trade, political considerations and Mexico's close ties to the United States have probably been a hindrance to closer ties. With regard to Iran, for example, total trade with Mexico in 2009 amounted to just $50 million, while Brazil's trade with Iran amounted to forty times that amount; that same year, Iran began to pursue deliberate outreach to Mexico to try to strengthen their relationship.[30] For its part, Mexico has expressed an interest in becoming more involved in the Middle East. For example, in 2000, the Zedillo administration signed a free trade agreement with Israel. This agreement more than doubled the total trade volume between the two countries over the course of a decade, and it is likely to produce further increases in trade since it was amended in April 2011 to allow commercial transshipment to Mexico via Canada and the United States.[31] Meanwhile, despite this trade relationship, Mexico has also taken a critical position toward Israel. In 2009, in the spirit of the principle of self-determination, Mexico condemned Israel's efforts to expand its settlements in Palestinian territories. Mexico maintains diplomatic offices in Ramallah and has expressed its support for an independent Palestinian state.[32]

Mexico's most recent efforts to play a larger role on the world stage have been primarily focused on diversifying and strengthening its relationship with countries other than the United States, which we discuss in further detail in the next chapter. The Fox administration was particularly active in pursuing this goal, drawing attention to Mexico's recent economic stability in order to generate greater trade and investment and forge new free trade agreements beyond NAFTA. Fox was also quick to capitalize on his country's successful transition to democracy—accepting an invitation for Mexico to join the Convening Group of the Community of Democracies and making a strong commitment to strengthen democracy and human rights protections both at home and abroad.[33]

President Calderón has attempted to build on the efforts of his predecessor, including a continued rejection of the Estrada Doctrine. Differing in important respects from past practice for much of the twentieth century, under Calderón Mexico has taken a more active and assertive role in international affairs and adopted a more discerning and sometimes critical position with regard to the status, decisions, and actions of other nations. For example, at the time this book went to press, in contrast to its past application of the Estrada Doctrine, Mexico still had not recognized the government of Kosovo, which declared its independence from Serbia in February 2008. As we discuss in the next chapter, Mexico has also taken a more vocally critical stance with regard to certain U.S. policies, such as the poor regulation of firearms trafficking and state-level laws that seek to regulate immigration.

In addition, as noted earlier, Mexico has also taken a more active role in international organizations. In President Calderón's words, "Instead of being mere observers, we must seek to participate actively in the construction of rules that will affect our country. The active participation of Mexico must allow us to . . . acquire a stronger influence in the geopolitical and geoeconomic arena."[34] Calderón's administration identifies among his foreign policy priorities the strengthening of Mexico's economic and cultural ties with Central and South America, and the intent to coordinate national efforts with those of European countries to combat environmental degradation, pandemics, and organized crime and to defend human rights.[35] In particular, Mexico has worked to engage countries like China to remain globally competitive, though it remains to be seen how these efforts will pay off in the long run.

CONCLUSION

Mexican foreign relations have changed substantially in the past several decades. It remains a very proud and independent-spirited country, but its governments are no longer as prone to fierce nationalism and over-defensiveness. While Mexico remains beholden to the core diplomatic principles enshrined in its constitution, it is also exploring new approaches to its relations in the international arena. The end of the Cold War and bipolarity have created new opportunities that not so long ago would have been considered unthinkable. As a result, Mexican foreign policy reflects a more global outlook for the twenty-first century—one that envisions the country as much more than an inferior neighbor to the world's greatest power. Today, Mexican leaders, business owners, and intellectuals talk realistically of regional leadership and strong economic ties to Europe and Asia. With strong economic relationships to a number of countries within and outside North America, membership in almost sixty major international organizations (e.g., the World Trade Organization, the Organisation for Economic Co-operation and Development, the Inter-American Development Bank, the Organization of American States, and the United Nations), and its pledge to promote democracy and human rights, Mexico is undeniably an important global economic actor.

Finally, Mexico's transition to democracy has also fundamentally altered the foreign policy process.[36] In the past, Mexican presidents, together with their foreign ministers, essentially dictated the country's foreign policy initiatives. Now the process is more dynamic, involving many political actors and interests. For example, once a rubber stamp, Congress now acts as a true check on the president's international agenda, debating, amending, and occasionally rejecting foreign policy initiatives. Public opinion is also important, since unpopular policy decisions can now credibly lead to a party's defeat in the next elections. Other actors that play an important role in the foreign policy process include influential interest groups (e.g., business), nongovernmental organizations (e.g., human rights groups), and subnational governments: it is now common for state governors to bypass the federal government and conduct their own negotiations with counterparts in the United States on trade, investment, tourism, and cultural exchange issues.[37]

The involvement of these actors in the foreign policy process has facilitated greater cooperation, particularly with actors in the United States, and to some degree, it has also potentially increased Mexico's leverage in bargaining situations by allowing the president to demand more or specific concessions from foreign actors, legitimately claiming that without them, he will be unable to convince relevant domestic interests to support and ratify the agreement. While these changes speak well of the development of Mexico's democracy and greater international clout, they also render the policy making process longer, more difficult, and less certain. Therefore, much like leaders in other democratic countries, President Calderón's foreign policy agenda faces close public scrutiny and is determined not just by the actions of his foreign counterparts, but also by the behavior of a plethora of relevant domestic political actors.

13

U.S.-Mexico Relations

The context of U.S.-Mexico relations has changed dramatically in recent years. Nearly a decade of increasing economic integration, demographic trends, and cultural influences tie the two nations more closely together than ever before. The immigration of millions of Mexicans is rapidly expanding the Latino population of the United States, and U.S. consumers have become dependent on immigrant labor for a broad range of low-cost services. Similarly, U.S. influences in Mexico have increased significantly, especially with the two countries' increasing economic integration, which has brought innumerable and sometimes unexpected influences to Mexico: well-known U.S. franchises (e.g., McDonald's, Starbucks), competition and instability in Mexico's agricultural sector, and large English-speaking retirement communities in states like Guanajuato and Baja California. Alongside these significant social and economic influences, there are also the violence and rule of law challenges posed by narcotrafficking from Mexico to the United States and the corresponding flow of illegal arms to Mexico from the United States.

Meanwhile, both countries have experienced domestic political changes that influence U.S.-Mexico relations. Mexico's democratization, for example, significantly altered the bilateral relationship in that its policy makers now benefit from greater legitimacy in the eyes of the United States. These same Mexican policy makers now operate in a political context in which they are limited by the checks and balances of the democratic process; this can slow or prevent the approval of policies and agreements that would have been easily implemented within a more authoritarian system and have implications for Mexico's relationship with the United States. At the same time, domestic political pressures—notably, public fears of possible terrorism against the United States and conflicting calls for immigration reform—significantly influenced the foreign policy outlook of U.S. policy makers, especially with regard to dealing with Mexico and the U.S.-Mexico border.

In short, the increasingly interdependent bilateral relationship between the United States and Mexico brings with it important policy considerations. What is more, challenging policy issues would be difficult if not impossible to address without significant binational cooperation: the two countries must inevitably work together to find constructive ways of dealing with them. To better understand these major challenges, we will first examine the historical trajectory of relations between the two countries and then discuss the three major issues affecting the contemporary bilateral U.S.-Mexico relationship: immigration, economic integration, and security. We close the chapter with a discussion of the U.S.-Mexico border, where these challenges are particularly acute.

EARLY MEXICO-U.S. RELATIONS

Mexico's relationship with the United States can be traced all the way back to the early nineteenth century, when the *criollos* of New Spain sought to diversify their trading partnerships and gain access to foreign markets. The United States was an important market for the colony's chief products: silver, animal hides, cotton, fibers, and sugar. After Mexico's independence in 1821, trade with the United States increased, and U.S. actors began to influence events in Mexico. For example, the first U.S. diplomat to travel to Mexico, Joel Poinsett, sought to influence the outcome of the struggle between elite factions seeking to assume national leadership. More pivotal was the annexation of Texas in 1845. A breakaway republic that was settled by U.S. citizens, Texas seceded from Mexico in 1836 and later sought to join the United States. Mexico saw U.S. actions to incorporate the territory as a direct insult, and the result was the Mexican-American War—or as it is known in Mexico, the War of the North American Invasion. The ensuing 1848 Treaty of Guadalupe Hidalgo ceded roughly half of Mexico's territory to the United States in exchange for $15 million in war indemnities. Mexico's territorial losses were compounded by the Gadsden Purchase of 1854, in which Mexico's leader, General López de Santa Anna, agreed to sell parts of southern Arizona and New Mexico to the United States for 10 million pesos (see figure 13.1).

For the United States, the outcome of its war with Mexico could hardly have been better. The war nearly doubled its territory, to include fertile and mineral-rich lands in what is now all or part of Texas, California, Arizona,

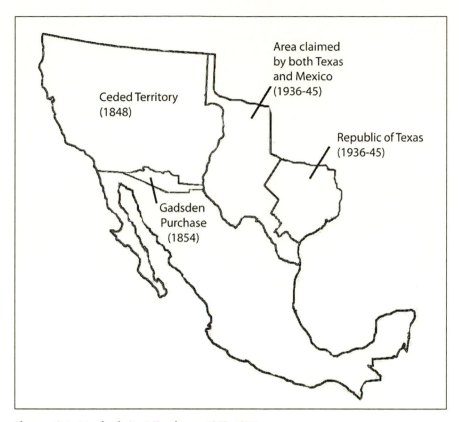

Figure 13.1. Mexico's Lost Territory, 1848–1854

New Mexico, Colorado, Nevada, and Utah. It also benefited from the addition of approximately one hundred thousand people to its population and workforce. For Mexico, the losses from the war were immeasurable—a fact that makes the War of the North American Invasion a painful and salient reminder of what many Mexicans, even today, perceive to be their northern neighbor's true intention to provoke war.

Mexico's relationship with the United States improved slightly during the period of liberal reform (1855–1867) and reached new heights during the Porfiriato, when U.S. financiers readily accepted the invitation to invest in Mexico. In 1897, U.S. investments in Mexico topped $200 million. By 1911 that figure had increased to $1 billion and represented more than all other domestic and foreign investment. Moreover, the United States consumed 74 percent of all Mexican exports.[1] U.S. economic interests became so firmly entrenched during the Porfiriato that when the Díaz regime was ousted by

Francisco Madero and other revolutionary forces, there was little doubt that the U.S. government would try to influence the outcome of the succession.

When Madero took office in 1911, the United States openly criticized him and demanded his resignation, and later supported Victoriano Huerta's counterrevolutionary coup. Once Madero was out of the picture, however, the United States turned against Huerta by selling arms to the revolutionary armies and applying military and economic pressure by occupying the port of Veracruz. Later, the United States was reluctant to recognize the Obregón government, believing he was too radical and would act against U.S. oil interests. Obregón's reassurances failed to quell U.S. fears, and in 1923 Mexico was pressured into signing the Bucareli Agreement, which required Mexico to compensate the United States for property damage sustained during the revolution and sought to protect U.S. oil interests.[2]

As we saw in chapter 2, the Bucareli Agreement did not guarantee anything in the long term. In the late 1930s, Mexico scored its first victory in its battle of wills with the United States when it nationalized the petroleum industry despite U.S. efforts to punish the action. Nationalization of the petroleum industry marked two important turning points for Mexico. First, it was a huge domestic victory for the Cárdenas administration, which not only stood up to the United States and essentially won, but also secured Mexico's control over its most valuable natural and economic resource.[3] Second, the pro-Mexican resolution of the dispute, together with pledges of various types of U.S. economic assistance, helped ensure Mexican and regional support of the United States and the Allied cause in World War II—an outcome that before 1939 was not a foregone conclusion.

From the 1940s to the early 1980s, there were no major disputes between the United States and Mexico on par with events mentioned above. The Cold War created an "us" versus "them" environment that in many ways brought the two countries together and gave them an opportunity to realize their shared economic interests. For example, in 1942 the United States worked with Mexico to initiate the Bracero Program, an agreement that allowed almost half a million agricultural laborers a year to work legally, if temporarily, in the United States, which was experiencing a labor shortage.[4] When the Bracero Program ended in 1964, Mexican laborers previously employed in the United States began to return home. In part to absorb these returning laborers, the Mexican government initiated a new program to promote economic development in the northern border region. That initiative was known as the Border Industrialization Program (BIP) and became the source of the vast *maquiladora* industry along the U.S.-Mexico border. The BIP allowed foreign-owned companies to set up labor-intensive assembly plants on the Mexican side of the border and to import, duty free, parts used in the assembly of a broad range of manufactured goods (e.g., electronics, machinery, automobile components) that were then returned to the United States, duty free, for sale to consumers in the United States and other foreign markets. This arrangement was mutually beneficial in that it created jobs for Mexicans and allowed foreign companies to increase their profit margin.

Still, despite their growing interdependence, Mexico and the United States were not always of like mind during this period—in part because the asymmetry in the relationship persisted, with the United States retaining the upper hand as the wage setter and provider of capital. So, although the two countries often found ways to work together, they also had substantially different attitudes on a number of policy issues. In the words of one leading expert on U.S.-Mexico relations, Mexico adopted "a strategic or geopolitical view of the world which—without being diametrically opposed to Washington's—[was] nevertheless contradictory."[5]

Most of the Mexican administrations that governed between 1960 and 1990 were genuinely committed to protecting the principles of national sovereignty and nonintervention, but their actions were often perceived as being anti-U.S. for the sake of being contrary. But if Mexico was simply trying to stick a thorn in the paw of the lion, what did it hope to gain? Some would argue that it was trying to extract concessions from the United States. If that was the case, the benefits were paltry indeed. The United States did grant some small concessions over the years, such as offers of financial aid in exchange for toning down the rhetoric, but these were relatively minor and arguably would have been forthcoming anyway given the importance of Mexican financial and political stability to the United States. Others would argue that Mexico's foreign policy stance vis-à-vis the United States provided important domestic political benefits for the PRI, since the government's defense of national sovereignty and criticism of U.S. imperialism almost always played well among Mexican intellectuals and some within the political elite.

Ironically, Mexico's greatest leverage with the United States was its massive debt. As we saw in chapter 9, Mexico's announcement in 1982 that it could no longer meet its debt obligation prompted other countries in similar situations to make the same claim and sent shockwaves through the financial world. This put the U.S. government in a difficult position because, with all of the U.S. capital invested in the country and the outstanding loans extended by U.S. banks, default would have devastated both economies. Therefore, the Reagan administration had little choice but to put together a bailout package. Without the help of the U.S. government, Mexico no doubt would have had a more difficult time negotiating with the international financial community.

CONTEMPORARY U.S.-MEXICO RELATIONS

The 1990s appeared to mark a new beginning for the relationship between the United States and all of Latin America. The end of the Cold War and a bipolar international environment allowed all countries to refocus their attention on issues of mutual interest, such as deepening democratic transitions and the emerging consensus regarding the need for neoliberal economic policies. While the 1990s did not, as some predicted, reduce the power asymmetries between the United States and its Latin American neighbors, it was a time in which relations within the region were more balanced and mutually respectful than they had been in the past. In this spirit, Mexico and the United States began to work more cooperatively to solve what have historically been the most intractable bilateral problems: addressing the myriad issues surrounding illegal Mexican migration to the United States, reducing trade barriers, and combating drug trafficking. On all of these issues both Mexican and U.S. policy makers openly acknowledged that solutions required bilateral cooperation and pledged to work together. Making good on their promises, the Clinton and Zedillo administrations worked hard to emphasize the countries' similarities and common interests rather than stressing their differences. This effort paid off particularly well in the area of commerce with the implementation of the North American Free Trade Agreement (NAFTA) beginning in 1994.

Almost everyone expected that the gains made in the 1990s would be reinforced by the elections of Vicente Fox and George W. Bush in 2000. By the early days of September 2001 the two countries seemed to be on track to make significant progress in achieving their goals. The two presidents met in a series of meetings to discuss long-standing issues and appeared to be committed to working together. Moreover, on September 9, 2001, the Bush White House feted Fox in its first state dinner, expressing appreciation for Fox's commitment to working with the United States.[6] But any progress made by Fox and Bush appeared to vanish overnight in the wake of the September 11, 2001, terrorist attacks in the United States. While the Canadian and British leaders immediately offered condolences and public shows of support, Fox remained oddly silent and his foreign minister, Jorge Castañeda, subsequently announced that under no conditions would Mexico provide troops or military support to any U.S. effort at retaliation.[7] Mexico's actions were particularly hurtful to the United States because they came in the wake of perhaps the most genuine display of cooperation and goodwill ever experienced between the two neighbors. Although Fox and the government moved relatively quickly to mend the damage, the incident marked the beginning of renewed bilateral tensions that lasted for several years, in large part because of Mexico's refusal to support U.S. use of military force in Iraq in 2003. By the end of Fox's administration, it was clear that what might have been a period of great collaboration and progress looked little different from past eras of suspicion and animosity. A great opportunity was lost due to unfortunate circumstances and missteps on both sides.

While President Fox was never able to achieve his foreign policy objectives with the United States, President Calderón has, for the most part, cultivated a positive and cooperative relationship with the United States. During his *sexenio*, he and his cabinet met several times with Presidents Bush and Obama, as well as with top U.S. officials, to renew Mexico's commitment to collaborate on immigration, trade, economic development, and security issues. More substantively, Calderón has demonstrated goodwill by extraditing several high-profile drug traffickers to the United States to stand trial and fostering increased cooperation with agencies such as the FBI, Homeland Security, and DEA on drug trafficking and other potential security issues. That said, the bilateral relationship has been strained by the escalation in drug violence. While the Obama administration has publicly and financially supported the Calderón administration's military strategy to combat drug-trafficking organizations, it has also complicated bilateral relations by referring to the problem as a "narco-insurgency" and openly discussing the possibility of Mexico becoming a "failed state." Perhaps the most serious blow to the relationship came in early 2011 when U.S. Ambassador Carlos Pascual's frank assessment of the Mexican army's shortcomings became public on WikiLeaks and he was forced to step down. The episode illustrated that while Mexico and the United States have strengthened their relationship in many ways, tensions and sensitivities have not completely disappeared. There is little doubt that the character of future relations between the two countries will depend on their ability to set aside these differences and to cooperate on what traditionally have been their most serious bilateral problems: immigration, trade disputes, and drug trafficking. We discuss each of these in greater detail below.

MEXICO-U.S. MIGRATION

In the fifteen-year period from 1994 to 2009, the United States granted more visas for legal permanent residency to Mexicans than to any other nationality, with an average of about 150,000 visas granted annually. Paradoxically, during this same period, Mexico was also the country that sent the largest number of undocumented immigrants to the United States. The estimated 9 million undocumented Mexican immigrants living in the United States represent almost 10 percent of Mexico's population. Today, people of Mexican origin make up the single largest immigrant group in the United States. In 2009, 38.5 million foreign-born people resided in the

United States, 30 percent of them from Mexico.[8] A significant percentage of Mexicans residing in the United States do not have proper visas, and they account for nearly 57 percent of all undocumented residents living in the United States.[9]

Why do they come? The availability of jobs with higher wages is probably the most important factor pulling Mexicans across the border into the United States. On average, a worker in the United States earns ten times more than another doing the same job in Mexico. Moreover, in the United States, jobs are readily available to anyone who is willing to accept low wages, and U.S. employers in sectors such as agriculture, meatpacking, domestic services, and construction have come to rely on Mexican immigrants as a primary source of relatively low-cost labor. Also, strong social networks create incentives for Mexicans to assume the risks of crossing the border, often illegally. Reunification with family members is a compelling reason to migrate, but social networks also have the effect of lowering the costs of migration by providing a ready-made community that can offer lodging, financial support, and a line on employment possibilities.

Yet if the demand for low-priced labor and social networks pull people across the border, there are also strong push factors emanating from Mexico. Political and especially economic crises that bring high levels of unemployment and low or stagnant wages serve as catalysts that force people to look for different economic survival strategies.[10] Migration to the United States is a strategy that has become embedded in the lives not just of individual Mexicans, but of entire communities, so that it is common for almost all able-bodied men in a Mexican village to live and work in the United States, supporting the family with remittances and returning only periodically.[11]

Although almost everyone in the United States agrees that the country's immigration policies are in dire need of reform, they disagree both about whether immigration is good or bad for the United States and about what kind of reform should occur (see textbox 13.1). These differences transcend partisan affiliation and have long contributed to U.S. policies that at best lacked coherence, and at worst were counterproductive. For its part, the Mexican government has rarely attempted to stop its citizens from leaving, prompting many to characterize its approach as "a policy of no policy." The following section provides a brief overview of each country's policies and discusses the most recent attempts by the U.S. government to implement immigration reform.

Migration Policy

Curiously, U.S. immigration policy has rarely been coherent or aimed at a clear goal. There have been a number of policy initiatives designed

Textbox 13.1. MEXICAN MIGRATION TO
THE UNITED STATES: GOOD OR BAD?

Those who oppose large-scale immigration (and particularly unauthorized immigration) and believe that U.S. immigration policy is not restrictive enough base their arguments on at least four different elements that are often combined into a single stance. First, they object to the fact that undocumented migrants flout U.S. immigration laws and sovereignty and argue that "illegals" should be punished and deported. Further, they stress the necessity of sealing the border in order to ensure national security. Another point of contention is that large numbers of unauthorized migrants put a strain on resources that more appropriately belong to law-abiding, taxpaying citizens. A related argument is that low-wage labor depresses wages and takes jobs from U.S. citizens, thereby contributing to unemployment and poverty. The effects of this dynamic are most acutely felt by members of the lower and working classes because they rely more heavily on government services and lack the education or job skills needed to broaden their economic opportunities. Finally, opponents claim that too much migration from a single country, particularly one that is linguistically different, threatens to unalterably change the cultural makeup of the United States. Mexican-origin immigrants have been vulnerable to this charge because until very recently, they tended to concentrate in specific geographic areas (e.g., the Southwest) and therefore had a disproportionate effect on those locations.

Advocates of more liberal immigration laws tend to focus on the contributions that immigrants make to U.S. society. While few would claim that illegal entry into the United States is unequivocally acceptable, they tend to stress the fact that Mexicans migrate to the United States only because of the high demand for their labor and their desperate wish for a better life. From this perspective, Mexican emigration is an economic calculation that minimizes the importance of national boundaries and legal status. Furthermore, advocates stress the entrepreneurial spirit among immigrant populations and argue that the notion that immigrants take jobs from natives is folly because of the social stigma associated with doing many "immigrant" jobs (e.g., picking fruits and vegetables, working as domestics, packing meat, etc.). Similarly, they dispute the claim that undocumented migrants do not pay into the system of public services that they use, since all residents, regardless of legal status, contribute equally to flat taxes (e.g., sales tax), social security (even if they are using stolen cards), and indirect taxes (e.g., property tax figured into the price of rent). Immigration advocates also point to the experience of other immigrant groups to show that at one time almost all immigrants (Germans, Irish, Italians, Poles, Jews) were accused of resisting assimilation and adopting

an "American" identity. Recent studies show that much like other immigrant groups, foreign-born and first-generation Mexican-origin immigrants acquire the English language slowly, while members of the second
generation become well integrated into U.S. society. Finally, holders of a
pro-immigrant stance acknowledge that there are economic costs associated with large immigrant populations in concentrated geographic areas,
but counter by saying that they provide net gains to society by reducing
the cost of many goods and services.

to strengthen border enforcement and punish employers who hire undocumented laborers. Yet there have also been large-scale efforts to attract
Mexicans to the United States, first for jobs and later to reunite with their
family members. Early in the twentieth century, Mexican immigrants were
given preferential treatment over their European counterparts because they
were thought to be less likely to be members of unions agitating for labor
reform. It was also easy to deport Mexicans in times of economic downturn
(e.g., the Great Depression). Mexican migrants benefited from the Bracero
Program, the bilateral agreement that allowed Mexican agricultural laborers to work legally but temporarily in the United States during wartime. By
the mid-1950s, public opinion turned against this practice, and in language
that both echoed the past and foreshadowed the future, Mexican migrants
were deemed undesirable because they purportedly depressed wages, displaced U.S. workers, and posed a threat to national security. In response,
the U.S. government launched the effective (if offensively named) Operation Wetback, which rounded up hundreds of thousands of undocumented
Mexicans and sent them to Mexico.[12]

The end of the Bracero Program in 1964 marked the first and last time
that the United States and Mexico jointly managed the large-scale flow of
migrants across their shared border, but it did not mean that U.S. immigration policy became more coherent. The next major reform, the Immigration
Reform and Control Act (IRCA) of 1986, reinforced the dual nature of U.S.
immigration policy by on the one hand penalizing those who knowingly
employed undocumented migrants while on the other providing a pathway
to legalization for those migrants who had U.S. residence before 1982 and
the creation of a temporary work program that facilitated legalization of
some agricultural workers.

In the end, IRCA disappointed those who wanted more restrictive immigration and did little to reduce the number of undocumented migrants
entering the United States. As a result, the issue of controlling immigration

flows resurfaced periodically throughout the 1990s in ways that were openly hostile to Mexicans. For example, in the early 1990s, Texas and California, the two states that probably bore the greatest costs associated with undocumented migration, sought to get a hold on the problem by building border fences and beefing up border security for the express purpose of dissuading and apprehending illegal crossers. In 1994 California passed Proposition 187, a law that made undocumented immigrants ineligible for government-funded services such as public education and health care. Most provisions of the legislation were ultimately deemed unconstitutional, but the measure reflected growing disillusionment with federal immigration laws that would come to have national resonance ten years later.

For its part, Mexico has historically done little to stem the flow of its citizens across the border, partly because it lacked the resources to police the northern border and partly because it benefited from the roughly $20 billion in remittances sent home annually. Hence, while Mexican migration to the United States has always been at the top of the bilateral agenda, it is also an issue that, until recently, was a relatively low foreign policy priority in Mexico. Rather than accept that Mexico's uneven rates of economic growth, poor job creation, low wages, and government inertia contributed to the high levels of emigration to the United States, many Mexicans and government officials instead focused on the difficult and dangerous conditions that characterize illegal crossings, the shoddy and exploitative treatment (both real and exaggerated) that many receive at the hands of border patrol agents, unscrupulous employers, and other U.S. actors and criticized the United States for its failure to protect the rights and lives of Mexican nationals. The Mexican media played a large role in shaping Mexicans' understanding of U.S. immigration policy, usually to ill effect.

Mexico's policy of no policy on emigration issues started to change in the early 1990s, as the government began to participate in high-level talks with Washington. Together with their American counterparts, Mexican officials helped draft a binational study of the problem in 1997. The government also stepped up its efforts to improve human rights conditions along the border and promote awareness about labor rights.[13] President Fox reiterated this priority and called for deepening regional integration to include the free flow of labor across national boundaries in a so-called NAFTA-plus relationship that more closely resembled the European Union. At the same time, he pledged to increase domestic economic growth and employment opportunities so that Mexicans would have greater incentives to stay home. President Bush supported many of these ideas and pledged to work steadily toward an agreement. As discussed earlier, the events of September 11, 2001, dramatically changed U.S. foreign policy priorities. However, even without the shift, it is likely that President Bush would have had a difficult time reforming immigration policy to include a path to citizenship and a guest worker program because the public and U.S. lawmakers were deeply divided about the issue. These divisions became starkly apparent in 2005 when the House of Representatives passed the Border Protection, Antiterrorism, and Illegal Immigration Control Act of 2005 (HR 4437), which would have significantly increased border surveillance and security, allowed for the construction of a seven-hundred-mile fence along the border, made unlawful presence a felony punishable with jail time, required local law enforcement agencies to enforce federal immigration laws, made it almost impossible for an undocumented migrant to gain legal status, and made it a felony for any individual or organization to aid undocumented migrants by providing them food, shelter, or aid of any kind.

This bill sparked enormous controversy both at home and in Mexico, and prompted the U.S. Senate to try to come up with an alternative. While disparate interest groups sought to influence the nature of the reform, lawmakers spent all of 2006 debating different proposals and holding regional hearings in an effort to draft a new, more comprehensive bill that could simultaneously address border security and the complexities of immigration reform. In the end, the U.S. Congress passed a bill calling for the construction of a seven-hundred-mile double-layered wall and beefed up border enforcement in the highest-traffic areas of the border. Notably absent were provisions for a temporary worker program and reforms to current U.S. immigration laws. This legislation was narrowly focused on border security because many legislators were unwilling to cast votes on the more contentious issue of immigration reform during a midterm election year.

Not surprisingly, the plan to build a wall was roundly criticized in Mexico. Although many publicly acknowledged that it is Mexico's responsibility to give its citizens reasons to stay home, they also expressed dismay, calling the legislation a slap in the face. President-elect Calderón stated that a fence "is not and cannot be a solution to the problem." Even with increased surveillance, a fence is unlikely to seal the border and provide the security or immigration control that its proponents claim it will. Evidence from similar efforts in San Diego and El Paso has shown that fences and more border patrol agents simply push would-be migrants to more inhospitable desert territory where they risk death from dehydration or exposure, and do very little, in the long term, to stem the flow of migrants across the border.

Although President Obama expressed an interest in undertaking immigration reform, the recession and contentious domestic political climate have so far prevented large-scale reform. What has changed with Obama is the federal government's approach to dealing with undocumented individuals in the United States. Under his administration, there has been a shift away from workplace raids and greater emphasis on enforcement of employer sanctions and deportations. Unsatisfied with these measures, a handful of U.S. states such as Arizona, Alabama, and Utah have passed strict laws intended to produce "attrition through enforcement." The goal of these laws is to make life so difficult that illegal immigrants will choose to leave. Yet so far neither federal- nor state-level efforts have succeeded in reducing the number of people residing illegally in the United States. Figures from the 2010 census show that between 2009 and 2010 the number of illegal immigrants stayed constant at approximately 11.2 million (of which Mexicans comprise approximately 58 percent).[14] These findings reiterate the importance of the United States and Mexico working together to create a sufficient number of permanent, high-paying jobs in Mexico to convince would-be migrants to stay home.

BILATERAL TRADE AND ECONOMIC RELATIONS

NAFTA has come to dominate most discussions about trade between Mexico and the United States, but long before 1994, the two countries had well-established economic ties. After Mexico's independence, the United States cultivated commercial ties, and especially during the Porfiriato, the United States became Mexico's most important trade partner and source of foreign investment. While bilateral trade declined during the revolution and the Great Depression, it took off again in the 1940s when the United States began to demand significantly more food and raw materials for the war efforts, first in Europe and Japan and later in Korea. This demand helped double Mexico's exports during this period. Similarly, U.S. investment in Mexico increased dramatically, doubling in the 1950s, tripling in the 1960s, and quadrupling in the 1970s.[15] Again, bilateral trade dropped off during the recessions and economic crises of the 1970s and 1980s, but it was revived in the late 1980s after Mexico signed the General Agreement on Tariffs and Trade (GATT), an international agreement designed to liberalize trade by reducing tariffs and other trade barriers.

As discussed in chapter 9, liberalizing trade was one of the measures taken by the de la Madrid administration to bring Mexico out of the debt crisis and to forge greater macroeconomic stability. Before Mexico's entry into GATT in 1986, it used tariffs to protect its domestic industries from foreign competition, but between 1982 and 1993 Mexican tariffs on U.S. goods were cut in half, from roughly 25 to 12 percent, and U.S. imports to Mexico increased significantly.[16] Below we consider the trajectory of the economic relationship between Mexico and the United States from the 1990s to the present.

NAFTA and Mexico's Economic Opening

NAFTA was an attempt to institutionalize freer trade and to boost economic growth by increasing the flow of trade and investment in Mexico, the United States, and Canada. It was the most important example of economic integration in the 1990s, after the European Union. But why did three countries that already had extensive trade relations and relatively low tariffs feel it was necessary to sign an international treaty that committed them to reduce the protection of domestic industries in favor of free trade? The answer to that question is multifaceted.[17] One important component was certainly the pervasiveness of the Washington Consensus (see textbox 9.2) and its emphasis on free trade as a key to promoting economic growth and democracy. In the wake of recurring economic crises and balance of payment deficits, Mexico, like most Latin American countries, found itself under pressure from multilateral lending institutions to reduce domestic barriers to trade in the 1980s.[18] Technocrats within the PRI (e.g., de la Madrid, Salinas, and Zedillo) also advocated free trade and other neoliberal policy prescriptions to structurally alter the national economy and make it bigger and more stable. Salinas, in particular, aimed to bring Mexico into the first world by linking it to the United States and Canada. Entry into NAFTA would not only give Mexico privileged access to one of the largest and most affluent markets in the world, it was also a way for Salinas to institutionalize neoliberalism in Mexico, since defenders of protectionism would have a difficult time overturning an international treaty.

The free trade agreement was also considered a way to ensure that Mexico would be insulated from any future movement within the United States to reinstate tariffs and other protectionist policies that could restrict Mexico's access to its market. Moreover, technocrats in Mexico saw NAFTA as part of the solid foundation necessary to attract more foreign investment from Europe and Japan, as well as the United States. Of course, the free trade proposal was not meant to benefit only Mexico: the United States had its own motivations for entering into NAFTA. Perhaps highest in the minds of many U.S. politicians was finding a way to stay competitive with the European Union. Easy access to low-wage Mexican labor was seen as an integral part of their strategy. Also important were U.S. desires to secure access to Mexican oil and to curtail Mexican emigration by creating new economic opportunities and incentives for Mexicans to stay in their homeland.

Thus NAFTA seemed like a winning proposal for both Mexican and U.S. interests, but not everyone was excited about the prospects of integrating the two economies (see textbox 13.2). Domestic groups within both countries raised strong objections to the initiative. In the United States, the most vocal opposition came from labor unions, which claimed that the agreement would lead to significant job losses and depressed wages.

Textbox 13.2. NAFTA: WHAT IT IS . . . AND IS NOT

What It Is . . .

On January 1, 1994, the North American Free Trade Agreement went into effect. The trilateral agreement, signed by Canada, Mexico, and the United States, had three main goals. First, it reduced barriers to trade among the signatories. All three countries pledged to reduce and eventually eliminate tariffs and other forms of protectionism on almost all manufactured and agricultural goods, financial and other services, transportation, and telecommunications within fifteen years, or by 2009. This allows all three countries' products to compete on a level playing field in all three markets. Second, it established an institutional framework to help the signatories coordinate their trade policies and resolve conflicts. The NAFTA Free Trade Commission strives to clarify rules and procedures and helps settle disputes when countries cannot resolve them on their own. Finally, the agreement required Mexico to strengthen its laws protecting intellectual property rights (e.g., copyrights, patents) and to reform other domestic laws in order to facilitate the flow of foreign investment into Mexico.

. . . and Is Not

While North America has the most extensive free trade area after the European Union, it stops short of promoting true regional integration. For example, NAFTA did not include the creation of any true governing institutions. All three countries retain complete sovereignty over their own affairs, including the freedom to decide whether to participate in conflict resolution mediated by the NAFTA Free Trade Commission and whether to abide by the commission's rulings. Unlike the European Union, where the smaller and poorer economies were given significant financial assistance to offset the short- and medium-term dislocations caused by the transition to free trade, NAFTA did not provide aid to Mexico, the smallest and poorest of the three signatories. In spite of the scale and importance of Mexican migration to the United States, the agreement included no provisions to regulate or facilitate the flow of labor across national borders. Instead, the three governments signed a supplemental agreement that committed each country only to enforcing its own domestic labor laws. Nor did the accord incorporate a legal framework to protect the environment from the negative effects of international trade. Like labor, the environment was addressed only in a side agreement that calls for, but cannot enforce, environmental protection laws.

Environmental advocates were also concerned about the negative effects of industry and increased trade, especially in the border region. While neither of these groups was able to exert enough pressure to defeat the proposal, they were successful in convincing the Clinton administration to require side agreements that would ensure the protection of both labor standards and the environment. After a protracted and bitter congressional debate, both houses approved the agreement in 1993.

In Mexico, many were concerned about the negative effects that a free trade agreement would have on the Mexican countryside and on small businesses unprepared to compete on the international market. There were also reservations about how long it would take Mexico to truly benefit from the agreement, since it was the country with the highest tariffs and least competitive industries, and therefore the one that would experience the greatest economic dislocation. Yet unlike their North American counterparts, opponents of NAFTA in Mexico were unable to exert enough pressure on the government to exact any concessions. In the words of Levy and Bruhn:

> Opponents to free trade within Mexico were ineffectively organized and politically marginalized. Salinas could count on a loyal legislature to approve the treaty without respect to its content. In fact, PRI legislators turned down opposition requests for regular updates on the progress of negotiations. In the end, the Mexican Congress approved the agreement essentially without debate.[19]

NAFTA went into effect on January 1, 1994, and since that time has had a significant effect on Mexico's economy and society. Mexico quickly rose to become the second most important source of U.S. imports, and increased trade with the United States has contributed to an increase in Mexico's GDP.[20] Thus, many of those who predicted that NAFTA would bring economic benefits to Mexico were vindicated by economic figures that demonstrated a significant increase in the volume of trade with the United States: whereas trade between the two countries amounted to $88 billion in 1993, that figure increased to $157 billion by 1997, and $250 billion in 2002.[21] Currently, the U.S. has a trade deficit with Mexico: in 2010 the United States exported $129 billion to Mexico, while Mexico exported $177 billion to the United States.[22] Proponents of NAFTA were also quick to point to the large increase in foreign direct investment in Mexico, from a pre-NAFTA average of $4 billion to $13 billion after the trade agreement went into effect. Furthermore, the Mexican government estimated that 1.7 million jobs were created as a result of NAFTA, while relatively few were lost in the United States—a big fear among U.S. detractors like organized labor.[23] Costs for consumers also dropped significantly thanks to NAFTA, as U.S. citizens and Mexicans can now purchase each other's goods without the extraordinarily high tariffs of the past. Other important benefits include the fact that Mexico now has a more diverse export-based economy, which means that it has somewhat reduced its dependence on oil exports for its income and, thanks to stronger economic ties to the United States, improved ability to weather economic hardship (e.g., the peso crisis of 1994).

Yet for all of its positive effects, NAFTA has its drawbacks, such as Mexico's increased dependence on the U.S. economy. As the recent global recession made clear, now more than ever, Mexico's economic fate is tied to that of the United States. Approximately 80 percent of Mexico's global exports are purchased by the United States, and Mexico does more business in a month with the United States than it does in an entire year with all twenty-seven countries of the EU combined.[24] NAFTA has also produced negative consequences for specific groups in Mexico because the gains of trade have not been equally distributed in society. Those individuals and regions with ties to investment and manufacturing have enjoyed growth in productivity, profits, and job creation. Meanwhile, agriculture has suffered significant losses as Mexican farmers struggle and fail to compete with U.S.-subsidized crops such as corn and sugar. Indeed, while Mexico now enjoys an overall trade surplus with the United States, its trade deficit in agricultural products has increased. The result is not only a loss of income as domestic agricultural prices become depressed, but the displacement of thousands of agricultural workers: between 1994 and 2004 the sector lost approximately 1.3 million jobs.[25] The majority of people who lost jobs have low levels of education, few job skills unrelated to agriculture, and virtually no safety net to facilitate a transition to another economic sector. While NAFTA has led to the creation of some new jobs, there are not nearly enough to absorb the nearly one million people entering the workforce every year. Nor has the agreement been able to offset job losses to countries in Central America and Asia, where labor and production costs are even lower than in Mexico. Thus it comes as no surprise that another negative effect of NAFTA is increased income inequality between the rich and poor: since 1994, "the top 10 percent of households have increased their share of national income, while the other 90 percent have lost income share or seen no change."[26] The effects of NAFTA are, therefore, mixed. The agreement brought Mexico important gains in the aggregate, but to those individuals and regions that experienced job and income losses, the effects of trade liberalization were devastating.

Today, Mexico has a better understanding of the benefits and limitations of NAFTA, but it must find a way to address the agreement's shortcomings if it is to more equitably distribute the gains from free trade and promote more broad-based economic growth and development. To this end, the Fox administration placed at the top of its bilateral policy agenda the resolution of outstanding problems with NAFTA's implementation and the pursuit of NAFTA-plus, an expanded version of the accord that included the free flow of labor among the three countries, common monetary policy, harmonized external tariffs, and compensatory funding—fiscal transfers from the United States and Canada to Mexico to offset the adjustment costs associated with liberalizing trade and investment.[27] Fox's strategy was to use Mexico's "democratic bonus," or increased clout as a democracy, to help convince the other signatories that further economic integration would benefit all three countries as they sought to remain globally competitive.[28] To their credit, presidents Fox and Bush resolved a number of ongoing trade disputes, including the U.S. refusal to comply with the terms of NAFTA that allowed Mexican trucks to cross the border and make deliveries in the United States. However, the Mexican leader's more ambitious plan for NAFTA-plus was irreversibly derailed by the shift in U.S. foreign policy priorities after the events of September 11, 2001.[29]

Despite Fox's limited success, many within Mexico still believe that the solution to problems created by NAFTA lies in deepening, rather than reversing, regional integration. For example, Felipe Calderón stated early in his *sexenio* that one of Mexico's most important challenges is to consolidate integration with the rest of North America, and he made it clear that further integration is the key not only to spurring the country's economic development, but also to solving the problems associated with Mexican emigration. Among his administration's top priorities were several initiatives to promote greater communication and cooperation among NAFTA's three signatories, and a plan to channel new investment from Canada and the United States into migrant-sending areas in order to create new jobs and infrastructure that will encourage would-be migrants to stay home.

Another of Calderón's goals was the reform of the North American Development Bank (NADBank), an organization created by the NAFTA treaty and funded by all three countries to finance environmental protection projects. Currently NADBank's mandate allows it to address only a narrow range of problems in the U.S.-Mexico border region. Building on a proposal introduced by the Fox administration, Calderón aimed to broaden the scope and reach of the institution, allowing it to finance a wider range of projects both within and outside of the border region. If reformed, NADBank funds might be used to offset some of the costs of job losses (e.g., education and retraining for displaced workers) and thus constitute a first and small step toward compensatory funding for Mexico. Yet Calderón achieved relatively little on these goals. Perhaps the main reason for this failure is that the global recession forced both Mexico and the United States to focus on immediate domestic economic priorities. Additionally, the Calderón administration was preoccupied by its war on drug trafficking, and the Obama administration's goal of health care reform and attention to the U.S. economy forced all other issues to the back burner. Therefore, while it is certain that NAFTA will remain in place for the foreseeable future, at this point there does not appear to be the political will in any of the signatory countries to revamp the agreement.

BINATIONAL SECURITY CHALLENGES

U.S.-Mexico collaboration is absolutely essential if the two countries are to get a handle on transborder crime and security challenges such as arms trafficking, narcotics and human smuggling, elevated levels of crime and violence, multiple forms of official corruption, and tensions over the appropriate goals and means for law enforcement. The Bush administration's early declarations that narco-trafficking and immigration stemmed from U.S. demand represented a long-overdue acknowledgment of a major shift in the U.S. perspective and paved the way for closer cooperation and new directions in policy formation. However, U.S. priorities after 9/11 quickly became focused on seeking and destroying terrorist threats abroad, and Mexico appeared to be the weak link in the North American security chain. Domestic rule of law challenges—and the porous nature of the U.S.-Mexico border—led to considerable speculation that Mexico could become an entry point for terrorist attacks against the United States.

To the frequent frustration of U.S. officials, persistent problems in Mexican law enforcement—from lack of adequate resources to outright corruption—often set limits on binational cooperation to address these challenges. Meanwhile, Mexican officials are mainly focused on their own domestic rule of law challenges, as well as addressing southbound flows of illegal arms, dangers posed to northbound migrants, growing domestic drug use, and unlawful behavior by U.S. visitors to Mexico. From the Mexican perspective, U.S. unilateralism and reluctance to share intelligence too often subvert or undermine the domestic law enforcement efforts of Mexican officials.

Furthermore, because U.S.-Mexico security collaboration depends heavily on goodwill and ad hoc initiatives rather than on institutionalized mechanisms, there is an unfortunate lack of consistency and continuity. As García points out, binational cooperation typically tends to be more focused on "reducing cross-border interagency irritants and misunderstandings" rather than on coordinated operations, and while occasionally stronger at the local level, interagency cooperation tends to vary "from place to place and time to time."[30] These perceptions were created by a number of high-profile setbacks that seriously undermined collaboration on security matters in the 1980s and 1990s. One of the earliest and most notable breakdowns in U.S.-Mexico security collaboration occurred in the wake of the torture and murder of DEA agent Enrique "Kiki" Camarena in 1985. Camarena was conducting an undercover narco-trafficking investigation in Mexico, when his cover was blown by a corrupt Mexican official. U.S. frustration over this severe breach of the investigation and perceptions that Mexican authorities were doing too little to investigate Camarena's murder resulted in an eight-day partial shutdown of the U.S.-Mexico border in February 1985. In addition, five years later—in retaliation for Camarena's murder—under evident direction from DEA officials, U.S. bounty hunters abducted a Mexican doctor from Guadalajara who was accused of collaboration in Camarena's torture. This extra-territorial abduction was eventually challenged before the U.S. Supreme Court, in the case of *United States v. Alvarez-Machain* (1992), but its legality was ultimately upheld. Mexican authorities were outraged, just as U.S. officials would have been if Mexican law enforcement unilaterally authorized the abduction of a U.S. citizen for trial in Mexico.

By the mid-1990s, binational security relations appeared to improve gradually. Within the Binational Commission originally formed in 1977 to allow annual meetings of U.S. and Mexican cabinet officials, presidents Zedillo and Clinton authorized the formation of a High-Level Contact Group in 1996 to specifically target narco-trafficking. However, bilateral efforts experienced another setback with the arrest of General Gutiérrez Rebollo, the head of the National Institute for Combating Drugs (Instituto Nacional para el Combate a las Drogas, INCD), when it was discovered that he had ties to the Juárez drug cartel.

Such incidents of corruption have contributed to the evident distrust of U.S. law enforcement toward Mexican authorities, as well as responses that contribute to further irritations in the U.S.-Mexico relationship. For example, in an effort to avoid possible leaks from corrupt Mexican authorities, U.S. authorities opted to pursue an extraterritorial investigation of money-laundering activities in Mexico through Operation Casablanca—the code name for a U.S. Customs investigation against operations of Colombia's Cali cartel on Mexican soil from 1995 to 1998. The operation was a success, but it brought significant criticism from Mexican authorities that saw the unauthorized operation of U.S. law enforcement in Mexico as an excessive violation of national sovereignty.[31] More recently, in February 2011, drug traffickers killed one and wounded another U.S. Immigration and Customs Enforcement agent operating in Mexico, leading U.S. officials to question Mexico's ability to protect foreign citizens from drug violence.

For their part, the Mexicans were incensed by the revelation that same month that the U.S. Bureau of Alcohol, Tobacco, Firearms, and Explosives (ATF) had allowed hundreds of guns to be illegally imported to Mexico. Dubbed Operation Fast and Furious, the ATF's goal was to monitor straw gun purchases in the United States and then follow the flow of guns to see if they ended up in the hands of drug traffickers in Mexico. Several whistle-blowers claim that the ATF allowed the guns to "walk" even after safety concerns were raised, and in a sad and ironic twist, it was subsequently discovered that one of the AK-47s involved in Fast and Furious was used to kill a U.S. border patrol agent in late 2010. Mexico has long criticized the United States for doing little to stop the flow of arms across its southern border. Its argument is made stronger by the fact that at least 70 percent of the firearms recovered by Mexican authorities in 2009 and 2010 came from the United States.[32]

Cross-Border Collaboration

Despite these setbacks, U.S.-Mexico collaboration on security matters has shown significant signs of improvement. One key area of collaboration between the United States and Mexico is the extradition of criminals and sharing of evidence for cross-border prosecutions. For most of the twentieth century, there was no formal agreement on the extradition process between Mexico and the United States, although some informal agreements existed (especially between local law enforcement agencies on either side of the border). In 1978, the United States and Mexico signed their current extradition treaty, which went into effect in 1980 with the provision that Mexico would refuse extradition in cases where defendants would be subject to the death penalty in the United States. In October 2001, the Mexican Supreme Court ruled that the extradition of criminals under charges that included life imprisonment represented a cruel and unusual punishment, and was therefore unconstitutional. This ruling frustrated U.S. prosecutors and law enforcement officials, who had to forgo both the death penalty and life imprisonment until a subsequent Mexican Supreme Court ruling in 2006 found that the domestic use of life imprisonment sentences was not unconstitutional, thereby permitting similar sentences to be applied in international extradition cases.

Notwithstanding the temporary prohibition of life imprisonment, extraditions from Mexico to the United States grew at record levels between 2001 and 2006. Indeed, during the later part of the 1990s, the number of extraditions from Mexico to the United States averaged around eleven per year, yet this rate more than tripled by the end of the Fox administration. The Calderón administration stepped up extradition efforts even more dramatically, sending a total of 285 suspects to the U.S. for prosecution between 2007 and 2009. In just three years, the administration extradited more suspects to the U.S. than had been sent between 1996 and 2000 (see figure 13.2). The most high-profile of these extraditions came in 2007 and 2011, when Osiel Cárdenas, leader of the northeastern Gulf cartel, and Benjamín Arellano Félix, leader of the Tijuana cartel, were sent to the United States to face drug-trafficking charges. The extraditions were hailed in both the United States and Mexico as an illustration of effective bilateral cooperation, and a sign of goodwill and mutual trust on the part of authorities in both countries.

Yet another area of cross-border law enforcement collaboration in recent years can be found in cross-border evidence sharing and prosecutions. Mexico and the United States share a Mutual Legal Assistance Treaty (MLAT), which allows law enforcement to share evidence in courtrooms for

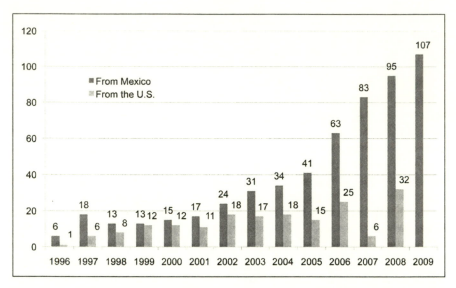

Figure 13.2. International Extraditions between Mexico and the United States, 1996–2009

Source: Embassy of Mexico Fact Sheet, "Rounding Up Fugitives," May 12, 2004; "U.S. and Mexico Team Up to Arrest Mexican Fugitive from Justice" (2004–2005); Matthew T. Hall, "Gonzales Lauds Mexico's extradition of 15 to U.S.," *San Diego Union Tribune*, January 21, 2007; e-mail inquiry to U.S. Embassy in February 2007; and press release by Ambassador Tony Garza on December 31, 2008. Data for first 10 months of 2009 reported in "Mexico-US hold extradition talks," *BBC News*, November 2, 2009.

criminal prosecutions. In addition, Article 4 of the Mexican Federal Penal Code also permits foreign law enforcement to present evidence in the domestic prosecution of Mexican nationals charged with committing crimes outside of Mexico.[33] In such cases, U.S. authorities can file briefs providing evidence that can be used against the accused in Mexican court. One caveat is that U.S. authorities cannot retry the individual upon return to the United States (because of the Fifth Amendment), even if the punishment is considered inadequate or the individual has evaded his or her complete sentence through bribery. Hence, U.S. law enforcement authorities tend to pursue prosecution through the Article 4 procedure only to prosecute serious felonies like murder or rape, when there is a strong indication that there will be adequate punishment.

Finally, this apparent trend toward greater bilateral U.S.-Mexico collaboration has been complemented by proposals for larger, regional security agreements involving Canada and Central America. After 9/11, some U.S. and Mexican authorities and security experts began to focus more on the big picture of North American security, with greater trilateral collaboration between Canada, Mexico, and the United States to address shared security threats. More specifically, some have called for a regional security perimeter that would extend beyond U.S. borders, with common security standards and greater information sharing in the North American context. In fact, such proposals have become a partial reality with initiatives such as the U.S.-Canada and U.S.-Mexico smart border agreements, which articulated specific objectives and areas for collaboration in ensuring secure and efficient cross-border flows. In March 2005, Canada, Mexico, and the United States went one step further by trilateralizing security collaboration with the creation of the Security and Prosperity Partnership (SPP), an agreement to identify shared goals and coordinate security strategies between the three countries. During President Bush's 2007 goodwill tour of Latin America, conversations with Felipe Calderón and Guatemalan president Óscar Berger laid the groundwork for the development of a regional security plan. The initial framework for that agreement was announced in May 2007, with an emphasis on countermeasures to combat drug and arms trafficking, control immigration, and combat transnational gangs.[34] The plan was further developed by presidents Bush and Calderón in what became known as the Mérida Initiative.

This initiative called for the United States to provide more than $1 billion in financial assistance to support Mexico's counternarcotics efforts in four areas: helicopters, equipment, and training to disrupt the capacity of organized crime to operate; training and aid to institutionalize the rule of law through justice sector reform; technology, infrastructure, and training to create a more secure border; and investment to build strong and resilient communities.

The possible end result of such an ambitious regional security agreement could be the development of a more comprehensive "NAFTA-plus" security regime. In the meantime, it is important to note that U.S.-Mexico collaboration on security matters has obtained a significant boost as a result of the so-called democratic bonus. That is, many U.S. authorities and law enforcement officials have evidenced a greater willingness to work with the governments of Vicente Fox and Felipe Calderón, who have been perceived as more legitimate and transparent than their PRI predecessors. Moreover, high-level officials now speak openly about their improved ability to work with one another. According to Alan Bersin, commissioner of U.S. Customs and Border Protection, in the past, "there was a separation and finger pointing on the various problems of drugs and immigration, [but] they created the conditions for joint approaches. . . . With President Calderón and President Obama, there's been a 180-degree turn."[35] Perhaps the most significant development in this area is the decision by the Obama administration to post CIA operatives and retired U.S. military personnel at Mexican military bases to help their counterparts collect information about drug-trafficking organizations and plan operations to combat them.

This level of cooperation was previously unthinkable and marks a sea change in cross-border collaboration.[36] Over the long term, a positive U.S. orientation toward Mexico's contemporary democratic leaders—as well as their genuine efforts to strengthen the rule of law as part of the process of democratic consolidation—may be the most important factor in improving the bilateral security relationship.

THE U.S.-MEXICO BORDER

Nowhere else are the contours of the U.S.-Mexico relationship—the opportunities and frustrations, the dynamism and inequities—more intensely illustrated than along their shared two-thousand-mile border. Whether regarding the issue of immigration, bilateral trade, or transnational security threats, the border region factors heavily into national level policy debates and negotiations between the United States and Mexico. Still, most U.S. and Mexican citizens lack familiarity with the border region, and they often fail to appreciate the enormous interdependence of U.S. and Mexican border communities. In terms of binational policy, the border region is of tremendous importance, and in terms of daily life, the border is very much a part of the U.S. and Mexican reality—at least 14 million U.S. and Mexican residents live in near proximity to the border. Below, we consider the development of the border region and the way that the bilateral policy issues already discussed above play out along the U.S.-Mexico border.

The Development and Significance of the U.S.-Mexico Border Region

Defining any region is often challenging, since—by definition—a region does not always conform strictly to formal political, cultural, or economic boundaries. Defining a border region is especially difficult, as one observer noted, because "its defining boundary runs *through* it rather than around it."[37] We must take into consideration the multiple ways of conceptualizing the region. In strictly political terms, the border region can be thought of as the widely expansive area that includes the four U.S. and six Mexican border states, or as the more limited set of county and municipal governments immediately adjacent to the border region.

However, the border region is clearly more complex and fluid than a set of political lines. For example, expanding migration patterns and dissemination of cultural elements representative of the border region—like cowboy boots, *corridos*, and burritos—have spread to other regions of the United States and Mexico. There also exist significant subregional variations along the border, with major geographic, demographic, and cultural differences between twin city regions like El Paso–Ciudad Juárez and San Diego–Tijuana.

The nature of the U.S.-Mexico border has shifted over time. Initially an area of political and territorial conflict, by the 1880s, the U.S.-Mexico border relationship arguably advanced to become more cordial and coexistent, with both countries generally recognizing each other's sovereignty and territorial delimitations.[38] At the turn of the twentieth century, the two countries began to see growing transborder cultural, social, or economic interaction. In the aftermath of the 1910 revolution and especially since the mid-1950s, the U.S.-Mexico border relationship has become increasingly interdependent, with the two sides reflecting significantly greater mutual dependence—thanks to growing cross-border trade and economic activity, population flows, and cultural integration. Despite this progression, the U.S.-Mexico border relationship has not yet become fully integrated or characterized by shared and overlapping political authorities, such as those found in the European Union. Whether the United States and Mexico will move toward greater shared governance remains to be seen. But for the time being, the border region is an important point of intersection for the two countries and embodies the much larger social, political, and economic dynamics of Mexico, the United States, and their bilateral relationship.

Without a doubt, the bilateral challenges discussed above play themselves out most acutely in the border region. For example, the United States focuses much of its immigration control strategy on patrolling the border. Initiatives in the mid-1990s, such as Operation Hold the Line (also called the Blockade) in Texas and Operation Gatekeeper in San Diego, enhanced border security primarily by establishing fencing, increasing the presence of border patrol personnel, and introducing lighting and high-tech surveillance equipment in major populated centers along the U.S.-Mexico border in order to deter undocumented migrants from entering the United States and apprehend them. *Securitization*

In focusing their immigration control strategies on the border, U.S. policies do little to deter undocumented migration and instead have other, sometimes unintended, effects. For example, rather than diminishing, undocumented migrant flows have been rerouted overland through dangerous desert and mountain areas, underground through sophisticated tunnel systems, and offshore along open U.S. coastal areas. As undocumented migrants seek to avoid the perils of desert and mountain crossings, there has been a proliferation of people-smuggling, document fraud, and visa overstays. Additionally, as a result of the new dangers involved in land-based crossings, too many migrants crossing in the border's scorching deserts and formidable mountainous regions suffer a horrible fate, with thousands dying in the process over the past decade.[39] More dangerous and difficult border crossings have created incentives for undocumented individuals to stay in the United States for longer periods of time, rather than returning home, as many did in the past. Ironically, the implementation of tougher border controls unintentionally contributed a greater tendency toward long-term unauthorized residency.

Similarly, the border is a key area for trade between Mexico and the United States, since a large portion of goods exported to the U.S. originates in this region. The economy of the U.S.-Mexico border region began to develop as early as the Porfiriato, but it experienced a boom in the mid-twentieth century that facilitated the development of sophisticated infrastructure and the *maquiladora* sector. Throughout the border region, the combined expansion of U.S. manufacturing and Mexican assembly plants—producing televisions, electric fans, and other consumer goods—enabled the border region to thrive as never before. By 2005, the U.S.-Mexico border processed roughly three times the amount of cross-border legal flows as the U.S.-Canada border, with some 643,739 persons and 264,939 vehicles legally crossing the U.S.-Mexico border each day through twenty-five major corridors and 312 individual ports of entry.[40] Today, thanks in large part to the booming import-export sector, the border region has experienced massive foreign investment from U.S., Japanese, South Korean, and (more recently) Chinese companies.

At the same time, significant gaps and notable social costs are associated with the border region's prodigious development over the last few decades. As prosperous as the region has been, both Mexican and U.S. communities along the border continue to reflect the enormous income inequality discussed in chapter 10. The high cost of living in some urban areas on both sides of the border contributes to long commutes and the formation of squatter settlements, both of which have spillover consequences for the environment and the quality of life in the border region (see textbox 13.3).

No discussion of U.S.-Mexico relations would be complete without consideration of the transnational security challenges that are so significantly manifested at the border. For example, although bigger budgets, new technologies, and increased manpower have created greater capacity for interdiction at the border, the elevated security has not necessarily curtailed illicit smuggling activities. Smugglers have simply become more creative in their efforts to move contraband into the lucrative U.S. black market. For example, some have modified SUVs with special armor and silicon-reinforced tires, and now brazenly crash these vehicles through port of entry facilities. Others have turned to subtler and more effective innovations, including sophisticated tunnel systems and maritime smuggling operations.

At the same time, the border region continues to confront other persistent law enforcement problems. Communities located near the border are

---

**Textbox 13.3. THE NATURAL RESOURCES AND
ENVIRONMENT OF THE BORDER REGION**

Rapid urbanization and industrialization have brought significant economic growth to the border region, but also formidable environmental challenges. Although NAFTA legislation charged the Border Environment Cooperative Commission (BECC) and the North American Development Bank (NADBank) with addressing the environmental implications of NAFTA, these entities have had mixed results in dealing with the monumental environmental challenges of the border region. Because natural resource, ecological, and environmental issues frequently cross political boundaries, they have consistently been a point of bilateral concern in the border region. Yet for the same reason, such issues have not always received sufficient attention from policy makers on either side of the border. Some of the environmental areas that most require binational attention include reducing and treating air pollution, hazardous industrial waste, and sewage runoff from squatter settlements, as well as increased demand for water and the disruption of wildlife corridors that span the border region. Although there are numerous governmental agencies and even more nongovernmental organizations attempting to address these issues, the broad scope of the problems makes environmental efforts appear disjointed in a manner that has the potential to impede comprehensive, sustainable environmental change. Recently, joint initiatives between the U.S. Environmental Protection Agency (EPA) and Mexico's Ministry of Environmental and Natural Resources (Secretaría de Medio Ambiente y Recursos Naturales, SEMARNAT) have contributed to encouraging progress. However, if binational environmental issues are not addressed in a comprehensive bilateral fashion, U.S. and Mexican communities along the border will likely continue to suffer the public health and long-term environmental consequences.

---

generally more likely than others to experience certain forms of violent and property crime. For example, auto theft represents approximately 20 percent of all major property crime in San Diego. Proximity to the border is paramount here, since autos stolen in the United States are often smuggled to chop shops in Mexico or are used by smugglers to reenter the United States.

More problematic from Mexico's point of view is the trafficking of arms that are readily available in the United States—including high-caliber automatic weapons. Guns are illegal in Mexico, so the United States effectively serves as a gray market for arms traffickers, and—ironically—as a source of weapons for criminal organizations active in narco-trafficking and other cross-border crimes.[41] Law enforcement officials on both sides of the border have lobbied for stricter controls of arms flows from the United States. However, these measures have so far had little effect.

The smart border agreement framework, which also sets new terms of cooperation between Canada and the United States, may prove useful in moving toward a trilateral NAFTA-plus security regime capable of addressing border crimes more effectively. What is clear is that, until a larger regional strategy develops, the border will likely remain at the center of U.S. and Mexican bilateral collaboration on security matters.

CONCLUSION

Over the past twenty-five years Mexico and the United States have become more interdependent. In every major arena—culture, economy, and security—the two countries are inextricably linked. Clearly, then, they cannot ignore each other. Nor can they revert to past practices of finger pointing and passing the buck when confronted with intractable problems like undocumented migration and drug trafficking. Instead, they must cooperate if they are to effectively address their shared challenges. Fortunately, despite the many obstacles to effective collaboration noted in this chapter, there appears to be a general willingness on the part of both U.S. and Mexican policy makers to work together. No doubt this sentiment stems from the mutual recognition that unilateral approaches to bilateral problems can never be fully successful. But most certainly the change in attitudes has also occurred as a result of Mexico's move away from authoritarianism. Electoral competition, power sharing, and increased voter sophistication have altered Mexican policy makers' perspectives and priorities. On the other side, the United States has shown greater willingness to trust and cooperate with Mexico's democratically elected leaders. Thus, improved bilateral relations appear to be yet another benefit of Mexico's embrace of democracy.

Conclusion

Some observers might conclude that Mexico is a country doomed to political chaos and economic failure. Headlines featuring Mexico invariably focus on the country's recent security challenges; the problems of corruption and political strife that plague Mexico's government; the inefficiencies, inequalities, and lack of competitiveness of its economy; or the plight of poor Mexican migrants in search of a better life and the problems they pose for the United States. To be sure, Mexico remains mired in a severe security crisis, with levels of crime and violence that are highly disturbing to Mexicans and foreigners alike. Meanwhile, although Mexico's political system continues to develop the hallmarks of a consolidated democracy that ensure effective contestation and representation in government, there are still many imperfections that limit overall transparency, accountability, and political efficacy. Furthermore, Mexico's mid-twentieth-century "economic miracle" is long forgotten, international investors are far more enamored with the so-called BRIC economies (Brazil, Russia, India, and China), and the average Mexican still identifies lack of economic opportunity among their greatest concerns. Perhaps most important, while the country may be home to the world's richest man, the face of Mexico that is most visible to the rest of the world is that of the Mexican migrant, whose very exodus paints a generally negative picture of conditions back home.

These are all certainly part of Mexico's contemporary reality, but focusing on only the country's problems ignores the enormous advances it has made over the last thirty years and also neglects its tremendous potential for progress in the medium- and long-term. Indeed, as observers of Mexican politics for more than two decades, we remain cautiously optimistic about

321

Mexico's future. In our final observations, we review some of the major issues that Mexico faces moving forward over the next few years, including
the implications of the 2012 election, ongoing drug violence, continuing
global economic uncertainty, and the increasingly interdependent relationship with the United States.

MEXICAN POLITICS AFTER 2012

As this book goes to press, Mexico's political fate appears to hinge on the
outcome of the 2012 elections. In the run-up to July 2012, all signs pointed
to a PRI victory in the presidential election and perhaps even a majority in
the legislature. A decade after its stunning defeat in 2000 and its humiliating third place finish in 2006, a steady series of victories at the subnational
level has gradually strengthened and restored the confidence of the PRI,
thanks in large part to a newfound spirit of consensus and collaboration
among party leaders. Although important divisions within the party remain, just one year before the July 2012 presidential election, out-going
Mexico state governor Enrique Peña Nieto was already the virtually assured
PRI nominee, with no other challengers officially seeking the nomination.
A Peña Nieto victory would demonstrate that the party's loss of the presidency was not the deathblow many had predicted, but it rather provided
evidence that the PRI could forge cooperation from its various internal factions and win elections in a truly competitive environment. If this formula
proves sustainable, it is likely that the PRI will be a difficult party to defeat
in future electoral contests in the coming years.

It would be easy to view the return of Mexico's old ruling party as a step
backward; indeed, in supporting the PRI many voters may be explicitly trying to evoke a return to the status quo ante, a time when life in Mexico may
have been less democratic but seemed to afford greater stability and predictability. Yet, Mexico's political system has moved dramatically away from
the entrenched authoritarian institutions and practices of the past. While
the PRI may not always be a model political party for a democracy, the days
of the *dedazo*, blatantly rigged elections, and unilateral efforts to amend the
constitution are over. In their place, Mexico has strong and impartial electoral institutions and a vibrantly competitive electoral environment with
several national parties capable of winning elections. That said, the PRI's
main political opponents—the PAN and the PRD—will need to regain the
confidence of voters who at different points have turned to them as an alternative to Mexico's once dominant and now resurgent party. While neither
has a clear front-runner in the lead-up to the 2012 presidential election,
both the PAN and the PRD have a nucleus of sharp, experienced, and dedicated leaders to move them forward. Equally important, these parties have

solid, loyal bases of support with no interest or intention of allowing the PRI to dominate the political arena. Furthermore, the Mexican electorate is now accustomed to free and fair elections, and civil society has repeatedly demonstrated its ability and willingness to mobilize when it is at odds with the state. Thus, while many would view a return of the PRI with dismay, it is far from guaranteed that a PRI victory would initiate a return to the past.

REDUCING CRIME AND VIOLENCE

Without a doubt, the highest-profile challenge Mexico faces today is the violence associated with the illicit drug trade. In the first five years of President Calderón's administration, the country saw more than forty thousand people murdered as a result of the drug war, including hundreds of federal and local police, prosecutors, military personnel, elected officials, and innocent victims.[1] Looking forward, there is no doubt that the drug war will continue to present serious security challenges for Mexico well beyond the Calderón administration. His successor will face the daunting task of deciding whether to continue to use a military strategy or to shift the government's focus to a different approach. In the short term, it seems unlikely that the military strategy will be abandoned, for the simple fact that the Mexican justice system (police forces, court system, jails, etc.) does not have the capacity to effectively address the problem on its own. In the medium and longer term, it is possible that other approaches will gain political and popular support. Already the calls for a more society-centered solution (e.g., greater attention to education, public health, and job creation) are beginning to gain traction—thanks in large part to the efforts of numerous Mexican nongovernmental organizations (NGOs) and private citizens to demand change and propose alternative strategies.

More controversial is the prospect of legalizing the psychotropic drugs that are so lucrative on the black market. Mexico has already legalized the possession of small amounts of marijuana, but there is no indication that this law will be expanded to include larger amounts or possession of other types of drugs. Similarly, in the United States, medicinal use of marijuana is legal in a small number of states, but there remains significant popular and political opposition to move further down the path of legalization. Therefore, legalizing drugs will not produce a rapid change in policy. In the meantime, in the absence of a more comprehensive, binational strategy, together with demand created by U.S. users (who evidently care little about the consequences that their actions have for Mexicans), Mexico will remain an important source and conduit for illegal drugs destined for the United States, even as drug traffickers increasingly turn to other new transit zones in Central America and elsewhere. Indeed, the unfortunate reality is that in the short term Mexico's best hope is that organized crime groups will stop fighting among themselves and get back to business as usual, or that drug-trafficking patterns will shift elsewhere and allow some restoration of normalcy.

Even if this were possible, though, Mexico continues to face other security challenges, including a rash of kidnappings, robberies, and other common forms of violent crime. For example, in August 2008, the abduction and brutal murder of Fernando Martí, the fourteen-year-old son of prominent Mexico City businessman Alejandro Martí, triggered a nationwide series of demonstrations involving hundreds of thousands of people. The Mexican public was particularly outraged upon discovery of the involvement of law enforcement—including federal police officers—in the kidnapping ring. Mr. Martí became a vocal activist, demanding justice for his son and creating an NGO (Sistema de Observación para la Seguridad Ciudadana, SOS) to press the government to improve public security and the rule of law in general. Similarly, in 2011, the activism of poet Javier Sicilia after the murder of his son, Juan Francisco, prompted tens of thousands to march in Mexico City, demanding that the government fundamentally alter its strategy for combating drug-trafficking organizations.

While tragic, these examples are also inspiring in that they spawned levels of engagement and articulated demands from society that raise expectations for Mexico's elected officials. Today, most Mexicans expect their government to respond to their needs and preferences to a degree that would have been unthinkable in the past. Indeed, Javier Sicilia's actions prompted President Calderón to sit down with him in a televised conversation about the government's strategy for dealing with drug-related violence. In another case, the families of several innocent teens murdered in Ciudad Juárez publicly took President Calderón to task for his inability to stop the violence. Their actions prompted the administration to redouble its efforts to deal with the explosion of violence in that city. Such activism and insistence bodes well for citizens' ability to pressure public officials to deliver better policies and service, and it is promising for the outlook of the democratic process in Mexico.

ECONOMIC GROWTH AND POVERTY

Mexico faces a number of pressing economic problems that will continue for the foreseeable future. Of particular importance is the country's ability to create enough jobs to absorb the economically active sector of the population. We have already seen that Mexico's lack of permanent jobs has a direct impact on the country's high levels of poverty and inequality, which in turn form the roots of many of the country's most serious social problems and can lead to violent protest rather than to peaceful negotiation or voting in elections. Over the last half-century, amid these patterns of chronic poverty, inadequate wages, and economic instability, the needs of Mexico's most desperate citizens were systematically ignored—or worse, taken advantage of—by self-seeking and rapacious politicians. From the look of things, little has changed. By mid-2011, as this book goes to press, Mexico's autonomous, federally funded National Council for the Evaluation of Social Development Policy (Consejo Nacional de Evaluación de la Política de Desarrollo Social, CONEVAL) found that the number of poor people in Mexico had reached 52 million (46.2 percent of the population) in 2010, with 11.7 million living in extreme poverty.[2]

Still, some things have indeed changed for the better. First, Mexico's economy grew 5.5 percent in 2010 and is on track to approximate the same rate in 2011. Its ability to rebound so quickly and strongly from the recession of the late 2000s is impressive evidence that the Mexican economy is more fundamentally sound and resilient than at any time in its past. Hence, recent increases in poverty must be considered in relation to Mexico's past economic crises—particularly those that occurred in 1976, 1982, and 1994—which eviscerated the value of the national currency, slashed the buying power of the average family, and drove generations of Mexicans to migrate in search of opportunities in the United States. Mexico withstood the twenty-first century's first global financial collapse, the worst economic crisis since the Great Depression, without the disastrous results seen in more developed economies like Greece, Iceland, Portugal, and Italy, all of which have struggled with serious debt crises in recent years.

That said, because Mexico's export earnings are so closely tied to the health of the U.S. economy, its ability to maintain such robust growth will depend greatly on the latter's willingness to buy Mexican products. Fortunately, in recent years, U.S. consumer demand for televisions, electronic devices, car parts, and other products assembled in the *maquiladora* plants has remained strong. Indeed, this demand has spurred job creation and investment in the manufacturing sector, as businesses expand or restart production disrupted by the recession. While more of both will be necessary to recapture losses sustained during the recession, Mexico again appears to be on the right track.[3] Also, while low wages continue to be a problem in much of the country, in many areas of north and central Mexico, the wage disparity between wages in the United States and Mexico has narrowed from 10 to 1 to just under 4 to 1, which helps explain how the Mexican middle class continues to expand, despite recent economic setbacks.[4]

Mexico's next president will face the daunting task of keeping the country on track to a brighter future. As the security situation gets under control, Mexico's leaders will need to begin courting tourists, businesses, and international investors to return to parts of the country that have been hard-struck by violence. Mexico will also need to address some of the long-standing problems in its economy, including those created by monopolistic practices in major industries (notably telecommunications), poor government collection and management of tax revenues, and the persistence of inefficiencies in government-run agencies like PEMEX. Above all, in the long run, Mexico's economic future will be tied to the investments it makes in the development of its workforce, primarily by promoting major advances in education and training programs to help Mexico become more competitive with the world's other emerging economies. These are all problems that will require both a long-term vision and much political compromise—things not easily achieved in contemporary Mexican politics. However, so long as Mexicans themselves remain vigilant and insistent, there is a real possibility for Mexico to rise to the challenge.

U.S.-MEXICO RELATIONS

Mexico's economic picture has important implications for U.S.-Mexico relations. In the post-NAFTA era, Mexico has become such a vital economic partner for the United States that many people take it for granted. Indeed, as we have discussed in earlier chapters, while Mexico is the second largest market for U.S. exports, U.S. businesses could sell still more goods there if its economy were more prosperous. As we have also seen, the limited fiscal capacity of Mexico's government means that the poor provision of certain public policies and services, like law enforcement and security, can work in opposition to the U.S. interest in combating transnational organized crime. At the end of the day, when the Mexican economy does well, it means greater prosperity for the United States and allows Mexico to be a better neighbor.

Perhaps the economic issue that U.S. citizens are most concerned about with regard to their country's relationship to Mexico is immigration. Today, Mexico is the largest source of immigration to the United States, both in terms of authorized and undocumented migration flows. When U.S. immigration controls were more lax, many undocumented immigrants came mainly for temporary and seasonal labor. As tougher border security made it more difficult to return home, more and more of them stay in the United States permanently, contributing to significant cultural changes and growing resentment in many parts of the country that are not accustomed to receiving immigrants from Mexico. Although undocumented immigration has dropped to its lowest levels in many years, there are still millions of people living in the United States without proper visas. For many frustrated U.S. citizens, the thought of people breaking the law to gain entry to the U.S. job market is already unacceptable. But, especially for the 25 million U.S. citizens who were unemployed in 2011, the thought of foreign workers taking U.S. jobs during a time of economic scarcity seems outrageous.

That said, there are enormous complexities and even absurdities of the U.S. immigration system, which contribute to the desperation that leads many to use improper channels to enter or remain in the United States. Also, those who fear that undocumented immigrants steal jobs often fail to recognize that most are employed in dirty, dangerous, and difficult jobs that most U.S. citizens would prefer not to have—even when few other jobs are available. Moreover, the bleak employment situation in the United States, higher wages in Mexico, smaller family sizes, and other improvements in the quality of life (such as expanded public services and greater educational opportunities) have contributed to a steep decline in emigration from Mexico. If this trend continues, it is quite likely that the problem of undocumented migration from Mexico to the United States will be solved not by fences or guest worker programs, but by Mexico's domestic economic and demographic trends. What is more, it is possible that the sharp drop in the supply of cheap, undocumented labor will prove problematic for the U.S. economy, which has a growing elderly population that is increasingly dependent on younger workers. A decade from now, U.S. employers may well lament the dearth of Mexican immigrant laborers that is likely to develop.

But for several years to come, immigration—both documented and undocumented—is likely to weigh heavily on the U.S.-Mexico relationship. Like Republican President Bush before him, Democratic President Obama has repeatedly expressed his interest in promoting comprehensive immigration reform. Even so, given strong resistance from many to both of these appeals, it seems unlikely that there will be significant headway toward the resolution of the immigration issue anytime in the near future. The failure to do so will no doubt make immigration one of the most polemical issues on the national agenda for many years to come. Over time, like every generation of immigrants before them, it is virtually certain that Mexican immigrants will become woven into the fabric of U.S. society, making the national tapestry stronger and more beautiful. Yet, also like previous generations of immigrants, this process of social integration and cultural blending is likely to involve many trials and moments of great tension in the process.

Meanwhile, with both the United States and Mexico voting in 2012 to determine who will lead their respective countries, the outcome of either contest may have significant implications for the U.S.-Mexico relationship. Regardless of the outcome, however, there is no doubt that relations between the two countries will remain of tremendous importance. New national leadership, diplomatic personnel, and policy agendas are unlikely to undo the foundations that structure how these two countries relate, nor the perennial concerns that have dominated the bilateral agenda for the last few decades. What does seem likely is that policy makers will continue to recognize the large and growing importance of the U.S.-Mexico relationship for each country's future.

FINAL THOUGHTS

This book has covered an enormous set of subjects in order to survey the landscape of contemporary Mexican politics. In the process, we have tried to provide a basic understanding of Mexico's historical development, the character of its political institutions, culture, and society, its most pressing domestic policy issues, and the foreign policy challenges it faces. There are, of course, many deserving topics that we could not cover in a single book, and many more that would require much deeper analysis for a proper understanding. Mexico is a land of many peoples, places, and stories, and no one book can do it justice. Thus, we can only hope that this book has helped pique the reader's interest and inspired some to learn more by continuing to study and, above all, explore Mexico and the many wonders it has to offer. Indeed, the best way to learn about Mexico is to travel to the country, listen to its people, and lose oneself in its alluring history, day-to-day realities, and enchanting dreams.

Notes

1 MEXICO'S HISTORICAL FOUNDATIONS

1. These early inhabitants likely came from Asia. See Michael D. Coe and Rex Koontz, *Mexico: From the Olmecs to the Aztecs* (New York: Thames & Hudson, 2002), 22.

2. It is also worth noting that slavery in Mesoamerica could be a temporal category (entered into by persons who became indebted and might one day win their freedom) or a terminal fate (especially for those captured in battle and sacrificed to the gods).

3. The true name of the Olmecs is unknown. "Olmec" is an Aztec reference meaning "people of the land of rubber" but was likely used to refer to different people who were their contemporaries.

4. Michael D. Coe, *America's First Civilization* (Princeton, N.J.: American Heritage, 1968).

5. Olmec society was also the only pristine civilization to develop in a lowland tropical forest. Richard A. Diehl, *The Olmecs: America's First Civilization* (London: Thames & Hudson, 2004), 12.

6. Ronald Spores, *The Mixtecs in Ancient and Colonial Times* (Norman: University of Oklahoma Press, 1984).

7. For example, the Maya utilized a unique and sophisticated iteration of a cyclical calendar that was probably passed on to them by the Olmecs, who may have developed it with the help of the Zapotecs. Geoffrey E. Braswell, *The Maya and Teotihuacán: Reinterpreting Early Classic Interaction* (Austin: University of Texas Press, 2003); Michael D. Coe, *The Maya* (New York: Praeger, 1970); Michael D. Coe, *Breaking the Maya Code* (New York: Thames & Hudson, 1992).

8. See A. Gómez-Pampa, M. F. Allen, S. L. Fedick, and J. J. Jiménez-Osornio, eds., *The Lowland Maya Area: Three Millennia at the Human-Wildland Interface* (Binghamton, N.Y.: Food Products Press, 2003).

9. For competing explanations of the sudden decline of the Maya, see Arlen Chase and Prudence M. Rice, eds., *The Lowland Maya Postclassic* (Austin: University of Texas Press, 1985); T. Patrick Culbert, ed., *The Classic Maya Collapse* (Albuquerque: University of New Mexico Press, 1991); Richardson B. Gill, *The Great Maya Droughts: Water, Life, and Death* (Albuquerque: University of New Mexico Press, 2000); and David Webster, *The Fall of the Ancient Maya: Solving the Mystery of the Maya Collapse* (London: Thames & Hudson, 2002).

10. Some scholars believe those caves were the reason why the Teotihuacanos, as the city's residents have become known, decided to settle there. Manuel Aguilar-Moreno, *Handbook to Life in the Aztec World* (New York: Facts on File, 2006).

11. Richard A. Diehl, *Tula: The Toltec Capital of Ancient Mexico* (London: Thames & Hudson, 1983).

12. Warwick Bray, *Everyday Life of the Aztecs* (New York: Peter Bedrick Books, 1991).

13. Aguilar-Moreno, *Handbook*.

14. Jared Diamond, *Guns, Germs, and Steel: The Fates of Human Societies* (New York: Norton, 1997); Ross Hassig, *Mexico and the Spanish Conquest* (Norman: University of Oklahoma Press, 2006); Miguel León-Portilla, ed., *The Broken Spears: The Aztec Account of the Conquest of Mexico* (Boston: Beacon, 2006).

15. Karl H. Schwerin, "The Indigenous Populations of Latin America," in *Latin America: Its Problems and Its Promise*, ed. Jan Knippers Black (Boulder, Colo.: Westview, 2005), 42.

16. Jean Gillespie, *Saints and Warriors: Tlaxcalan Perspectives on the Conquest of Tenochtitlán* (New Orleans, La.: University Press of the South, 2004).

17. Camilla Townsend, *Malintzin's Choices: An Indian Woman in the Conquest of Mexico* (Albuquerque: University of New Mexico Press, 2006).

18. Hassig, *Mexico*, 142.

19. Hernán Cortés, *Letters from Mexico* (New York: Grossman, 1971); Bernal Díaz del Castillo, *The Conquest of New Spain* (Baltimore: Penguin, 1963).

20. Richard F. Townsend, *The Aztecs* (New York: Thames & Hudson, 2000).

21. Ross Hassig, *War and Society in Ancient Mesoamerica* (Berkeley: University of California Press, 1992), 135–64.

22. Hassig, *Mexico*.

23. Carlos Romero Giordano, *Moctezuma II: El misterio de su muerte* (Mexico City: Panorama Editorial, 1986).

24. Centro de Estudios Históricos, ed., *Historia General de México* (Mexico City: El Colegio de México, 2000), 257.

25. Robert B. Ekelund and Robert D. Tollison, *Politicized Economies: Monarchy, Monopoly, and Mercantilism* (College Station: Texas A&M University Press, 1997).

26. Alicia Hernández Chávez, *Mexico: A Brief History* (Berkeley: University of California, 2000), 46–56.

27. Hugo G. Nutini, "Class and Ethnicity in Mexico: Somatic and Racial Considerations," *Ethnology* 36, no. 3 (1997): 227–38.

28. Susan Schroeder and Stafford Poole, eds., *Religion in New Spain* (Albuquerque: University of New Mexico Press, 2007).

29. Martin Austin Nesvig, ed., *Local Religion in Colonial Mexico* (Albuquerque: University of New Mexico, 2006).

30. Richard L. Garner, *Economic Growth and Change in Bourbon Mexico* (Gainesville: University Press of Florida, 1993).

31. Enrique Krauze Magú, *Hidalgo y sus gritos* (Mexico City: Hoja Casa Editorial, 1993).

32. Virginia Guedea, "The Conspiracies of 1811: How the Criollos Learned to Organize in Secret," in *The Birth of Modern Mexico, 1780–1824*, ed. Christon I. Archer (Wilmington, Del.: Scholarly Resources, 2003).

33. José Manuel Villalpando and Alejandro Rosas, *Historia de México: A través de sus gobernantes* (Mexico City: Planeta, 2003).

34. John S. D. Eishenhower, *So Far from God: The U.S. War with Mexico, 1846–1848* (Norman: University of Oklahoma Press, 2000).

35. The losses sustained by U.S. forces are remembered by the Marines to this day, who memorialize the Mexico City campaign in their military anthem ("from the halls of Montezuma"). Gabrielle M. Neufeld Santelli, *Marines in the Mexican War* (Washington, D.C.: History and Museums Division, Headquarters, U.S. Marine Corps, 1991).

36. Santa Anna continued to exercise power behind the scenes and then re-emerged as president just long enough to arrange the Gadsden Purchase in 1854—an agreement that sold much of what is now southern New Mexico and Arizona to the United States for $10 million.

37. Richard O'Connor, *The Cactus Throne: The Tragedy of Maximilian and Carlotta* (New York: Putnam, 1971).

38. Other "liberal dictators" who ruled in a similar style included Juan Manuel de Rosas of Argentina and Juan Vicente Gómez of Venezuela.

39. Turner was praised by Francisco I. Madero for helping expose the nature of the Díaz regime, thereby contributing to the overthrow of the Porfiriato. John Kenneth Turner, *Barbarous Mexico* (Austin: University of Texas Press, 1969).

40. Most of the Yaqui prisoners died within a year. Michael J. Gonzales, *The Mexican Revolution, 1910–1940* (Albuquerque: University of New Mexico Press, 2002), 32.

41. Fernando Paz Sánchez, *La política económica del Porfiriato* (Mexico City: Instituto Nacional de Estudios Históricos de la Revolución Mexicana, 2000).

42. Michael C. Meyer, William L. Sherman, and Susan M. Deeds, *The Course of Mexican History*, 8th ed. (Oxford, UK: Oxford University Press, 2007), 386.

43. José F. Godoy, *Porfirio Díaz, President of Mexico: The Master Builder of a Great Commonwealth* (New York, London: Knickerbocker Press, 1910), 200.

44. Godoy, *Porfirio Díaz*, 188.

45. William D. Raat, "Ideas and Society in Don Porfirio's Mexico," *The Americas* 30, no. 1 (1973): 32–53.

2 THE MEXICAN REVOLUTION AND ITS LEGACY

1. There are many excellent comprehensive treatments of the Mexican Revolution available in English and Spanish. See, for example, Héctor Aguilar Camín

and Lorenzo Meyer, *In the Shadow of the Mexican Revolution: Contemporary Mexican History, 1910–1989* (Austin: University of Texas Press, 1993); Michael J. Gonzales, *The Mexican Revolution, 1910–1940* (Albuquerque: University of New Mexico Press, 2002); John Mason Hart, *Revolutionary Mexico: The Coming and Process of the Mexican Revolution* (Berkeley: University of California Press, 1987); Alan Knight, *The Mexican Revolution* (Cambridge, UK: Cambridge University Press, 1986).

2. Kevin J. Middlebrook, *The Paradox of Revolution: Labor, the State, and Authoritarianism in Mexico* (Baltimore: Johns Hopkins University Press, 1995).

3. Gonzales, *Mexican Revolution*, 52.

4. Hart, *Revolutionary Mexico*, 188.

5. There were as many as 750,000 slaves during the Porfiriato. Donald Clark Hodges and Daniel Ross Gandy, *Mexico: The End of the Revolution* (Westport, Conn.: Praeger, 2002), 13.

6. Luis González, "El liberalismo triunfante," in *Historia General de México*, ed. El Colegio de México (Mexico City: El Colegio de México, 2000), 696–97.

7. Enrique Krauze, *Mexico: Biography of Power: A History of Modern Mexico, 1810–1996* (New York: HarperPerennial, 1997).

8. Brian Hamnett, *A Concise History of Mexico* (Cambridge, UK: Cambridge University Press, 1999), 178; Krauze, *Mexico*, 256–57.

9. Historians continue to debate many details of Villa's early life. See Friedrich Katz, *The Life and Times of Pancho Villa* (Stanford, Calif.: Stanford University Press, 1998); Frank McLynn, *Villa and Zapata: A Biography of the Mexican Revolution* (London: Jonathan Cape, 2000).

10. Pablo Moctezuma Barragán, *Vida y lucha de Emiliano Zapata: Vigencia histórica del héroe mexicano* (Mexico City: Grijalbo, 2000); John Womack, *Zapata and the Mexican Revolution* (New York: Knopf, 1969).

11. McLynn, *Villa and Zapata*, 78.

12. Lowell L. Blaisdell, "Henry Lane Wilson and the Overthrow of Madero," *Southwestern Social Science Quarterly* 43 (1962): 126–35.

13. Michael C. Meyer, William L. Sherman, and Susan M. Deeds, *The Course of Mexican History*, 6th ed. (Oxford, UK: Oxford University Press, 1999), 523–25.

14. José Rubén Romero, *Obregón: Aspectos de su vida* (Mexico City: Editorial Cultura, 1935); Enrique Krauze, Aurelio de los Reyes, and Margarita de Orellana, *El vértigo de la victoria: Álvaro Obregón* (Mexico City: Fondo de Cultura Económica, 1987).

15. Krauze, *Mexico*, 427.

16. Peter Calvert, *Mexico: Nation of the Modern World* (New York: Praeger, 1973).

17. So pervasive was Calles's influence during the *maximato* that although Maximilian's Castle of Chapultepec then served as the presidential residence, Calles's home in a nearby neighborhood was seen as the real seat of power. The saying went, "The president lives in Chapultepec Castle; the man who rules lives in front." Calvert, *Mexico*.

18. Calvert, *Mexico*, 264.

19. Fernando Benítez, *Lázaro Cárdenas y la Revolución Mexicana* (México City: Fondo de Cultura Económica, 1977).

20. Quiroga empowered locals with artisan skills that persist even today in the works of craftsmen in Michoacán's Pátzcuaro region.

21. Meyer, Sherman, and Deeds, *Course of Mexican History*.

22. Cárdenas's challengers were Antonio Villareal (CRPI), Adalberto Tejada (Socialist Party), and Hernán Laborde (Communist Party). Calvert, *Mexico*, 259.

23. Calvert, *Mexico*, 259.

24. Lombardo had established the CTM in 1936, fusing formerly independent unions to challenge the crumbling CROM, with furtive backing from Cárdenas. Lombardo's orchestration of a wave of strikes from 1934 to 1936 had previously provoked the final showdown between Cárdenas and Calles. Calvert, *Mexico*, 259.

25. Figures representing the total amount of land redistributed by Mexican presidents vary depending on the source. Estimates for Cárdenas's term range from 17 million to more than 20 million acres. Calvert, *Mexico*, 259.

3 POSTREVOLUTIONARY MEXICAN POLITICS, 1940–1968

1. Robert R. Kaufman, "Mexico and Latin American Authoritarianism," in *Authoritarianism in Mexico*, ed. José Luis Reyna and Richard S. Weinert (Philadelphia: Institute for the Study of Human Issues, 1977).

2. Many feel that Peruvian novelist Mario Vargas Llosa said it best when he referred to Mexico's unique political arrangement as the "perfect dictatorship." Dan A. Cothran, *Political Stability and Democracy in Mexico: The "Perfect Dictatorship"?* (Westport, Conn.: Praeger, 1994).

3. Magaloni describes Mexico's classical political system as electoral authoritarianism. Beatriz Magaloni, *Voting for Autocracy: Hegemonic Party Survival and Its Demise in Mexico* (New York: Cambridge University Press, 2006), 7.

4. David Collier and Steven Levitsky, "Democracy with Adjectives: Conceptual Innovation in Comparative Research," *World Politics* 49, no. 3 (1997): 430–51.

5. Wayne A. Cornelius, Judith Gentleman, and Peter H. Smith, *Mexico's Alternative Political Futures* (La Jolla: University of California-San Diego, Center for U.S.-Mexican Studies, 1989).

6. Ilene V. O'Malley, *The Myth of the Revolution: Hero Cults and the Institutionalization of the Mexican State, 1920–1940* (New York: Greenwood, 1986).

7. Juan Molinar Horcasitas, *El tiempo de la legitimidad: Elecciones, autoritarismo, y democracia en México* (Mexico City: Cal y Arena, 1991).

8. Joy Langston, "Breaking Out Is Hard to Do: Exit, Voice, and Loyalty in Mexico's One-Party Hegemonic Regime," *Latin American Politics and Society* 44, no. 3 (2002): 61–88.

9. Diane E. Davis, "Uncommon Democracy in Mexico: Middle Classes and the Military in the Consolidation of One-Party Rule, 1936–1946," in *The Social Construction of Democracy, 1880–1990*, ed. Herrick Chapman and George Reid Andrews (London: Macmillan, 1995).

10. Octavio Rodríguez Araujo, "Partidos políticos y elecciones en México, 1964 a 1985," *Revista Mexicana de Sociología* 47, no. 1, Número conmemorativo del XX aniversario de la publicación de "La democracia en México" (January–March 1985), 41–104.

11. Peter H. Smith, *Labyrinths of Power* (Princeton, N.J.: Princeton University Press, 1979); Roderic Ai Camp, *Mexico's Mandarins: Crafting a Power Elite for the Twenty-First Century* (Berkeley: University of California Press, 2002).

12. *Camarillas* were commonly reshuffled following the *destape,* or unveiling of a president's successor. Once the chosen candidate was publicly identified, *camarilla* members of the losing contenders faced the difficult task of positioning themselves well for the incoming administration.

13. Jeffrey A. Weldon, "Changing Patterns of Executive-Legislative Relations in Mexico," in *Dilemmas of Change in Mexican Politics,* ed. Kevin J. Middlebrook (London: Institute of Latin American Studies, University of London, 2003).

14. Similar factional divisions emerged in other single-party-dominated systems, like South Korea and Taiwan. Dorothy J. Solinger, "Ending One-Party Dominance: Korea, Taiwan, Mexico," *Journal of Democracy* 12, no. 1 (2001): 30–42.

15. Enrique Krauze, *Mexico: Biography of Power: A History of Modern Mexico, 1810–1996* (New York: HarperPerennial, 1997).

16. The PRI swung back to the right during the late 1960s, and left again in the early 1970s, until the pendulum settled at the right of the political spectrum in the 1980s. Wayne Cornelius and Ann Craig, *The Mexican Political System in Transition* (La Jolla: University of California, Center for U.S.-Mexican Studies, 1991), 39–40.

17. Victoria E. Rodriguez and Peter M. Ward, "Disentangling the PRI from the Government in Mexico," *Mexican Studies/Estudios Mexicanos* 10, no. 1 (Winter 1994).

18. Victoria Elizabeth Rodríguez, *Decentralization in Mexico: From Reforma Municipal to Solidaridad to Nuevo Federalismo* (Boulder, Colo.: Westview, 1997); Blanca Torres Ramírez, *Decentralización y democracia en México* (México, D.F.: El Colegio de México, 1986).

19. As noted in chapter 2, the principle of no reelection was abrogated somewhat by Obregón's reelection but reinstated (along with a shift from four- to six-year terms) shortly after he was assassinated.

20. Michael C. Taylor, "Constitutional Crisis: How Reforms to the Legislature Have Doomed Mexico," *Mexican Studies/Estudios Mexicanos* 13, no. 2 (Summer 1997): 299–324; Weldon, "Changing Patterns."

21. Jorge Castañeda, *Perpetuating Power: How Mexican Presidents Were Chosen* (New York: New Press, 2000).

22. The same applied to governors and mayors to a lesser extent within their own jurisdictions, since they too were assured of PRI dominance and cooperation (unless their superior decided otherwise).

23. Javier Hurtado, *El sistema presidencial mexicano: Evolución y perspectivas* (Guadalajara: University of Guadalajara, 2001).

24. Luis Javier Garrido, "The Crisis of Presidencialismo," in *Mexico's Alternative Political Futures,* ed. Wayne A. Cornelius, Judith Gentleman, and Peter H. Smith (La Jolla: University of California–San Diego, Center for U.S.-Mexican Studies, 1989).

25. Magaloni, *Voting for Autocracy.*

26. Soledad Loaeza, *El Partido Acción Nacional, la larga marcha, 1939–1994: Oposición leal y partido de protesta* (Mexico City: Fondo de Cultura Económica, 1999); Donald J. Mabry, *Mexico's Acción Nacional: A Catholic Alternative to Revolution* (Syracuse, N.Y.: Syracuse University Press, 1973); Yemile Mizrahi, *From Martyrdom to Power: The Partido Acción Nacional in Mexico* (Notre Dame, Ind.: University of Notre Dame Press, 2003); David A. Shirk, *Mexico's New Politics: The PAN and Democratic Change* (Boulder, Colo.: Lynne Rienner, 2005).

27. Ramón Miró, *Organized Crime and Terrorist Activity in Mexico, 1999–2002* (Washington, D.C.: Library of Congress, 2003).

28. Howard Handelman, "The Politics of Labor Protest in Mexico: Two Case Studies," *Journal of Interamerican Studies and World Affairs* 18, no. 3 (1976): 267–94; Raquel Tibol, *Siqueiros, vida y obra* (Mexico City: Departamento del Distrito Federal Secretaría de Obras y Servicios, 1974).

29. Shirk, *Mexico's New Politics.*

30. Mariano Herrera Motte, *1968, lo peor y lo mejor de México* (Mexico City: Federación Editorial Mexicana, 1975); Donald J. Mabry, *The Mexican University and the State: Student Conflicts, 1910–1971* (College Station: Texas A&M University Press, 1982).

31. Christopher Brasher, *Mexico 1968: A Diary of the XIXth Olympiad* (London: S. Paul, 1968); Oferta Olímpica Mexico, *La Olimpiada en México, 1968* (Mexico City, 1968).

32. Judith Adler Hellman, *Mexico in Crisis* (New York: Holmes & Meier, 1988).

33. Hellman, *Mexico in Crisis.*

34. Many media sources at that time were coopted through their dependence on lucrative government advertising contracts, subsidies, and even direct payoffs to reporters to favor the PRI. Hence, with the help of the official media, the massacre was essentially swept under the rug.

35. See, for example: Gerardo Estrada Rodríguez, *1968, Estado y universidad: orígenes de la transición política en México* (México, D.F.: Plaza Janés, 2004); José Luis Tejeda, *El proceso de democratización en México, 1968–1982* (Álvaro Obregón, D.F.: Praxis, 1991).

4 MEXICAN DEMOCRATIZATION, 1968 TO THE PRESENT

1. Kenneth Greene, *Why Dominant Parties Lose: Mexico's Democratization in Comparative Perspective* (Cambridge, UK: Cambridge University Press, 2007).

2. This section draws on Judith Adler Hellman's thorough discussion of the 1970s and 1980s in *Mexico in Crisis,* 2nd ed. (New York: Holmes & Meier, 1988), 187–216.

3. Adler Hellman, *Mexico,* 229.

4. Although the amendment to Article 115 of the Mexican constitution was supposed to empower local governments, it had the effect of requiring them to assume financial and administrative responsibility for public services they had neither the resources nor training to provide. See R. Andrew Nickson, *Local Government in Latin America* (Boulder, Colo.: Lynne Rienner, 1995); Victoria Rodriguez, *Decentralization in Mexico: From Reforma Municipal to Solidaridad to Nuevo Federalismo* (Boulder, Colo.: Westview, 1997).

5. The 1986 reforms also gave the federal executive the power to name the presidents of all electoral authorities from the Federal Electoral Commission down to the polling places. Clearly this did nothing to increase the transparency or equity of the electoral process.

6. On the rise of the technocrats in the PRI, see Miguel Angel Centeno, *Democracy within Reason: Technocratic Revolution in Mexico* (University Park: Pennsylvania State University Press, 2004).

7. Miguel de la Madrid Hurtado, *Cambio de rumbo: Testimonio de una presidencia, 1982–1988* (Mexico City: Fondo de Cultura Económica, 2004).

8. Wayne A. Cornelius, Ann L. Craig, and Jonathan Fox, eds., *Transforming State-Society Relations in Mexico: The National Solidarity Strategy* (La Jolla: Center for U.S.-Mexican Studies, 1994).

9. Juan Molinar Horcasitas and Jeffrey Weldon demonstrated that municipalities and communities that had supported Cuauhtémoc Cárdenas in the 1988 election received a disproportionate amount of the program's resources, seemingly to ensure that they would support the PRI in future elections. "Electoral Determinants and Consequences of National Solidarity," in *Transforming State-Society Relations*, ed. Cornelius, Craig, and Fox, 123–42.

10. The impetus for this round of reforms came from the fact that after 1988, it was impossible for the PRI to win an election without the opposition crying foul. Salinas was concerned that the 1994 presidential election would be marred by such claims. Furthermore, Salinas was eager to demonstrate to the U.S. Congress, which at the time was debating whether to ratify NAFTA, that Mexico had a strong commitment to democratizing its political system.

11. Other events that worried investors included the kidnapping of businessman Alfredo Harp in June, as well as the September murder of José Francisco Ruiz Massieu, the brother-in-law of Carlos Salinas and secretary-general of the PRI.

12. For some, the biggest surprise of 1994 was that, amid all the political unrest that was so clearly directed at or emanating from the PRI, Zedillo was able to win the election, especially given the fact that he was running against Cuauhtémoc Cárdenas on the left and Diego Fernández de Cevallos, a strong candidate on the right. Yet he did win, largely because his campaign succeeded in branding his strongest challenger, Cárdenas, as a potentially dangerous option.

13. One of the reasons that the opposition was so successful at winning subnational elections in the 1990s was that its internal primaries generated strong candidates with popular appeal.

14. On the events leading up to the 2000 elections, see David A. Shirk, *Mexico's New Politics: The PAN and Democratic Change* (Boulder, Colo.: Lynne Rienner, 2005), chapter 5.

15. Evidence of this is found in the PAN's incremental but consistent improvement in electoral contests between 1988 and 2000. The three presidential candidates received, respectively, 17, 27, and 42.5 percent of the vote. During the same time period, the PAN's share of the vote in the Chamber of Deputies also increased substantially.

16. In late 2003, it appeared that Fox's proposal might receive enough support from the PRI to pass, until the prospect of cooperating with the PAN in support of a regressive tax led to a bitter public feud within the PRI and undermined the reform. See Emily Edmonds-Poli, "Decentralization under Fox: Progress or Stagnation?" *Mexican Studies/Estudios Mexicanos* 22, no. 2 (Summer 2006): 387–416.

17. This law has been used to great effect to uncover the truth about the nature of the government's actions in the 1968 Tlatelolco massacre.

18. Alberto Aguirre, "Rechaza AMLO dialogo con gobierno," *Reforma*, December 12, 2006.

19. "Economía, gobierno, y política," *Consulta Mitofsky*, January 2010; William Finnegan, "Silver or Lead," *New Yorker*, May 31, 2010; Elly Castillo, "Muestran apoyo a *La Familia* en Apatzingán," *El Universal*, December 12, 2010.

20. Fabiola Martinez, "Prepara el blanquiazul la estrategia para cabildear y defender la iniciativa," *La Jornada*, February 11, 2010; Felipe Calderón Hinojosa, "Reforma en favor de los ciudadanos: del sufragio efectivo a la democracia efectiva," *Milenio*, February 3, 2010; Elba Monica Bravo, "Pide Calderón pasar de amenazas a consensus," *Milenio*, February 6, 2010; Roberto Garduño and Enrique Méndez, "Condenan PRI, PRD, y PT el apoyo del ejercito a reforma politica de Calderón," *La Jornada*, February 11, 2010; Ricardo Gomex, "Por qué tropezó la reforma politica antes de caminar?" *El Universal*, February 11, 2010.

5 GOVERNMENT STRUCTURE AND PROCESSES

1. Matthew Soberg Shugart and Scott Mainwaring, "Presidentialism and Democracy in Latin America: Rethinking the Terms of the Debate," in *Presidentialism and Democracy in Latin America*, ed. Scott Mainwaring and Matthew Soberg Shugart (New York: Cambridge University Press, 1997).

2. This discussion draws on Jeffrey Weldon, "Political Sources of Presidencialismo in Mexico," in *Presidentialism and Democracy*, ed. Mainwaring and Shugart; and Weldon, "Changing Patterns of Executive-Legislative Relations in Mexico," in *Dilemmas of Political Change in Mexico*, ed. Kevin J. Middlebrook (London: Institute of Latin American Studies, University of London, 2004), 133–67.

3. The Mexican presidency also enjoyed what one author has called anticonstitutional powers—for example, the power to declare legal or fraudulent any election results, and the ability to extend immunity to any public official. These powers stemmed from the same three conditions described above and from the fact that they guaranteed that the legislature would not exercise its power of legislative review. See Luis Javier Garrido, "The Crisis of Presidencialismo," in *Mexico's Alternative Political Futures*, ed. Wayne A. Cornelius, Judith Gentleman, and Peter H. Smith (La Jolla: University of California–San Diego, Center for U.S.-Mexican Studies, 1989).

4. All of Mexico's presidents between 1946 and 1976 served as interior minister before their election, and in subsequent years the head of this agency was almost always a serious contender for the PRI's presidential candidate. This tradition continued into the Fox administration, when Santiago Creel entered the presidential horse race for the 2006 election.

5. Proportional representation seats are distributed without regard to state.

6. While the PRD itself may be underrepresented, in the 2006 election it was part of a three-party coalition, and when taken together, the coalition's senatorial seats do come close to matching its proportion of the national vote. It is quite common for countries to employ electoral systems that distribute seats in ways that are not perfectly proportional to the popular vote.

7. When President Fox exercised this power by vetoing the budget in 2004, there was some ambiguity about this issue. Although the Mexican presidency does have veto power, the constitution states that it can only be used on bills approved by both houses of Congress. Since the Chamber of Deputies is the only one with authority to approve the budget, some questioned the president's authority to veto the budget. See Weldon, "Changing Patterns," 146, n. 31; and David Gaddis Smith,

"Mexican Congressman Prods Government with Challenges," *San Diego Union Tribune,* January 22, 2006.

8. Jeffrey Weldon, "Committee Power in the Mexican Chamber of Deputies," paper presented at the Twenty-First Chamber of Deputies International Congress of the Latin American Studies Association, Chicago, September 1998.

9. Indeed, the presidents' bills enjoyed a success rate of 98 percent between 1988 and 1997. This was significantly better than the Chamber's showing, which averaged 23.4 percent. See Weldon, "Changing Patterns," 159, tables 5.7 and 5.8.

10. The PRI's representation in the Senate follows a similar pattern. Whereas the PRI consistently won 60 to 75 percent of Senate seats before 1994, its share had declined to 47 percent in 2000.

11. Weldon, "Changing Patterns," 156, table 5.4.

12. The remaining 2.8 percent were sponsored by state legislatures. Weldon, "Changing Patterns," 158, table 5.6.

13. "His Congress Says No, No, Zedillo," *New York Times,* November 9, 1997; and Sam Dillon, "Newly Elected Mexican Opposition to Fight President's Economic Plan," *New York Times,* November 9, 1997.

14. This situation has begun to change. Much of this information is now available online or in one of the congressional research institutes.

15. Roderic Ai Camp, "Mexico's Legislature: Missing the Democratic Lockstep?" in *Legislatures and the New Democracies in Latin America,* ed. David Close (Boulder, Colo.: Lynne Rienner, 1995).

16. This discussion draws on Jeffrey Weldon, "The Prohibition on Consecutive Reelection in the Mexican Congress," *Election Law Journal* 3, no. 3 (2004): 574–79.

17. Michael Taylor, "Constitutional Crisis: How Reforms to the Legislature Have Doomed Mexico," *Mexican Studies/Estudios Mexicanos* 13, no. 2 (1997): 299–324.

18. Beatriz Magaloni, "Authoritarianism, Democracy, and the Supreme Court: Horizontal Exchange and the Rule of Law in Mexico," in *Democratic Accountability in Latin America,* ed. Scott Mainwaring and Christopher Welna (New York: Oxford University Press, 2003), 281.

19. The law granted the same powers to state supreme courts.

20. Magaloni, "Authoritarianism," 281.

21. Jeffrey Staton, *Lobbying for Judicial Reform: The Role of the Mexican Supreme Court in Institutional Selection,* USMEX 2003–04 Working Paper Series (La Jolla: University of California–San Diego, Center for U.S.-Mexican Studies, 2003).

22. Kevin Sullivan and Mary Jordan, "Mexican Supreme Court Refuses to Take Back Seat," *Washington Post,* September 10, 2000, A31.

23. For more on these cases, see Jodi Finkel, "Judicial Reform as Insurance Policy: Mexico in the 1990s," *Latin American Politics and Society,* 47, no. 1 (Spring 2005): 87–113.

24. Jodi Finkel, "Supreme Court Decisions on Electoral Rules after Mexico's 1994 Judicial Reform: An Empowered Court," *Journal of Latin American Studies* 35 (2003): 777–99.

25. Kevin Sullivan, "Mexican Court Rejects Part of Genocide Appeal," *Washington Post,* February 24, 2005, A18.

26. BANAMEX, "Review of the Economic Situation of Mexico," Working Paper Series 81, no. 949 (2005).

27. The Supreme Court has two sessions per year: early January to mid-July and early August to mid-December. The constitution allows a single Supreme Court justice to address emergency issues during a recess that would normally require the consideration of the full court.

28. This discussion draws on Magaloni, "Authoritarianism"; and Beatriz Magaloni and Guillermo Zepeda, "Democratization, Judicial and Law Enforcement Institutions, and the Rule of Law in Mexico," in *Dilemmas of Political Change in Mexico*, ed. Kevin J. Middlebrook, 168–97.

29. Magaloni and Zepeda, "Democratization," 194.

30. Mexican municipalities are the rough equivalent of U.S. city governments. In 2005, INEGI reported 2,451 municipalities in Mexico. This number tends to increase slightly every year.

31. The *cabildo* is comprised of *regidores* (aldermen) and *síndicos* (trustees). The exact number of these positions depends upon the size of the municipality. Together, the municipal presidency and the *cabildo* are known as the *ayuntamiento*.

32. Peter M. Ward and Victoria Rodríguez, *New Federalism and State Government in Mexico: Bringing the States Back In*, U.S.-Mexican Policy Studies Program, Report no. 9 (Austin: University of Texas, Lyndon B. Johnson School of Public Affairs, 1999).

33. The seminal work on local government in a PRI-dominated political system is Richard Fagen and William Tuohy, *Politics and Privilege in a Mexican City* (Stanford, Calif.: Stanford University Press, 1972).

34. Victoria Rodríguez, *Decentralization in Mexico: From Reforma Municipal to Solidaridad to Nuevo Federalismo* (Boulder, Colo.: Westview, 1997).

35. Juan Molinar Horcasitas and Jeffrey Weldon, "Electoral Determinants and Effects of PRONASOL," in *Transforming State-Society Relations in Mexico: The National Solidarity Strategy*, ed. Wayne Cornelius, Ann Craig, and Jonathan Fox (La Jolla: University of California–San Diego, Center for U.S.-Mexican Studies, 1994).

36. On the early experiences of the opposition at the subnational level, see the work of Victoria E. Rodríguez and Peter M. Ward, *Policymaking, Politics, and Urban Governance in Chihuahua: The Experience of Recent Panista Governments* (Austin: University of Texas, Lyndon B. Johnson School of Public Affairs, 1992); Rodríguez and Ward, *Political Change in Baja California: Democracy in the Making?* Monograph Series 40 (La Jolla: University of California–San Diego, Center for U.S.-Mexican Studies, 1994); and Rodríguez and Ward, eds., *Opposition Government in Mexico* (Albuquerque: University of New Mexico Press, 1995).

37. The Law of Fiscal Coordination mandates that 20 percent of national revenue be transferred to states and municipalities.

38. For more on the challenges of creating a federal arrangement that can function amid extreme economic inequalities, see Alberto Diaz-Cayeros, "Decentralization, Democratization, and Federalism in Mexico," in *Dilemmas of Political Change in Mexico*, ed. Kevin J. Middlebrook, 198–234.

39. States and municipalities do have some taxation authority. For example, states can levy a tax on the sale of new automobiles, and municipalities can collect property taxes.

40. In some respects, *presidencialismo* is more alive in the states than it is at the national level because some state congresses have been slower to check executive authority. For more on this issue, see Wayne A. Cornelius, "Blind Spots in

Democratization: Sub-national Politics as a Constraint on Mexico's Transition," *Democratization* 7, no. 3 (2000): 117–32; and Chappell Lawson, "Mexico's Unfinished Transition: Democratization and Authoritarian Enclaves in Mexico," *Mexican Studies/Estudios Mexicanos* 16, no. 2 (2000): 267–87.

6 POLITICAL PARTIES AND ELECTIONS IN MEXICO

1. On the PRI both before and after 2000, see José Antonio Crespo, *PRI: de la hegemonía a la oposición, un estudio comparado 1994–2001* (Mexico City: Centro de Estudios de Política Comparada, 2001); Kenneth F. Greene, *Why Dominant Parties Lose: Mexico's Democratization in Comparative Perspective* (Cambridge, UK: Cambridge University Press, 2007); and Beatriz Magaloni, *Voting for Autocracy: Hegemonic Party Survival and Its Demise in Mexico* (Cambridge, UK: Cambridge University Press, 2006).

2. Consulta Mitofsky, "2012: La elección: Variables fundamentales para seguir el proceso electoral, Abril 2011." http://www.consulta.mx/Estudio.aspx?Estudio =variables-fundamentales.

3. For more on the history and development of the PAN, see Soledad Loaeza, *El Partido Acción Nacional, la larga marcha, 1939–1994: Oposición leal y partido de protesta* (Mexico City: Fondo de Cultura Económica, 1999); David Shirk, *Mexico's New Politics: The PAN and Democratic Change* (Boulder, Colo.: Lynne Rienner, 2005); Yemile Mizrahi, *From Martyrdom to Power: The Partido Acción Nacional in Mexico* (Notre Dame, Ind.: University of Notre Dame, 2003); and Vikram Chand, *Mexico's Political Awakening* (Notre Dame, Ind.: University of Notre Dame, 2001).

4. Cited in Mizrahi, *From Martyrdom to Power*, 23.

5. See Shirk, *Mexico's New Politics*, 23 (figure 2.1) and 207 (figure 4.1).

6. Joseph Klesner argues that in the 1990s, this cleavage overshadowed ideology and induced parties to pursue broad nonideological platforms in order to attract voters. See "Electoral Competition and the New Party System in Mexico," *Latin American Politics and Society* 47, no. 2 (Summer 2005): 103–42.

7. Consulta Mitofsky, "2012: La elección"; Miguel Angel Gutierrez, Reuters, "Mexico's Cordero takes aim at presidency in 2012," May 26, 2011.

8. On the formation of the PRD, see Kathleen Bruhn, *Taking on Goliath: The Emergence of a New Left Party and the Struggle for Democracy in Mexico* (University Park: Pennsylvania State University Press, 1997).

9. This was the official figure, though many suspected that popular support for the FDN was actually higher—an accomplishment that was deliberately destroyed by the PRI's electoral shenanigans.

10. These factors are identified and discussed by Kathleen Bruhn in "The Partido de la Revolución Democrática: Diverging Approaches to Competition," in *Governing Mexico: Political Parties and Elections*, ed. Mónica Serrano (London: University of London, Institute of Latin American Studies, 1998).

11. Consulta Mitofsky, "2012: La elección."

12. Among the types of fraud commonly employed by the PRI were stuffing ballot boxes, buying votes, coercing voters, physically delivering citizens to the polls and monitoring their votes, allowing voters to cast more than one ballot, and including names of the deceased on voting lists.

13. One notable exception regarding the reelection rule pertains to *suplentes,* or substitute candidates who are formally identified on the ballot as stand-ins for an elected official in the event that he or she dies or leaves the post before finishing office. While a *suplente* who was not called into duty may run as a candidate for the same office in the next election, a sitting elected official may not serve as a *suplente* for a candidate running for the same office.

14. Ten years earlier, the PRI had also introduced a law that would penalize parties and politicians for boycotting the system by refusing to assume their elected posts and thus damaging Mexico's competitive image. The law enacted in 1963 was a response to PAN efforts to do just this in the 1958 presidential election. It stated that candidates who refused to assume their elected posts would forfeit their political rights for three years and their parties would lose their registration. José Antonio Crespo, "Party Competition in Mexico: Evolution and Prospects," in *Dilemmas of Political Change in Mexico,* ed. Kevin J. Middlebrook (London: Institute of Latin American Studies, University of London, 2004), 68.

15. No party ever passed the 20 percent threshold while the law was in effect. The PAN came the closest in 1973 but still fell short by five percentage points. See Shirk, *Mexico's New Politics,* 22–23.

16. Alternatively, parties established definitive registration by providing a copy of party statutes and evidence of 65,000 members, 3,000 in half of the states plus one, or 300 in half plus one of all federal electoral districts.

17. For a thorough discussion of the political role of Mexico's media, see Chappell Lawson, *Building the Fourth Estate: Democratization and the Rise of a Free Press in Mexico* (Berkeley: University of California Press, 2002).

18. The creation of the IFE was not the only concession that the PRI granted to the opposition in exchange for its support of COFIPE. Equally important for the PAN was the fact that the government agreed to recognize *panista* victories in state and local elections. A similar concession was not made to the PRD, and not surprisingly, that party refused to support the passage of the COFIPE.

19. Salinas's motivation for the electoral reforms of the early 1990s was also driven by his desire to show the world that Mexico was becoming more democratic. The state of Mexico's democracy was of particular interest to the U.S. Congress, which was hotly debating whether to ratify NAFTA.

20. Crespo, "Party Competition," 71.

21. Mony de Swann, Paola Martorelli, and Juan Molinar Horcasitas, "Public Financing of Political Parties and Electoral Expenditures in Mexico," in *Governing Mexico: Political Parties and Elections,* ed. Mónica Serrano (London: University of London, Institute of Latin American Studies, 1998), 157.

22. Chand, *Mexico's Political Awakening,* 273; de Swann et al., "Public Financing," 159.

7 MEXICAN POLITICAL CULTURE

1. Gabriel Almond and Sidney Verba, *The Civic Culture: Political Attitudes and Democracy in Five Nations* (Princeton, N.J.: Princeton University Press, 1963).

2. A related problem, even in country surveys using a single language, is that survey respondents are often forced to have an opinion about issues that they have not seriously considered but that are deemed relevant by pollsters. Hence, even when questions are carefully crafted, survey responses can sometimes reflect gut reactions or glib thoughts, rather than deeply held beliefs and attitudes.

3. Early studies of Mexican political culture used a psychological approach that made inferences based on a relatively small, regionally specific group. See, for example, Erich Fromm and Michael Maccoby, *Social Character in a Mexican Village* (Englewood Cliffs, N.J.: Prentice-Hall, 1970); Richard Fagen and William Tuohy, *Politics and Privilege in a Mexican City* (Stanford, Calif.: Stanford University Press, 1972); and Rafael Segovia, *La politización del niño mexicano* (Mexico City: El Colegio de México, 1975). Ann Craig and Wayne Cornelius provide an insightful review of these and other studies in "Political Culture in Mexico: Continuities and Revisionist Interpretations," in Gabriel Almond and Sidney Verba, eds., *The Civic Culture Revisited* (Boston: Little, Brown, 1980), 325–83.

4. In the 1963 Almond and Verba study, the rural sector represented two-thirds of the entire population but was ignored. Today, rural dwellers represent only a quarter of the population but remain less likely than their urban counterparts to have access to basic public services, regular contact with government institutions, and opportunities to participate in politically active organizations.

5. For example, another problem with evaluating political culture is that researchers assume they can properly interpret people's internal motivations based on how they respond to survey questions and other forms of external observation. This assumes that survey respondents fully understand the questions they are being asked and that they accurately (and sincerely) communicate their responses.

6. See Alberto Hernández Medina and Luis Narro Rodríguez, *Como somos los mexicanos* (Mexico City: Centro de Estudios Educativos, 1987).

7. Craig and Cornelius, "Political Culture," 371–78.

8. For example, Protestantism is said to have played a direct role in the development of capitalism. See Max Weber in *The Protestant Ethic and the Spirit of Capitalism* (New York: Scribner's, 1958).

9. For example, Wiarda's early work asserted that Latin American political culture—including a tendency toward authoritarianism and corporatism—is attributable to the legacy of "a peculiarly Iberic-European tradition dating from approximately 1500, with a political culture and socio-political order that at its core was essentially two-class, authoritarian, traditional, elitist, patrimonial, Catholic, stratified, hierarchical, and corporate." Howard J. Wiarda, "Toward a Framework for the Study of Political Change in the Iberic-Latin Tradition: The Corporative Model," *World Politics* 25, no. 2 (1973): 209.

10. Wayne Cornelius and Jeffrey Weldon, "Politics in Mexico," in *Comparative Politics Today: A World View*, ed. Gabriel Almond, G. Bingham Powell, Kaare Strom, and Russell Dalton (New York: Pearson Longman, 2004).

11. Ilene V. O'Malley, *The Myth of the Revolution: Hero Cults and the Institutionalization of the Mexican State, 1920–1940* (New York: Greenwood, 1986).

12. Jorge Domínguez and James McCann, *Democratizing Mexico: Public Opinion and Electoral Choices* (Baltimore: Johns Hopkins University Press, 1996), chap. 2.

13. It is important to point out, however, that when asked whether "a few strong leaders would do more for Mexico than all the laws and talk," 54 percent of all respondents agreed. This suggests that during the mid-1990s, roughly half of the population still believed that strong leadership is more effective than laws and institutions. See Domínguez and McCann, *Democratizing Mexico*, 41, table 2.7.

14. Specifically, the Latinobarómetro survey asks whether respondents believe that democracy is preferable to any other type of government (www.latinobarometro.org).

15. Domínguez and McCann demonstrate that in 1988, voters made their decisions in a two-step process. First, they made a strategic choice about whether to support the PRI. This decision was based on the voters' assessment of the PRI's strength and whether altering the status quo would be disruptive or beneficial. Voters who opted for the opposition then chose a candidate based either on their perception of which candidate had the best chance of defeating the PRI or, in some cases, on their assessment of which candidate best represented his norms and beliefs. Domínguez and McCann, *Democratizing Mexico*, chaps. 3–4.

16. Domínguez and McCann, *Democratizing Mexico*, 206, table E-3.

17. UN Development Programme, *Democracy in Latin America: Towards a Citizens' Democracy* (New York: United Nations Development Programme, 2004), 236.

18. Consulta Mitofsky survey, *Identidad Partidista*, August 2010.

19. Alejandro Poiré, "Retrospective Voting, Partisanship, and Loyalty in Presidential Elections: 1994," in *Toward Mexico's Democratization: Parties, Campaigns, Elections, and Public Opinion*, ed. Jorge Domínguez and Alejandro Poiré (New York: Routledge, 1999), 24–56; and Beatriz Magaloni, "Is the PRI Fading? Economic Performance, Electoral Accountability, and Voting Behavior in the 1994 and 1997 Elections," in *Toward Mexico's Democratization*, ed. Domínguez and Poiré, 203–36.

20. Jonathan Fox, "The Difficult Transition from Clientelism to Citizenship: Lessons from Mexico," *World Politics* 46, no. 2 (1994): 151–84.

21. UN Development Programme, *Democracy in Latin America*, 224–25.

22. UN Development Programme, *Democracy in Latin America*, 233–35.

23. The question asked was, "In a scale like the one used in the school where 0 is nothing and 10 is a lot, please tell me how much do you trust in . . . ?" Consulta Mitofsky, "Confianza en Instituciones," *National Home Survey*, July 2005, 3.

24. According to UNESCO media statistics, there was approximately one television set to every four Mexicans in 2003.

8 MEXICAN CIVIL SOCIETY

1. María Fernanda Somuano, "Las organizaciones civiles: formación y cambio," in *Los grandes problemas de México*, vol. 14, *Instituciones y procesos políticos*, ed. Soledad Loaeza and Jean François Prud'homme (Mexico City: El Colegio de México, 2010), 184.

2. Alexis de Tocqueville, *Democracy in America* (New York: Perennial Classics, 2000). Robert Putnam, *Making Democracy Work: Civic Traditions in Modern Italy* (Princeton, N.J.: Princeton University Press, 1993).

3. Mariclaire Acosta, "The Role of Civil Society," in *Mexico's Democratic Challenges: Politics, Government, and Society*, ed. Andrew Selee and Jacqueline Peschard (Washington, D.C.: Woodrow Wilson Center Press, 2010), 275.

4. Fernanco Somuano, "Las organizaciones civiles," 197–204.

5. This discussion is not meant to imply that all workers or unions were quiescent. In a number of instances, labor in particular industries challenged state-labor relations, with differing results. For example, in the 1970s, automobile industry unions fought for and won greater internal democracy and autonomy from the Confederation of Mexican Workers (Confederación de Trabajadores de México, CTM).

6. Kevin J. Middlebrook, *The Paradox of Revolution: Labor, the State, and Authoritarianism in Mexico* (Baltimore: Johns Hopkins University Press, 1995), 256.

7. Graciela Bensusán, "A New Scenario for Mexican Trade Unions: Changes in the Structure of Political and Economic Opportunities," in *Dilemmas of Political Change in Mexico*, ed. Kevin J. Middlebrook (London: Institute of Latin American Studies, University of London, 2004), 248–50.

8. Noé Cruz Serrano, "Sindicato de Pemex se da bono de 21%," *El Universal*, September 30, 2009.

9. Joaquim Ibarz, "Felipe Calderón afronta el reto de la ineficiencia y la corrupción," *La Vanguardia*, October 12, 2009; "Movilizaciones en seis estados en apoyo al Sindicato Mexicano de Electricistas," *La Jornada*, October 13, 2009; José de Córdoba, "Mexico Power Takeover Creates Sparks," *Wall Street Journal*, October 12, 2009.

10. Many argue that Gordillo's support for Calderón in the 2006 presidential election was pivotal in his victory and that this helps explain her close working relationship with him throughout his *sexenio*.

11. "Se reúnen Gordillo y Peña Nieto," *El Universal*, November 29, 2010.

12. "Intelectuales piden a Calderón separarse de SNTE," *El Universal*, November 21, 2010; "El SNTE dice no a consejos de OCDE," *El Universal*, October 21, 2010.

13. Marion Lloyd, "'The Teacher' holds sway in Mexico," *Houston Chronicle*, May 25, 2008.

14. Lucrecia Santibañez and Brenda Jarillo Rabling, "Conflict and Power: The Teacher's Union and Education Quality in Mexico," *Well Being and Social Policy* 3, no. 2, (2007): 21–40.

15. Enrique Cárdenas Sánchez, "Mexico's Private Sector, Then and Now," in *Mexico's Private Sector: Recent History, Future Challenges*, ed. Riordan Roett (Boulder, Colo.: Lynne Rienner, 1998).

16. Ben Ross Schnieder, "Why Is Mexican Business So Organized?" *Latin American Research Review* 37, no. 1 (2002): 77–118.

17. Matilde Luna, "Business and Politics in Mexico," in *Dilemmas of Political Change in Mexico*, ed. Middlebrook.

18. See Vikram Chand, *Mexico's Political Awakening* (Notre Dame, Ind.: Notre Dame Press, 2001); and Yemile Mizrahi, *From Martyrdom to Power: The Partido Acción Nacional in Mexico* (Notre Dame, Ind.: University of Notre Dame Press, 2003).

19. Kristin Johnson Ceva, "Business-Government Relations in Mexico Since 1990: NAFTA, Economic Crisis, and the Reorganization of Business Interests," in *Mexico's Private Sector*, ed. Riordan Roett, 125–57. See also Schnieder, "Why Is Mexican Business So Organized?" 100–103.

20. Kenneth Shadlen, *Democratization without Representation: The Politics of Small Industry in Mexico* (University Park: Pennsylvania State University Press, 2004).

21. Chappell Lawson, *Building the Fourth Estate: Democratization and the Rise of a Free Press in Mexico* (Berkeley: University of California Press, 2002), 8.

22. Chappell Lawson, "Building the Fourth Estate: Media Opening and Democratization in Mexico," in *Dilemmas of Political Change*, ed. Middlebrook, 381–82.

23. Lawson, *Building the Fourth Estate* (2002), 118.

24. Lawson, "Building the Fourth Estate" (2004), 396.

25. Committee to Protect Journalists, "Attacks on the Press 2010: Mexico," http://www.cpj.org/2011/02/attacks-on-the-press-2010-mexico.php.

26. Sallie Hughes, *Newsrooms in Conflict: Journalism and the Democratization of Mexico* (Pittsburgh, Pa.: University of Pittsburgh Press, 2006), 88–107.

27. Chand, *Mexico's Political Awakening*, 153–54.

28. Roberto Blancarte, "Churches, Believers, and Democracy," in *Mexico's Democratic Challenges: Politics, Government, and Society*, ed. Selee and Peschard.

29. Roberto Blancarte, "Religion, Church, and State in Contemporary Mexico," in *Changing Structure of Mexico: Political, Social, and Economic Prospects*, ed. Laura Randall (Armonk, N.Y.: M.E. Sharpe, 2006): 428–29; Roderic Ai Camp, *Politics in Mexico: The Democratic Consolidation*, 5th ed. (New York: Oxford University Press, 2007), 146.

30. Blancarte, "Religion, Church, and State," 425. See also Alberto Olvera, "Civil Society in Mexico at Century's End," 415 in the same volume.

31. Important exceptions to this are conservative Catholic groups like Opus Dei and El Yunque (The Anvil), whose goals include influencing Mexico's political trajectory by successfully placing their members in public office where they will then be in a position to enact policies in line with their conservative religious beliefs.

32. Helga Baitenmann, Victoria Chenaut, and Ann Varley, eds. *Decoding Gender: Law and Practice in Contemporary Mexico* (New Brunswick, N.J.: Rutgers University Press, 2007).

33. Michael Meyer, William Sherman, and Susan Deeds, *The Course of Mexican History*, 7th ed. (New York: Oxford University Press, 2003), 533. See also Jocelyn Olcott, *Revolutionary Women in Postrevolutionary Mexico* (Durham, N.C.: Duke University Press, 2005).

34. Victoria Rodríguez, *Women in Contemporary Mexican Politics* (Austin: University of Texas Press, 2003), 98–101.

35. National Women's Institute website: http://www.inmujeres.gob.mx/ique-es-el-inmujeres/historia.html (accessed December 2, 2010).

36. In Rodríguez's words, "The 'woman' question of yesteryear is now a part of the organizational and official discourse." Rodríguez, *Women in Contemporary Mexican Politics*, 110.

37. The bill passed 46 to 19, with the opposition coming mainly from members of the PAN. James McKinley Jr., "Mexico City Legalizes Abortion Early in Term," *New York Times*, April 24, 2007. Subsequently, seventeen states have changed their constitutions to say that life begins at the moment of conception and have used murder laws to prosecute women who have abortions. See Grupo de Información en Reproducción Elegida, www.gire.org.mx.

38. INMujeres, *Cuarto informe de labores, 2004–2005* (Mexico City: Instituto Nacional de las Mujeres, 2005), 58, table 1.11.

39. Kathleen Bruhn, "Whores and Lesbians: Political Activism, Party Strategies, and Gender Quotas in Mexico," in *Electoral Studies* 22, no. 1 (2003): 101–19.

40. Lisa Baldez, "Elected Bodies: The Gender Quota Law for Legislative Candidates in Mexico," *Legislative Studies Quarterly* 29, no. 2 (2004): 27; "Primaries vs. Quotas: Gender and Candidate Nominations in Mexico, 2003," *Latin American Politics and Society* 49, no. 3 (2007): 69–96.

41. Bruhn argues that the PRD adopted the quota, in part, because of the pressure of women activists within the party. See "Whores and Lesbians."

42. Robles was chosen to take over for Cuauhtémoc Cárdenas when he left the position to launch his presidential campaign in 1999.

43. Now that the gender quota is in effect for all parties, the PAN, like the PRI, has found ways around it. For example, women within the party complain that they are chosen as candidates only in districts where the party's chances of winning are slim to none. Another common practice is for women candidates to run as an alternate candidate (*candidato suplente*) to the principal candidate. Alternates assume office only if the "real" candidate resigns or is unable to serve the full term of office. See Bruhn, "Whores and Lesbians."

44. Roderic Camp, "Women and Men, Men and Women: Gender Patterns in Mexican Politics," in *Women's Participation in Mexican Political Life*, ed. Victoria Rodríguez (Boulder, Colo.: Westview, 1998).

45. It is important to note, however, that in a number of states and in the Federal District, women regularly made up between 20 and 30 percent of the local legislatures. INMujeres, *Cuarto informe*, 59; INMujeres, *Quinto informe de labores, 2005–2006* (Mexico City: Instituto Nacional de las Mujeres, 2006), 41.

46. INMujeres, *Cuarto informe*, 62.

47. Vivienne Bennett skillfully recounts the events leading up to this victory in *The Politics of Water: Urban Protest, Gender, and Power in Monterrey, Mexico* (Pittsburgh, Pa.: University of Pittsburgh Press, 1995).

48. Vivienne Bennett, "Everyday Struggles: Women in Urban Popular Movements and Territorially Based Protests in Mexico," in *Women's Participation*, ed. Rodríguez, 124.

49. In response, Governor Ulíses Ruíz Ortiz ordered state police to forcibly remove the demonstrators from the central square. Subsequent clashes turned violent, and hundreds of protesters were injured and arrested as the police used excessive force to subdue them. In October, another confrontation resulted in three deaths and prompted President Fox to send in the federal police. Even after the federal police arrived, the protests and violence continued, culminating in the bombing of two financial buildings in Mexico City in early November. Promising to use a firm hand against lawbreakers, incoming President Calderón immediately secured the arrest of the APPO's leader and the mass detention of its supporters. Although these moves initially took the wind out of the APPO's sails, the next summer the group was once again organizing demonstrations in Oaxaca.

50. "Mass anti-crime rallies in Mexico," *BBC News*, August 31, 2008. http://news.bbc.co.uk/2/hi/americas/7590272.stm.

51. Laura Carlsen, "Mexico's Anti-Drug War March Demands Far-Reaching Political Reforms," *Americas Program*, www.cipamericas.org/archives/4459.

52. Olvera, "Civil Society in Mexico," 431.

53. While Alianza Cívica operates independently and in fact eschews relationships with political parties, it is widely perceived to be leftist in its ideological orientation.

54. Olvera, "Civil Society in Mexico," 430–31.

55. Alianza Cívica, www.alianzacivica.org.mx (accessed June 1, 2011).

56. The EZLN was not the first indigenous effort at resistance in Chiapas. Bill Weinberg, *Homage to Chiapas: The New Indigenous Struggles in Mexico* (New York: Verso, 2000).

57. A number of excellent books analyze the Zapatista uprising: George Collier, with Elizabeth Lowery Quaratiello, *Basta! Land and the Zapatista Rebellion in Chiapas* (Oakland, Calif.: Institute for Food and Development Policy, 1994); Neil Harvey, *The Chiapas Rebellion: The Struggle for Land and Democracy* (Durham, N.C.: Duke University Press, 1998); and Andres Oppenheimer, *Bordering on Chaos: Mexico's Roller-Coaster Journey toward Prosperity* (New York: Little, Brown, 1996).

58. Cited in Rodolfo Stavenhagen, "Mexico's Unfinished Symphony: The Zapatista Movement," in *Mexico's Politics and Society in Transition*, ed. Joseph Tulchin and Andrew Selee (Boulder, Colo.: Lynne Rienner, 2003), 112.

59. Luis Hernández and Laura Carlsen, "Indigenous Rights: The Battle for Constitutional Reform in Mexico," in *Dilemmas of Political Change*, ed. Middlebrook, 451–52.

60. However, it should be noted that the use of *usos y costumbres* is not without its problems. For some shortcomings, see Hernández and Carlsen, "Indigenous Rights," 447. See also Laura Carlsen, "Autonomía indígena y usos y costumbres: La innovación de la tradición," *Chiapas* 7 (1999). www.ezln.org/revistachiapas/No7/ch7carlsen.html (accessed January 23, 2006).

9 MEXICO'S POLITICAL ECONOMY

1. Mexico was not the only country to employ the export-oriented model. It was used almost exclusively in Latin America and in many other parts of the developing world at least until the 1930s.

2. As noted in chapter 1, the belief that foreigners ought to play a central role in Mexico's economic development was partly grounded in the culturally biased (if not racist) view of Díaz and the *científicos*, who believed that Europeans were inherently superior to other peoples. Roger Hansen, *The Politics of Mexican Development* (Baltimore: Johns Hopkins University Press, 1971), 18–20.

3. See Hansen, *Politics of Mexican Development*, 16–17.

4. Brian Hamnett, *A Concise History of Mexico* (Cambridge, UK: Cambridge University Press, 1999).

5. See Hansen, *Politics of Mexican Development*, 23–29.

6. The ISI model was used widely throughout Latin America. For a concise description of the model and an assessment of its effects in the region, see Patrice Franko, *The Puzzle of Latin American Economic Development* (Lanham, Md.: Rowman & Littlefield, 2007), chap. 3.

7. One of the most common was to pay a Mexican citizen for the use of his name, a *prestanombre* that served as a front for a foreign firm yet gave the appearance of local ownership.

8. Further exacerbating the problem was the fact that Mexico had one of the highest rates of population growth in the world in the 1960s, thus making it less likely that economic growth alone would lead to an improved standard of living.

9. Exemplifying the discontent among middle sectors was the doctors' strike that occurred at the outset of Díaz Ordaz's term. Some doctors were arrested and beaten before they agreed to go back to work. Díaz Ordaz also had to resort to hard-line tactics to deal with insurgent labor groups, notably oil workers and Mexico City truck drivers. Raul Trejo Delarbe and Anibal Yanez, "The Mexican Labor Movement: 1917–1975," *Latin American Perspectives* 3, no. 1 (1976): 133–53.

10. The entrenched political interests of larger manufacturing industries—which benefited from the status quo and the accessibility of cheaper, high-quality foreign inputs—made it difficult to move toward the domestic development of input production.

11. In the United States, high consumer spending, increased public sector spending on social welfare programs, and military expenditures during the Vietnam War combined to create a significant U.S. imbalance of payments.

12. Thomas D. Lairson and David Skidmore, *International Political Economy: The Struggle for Power and Wealth*. 3rd ed. (Belmont, Calif.: Thomson-Wadsworth, 2003).

13. Rene Villarreal and Rocio de Villarreal, "Mexico's Development Strategy," *Proceedings of the Academy of Political Science* 34, no. 1 (1981): 97–103; Thomas Skidmore and Peter Smith, *Modern Latin America* (New York: Oxford University Press, 2005), 283; Lynn Foster, *A Brief History of Mexico* (New York: Checkmark, 2004), 212.

14. Although Mexico's oil deposits were at one time expected to surpass those of Saudi Arabia, in the early days of the boom it was ill equipped to capitalize on its treasure because the industry was in disarray. Thirty-five years under national control had taken their toll: the necessary technical expertise, training, modern equipment, and adequate infrastructure were all absent. Therefore, the government had to make significant investments in modernizing the industry before it could fully exploit its oil reserves. See Judith Adler Hellman, *Mexico in Crisis*, 2nd ed. (New York: Holmes & Meier, 1988), 74–76.

15. Even though the oil boom created millions of jobs, it fell far short of creating enough jobs to substantially reduce unemployment, especially in rural areas.

16. Global interest rates increased significantly as the United States sought to tighten its money supply to get a handle on stagflation—inflation at a time of low growth.

17. Although Mexico was the first to announce its inability to service its debt, many other countries in Latin America and elsewhere found themselves in similar circumstances. Low prices for many export commodities combined with heavy indebtedness to finance ISI and rising international interest rates made it nearly impossible for even relatively strong economies like Argentina's, Brazil's, and Venezuela's to make good on their loans. See Franko, *Puzzle*, 97–98.

18. Foster, *Brief History of Mexico*, 215.

19. Skidmore and Smith, *Modern Latin America*, 285.

20. This goal was achieved with the help of U.S. Treasury Secretary James Brady. The so-called Brady Plan allowed highly indebted countries like Mexico to reduce their debt with "buybacks" in the secondary market, to structure repayment over a longer period of time, or to take out new loans from the IMF. See Franko, *Puzzle*, 97–98.

21. The government's sale of industries that were previously owned by the state brought in much-needed capital to the public coffers and arguably improved the efficiency of the industries by placing them in private hands. Yet equally important is the fact that the sell-off benefited a select group of Mexican entrepreneurs that had ties to the Salinas family. For example, Carlos Slim, a Mexican businessman, purchased the formerly state-owned telecommunications company, Telmex, at well below market price and converted it into a privately held monopoly.

22. The United States already had a free-trade agreement with Canada. The latter agreed to become part of NAFTA in the hopes of retaining its privileged access to the U.S. market, not so much because it had a compelling interest in free trade with Mexico.

23. Mexicans were incensed by the fact that many of the loans were made to politically well-connected business interests who were not creditworthy and gambled that the government would not allow a mass default.

24. Russell Crandall, "Mexico's Domestic Economy: Policy Options and Choices," in *Mexico's Democracy at Work: Political and Economic Dynamics*, ed. Russell Crandall, Guadalupe Paz, and Riordan Roett (Boulder, Colo.: Lynne Rienner, 2005), 71–72.

25. Marla Dickerson, "Fox Not Shy in Touting Record," *Los Angeles Times*, March 21, 2006.

26. Adding insult to injury was the fact that Mexico was displaced by China, its biggest economic rival, as the United States' number two source of imported goods.

27. All figures GDP in purchasing power parity. www.oecd-library.com/economics/country-statistical-profile-mexico and https://www.cia.gov/library/publications/the-world-factbook/geos/mx.html (accessed January 14, 2011).

28. Tracy Wilkinson, "Mexican Titans Wage Telecom War," *Los Angeles Times*, May 17, 2011.

29. http://latino.foxnews.com/latino/money/2011/01/04/mexico-touts-fastest-job-creation-years/ (accessed January 4, 2011).

10 POVERTY, INEQUALITY, AND SOCIAL WELFARE POLICY

1. Mexico's 1917 constitution explicitly mandates the establishment of a minimum wage. The minimum is set by the National Minimum Wage Commission according to the price of a basket of food products. The minimum wage for the north and in tourist areas (about US$4.50 per day) is slightly higher than that in other regions (e.g., the center, US$4.37 per day, and the south, US$4.25 per day).

2. This is a different definition of extreme poverty than the one used by the United Nations, which sets the rate as those persons earning less than $1 per day.

3. One problem with measuring poverty in this way is that wages may not represent all of a household's sources of income. In Mexico, many poor people often earn money through ways that are not easily monitored by the government, such as working as a street vendor or a domestic servant. Income from this vast informal economy is not registered.

4. This measure of purchasing power is usually indexed to the U.S. dollar, and it represents the relative value of income, controlling for the cost of living.

5. CIA World Factbook, https://www.cia.gov/library/publications/the-world-factbook/geos/mx.html (accessed January 14, 2011).

6. UN Development Programme, "Human Development Report: The Human Development Index (HDI)." http://hdr.undp.org/en/statistics/hdi/ (accessed February 1, 2011).

7. Julio Boltvinik, "Welfare, Inequality, and Poverty in Mexico," in *Confronting Development: Assessing Mexico's Economic and Social Policy Challenges*, ed. Kevin J. Middlebrook and Eduardo Zepeda (Standford, Calif.: Stanford University Press, 2003).

8. Juan Pardinas, "Fighting Poverty in Mexico: Policy Changes," in *Mexico under Fox*, ed. Luis Rubio and Susan Kaufman Purcell (Boulder, Colo.: Lynne Rienner, 2004), 65–86; Sergio Aguayo, *Almanaque Mexicano* (Mexico City: Aguilar, 2007). See also the SEDESOL website, http://www.sedesol.gob.mx/.

9. See Dorte Verner, "Activities, Employment, and Wages in Rural and Semi-Urban Mexico," World Bank Policy Research Working Paper 3561 (April 2005), 7, table 2.1.

10. Mexico was not alone in this experience. By the early 1990s, the number of persons living in poverty in Latin America nearly doubled from 78 million in 1982 to 150 million in 1993. By the mid-1990s, the number of poor people climbed to 210 million—a proportional increase in the number of poor people from 35 percent in the 1980s to 41 percent in the 1990s. According to some analysts, Latin American income disparities became the worst in the entire world in the 1990s. See Roberto Patricio Korzeniewicz and William C. Smith, "Poverty, Inequality, and Growth in Latin America: Searching for the High Road to Globalization," *Latin American Research Review* 35, no. 3 (2000): 9.

11. Sara R. Gordon, "Nuevas desigualdades y política social," in *Las políticas sociales de México al fin del milenio: Descentralización, diseño y gestión*, ed. Rolando Cordera and Alicia Ziccardi (Mexico City: Coordinación de Humanidades, Facultad de Economía and Instituto de Investigaciones Sociales, UNAM, 2000), 57–70.

12. Vivienne Bennett, "The Evolution of Urban Popular Movements in Mexico between 1968 and 1988," in *The Making of Social Movements in Latin America* (Boulder, Colo.: Westview, 1992), 240–59.

13. The agency was formerly the Ministry of Public Works (1959–1976), the Ministry of Human Settlements and Public Works (1976–1982), and the Ministry of Urban Development and Ecology (1982–1992). It received its most recent title and mission under President Salinas.

14. The Ministry of Health was predated by the Ministry of Wellness and Hygiene in the 1920s and 1930s, when the primary functions of the agency were focused on health. However, when the Ministry of Social Assistance (Secretaría de Asistencia Social, SAS) was created in 1938, it took on many public health functions. In 1940, the agency was renamed the Ministry of Health and Welfare (Secretaría de Salubridad y Asistencia, SSA) until it was given its current title in 1982.

15. Programa de Apoyo al Ingreso Agropecuario, PROCAMPO para Vivir Mejor: Resultados Principales del Primer Trimestre, Informe Enero-Marzo 2011. http://www.aserca.gob.mx/artman/uploads/Informe_PROCAMPO_2011_marzo.pdf.

16. Rose Spalding, "Early Social Policy Initiatives in the Fox Administration," paper presented at the Twenty-Third International Congress of the Latin American Studies Association, Washington, D.C., September 6–8, 2001), 4.

17. According to Spalding, Fox and his close advisers believed that Progresa had been used as a "stick" to threaten voters, who were told that if Fox was elected they would no longer receive its benefits. "Early Social Policy Initiatives," 7.

18. Spalding, "Early Social Policy Initiatives," 4.

19. See "Padrón Inicial Correspondiente al Ejercicio Fiscal 2007," www .oportunidades.gob.mx.

20. The Fox administration argued that, without adequate highways, ports, airports, and telecommunications infrastructure, these areas were prevented from taking full advantage of the opportunities of the global economy.

21. These figures are based on preliminary data from the start of the program in 2001 to July 2006, as posted on the PRONAFIM website, www.pronafim.gob.mx (accessed July 18, 2007).

22. David Arellano Gault, Victor G. Carreón Rodríguez, Gustavo A. Del Angel Mobarak, and Fausto Hernández Trillo, "Evaluación de Resultados del Programa Nacional de Financiamiento al Microempresario (PRONAFIM) Correspondiente al Ejercicio Fiscal 2006," Evaluación Parcial: Enero—Agosto de 2006, Centro de Investigación y Docencia Económicas, A.C., 83.

23. "Compartamos: From Nonprofit to Profit," Bloomberg.com, December 13, 2007.

24. According to external analyses funded by SEDESOL, in terms of distribution, the program made its largest investments in poor, high-migrant-sending communities. Servicios Profesionales Para el Desarrollo Económico, Secretaría de Desarollo Social (SEDESOL), "Tablados de Información de Gabinete," *Evaluación Externa del Programa 3x1 para Migrantes*, 2005.

25. Similar criticisms were made of U.S. progressive reformers who toppled political machines like New York's Tammany Hall and laid the foundation for conservative local governments in much of the postwar Southwest. See Amy Bridges, *Morning Glories: Municipal Reform in the Southwest* (Princeton, N.J.: Princeton University Press, 1997); see also Steven Erie, *Rainbow's End* (Berkeley: University of California Press, 1988).

26. This is due to a 2002 constitutional amendment that made it obligatory to attend preschool—the equivalent of kindergarten in the United States—beginning in 2004 for age five, in 2005 for age four, and in 2008 for age three. "Sistema Educativo de los Estados Unidos Mexicanos, Principales Cifras, Ciclo Escolar 2005–06," Secretaría de Educación Pública, Dirección General de Planeación y Programación, Unidad de Planeación y Evaluación de Políticas Educativas, 41.

27. Preparatory or baccalaureate school is frequently referred to as "middle" school education (*educación media superior*) but is essentially equivalent to U.S. high school.

28. Statistical analyses carried out in the United States and Latin America show that those who attend preschool have increased high school graduation rates, improved performance on standardized tests, reduced crime and delinquency, lower rates of teen pregnancy, and better economic opportunities. Albert Wat, "Dollars and Sense: A Review of Economic Analyses of Pre-K," Pre-K Now Research Series, (Washington, D.C.: Pre-K Now, 2007); J. Flip and E. Schiefelbein, "Efecto de la educación pre-escolar sobre el rendimiento a fines de primaria en Argentina, Bolivia, Colombia, y Chile," *Revista Latinoamericana de Estudios Educativos* 7 (1982): 9–41.

29. Tuition calculations are based on majors in political science and international relations; tuition in other majors (e.g., law) may vary. UNAM, *2006 Agenda Estadística*, Dirección General de Planeación, www.planeacion.unam.mx. For a useful discussion of UNAM and its historical development, see Robert A. Rhoads, "Power and Politics in University Governance: Organization and Change at the Universidad Nacional Autónoma de México," *Journal of Higher Education* 76, no. 2 (2005): 234–37. Data for ITESO obtained from website, www.uia.mx.

30. www.oecd.org (accessed January 18, 2011).

31. OECD Programme for International Student Assessment (PISA), http://www.oecd.org/dataoecd/34/60/46619703.pdf.

32. Eligibility for pension benefits begins after a defined period of approximately ten years or five hundred weeks of formal employment. Gloria Grandolini and Luis Cerda, "Mexico: The 1997 Pension Reform in Mexico," *World Bank*, April 22, 1998, 5.

33. Because of its strong research emphasis, the Ministry of Health is a useful place for obtaining national- and state-level Mexican health statistics. It maintains a website at www.salud.gob.mx. Statistics are also available from the Mexican Foundation for Health, www.funsalud.org.mx.

34. Enrique Rios, "The Mexican Health Care System: A Federal Perspective," presentation at the Trans-Border Institute, August 2006, www.sandiego.edu/tbi/events.

35. Overall spending on health care amounted to only 6.1 percent of GDP, or about $360 per person, a figure below the average for Latin American countries. Spending on health care in Mexico varied widely by state, with the richest states spending five times as much on health care as poor states. Felicia Marle Knaul and Julio Frenk, "Health Insurance in Mexico: Achieving Universal Coverage through Structural Reform," *Health Affairs* 24, no. 5 (2003): 1467–1469.

36. L. Jacobo Rodríguez, "In Praise and Criticism of Mexico's Pension Reform," *Policy Analysis*, April 14, 1999.

37. See Grandolini and Cerda, "Mexico," 6.

38. This pension reform was first implemented in 1992 and modified through new congressional legislation beginning in 1995. Furthermore, the Mexican Central Bank guaranteed private banks a 2 percent minimum annual rate of return on these accounts. Federal Reserve Bank of Dallas, "Pension Reform in Mexico," *Financial Industry*, 3rd/4th Quarter 1996, 2.

39. Grandolini and Cerda, "Mexico," 9–11.

40. Olivia S. Mitchell, "Evaluating Administrative Costs in Mexico's AFORES Pension System," Pension Research Council Working Paper 99-1, January 1999, 33.

41. Similar reforms had been implemented in Chile in 1981 and Argentina in 1994. While the savings rate fell slightly in Argentina, in Chile domestic savings went from 16 percent to 29 percent of GDP from the mid-1980s to the early 1990s. Federal Reserve Bank of Dallas, "Pension Reform," 1–4.

42. Regarding Mexico's uninsured population, see Grandolini and Cerda, "Mexico," 4.

43. See Knaul and Frenk, "Health Insurance in Mexico," 1468.

44. *Plan Nacional de Desarrollo, 2006–2012*, www.presidencia.gov.mx (accessed July 21, 2006).

45. See Emilio Zebadúa, "Seguridad social, pasado y futuro," *El Universal*, May 11, 2007; Artemio Ortiz, "Por qué rechazar la nueva ley," *El Universal*, May 11, 2007.

46. Ricardo Jiménez, "Riesgo país, en su menor nivel del año," *El Universal*, May 29, 2007.

11 THE RULE OF LAW IN MEXICO

1. Some analysts describe Mexico as a narco-state overrun by violence, corruption, and narco-terrorism. Barnard R. Thompson, "The Drug War in Mexico: By Any Other Name It's Terrorism," *Mexidata*, August 9, 2010. Others, influenced by recent military doctrine, have tended to portray Mexico's recent violence as the equivalent of a domestic insurgency. John P. Sullivan and Adam Elkus, "State of Siege: Mexico's Criminal Insurgency," *Small Wars Journal*, August 2008.

2. Specifically, the report asserted, "In terms of worst-case scenarios for the Joint Force and indeed the world, two large and important states bear consideration for a rapid and sudden collapse: Pakistan and Mexico." United States Joint Forces Command, *Joint Operating Environment* (Norfolk, Va.: 2008).

3. 2010 Failed State Index. http://alturl.com/cfhzs.

4. Russell D. Howard and Reid L. Sawyer, *Terrorism and Counterterrorism: Understanding the New Security Environment, Readings and Interpretations*, rev. ed. (Guilford, Conn.: McGraw-Hill/Dushkin, 2004).

5. "Lidera Sedena quejas presentadas a CNDH," *Reforma*, December 26, 2008; Marcos Pablo Moloeznik, "Principales efectos de la militarización del combate al narcotráfico en México," *Renglones*, 2009; Moloeznik, "The Militarization of Mexican Public Security and the Role of the Military in Mexico," in *Police and Public Security in Mexico*, ed. Robert A. Donnelly and David A. Shirk (San Diego: Trans-Border Institute, 2009); Carlos Antonio Flores Pérez, "Organized Crime and Official Corruption in Mexico," in *Police and Public Security in Mexico*, ed. Donnelly and Shirk.

6. Daniel Kaufman, *Misrule of Law* (Washington, D.C.: World Bank Institute, 2001); Rachel Kleinfeld Belton, *Competing Definitions of the Rule of Law: Implications for Practitioners*, Carnegie Papers Rule of Law Series (Washington, D.C.: Carnegie Endowment for International Peace, 2005); José María Maravall and Adam Przeworski, eds., *Democracy and the Rule of Law* (Cambridge: Cambridge University Press, 2003).

7. There are significant problems with crime data collection in Mexico, including low rates of reporting by victims and sometimes inaccurate and sporadic reporting by government agencies. Nevertheless, the data give us a useful snapshot of how crime rates in Mexico have varied over time.

8. In 1999, for example, when they were graduate students, the authors of this book fell victim to a classic small-time theft operation at Mexico City's northern bus station. While rushing through the terminal, the two were politely informed by a cunning thief that there was ketchup on the back of Shirk's shirt. When he went to clean the mess, an accomplice distracted Edmonds and stole her laptop! Unlike the authors, most of Mexico's countless crime victims do not benefit from the security of travelers' insurance, which in this case enabled Edmonds to recover her losses and finish her doctoral dissertation.

9. Wayne A. Cornelius and David A. Shirk, eds., *Reforming the Administration of Justice in Mexico* (La Jolla, Calif.: Center for U.S.-Mexican Studies, 2007).

10. José Brambila Macias, *Modeling the Informal Economy in Mexico. A Structural Equation Approach*, Munich, 2008. http://mpra.ub.uni-muenchen.de/8504/.

11. Roderic Ai Camp, "Armed Forces and Drugs: Public Perceptions and Institutional Challenges" in *Shared Responsibility: U.S.-Mexico Policy Options for Confronting Organized Crime*, ed. Eric L. Olson, David A. Shirk, and Andrew Selee (Washington D.C.: Woodrow Wilson International Center for Scholars, 2010).

12. David A. Shirk, *Drug Violence in Mexico: Data and Analysis from 2001–2009* (San Diego, Calif.: Trans-Border Institute, 2010).

13. Once charges were levied, however, a defendant's odds of being sentenced proved extremely high. An estimated 1.2 out of 1.6 (75%) of prosecutions were brought to trial, and 1.1 (92%) of those 1.2 crimes resulted in sentences. G. Zepeda Lecuona, *Crimen sin castigo: Procuración de justicia penal y ministerio público en México* (Mexico City: Centro de Investigación Para el Desarrollo, A.C. Fondo de Cultura Económica, 2004).

14. Elena Azaola and Marcelo Bergman, "Crime and Punishment in Mexico: Insights from the Mexican Prison System," in *Reforming the Administration of Justice in Mexico*, ed. Cornelius and Shirk. See also "News Report," Justice in Mexico Project, January 2007. www.justiceinmexico.org.

15. UN Development Programme, *Democracy in Latin America: Towards a Citizens' Democracy* (New York: UN Development Programme, 2004), 261–65.

16. UN Development Programme, *Democracy in Latin America*, 258.

17. In modern commercial usage, the term *cartel* draws from the German word *Kartell*, which has earlier uses derived from Latin, French, and Italian, beginning with the use of written charters in the exchange of prisoners of war. In the conventional sense, a cartel refers to formal agreements among business associations, or firms, to control production, fix prices, limit competition, and/or segment markets (by product, clientele, or territory). The term *drug cartel* is frequently used to describe organized crime syndicates involved in the production, distribution, and sale of psychotropic substances. While these organizations rarely conspire to fix prices, they often engage in other behaviors typically identified by economists with cartels. However, usage of the term *cartel* is sometimes considered controversial because of the widespread view of cartels as *only* price-fixing arrangements.

18. The Guadalajara cartel included members of the Arellano Félix family, Rafael Caro Quintero, Amado Carrillo Fuentes, Juan José "El Azul" Esparragoza, Ernesto Fonseca, Eduardo González Quirarte, Joaquín Guzmán Loera, Héctor "El Güero" Palma, Manuel Salcido, and Ismael Zambada, among others.

19. Jason Trahan, Ernesto Londoño, and Alfredo Corchado, "Drug Wars' Long Shadow," *Dallas Morning News*, December 13, 2005.

20. Transparency International, 2010, www.transparency.org.

21. Transparencia Mexicana, *Encuesta nacional de corrupción y buen gobierno*, 2001, 2003, 2005. www.transparenciamexicana.org.mx/ENCBG.

22. See, for example, the following examples: David J. Gould, *Bureaucratic Corruption and Underdevelopment in the Third World: The Case of Zaire* (New York: Pergamon Press, 1980); Robin Theobald, *Corruption, Development, and Underdevelopment* (Durham, N.C.: Duke University Press, 1990); Transparencia Mexicana, *Encuesta Nacional*.

23. See Alan Knight, "Corruption in Twentieth-Century Mexico," in *Political Corruption in Europe and Latin America* (New York: St. Martin's Press, 1996); S. D. Morris, *Corruption and Politics in Contemporary Mexico* (Tuscaloosa: University of Alabama Press, 1991).

24. Thirty-eight mayors, state officials, police chiefs, public security secretaries, and other state and local officials were arrested on May 26, 2009, during an unprecedented federal operation in at least 12 of the state's 113 municipalities. By October 2010, all but one of the officials—Armando Medina Torres, former mayor of Múgica—had been released without a criminal conviction. María de la Luz González and Francisco Gómez, "Histórico: PGR pega al gobierno en Michoacán," *El Universal,* May 27, 2009; "De 38 detenidos por *Michoacanazo,* 37 libres," *El Universal,* September 28, 2010.

25. Sandra Dibble, "Mexican military detains former Tijuana Mayor Jorge Hank Rhon," *San Diego Union Tribune,* June 4, 2010.

26. Richard Serrano,"Ex-Cancun mayor extradited to U.S. on drug charges," *Los Angeles Times,* May 11, 2010.

27. Kathleen Staudt and Irasema Coronado, "Binational Civic Action for Accountability: Antiviolence Organizing in Ciudad Juárez–El Paso," in *Reforming the Administration of Justice in Mexico,* ed. Cornelius and Shirk.

28. For example, in addition to the above noted films produced by Layda Negrete and Roberto Hernández, lawyers like Ana Laura Magaloni and Javier Cruz have championed the cause of due process by defending the rights of indigenous persons detained in relation to the 1997 Acteal massacre.

29. "'Narcos' mexicanos apuntan contra religiosos: Iglesias," *La Jornada,* August 19, 2010; Ignacio Alvarado Álvarez, "Narcotraficantes atacan y extorsionan a iglesias," *El Universal,* August 16, 2010.

30. Luis González Placencia, Layda Negrete Sansores, and Guillermo Zepeda Lecuona, *Analisis tecnico de la propuesta de reforma al sistema de justicia mexicano,* Project on Reforming the Administration of Justice in Mexico (Mexico City: Instituto de Investigaciones Legislativas del Senado de la República (IILSEN); La Jolla, Calif.: Center for U.S.-Mexican Studies, 2005).

31. Miguel Ruiz-Cabañas, "La campaña permanente de México: costos, beneficios y consecuencias," in *El combate a las drogas en América,* ed. Peter Smith (Mexico City: Fondo de Cultura Económica, 1993); Luis Alejandro Astorga Almanza, *Drogas sin fronteras* (Mexico City: Grijalbo, 2003); Astorga Almanza, *Seguridad, traficantes y militares: el poder y la sombra* (Mexico City: Tusquets, 2007).

32. Donald E. Schulz, *Between a Rock and a Hard Place: The United States, Mexico, and the Agony of National Security,* SSI special report (Carlisle Barracks, Pa.: Strategic Studies Institute Army War College, 1997).

33. In July 2011, such concerns led the Mexican Supreme Court to rule unanimously that cases of military abuses must be tried in civilian courts, but skeptics worried that the military would not comply. Tracy Wilkinson, "Mexico to Get Civilian Trials for Military," *Los Angeles Times,* July 13, 2011.

34. "Lidera Sedena quejas presentadas a CNDH"; Moloeznik, "Principales efectos de la militarización del combate al narcotráfico en México"; Moloeznik, "The Militarization of Mexican Public Security and the Role of the Military in Mexico"; Flores Pérez, "Organized Crime and Official Corruption in Mexico."

12 MEXICAN FOREIGN POLICY

1. Remarks by Patricia Espinosa, Secretariá de Relaciones Exteriores de México, at the London School of Economics and Political Science, June 16, 2008. http://www2.lse.ac.uk/publicEvents/events/2008/20080509t1108z001.aspx (accessed June 1, 2011).

2. For more information on Mexico's embassies and consulates, see www.sre.gob.mx/.

3. The authors happened to be conducting an interview with Senate Foreign Relations Committee Chairwoman Rosario Green when this controversy developed, and we had to suspend our conversation while Senator Green excused herself to ensure a successful vote to approve the four nominees.

4. Francisco Reséndiz, "Voto en el exterior tendrá 75 días de anticipación," *El Universal*, April 16, 2011.

5. "Con voto diferenciado el Senado aprueba cónsules en EE.UU," March 25, 2011. http://www.diariocritico.com/mexico/2011/Marzo/noticias/261574/con-voto -diferenciado-el-senado-aprueba-consules-en-eeuu.html.

6. By comparison, Brazil has served on ten occasions, Argentina on eight occasions, and Chile on four occasions. http://www.un.org/sc/members.asp (accessed June 11, 2011).

7. Authors' translation of the 2009 Mexican constitution.

8. Fayette Robinson, *Mexico and Her Military Chieftains, from the Revolution of Hidalgo to the Present Time* (Glorieta, N.M.: Rio Grande Press, 1970).

9. The roots of this national security crisis date back to the controversial 1828 presidential election of General Manuel Gómez Pedraza, an officer in the Spanish royal forces who joined Iturbide in fighting for Mexico's independence. Gómez Pedraza's 1828 presidential victory was violently contested by liberal political forces loyal to the opposing candidate, General Vicente Guerrero. Guerrero's supporters succeeded in ousting Gómez Pedraza, but the resulting violence and property damages caused some French nationals—including an audacious pastry chef—to demand reparations from the Mexican government.

10. After 2000, Mexico deliberately deviated from the Estrada Doctrine by adopting what some have called the Castañeda Doctrine, articulated by Secretary of Foreign Relations Jorge Castañeda during the Fox administration.

11. George W. Grayson, *Oil and Mexican Foreign Policy* (Pittsburgh, Pa.: University of Pittsburgh Press, 1988).

12. At one time, Brazil, Argentina, Chile, Colombia, Mexico, Peru, and Bolivia all had substantial partnerships of one kind or another with Hitler's government. Peter Smith, *Talons of the Eagle: Dynamics of U.S.-Latin American Relations* (New York: Oxford University Press, 2000), 74–78, and 372, table A2.

13. This gesture is memorialized to this day by the square that bears Mexico's name in the capital city of Addis Ababa and by the Ethiopia metro stop in Mexico City, which was once a square.

14. http://www.mexconnect.com/articles/678-mexico-forgotten-world-war-ii-ally.

15. After the end of the Cold War, the pact was widely seen as outdated, and Mexico had planned to withdraw even before the terrorist attacks of 2001 occurred.

After 9/11, Mexico postponed its withdrawal, toning down the event to avoid any appearance that it was distancing itself from the United States. Harold Molineu, *U.S. Policy toward Latin America: From Regionalism to Globalism*, 2nd ed. (Boulder, Colo.: Westview, 1990), 25–26.

16. From 1945 to the 1980s, Mexico's votes in the United Nations consistently opposed those of the United States. See Robert Pastor, "U.S. Foreign Policy," in Robert Pastor and Jorge Castañeda, eds. *Limits to Friendship: The United States and Mexico* (New York: Alfred A. Knopf, 1988), 165–66.

17. Jorge Castañeda, "Mexican Foreign Policy," in Pastor and Castañeda, *Limits to Friendship*, 176–77.

18. Smith, *Talons of the Eagle*, 209.

19. There are other reasons why Mexico's stance toward Central America changed after 1982. In particular, the debt crisis that began that year made it essential that the country maintain a cordial and cooperative relationship with the United States. Economic hardship also meant that Mexico had fewer resources available for foreign aid to its southern neighbors.

20. Jorge Castañeda, "Mexican Foreign Policy," in Pastor and Castañeda, *Limits to Friendship*, 182.

21. The Sandinistas and FMLN also lost faith in the initiative when convinced that it was insufficient for bringing out lasting peace—in large part because the United States was not on board.

22. During this time Mexico also joined or increased its role in a number of multilateral economic organizations. For example, it is now a member of the Inter-American Development Bank, the International Monetary Fund, and the World Bank, and it was the first Latin American country to be admitted to the Organisation for Economic Co-operation and Development.

23. Riordan Roett, "Mexico and the Western Hemisphere," in *Mexico's Democracy at Work: Political and Economic Dynamics*, ed. Russell Crandall, Guadalupe Paz, and Riordan Roett (Boulder, Colo.: Lynne Rienner, 2005), 167.

24. Javier Santiso offers an analysis of why Mexico lagged behind South America in European trade and investment in "Mexico's Economic Ties with Europe: Business as Unusual?" in Crandall, Paz, and Roett, *Mexico's Democracy at Work*, 173–88.

25. Santiso, "Mexico's Economic Ties with Europe," 182.

26. Japanese firms employ approximately 7 percent of the workers in the *maquiladora* industry.

27. Russell Crandall, "Mexico's Domestic Economy: Policy Options and Choices," in Crandall, Paz, and Roett, *Mexico's Democracy at Work*, 78.

28. According to SRE, Mexico maintains embassies in Algeria, Egypt, Ethiopia, Kenya, Morocco, Nigeria, and South Africa.

29. "Zuma in Mexico to Enhance Relationships," *Mail & Guardian Online*, December 8, 2010. http://mg.co.za/article/2010-12-08-zuma-goes-to-build-mexican-relationship.

30. Alexandra Olson, "Iran Eyes Mexico in Deepening Latin America Ties," Associated Press, February 26, 2009; "Deputy Minister Meets with Foreign Affairs Minister of Iran to the Americas," Secretary of Exterior Relations, February 27, 2009.

31. "Mexico and Israel Sign a Free Trade Agreement," U.S.-Mexico Chamber of Commerce. http://www.usmcoc.org (accessed June 11, 2011).

32. "Mexico Supports the Middle East Peace Process and the Creation of a Sovereign Palestinian State," Press Release 296. Mexico City: Secretaría de Relaciones Exteriores, October 20, 2009. http://portal3.sre.gob.mx/english/index.php?option=com_content&task=view&id=296&Itemid=9.

33. To this end, a new position, undersecretary for human rights and democracy affairs, was created within the foreign ministry. Mexico also signed a number of international human rights agreements, most notably an accord with the UN High Commissioner for Human Rights to evaluate the country's human rights record. See Andrés Rozental, "Fox's Foreign Policy Agenda: Global and Regional Priorities," in *Mexico under Fox*, ed. Luis Rubio and Susan Kaufman Purcell (Boulder: Lynne Rienner, 2004), 92.

34. Excerpt from "Felipe Calderón's Foreign Policy," presentation at the Mexican Council on Foreign Relations, March 2006.

35. Other goals include the establishment of a program to attract North American capital investment to migrant-sending regions in Mexico, the reduction of the costs associated with sending remittances, the resumption of trilateral talks to design a North American alliance for security and prosperity, and reform of the Mexican foreign service. See chapter 13 for further discussion of these issues.

36. These and other effects of democratization on Mexico's foreign policy process are discussed by Luis Carlos Ugalde, "U.S.-Mexican Relations: A View from Mexico," and Susan Kaufman Purcell, "The Changing Bilateral Relationship: A U.S. View," in Rubio and Purcell, *Mexico under Fox*, 115–41.

37. Ugalde, "U.S.-Mexican Relations," 119.

13 U.S.-MEXICO RELATIONS

1. James Cockcroft, *Mexico: Class Formation, Capital Accumulation, and the State* (New York: Monthly Review Press, 1990), 93.

2. The agreement also guaranteed in writing that Article 27 of the constitution, which revoked foreign subsoil rights, was not retroactive. In return, Mexico received some concessions on repayment of its external debt, which had skyrocketed as a result of the revolution, and official recognition of the Obregón administration. Cockcroft, *Mexico*, 110, 117.

3. Skidmore and Smith counter that Mexico's victory was a pyrrhic one because, for the next thirty years, the U.S. government and foreign oil companies continued to informally enforce the boycott on Mexican oil and prevent Mexico from obtaining equipment from foreign suppliers. This hindered the development of PEMEX, the state-owned oil monopoly. Thomas Skidmore and Peter Smith, *Modern Latin America* (New York: Oxford University Press, 2005), 273.

4. Kitty Calavita, *Inside the State: The Bracero Program, Immigration, and the INS* (New York: Routledge, 1992).

5. Jorge Castañeda, "Mexican Foreign Policy," in Robert Pastor and Jorge Castañeda, eds., *Limits to Friendship: The United States and Mexico* (New York: Knopf, 1988), 171.

6. The Fox administration took the unprecedented step of policing dangerous sections of its northern border in an effort to impede would-be migrants from crossing; It also began to work more closely with U.S. authorities to apprehend narco-traffickers and publicly distanced itself from Fidel Castro's Cuba.

7. Jeffrey Davidow, *The U.S. and Mexico: The Bear and the Porcupine* (Princeton, N.J.: Markus Wiener, 2004), 4–10.

8. U.S. Census Bureau, *American Community Survey, 2009.* www. census.gov/prod/ 2010pubs/acsbr09-15.pdf (accessed September 15, 2011).

9. Michael Hoefer, Nancy Rytina, and Christopher Campbell, *Estimates of the Unauthorized Immigrant Population Residing in the United States: January 2006*, Department of Homeland Security Report, August 2007. www.dhs.gov/ximgtn/statistics/ publications/index.shtm.

10. It is not surprising that the largest waves of unregulated Mexican emigration to the United States occurred during the most tumultuous times in Mexico, the revolution (1910–1920) and the economic crises of the 1930s, 1970s, 1980s, and 1990s.

11. This phenomenon is especially common in the states of Michoacán and Zacatecas.

12. In 1982, the U.S. government used this tactic again in Operation Jobs, a mass deportation of undocumented Mexicans in response to rising unemployment and economic recession in the United States.

13. For example, it created the Grupo Beta police force to rescue would-be migrants in danger and provide information on their human and labor rights. Marc Rosenblum, "Moving beyond the Policy of No Policy: Emigration from Mexico and Central America," *Latin American Politics and Society* 4, no. 1 (2004).

14. Julia Preston, "11.2 Million Illegal Immigrants in U.S. in 2010, Report Says; No Change From '09," *New York Times*, February 1, 2011.

15. James Cockcroft, *Mexico*, 151.

16. Daniel C. Levy and Kathleen Bruhn, *Mexico: The Struggle for Democratic Development* (Berkeley: University of California Press, 2006).

17. Peter Smith discusses the motivations behind NAFTA in *Talons of the Eagle*, 260–62. See also Levy and Bruhn, *Mexico*, 247–50.

18. For its part, Canada had many of the same interests when it signed its first free trade agreement with the United States in 1989.

19. Levy and Bruhn, *Mexico*, 248.

20. Other factors such as the decline in the value of the peso in the mid-1990s, and sustained growth in the U.S. economy during the same period, also contributed greatly to the flow of goods and services across the border. *The Effects of NAFTA on U.S.-Mexican Trade and GDP*, a study conducted by the U.S. Congressional Budget Office in 2003. www.cbo.gov/ftpdocs/42xx/doc4247/Report.pdf.

21. Gary Gereffi and Martha Martinez, "Mexico's Economic Transformation under NAFTA," in *Mexico's Democracy at Work: Political and Economic Dynamics*, ed. Russell Crandall, Guadalupe Paz, and Riordan Roett (Boulder, Colo.: Lynne Rienner, 2005), 122. Trilateral trade also increased dramatically. In 1993, Mexico, Canada, and the United States traded $306 billion; by 2000, $621 billion. Jorge Castañeda, "NAFTA at 10: A Plus or a Minus?" *Current History*, February 2004, 51–55.

22. U.S. Department of State. http://www.state.gov/r/pa/prs/ps/2010/05/142020.htm (accessed February 1, 2010).

23. Many of the jobs created by NAFTA disappeared during subsequent economic downturns; roughly two-thirds of the 150,000 jobs lost in 2001 were in the *maquiladora* industry. Levy and Bruhn, *Mexico*, 252–53; Russell Crandall, "Mexico's Domestic Economy: Policy Options and Choices," in *Mexico's Democracy at Work*, ed. Crandall, Paz, and Roett.

24. U.S. Department of State. http://www.state.gov/r/pa/prs/ps/2010/05/142020.htm (accessed February 1, 2010).

25. Castañeda, "NAFTA at 10," 52.

26. John J. Audley, Demetrios G. Papademetriou, Sandra Polaski, and Scott Vaughan, *NAFTA's Promise and Reality: Lessons from Mexico for the Hemisphere* (Washington, D.C.: Carnegie Endowment for International Peace, 2004), 13.

27. Susan Kaufman Purcell, "The Changing Bilateral Relationship," in *Mexico under Fox*, ed. Luis Rubio and Susan Kaufman Purcell (Boulder, Colo.: Lynne Rienner, 2004), 149.

28. Andrés Rozental, "Fox's Foreign Policy Agenda," in *Mexico under Fox*, ed. Rubio and Purcell, 99–100.

29. Many have noted that given the domestic political climate of both the United States and Canada at the time, Fox probably would not have been able to achieve measurable success on any of these goals, even if the events of September 11 had not occurred.

30. J. Z. García, "Security Regimes on the U.S.-Mexican Border," in *Transnational Crime and Public Security: Challenges to Mexico and the United States*, ed. J. J. Bailey and J. Chabat (La Jolla, Calif.: Center for U.S.-Mexican Studies, 2002).

31. Davidow, *The U.S. and Mexico*, 19–29.

32. Evan Perez, "Mexican Guns Tied to U.S.," *Wall Street Journal*, June 10, 2011.

33. This procedure may be used for the prosecution of non-Mexicans arrested and tried in Mexico for a crime committed outside of Mexico, if the case involves a Mexican victim.

34. "Frente multinacional contra narco, migración y 'maras,' " *El Universal*, May 23, 2007.

35. "Order on the Border?" *San Diego Union Tribune*, January 30, 2011.

36. Ginger Thompson, "New U.S. Role in Mexico Drug War," *New York Times* News Service, August 7, 2011.

37. David E. Lorey, *The U.S.-Mexican Border in the Twentieth Century* (Wilmington, Del.: Scholarly Resources, 1999), 6.

38. Oscar J. Martínez outlines these typologies in *Border People: Life and Society in the U.S.-Mexico Borderlands* (Tucson: University of Arizona Press, 1994), 28.

39. A 2006 border patrol report estimated that 4,045 migrants had died of extreme temperatures and other hazards since 1995. A record 472 of those lives were lost in 2005.

40. Bureau of Transportation Statistics (BTS). www.transtats.bts.gov.

41. L. Lumpe, "The US Arms Both Sides of Mexico's Drug War," *Covert Action Quarterly* 61 (1997): 39–46.

CONCLUSION

1. Viridiana Ríos and David A. Shirk, "Drug Violence in Mexico: Data and Analysis through 2010," Trans-Border Institute, University of San Diego, February 2011. http://justiceinmexico.files.wordpress.com/2011/03/2011-tbi-drugviolence.pdf.

2. Tracy Wilkinson, "Poverty Grew in Mexico to Nearly Half the Population, Study Finds," *Los Angeles Times*, July 29, 2011.

3. Randal Archibald, "Despite Violence, U.S. Firms Expand in Mexico," *New York Times*, July 11, 2011.

4. Damien Cave, "For Mexicans Looking North, a New Calculus Favors Home," *New York Times*, July 5, 2011.

Index

About the Authors

Emily Edmonds-Poli is associate professor of political science at the University of San Diego. She received her PhD in political science at the University of California–San Diego in 2001. She was awarded a Fulbright-Garcia Robles fellowship in 1998–1999 and a Ford Foundation Fellowship in 1999–2000. During the 2000–2001 academic year, she was a fellow at UCSD's Center for U.S.-Mexican Studies. Dr. Edmonds's research focuses on Mexican politics and decentralization and local democratic governance in Mexico. Her most recent article, "Decentralization under the Fox Administration: Progress or Stagnation?" was published in *Mexican Studies/ Estudios Mexicanos.*

David A. Shirk is director of the Trans-Border Institute and associate professor in the Political Science Department at the University of San Diego. He received his PhD in political science at the University of California–San Diego and was fellow at the Center for U.S.-Mexican Studies in 1998–1999 and 2001–2003. He conducts research on Mexican politics, U.S.-Mexican relations, and law enforcement and security along the U.S.-Mexican border. Dr. Shirk is currently the principal investigator for Justice in Mexico (www.justiceinmexico.org), a binational research initiative on criminal justice and the rule of law in Mexico. Book publications by Dr. Shirk include *Shared Responsibility: U.S.-Mexico Policy Options for Confronting Organized Crime* (2010), coedited with Eric Olson and Andrew Selee; *Police and Public Security in Mexico* (2009), coedited with Robert Donnelly; *Reforming the Administration of Justice in Mexico* (2007), coedited with Wayne Cornelius; *Evaluating Accountability and Transparency in Mexico: Local, National, and Comparative Perspectives* (2007), coedited with Alejandra Ríos Cázares; and *Mexico's New Politics: The PAN and Democratic Change* (2005).

CPSIA information can be obtained at www.ICGtesting.com
Printed in the USA
BVOW072134190212

283213BV00001B/4/P